GLOBALISATION AND LABOUR RIGHTS

In a world of work that has changed dramatically over the last few years, states are confronted with new actors and conflicting international legal obligations. This book examines the tensions between core labour rights as defined by the International Labour Organization, and the interests of international economic institutions (such as the WTO, IMF, World Bank, and OECD). It provides an analysis of the legal interactions between international regulations and state policy with regard to potential regulatory conflicts, at both horizontal and vertical levels. The study suggests a model of multilevel consistency as a way of reconciling the highly specialised and fragmented legal systems of core labour rights on the one hand, and trade liberalisation on the other, to form the coherent framework of a consistent legal order. Its detailed analysis and recommendations are designed for both academic readers and practitioners in international organisations and governments.

Studies in International Trade Law: Volume 5

Studies in International Trade Law
Titles in this series:

Volume 1 *Basic Legal Instruments for the Liberalisation of Trade*
Federico Ortino

Volume 2 *The Power to Protect: Trade Health, and Uncertainty in the WTO*
Catherine Button

Volume 3 *The WTO, the Internet and Trade in Digital Products*
Sacha Wunsch-Vincent

Volume 4 *Good Faith in the Jurisprudence of the WTO: The Protection of Legitimate Expectations, Good Faith Interpretation and Fair Dispute Settlement*
Marion Panizzon

Globalisation and Labour Rights

The Conflict between Core Labour Rights and International Economic Law

Christine Breining-Kaufmann

·HART·
PUBLISHING

OXFORD AND PORTLAND, OREGON
2007

Published in North America (US and Canada) by
Hart Publishing
c/o International Specialized Book Services
920 NE 58th Avenue, Suite 300
Portland, OR 97213-3786
USA
Tel: +1-503-287-3093 or toll-free: 1-800-944-6190
Fax: +1-503-280-8832
E-mail: orders@isbs.com
Website: www.isbs.com

Hart Publishing, 16C Worcester Place, Oxford OX1 2JW
Tel: 01865 517530
Fax: 01865 510710
E-mail: mail@hartpub.co.uk
Website: www.hartpub.co.uk

British Library Cataloguing in Publication Data
Data Available
ISBN-13: 978-1-84113-599-1 (hardback)
ISBN-10: 1-84113-599-2 (hardback)

Typeset by Hope Services, Abingdon
Printed and bound in Great Britain by
Biddles Ltd, King's Lynn, Norfolk

Acknowledgements

The idea for this book originated from experiences and insights that I gained while working for the Swiss central bank. Many people and institutions contributed to further development of the concept and the completion of the book: first of all, the University of Michigan Law School provided me with an invaluable research atmosphere, inspiring discussions with colleagues and opportunities to meet people who forced me to rethink and refine many points. I am particularly grateful to Virginia Gordan, Robert Howse, Christopher McCrudden, Christine Chinkin, Donald Regan, Mark Rosenbaum and Bruno Simma. Special thanks are also due to the reviewers of my habilitation thesis at the University of Zurich, Giovanni Biaggini and Dietrich Schindler, and to Thomas Cottier and my colleagues at the World Trade Institute in Berne for their valuable comments.

Friends, family and colleagues offered feedback, constructive criticism and moral support every step of the way—this book would not have been completed without them.

I would also like to thank the Stiefel Zangger Stiftung at the University of Zurich for supporting my stay at the University of Michigan Law School with a research grant.

Last but not least, I am indebted to Marianne Peter for her administrative assistance above and beyond the call of duty, to Michelle Foster, Susan Kaplan and Lisa Gourd for their careful review of the manuscript, and finally to Richard Hart for his encouragement and advice.

Summary of Contents

Contents

List of Figures

Abbreviations

AC	Law Reports, Appeal Cases (United Kingdom)
ACP States	African, Caribbean and Pacific States
AJIL	American Journal of International Law
AJP	Allgemeine Juristische Praxis
AFL-CIO	American Federation of Labor and Congress of Industrial Organizations
Art	article
AS	Amtliche Sammlung der Bundesgesetze und Verordnungen der Schweizerischen Eidgenossenschaft
ASEAN	Association of South East Asian Nations
ASIL	American Society of International Law
ATCA	Alien Tort Claims Act
BBl	Schweizerisches Bundesblatt
BCCI	Bank for Commerce and Credit International
BCLR	Butterworths Constitutional Law Reports (South Africa Constitutional Court)
BGE	Entscheide des Schweizerischen Bundesgerichts
BIAC	Business Industry Advisory Committee (OECD)
BJM	Basler Juristische Mitteilungen
BV	Schweizerische Bundesverfassung
BverfG	Bundesverfassungsgericht (Germany)
BWIs	Bretton Woods Institutions
CAS	Country Assistance Strategy
CC	Constitutional Court (South Africa)
CDF	Comprehensive Development Framework
CEDAW	Convention on the Elimination of All Forms of Discrimination against Women
CESCR	Committee on Economic, Social and Cultural Rights
CFA	Committee on Freedom of Association (ILO)
CFR	Code of Federal Regulations (United States)
CIME	Committee on International Investment and Multinational Enterprises (OECD)
Cir	Circuit
CMLR	Common Market Law Review
COMECON	Council for Mutual Economic Assistance
Cong	Congress
DEZA	Direktion für Entwicklung und Zusammenarbeit
EC	European Community

ECHR	European Convention on Human Rights
ECtHR	European Court of Human Rights
ECJ	European Court of Justice
ECOSOC	United Nations Economic and Social Council
ECR	Reports of Cases before the Court of Justice of the European Community
ESAF	Enhanced Structural Adjustment Facility
ESCOR	Economic and Social Council Official Records (United Nations)
EU	European Union
EWR	Europäischer Wirtschaftsraum
F, F.2d, F.3d	Federal Reporter (United States, Courts of Appeals)
Fed Reg	Federal Register (United States)
F Supp	Federal Supplement (Untied States, District Courts)
FDI	Foreign Direct Investment
GA	United Nations General Assembly
GATS	General Agreement on Trade in Services
GATT	General Agreement on Tariffs and Trade
GB	Governing Body (ILO)
GDP	gross domestic product
GNI	gross national income
GPA	Agreement on Government Procurement
GSP	Generalized Tariff Preferences (EU), Generalized System of Preferences (US)
HPIC	Heavily Indebted Poor Countries Initiative
HR	House of Representatives
HRQ	Human Rights Quarterly
IAIS	International Association of Insurance Supervisors
IBRD	International Bank for Reconstruction and Development
ICCPR	International Covenant on Civil and Political Rights
ICESCR	International Covenant on Economic, Social and Cultural Rights
ICFTU	International Conference of Free Trade Unions
ICHRP	International Council on Human Rights
ICJ	International Court of Justice
IDA	International Development Association
IFC	International Finance Corporation
ILC	United Nations International Law Commission
ILO	International Labour Organization
IMF	International Monetary Fund
IOSCO	International Organization of Securities Commissions
IR	Irish Reports (Supreme Court, Republic of Ireland)
ITO	International Trade Organisation

MAI	Multinational Agreement on Investment
MFN	Most Favoured Nation Principle
MIGA	Multinational Investment Guarantee Agency
MNE	Multinational enterprise
NAALC	North American Agreement on Labor Cooperation
NAFTA	North American Free Trade Agreement
NAIRU	Non-accelerating inflation rate of unemployment
NAO	National Administration Office (NAFTA)
NBER	National Bureau of Economic Research
NGO	non-governmental Organisation
OECD	Organisation for Economic Co-operation and Development
OEEC	Organisation for European Economic Co-operation
OJ	Official Journal of the European Community
PCIJ	Permanent Court of International Justice
PIN	Public Information Notice
PPM	Process and Production Method
PRGF	Poverty Reduction and Growth Facility
PRSP	Poverty Reduction Strategy Papers
PubL	Public Law (United States)
Res	Resolution
Rz	Randziffer
SAF	Structural Adjustment Facility
SC	United Nations Security Council
SCR	Supreme Court Reporter (United States)
SR	Systematische Sammlung des Schweizerischen Bundesrechts
Stat.	United States Statutes at Large
TBT	Agreement on Technical Barriers to Trade
TPA	Trade Promotion Authority Act
TRIPS	Agreement on Trade-Related Aspects of Intellectual Property Rights
TUAC	Trade Union Advisory Committee (OECD)
TVPA	Torture Victim Protection Act
UN	United Nations
UNCLOS	United Nations Convention on the Law of the Sea
UNCTAD	United Nations Conference on Trade and Development
UNDP	United Nations Development Programme
UNICEF	United Nations Children's Fund
UNTS	United Nations Treaty Series
USR	United States Reports (Supreme Court)
USC	United States Code
USCA	United States Code Annotated
USTR	United States Trade Representative
VCLT	Vienna Convention on the Law of Treaties

VEB	Verwaltungsentscheide der Bundesbehòrden
VPB	Verwaltungspraxis der Bundesbehörden
WDI	World Development Index
WTO	World Trade Organization

Note on Spelling

British English spelling has been used throughout the book, except when quoting directly or when referring to names of organisations, in which case standard spelling conventions have been followed. In other words, eg, the ILO is spelled as International Labour Organization, while the OECD is spelled Organisation for Economic Co-operation and Development.

Table of Cases

European Court of Human Rights

European Court of Justice and Court of First Instance

GATT/WTO

Germany

Human Rights Committee

International Court of Justice

International Criminal Tribunal for the Former Yugoslavia (ICTY)

Ireland

NAFTA

Nuremberg Military Tribunal

South Africa

Switzerland

United Kingdom

United States of America

Table of Legislation

Belgium

Bretton Woods Institutions

China

Council of Europe

Denmark

European Community

Directives

Regulations

Germany

International Labour Organization

International

Switzerland

United Kingdom

United Nations

United States of America

World Trade Organization

Introduction

Setting Out the Problems

OVER THE LAST few years, the world of work has changed dramatically. Technological innovation and globalisation have led to the establishment of global markets, which do not follow any single cultural or political pattern. The challenge for industry to remain competitive in new markets has already brought about a consolidation in domestic markets and will now be followed by global structural change. The large number of recent international mergers and acquisitions are symptomatic of this trend.

These changes have a serious impact on the meaning of work and on the working population. Moreover, the shift away from states and towards markets has an equally serious impact on the roles of states, international organisations and the international community. States are faced with the challenge of accommodating the consequences in the labour market that are brought about by technological development, globalisation and other ongoing structural change.

I.1. MEANINGS OF WORK

I.1.1. Work, Labour and Leisure

The definitions and scope of work, labour and leisure are of key importance since they form the basis of all labour rights and standards. What is work? The Concise Oxford English Dictionary defines it as "expenditure of energy, striving, application of effort or exertion to a purpose". However, there are many ways of deliberately expending energy that do not count as "work", such as playing tennis. On the other hand, defining work solely in terms of paid employment is also insufficient, because paid employment is a relatively modern development in human history and such a narrow definition would exclude unpaid work by housewives, children, the unemployed and retired.[1] Unsurprisingly, philosophers have hotly debated the meaning of work since the times of the Homeric Society.[2]

[1] Thomas (1999) at xiii.
[2] For a historical overview, see Applebaum (1995) 48–65.

In an attempt to reconcile the different schools of thought in the early twentieth century,[3] the 1944 Declaration Concerning the Aims and Purposes of the International Labour Organization (ILO) stated that:

> . . . all human beings, irrespective of race, creed, or sex, have the right to pursue both their material well-being and their spiritual development in conditions of freedom and dignity, of economic security, and equal opportunity . . .[4]

A few years later, in 1958, Hannah Arendt published *The Human Condition*, in which she further developed the ideas of Karl Marx and Henri Bergson. She distinguished between labour and work, defining labour as "the undifferentiated use of the body to perform work, while work is the use of the hands and head to create man-made things that are durable and that can be used to create other things."[5] Work thus becomes the defining characteristic of *homo faber*.

The late Pope John Paul II affirmed this humanistic approach in his encyclical letter "Laborem exercens" ("On Human Work"): "Everyone becomes a human being through, among other things, work."[6] Following the teachings of Saint Paul, the Pope viewed work as an obligation to society and community. Because each person has the moral obligation to work, each person has fundamental rights both as a person and as a worker.

Given the tremendous impact of technology on work towards the end of the twentieth century and the trend towards humanising work, some contemporary philosophers such as André Gorz share with Aristotle the belief that non-economic activities are the very fabric of life. The only work that should be performed for the sake of money is that dedicated to producing the necessities of life. The rest of one's time can be spent in form of voluntary work or activity that is free, self-determined, and taken up for pleasure.[7] Gorz therefore defines work as:

> . . . a paid activity, performed on behalf of a third party (the employer), to achieve goals we have not chosen for ourselves and according to procedures and schedules laid down by the person paying our wages.[8]

He distinguishes three types of work: work for economic ends, domestic labour or work for oneself and autonomous activity. Only the first type is covered by his definition. Gorz strongly opposes the treatment of housework as paid work and the provision of a wage (in the form of a public allowance) to those undertaking it (mostly women, of course),[9] thus denying the social utility of such

[3] The main scholars influencing the Declaration were Friedrich Hegel, Karl Marx, Henri Bergson and Hendrik de Man.

[4] Adopted at the 26th General Conference of the ILO in Philadelphia on 10 May 1944 as an Annex to the ILO Constitution, para II(a) [hereinafter Philadelphia Declaration]. Available at http://www.ilo.org/public/english/overview/iloconst.htm.

[5] Arendt, quoted in Applebaum (1995) 64.

[6] Pope John Paul II (1982) at para 9.

[7] Gorz (1989) 233.

[8] Gorz (1999a) 43.

[9] On the impacts of the public/private distinction, see Chinkin (1999) 389–90.

work. Gorz argues that domestic labour is not socially useful work, because it aims at the fulfilment of purely individual needs. He rejects a "totalitarian" conception of society in which there is no place for the uniqueness and singularity of the individual or the private sphere. For Gorz, this sphere is by nature exempt from social control and the criterion of public utility.[10]

Whether or not one agrees with Gorz, the significance of his ideas lies in his concept that the future of work and the future of society are inevitably intertwined. A good life in Gorz' and Aristotle's view is one that eliminates the constraint of necessity.[11] Yet the question remains whether the notion of work should—as according to Gorz—be understood in a narrow sense, excluding voluntary activities and activities that are not pursued with payment in mind. To answer this question a look at developments in the automobile industry is worthwhile.

In 1908, the first automobile assembled using mass production technology, the Ford T, rolled off the ramp of Henry Ford's factory in Detroit. Applying the theory of Frederick Winslow Taylor, Ford was the first to install assembly lines in his Detroit plant in 1913. The "age of the mass worker" peaked after World War II, when gigantic factories produced millions of consumer goods. However, higher efficiency and productivity took a high toll on workers: work became so intense that it reached and sometimes went beyond human tolerance limits.[12] Following the introduction of new production methods in the 1960s and 1970s, workers took to the streets in France, Germany and Italy, and many plants were disrupted by worker revolts. This was followed by major changes in production, initially in Japan and Sweden. Driven by the need to increase productivity and quality simultaneously, Japanese car manufacturers came up with the "Toyota system", which is based on outsourcing and "just-in-time" management of resources. Volvo took up the Japanese approach and developed it further by combining higher productivity with "work humanisation" measures. The assembly line was partly replaced by self-organised production islands, which meant that teams took on the responsibility for assembling a whole car, thus allowing them to take pride in creating a new product.

However, the recession of the 1990s led to another U-turn in industrial policy. A book published in 2000 by Daimler-Chrysler manager Roland Springer entitled *Return to Taylorism?* can be seen as a sign of what to expect in the near future.[13] The automobile industry was just the beginning: we are now facing a new trend toward fragmented work even in areas that previously seemed to be resistant to any form of Taylorism.

In response to these challenges, the ILO has announced a new programme for "Decent Work". Decent work, in the terminology of the ILO, means work that

[10] Gorz (1999a) 44.
[11] Applebaum (1995) 70–71; Gorz (1999b) 93–100.
[12] Kempe (2001) 19.
[13] Schumann (2001) 113–17.

is carried out in conditions of freedom, equity, security and human dignity.[14] While it does make sense to distinguish between labour, work and leisure, recent developments in the workplace require equal treatment of work that involves personal satisfaction and labour that is mainly physical activity. For the purpose of this book, we will therefore consider work as encompassing every activity undertaken with the aim of earning a living or fulfilling essential human needs including affirming one's own identity.[15]

I.1.2. Formal and Informal Sectors

A new debate similar to that about the meaning of work arose in the 1970s about the so-called informal economy.[16] It was meant as a label for work taking place outside government regulations and formal systems of labour and social protection. First applied to developing countries, it was soon also being used with reference to industrialised countries to describe the "hidden", "underground" or "black" economy. The informal sector was seen as a major force for national development.[17] Critics claimed that the concept was masking the exploitative nature of this economic area and that from a theoretical point of view, it lacked analytical precision.

It is in fact difficult to make the distinction between formal and informal work. Depending on the state of development of a society, different phenomena will be considered "irregular" and therefore part of the informal sector. Increased competitiveness, together with technological innovation, has led to fragmentation and relocation of production processes and to deregulation of labour markets.[18] As a result, informalisation has evolved simultaneously with technologically sophisticated global production systems.[19] Non-standard forms of employment and increased flexibility of the workforce call into question the value of labour rights. Labour rights are increasingly seen as costs, hampering competitiveness and thus encouraging non-registered or "black" working.[20]

According to the Fifteenth International Conference of Labour Statisticians, held in January 1993, the informal sector consists of production units that:

> . . . typically operate at a low level of organisation, with little or no division between labour and capital . . . and on a small scale . . .. Labour relations—where they exist—are based mostly on casual employment, kinship or personal and social relations rather than contractual arrangements with formal guarantees.[21]

[14] ILO (1999b) chapter 1; Somavia (1999) para 8.
[15] For a similar conclusion, see ILO (2001b) 5–7.
[16] Newman, Eatwell and Milgate (1987) vol 2, 845–46.
[17] For a detailed analysis, see Sethuraman (1982).
[18] Tomei (1999) 1.
[19] ILO (1999a) 27.
[20] Tomei (1999) 2.
[21] http://www.ilo.org/public/english/employment/skills/informal/index.htm.

In 1999, the international symposium organised by the ILO and the International Conference of Free Trade Unions (ICFTU) on the informal sector, proposed that the informal sector workforce be categorised into three broad groups: (a) owner-employers of micro-enterprises, which employ a few paid workers, with or without apprentices; (b) own-account workers, who own and operate one-person businesses, working alone or with the help of unpaid workers (generally family members and apprentices); and (c) dependent workers, paid or unpaid, including wage workers in micro-enterprises, unpaid family workers, apprentices, contract labour, home workers and paid domestic workers.[22]

At present, the majority of people worldwide work in the informal economy.[23] However, not only has the number of people working in the informal economy changed, but the way in which formal and informal economies interact has also evolved. The informal economy can no longer be defined as everything that is not included in the formal economy, because such a narrow concept fails to include the increasing mobility of workers between the two. The new phenomenon referred to by economists as "neo-informality" differentiates between three scenarios.[24]

In the first scenario, urban economic activity is performed by the owner of a small business and unpaid family members. The activities are a means to survival, mainly driven by poverty. As a rule, this scenario is excluded from the globalisation process and its possible benefits.

The second scenario is linked to the fragmentation of production processes and consists of activities in subordinated sectors through subcontracting arrangements. These activities are part of the globalisation process and motivated by the entrepreneurial goal to reduce labour costs and achieve greater production flexibility.

Finally, the third scenario refers to the agglomeration of small businesses with various degrees of formality and informality, with the borderline between the two not always being clear. The success of these promising organisations depends on which country they are located in and that country's participation in the global economy.

While all these scenarios contain some degree of informalisation, their underlying motivations vary and therefore need to be addressed by different policies. Accordingly, the role of the state is different in each scenario. Whereas the first scenario can be addressed best within the framework of poverty-alleviation programmes, the second and third require more specific labour-market-related policies.[25]

[22] *Ibid.*

[23] In Africa, the informal economy has accounted for about 60% of the urban labour force and 90% of the new urban jobs during the past decade. In Latin America, eight out of ten new jobs are created in the informal economy. See: ILO (1999b) 7, 60–61; Tomei (1999) 3–4; ILO, "Key Indicators of the Labour Market 2001/2002", Figure 7a.

[24] Pérez Sainz (1998) Table 1 at 162.

[25] Tomei (1999) 5.

Given the importance of the informal economy worldwide and the increasing difficulty of defining the boundary between the informal and formal economies, state activities can be effective only if they refer to the whole world of work. Within the broad conception of work as outlined above, this leads to the conclusions of the Director-General of the ILO: "Those who work should have rights at work."[26]

At the state level, the described changes in the production process result in shifts in competencies at different levels: internally, the executive branch will be vested with increased powers in order to participate efficiently in international negotiations. Externally, international organisations become more influential in regulating production, from trade regulation to labour standards. Both phenomena can be addressed under the notion of globalisation.

I.2. GLOBALISATION AND ITS EFFECTS

I.2.1. The Notion of Globalisation

Since the 1990s globalisation has become a buzzword, but what does it really mean? Is it something new? Globalisation is indeed a phenomenon that escapes easy definition. The elusive nature of globalisation might be one of the reasons why some authors, although a minority, more or less deny its existence.[27] Among those who accept that globalisation is real, there is no consensus as to whether it is a completely new phenomenon or has existed for a long time, since before the rise of the nation state.[28] While the so-called "hyperglobalisers" argue that globalisation is bringing about a "denationalisation" of economies through the establishment of transnational networks of production, trade and finance,[29] "transformationalists" go a step further by seeing globalisation as the driving force behind the rapid changes—not only economic but also social and political—that are reshaping modern societies and the world order.[30] Yet most authors agree that globalisation is not a fixed state of affairs or a single condition but a continuous process or set of processes.[31] Technological progress has made it possible to overcome territorial boundaries and time zones, therefore contributing largely to globalisation as a "time-space distanciation."[32]

[26] ILO (1999b) 7.

[27] Held, McGrew, Goldblatt and Perraton (1999) 5–7. For a sceptical view, see Hirst and Thompson (1999) 37–39.

[28] Delbrück (2001) 14; Thürer (2000) 107; Temin (1999) 77–86.

[29] For example, see Beck, 34: "For as we have seen, globalization means one thing above all else: *de*nationalization—that is, erosion of the national state, but also its possible transformation into a transnational state." (translation by the author)

[30] Held, McGrew, Goldblatt and Perraton (1999) 3, 7.

[31] *Ibid*, 27; Delbrück (2001) 14; Temin (1999) 87: "Policy-makers will not be faced with the choice of globalization or not, but rather with the question of how best to manage it."

[32] Giddens (1990) 14; Cotesta (1999) 30–33.

Globalisation is often understood as a deliberate effort to liberalise and deregulate markets. In Thomas Friedman's words, globalisation

> . . . is the inexorable integration of markets, nation-states and technologies to a degree never witnessed before—in a way that is enabling individuals, corporations and nation-states to reach around the world farther, faster, deeper and cheaper than ever before, and in a way that is enabling the world to reach into individuals, corporations and nation-states farther, faster, deeper, cheaper than ever before.[33]

This definition reflects the common perception of globalisation as a concept used to overcome national boundaries and to universalise aspects of everyday life in the political, economic and social arenas. However, globalisation must not be confused with internationalism or universalism. What makes it unique as a concept is not the liberalisation of markets but the shift in focus from the nation-state to values of transnational concern. Understood in this sense, globalisation is far more than a capitalist tool for increasing profits. Jost Delbrück provides a definition of globalisation that takes into account this distinction:

> [G]lobalization can be defined as the process or the processes of denationalization/deterritorialization of politics, markets, and laws or, more specifically, process of denationalization/deterritorialization of clusters of political, economic and social transactions involving national and international actors, public and private, leading to a global interconnectedness of these actors in time and space including individuals.[34]

Importantly, however, globalisation is not the only economic, social and political component of the global sphere it creates; and therefore, it does not exclude local difference and particularity.[35] Disintegrating effects can be the result[36] and are one of the reasons for the current marked increase in nationalism and ethnicism.[37]

Globalisation has several effects in the world of work:[38] it entails new markets, new products, new mindsets, new competencies and new ways of thinking about business.[39] Global competition is keeping businesses on their toes by requiring not only the application of new technologies and sharing of information, but also the capability to meet local needs. This requires a new form of management that accommodates different cultures and religions and is aware of local differences and particularities. In spreading the production of many goods and services all over the world, businesses face different labour laws and employment regulations imposed upon them by different states. Not surprisingly, the business community is pushing hard for harmonised regulations that would align the legal world with market reality and allow for rapid changes in business strategy to be made without the hamper of legal obstacles.

[33] Friedman, Th (2000) 9.
[34] Delbrück (2001) 16.
[35] Holton (1998) 16–17.
[36] Habermas (1998) 107–11.
[37] McGrew (1992) 74.
[38] For an overview, see ILO (1999a) para 1.
[39] Ulrich (1997) 2.

For individuals, globalisation has different effects depending on their particular jobs. Whereas skilled workers find themselves under greater pressure to share information and be flexible when it comes to working abroad,[40] unskilled workers feel threatened not only by new technologies that can increasingly replace humans in the manufacturing industries but also by the fact that worldwide competition among countries to attract businesses makes them more replaceable. Thus, unions complain that their bargaining position is often weakened.[41] Here too, the state has been called upon to establish minimum standards for working conditions and to prevent regulatory competition.

In sum, globalisation in the world of work affects all players in the labour market and calls for differing state actions: while from employers' and manufacturers' points of view national regulations should be reduced to make room for economic integration, unions fear a "race to the bottom" and therefore support protective measures and regulations.

I.2.2. The Effects of Globalisation on the International Community

Traditional international law is based on the concept of the sovereign territorial nation state. Although territorial integrity is defined as a relative and not an absolute concept in Article 2(4) of the UN charter, growing international concern over the protection of human rights has modified this principle to a degree probably unforeseen by the founders of the United Nations (UN).[42] Globalisation is further accelerating this development:

Understood as a dynamic process, globalisation not only entails new markets and new tools but also changes the rules of the game by empowering new actors such as the World Trade Organization (WTO), multinational enterprises, networks of non-governmental organisations (NGOs) and other groups.[43] In the context of work, this development results in a tension between core labour rights and international economic institutions.

National boundaries are becoming less important for the exercise of regulatory power because state borders no longer confine the "target" of such regulations. In

[40] OECD (2001b) at 95, 160.

[41] An example is the petition by the American Federation of Labor and Congress of Industrial Organizations (AFL-CIO) filed with the USTR on 16 March 2004 under section 301 of the Trade Act 1974 on behalf of its 13 million members. The petition alleges that "China's brutal repression of internationally recognised workers' rights constitutes an unfair trade practice under Section 301(d) of the Trade Act" and thereby results in burdening and or restricting US commerce. The cost advantage thereby gained by China—according to the complaint—translated into the loss of 727,000 jobs in the US (available at: http://www.aflcio.org). The complaint was later endorsed by Human Rights Watch and Amnesty International: Joint HRW–AI-USA Letter to United States Trade Representative Robert B Zoellick, 13 April 2004, available at: http://www.hrw.org/english/docs/2004/04/13/china8428.htm. The administration rejected the complaint on 29 April 2004.

[42] Delbrück (2001) 32–33.

[43] UNDP (1999) 1.

addition, integrated markets create a higher risk of national crises being spread to other countries. In the financial world, the collapse of the Bank for Commerce and Credit International (BCCI) in the early 1990s shook regulators by demonstrating how contagious the problems of a single institution can be and how vulnerable the global financial system has become. Although the fall of the BCCI left most individuals unaffected and, almost miraculously, did not spread to other sectors and countries, the financial turmoil in East Asia in 1997–99 did. The situation was impossible for single countries to withstand on their own, so bankruptcies spread, and education and health budgets came under pressure. The crisis had severe repercussions for labour markets in East and South-East Asia,[44] and the governments of the affected countries were left to stand by somewhat helplessly. This leaves us with the question as to whether, at the national level, globalisation undermines the ability of national governments to provide the public goods that their citizens have come to expect.[45]

How can a national government react to the perils of globalisation?[46] International teams of experts are increasingly involved in tailoring national policies. A recent example is the International Monetary Fund (IMF) and its proposed tax reform package for Argentina. When the reforms were altered during debate in parliament, the IMF announced that it would cancel its loan if the parliament did not annul its decision. Finally, the parliament passed a tax bill that complied with the IMF's conditions.[47] This example demonstrates the central role played by international experts when they formulate economic policies and reveals how this process can weaken democratic procedures.

The importance of remaining internationally competitive has narrowed the options for national policy makers.[48] In the world of work, the need to reduce labour costs in order for enterprises to stay in the market has led to a significant reduction of employment benefits. It has been argued that states must inevitably deregulate the labour market to allow for more flexibility. A possible "race to the bottom" as far as labour standards are concerned is therefore seen as one of the major threats of globalisation.

On the other hand, several European states have demonstrated that maintaining labour market policies that increase the overall cost of labour is still possible. However, these countries (France, Germany and Italy) paid a high price, with structural unemployment rates increasing significantly in the 1990s.[49] They experienced what Dani Rodrik called the "key tension of globalisation":

> In the markets for goods, services, labor and capital, international trade creates arbitrage—the possibility of buying (or producing) in one place at one price and selling at a

[44] For a detailed discussion, see Horton and Mazumdar (2001).

[45] Rodrik (1997) 21.

[46] UNDP (1999) 7–8, defines the "pernicious trends of globalization" as growing marginalisation, growing human insecurity and growing inequality.

[47] For a detailed overview on the Argentina crisis, see Setser and Gelpern (2006).

[48] OECD (1998) para 34.

[49] *Ibid.*

> higher price elsewhere. Prices thus tend to converge in the long run, this convergence being the source of the gains from trade. But trade exerts pressure toward another kind of arbitrage as well: arbitrage in national norms and social institutions. This form of arbitrage results, indirectly, as the costs of maintaining divergent social arrangements go up. As a consequence, open trade can conflict with long-standing social contracts that protect certain activities from the relentlessness of the free market.[50]

By providing expert advice for domestic regulation, international economic institutions such as the World Trade Organization (WTO) and the Bretton Woods Institutions (BWIs) are taking on responsibilities and tasks that are governmental in character. In relying mainly on economic considerations, conflicts with core labour rights, as the ILO has defined them, may arise. The result is a situation in which states find themselves confronted with conflicting international obligations.

The options of the state in this situation depend on two factors: first, the way in which the public goods it must provide to its citizens are defined; and second, how much room for national regulation is left given increasing demands for international co-operation.

I.3. THE AGENDA OF THIS BOOK

This book aims to put the debate about the role of the traditional nation state in a broader context by examining the tensions between core labour rights and international economic institutions. Historically, this tension is a relatively new phenomenon.

When Winston Churchill and Franklin Delano Roosevelt met on a battleship in the Atlantic Ocean in 1941, their vision of a peaceful world order after the Second World War—spelled out in the Atlantic Charter[51]—was essentially based on three pillars: peace, economic stability and trade between equal nations. The new economic framework was the topic of the conference held in Bretton Woods, New Hampshire, in 1944. The goal of this conference and its follow-ups for establishing an International Trade Organisation held in London (1946), Lake Success and Geneva (1947) and Havana (1948) was "to win the peace". A legal framework for stable monetary and financial conditions, combined with a plan for reconstruction after the war, was created with the founding of the IMF and the World Bank. In addition, liberalisation of international trade was seen as a means to re-establish peaceful international relations and ultimately enhance human welfare and democracy.

In the spirit of traditional international law, peaceful co-operation of equal sovereign states in the Westphalian sense stood at the centre of the deliberations on a new international trade organisation. What the drafters of what later

[50] Rodrik (1997) 27.
[51] Reprinted in Rosenman (1938) 314.

became the General Agreement on Tariffs and Trade (GATT) had in mind was not some abstract economic policy goal but to overcome the results of an era marked by totalitarian regimes and disrespect for human dignity. Human rights and the development of a general legal framework for a peaceful post-war order were left to the new United Nations. In hindsight, this early crossroads already seems to symbolise the different conceptual avenues that core labour rights and international economic institutions would take in the years to follow.

This book will show how the different concepts share a common general objective of enhancing human welfare but have developed in very different ways over the years, resulting in the fragmentation of international law into the highly specialised international legal systems with which we are faced today. The key aim of the study is to bring the different legal systems into a coherent framework, a consistent legal order.

It will start with an outline of the conceptual framework for core labour rights and international economic institutions, pointing out existing incompatibilities and/or conflicts of interest. The analysis will not stop at the conceptual level but will turn to concrete conflicts and ask: where do they occur? One of the questions to be explored is how trade liberalisation and structural adjustment programmes affect core labour rights. Within this broader context, the role of states in the international community and possible new forms of co-operation will also be addressed.

With the hypothesis that regulatory conflicts occur not only at the international level between different international organisations but also at the vertical level between international organisations and the state, we need to understand how international regulations and state policy interact. Chapter 1 will therefore outline the basic principles and the legal framework for core labour rights, in both domestic and international law. In the domestic context, the principles that govern economic policy also determine to what extent labour rights are to be protected. This is illustrated by a brief discussion of the evolution of the modern welfare state and its impact on the development of a core concept of labour rights. Within the economic and social policy framework, the content of core labour rights is then defined by international instruments such as the Conventions of the ILO and once again domestic law. The study shows first that core labour rights have their conceptual basis in human rights and therefore imply state obligations to respect, protect and fulfil such rights. A discussion will then follow about the development of a broad consensus on a set of core labour rights among the international community, which resulted in the 1998 ILO Declaration on Fundamental Principles and Rights at Work.

In light of the increasing influence of international economic organisations, chapter 2 will focus on the role of such organisations in enhancing core labour rights, first pointing out the extent to which their conceptual framework differs from the core labour rights approach. It will then show that international economic organisations can affect core labour rights: they can respect them by adopting a "do no harm policy" and complying with core labour rights in their own activities. In addition, it will argue that despite conceptual differences, there are possibilities for international economic organisations to go a step further and actively protect core labour rights by incorporating them into their own policies in the same way as the World Bank does with child labour and gender equality.

After the legal framework has been defined, chapter 3 will look at areas where conflicts between core labour rights and the objectives of international economic organisations may arise. In this context, multinational enterprises (MNEs) play an important role. Since traditional, state-based international law only partially accommodates this phenomenon, new approaches on holding them accountable, such as the new proposal by the United Nations Human Rights Commission for norms on responsibility of transnational corporations, will be discussed.

Finally, chapter 4 will describe the impact of these conflicts on the functioning of international organisations and the role of the state. It will conclude with a proposal on how to reconcile core labour rights with the interests of international economic organisations and the legal obligations related to them.

1

The Legal Framework for Core Labour Rights

> We hold these truths to be self-evident, that all Men are created equal, that they are endowed by their Creator with certain inalienable Rights, that among these are life, liberty, and the Pursuit of Happiness—that to secure these rights, Governments are instituted among men . . .
>
> Declaration of Independence, 1776

THE WORLD OF work for any body of citizens is largely affected by three interconnected forces. First, the internal constitution provides the foundation for the political, social and economic systems and sets out the framework in which the state operates. Second, human rights in the form of international (treaty) law provide additional guidelines with regard to individual liberties. Finally, the role of international economic organisations must be taken into account. This chapter will first look at the legal framework for economic and social policy and then move on to discuss the different instruments for protecting labour rights at the international and domestic levels. Chapter 2 will then examine the emergence of international economic organisations as important players in the world of work.

1.1. NATIONAL ECONOMIC AND SOCIAL POLICY

1.1.1. Free Market and Social Welfare

1.1.1.1. Theoretical Conceptions: Market versus Government Failure

The modern welfare state[1] is a relatively recent phenomenon. The first tentative attempts were seen towards the middle and end of the nineteenth century when a few industrialised countries started to develop modest policies to attenuate the

[1] The term did not actually enter the English language until 1941 when Archbishop Temple coined the phrase to differentiate wartime Britain from the "warfare" state of Nazi Germany. But it was Germany that pioneered both modern social insurance as early as the 1880s, and the concept of the *Wohlfahrtsstaat* in the 1920s. Newman, Eatwell and Milgate (1987) vol 4, at 895.

harshness of the industrial revolution.[2] Although the development of social protection schemes received a boost during the "New Deal" in the United States,[3] it was not until after the Second World War that the modern welfare state fully emerged in the countries associated with the Organisation for Economic Co-operation and Development (OECD) and in Eastern Europe. At this time, many developing countries also started to introduce social protection measures such as safety nets and pension schemes, unemployment benefits and health insurance for formal sector workers.[4]

Economically speaking, the labour market is a market like any other, driven by supply and demand. But, what happens in the labour market is of crucial importance for the lives of most people. A person's work is closely linked to his or her social status. Thus, being unemployed often amounts to exclusion from social life.[5] Because of the important role played by work in our society, regulating the labour market can be very tempting. On the one hand, high unemployment rates[6] and an increasing number of people who work but do not earn enough to make a living (the working poor) have resulted in calls—especially by left-wing politicians—for state action and new labour market policy.[7] On the other hand, conservatives and neo-liberals argue that the current problems are not caused by market failure but rather by misguided state intervention. As a remedy, they prescribe a course of deregulation, eg lowering minimum wages and reducing unemployment benefits.

While the need for social policies that complement economic liberties is widely acknowledged, the question of how far social policy should go is still being debated among economists and lawyers. The different views revolve around the underlying concept of human nature[8] and the degree to which the state should intervene in the market.

State activities have increased significantly over the last century. To explain this phenomenon, several theories refer to the concept of market failure.[9] However, the definitions of what conditions can be defined as market failure and thus justify state interventions vary.

In modern welfare economics it is argued that the state should intervene to re-establish ideal (ie, Pareto efficient) conditions in the market. This argument is

[2] The modern welfare state was inaugurated with the provision of public elementary education in Germany in 1850 (followed by the United States in 1870) and confirmed by the enactment of the first of Bismarck's social insurance schemes in 1883.

[3] Social Security Act of 1935, 42 USCA § 657. For a history of the New Deal legislation, see Malamud (1998).

[4] World Bank (2001b) 1.

[5] For a general description, see Sennett (1998).

[6] The OECD average standardised unemployment rate rose from just over 3 per cent in 1973 to 7.3 per cent in 1997. Martin (1998) para 1.

[7] For example, Gorz (1999a) 49–63.

[8] Economists often refer to a fictional *homo oeconomicus* whose behaviour is driven by rational decisions. Richli (2000) 121. Lawyers on the other hand, often tend towards the concept of what Peter Häberle once called the *homo socialis*. Häberle (1984) 95–98, 102.

[9] Watrin (1985) 138–44.

based on the *theorem of the invisible hand* developed by Adam Smith.[10] It implies that consumers and firms will make independent, rational decisions to maximise utility or profit. As a result, the general equilibrium established under the condition known as "perfect competition" is socially optimal.[11] It is important to note that the term "social optimum" has a special meaning in welfare economics. It acknowledges the fact that individual gains cannot be compared, and therefore focuses on the basis for the Pareto efficiency theorem.[12] The equilibrium is optimal because it is efficient with respect both to the production of goods and to their allocation to consumers. Hence, it is not possible to make any consumer better off without making some other consumer worse off.[13] The state should apply corrective measures and interfere with individual liberties only when this equilibrium is threatened. For welfare economists, state intervention can thus only be justified by economic reasons.[14] In this liberal concept, the commonly accepted reasons for intervention are external effects, public goods and natural monopolies.[15]

Two major theories emphasise the stability of the market as a critical criterion: *Keynesians* maintain that the market tends to be unstable, thus allowing a broad range of state interventions. On the other hand, *monetarists* assume the market to be stable as long as the state ensures stable monetary conditions, for example, by granting independence to central banks.[16]

A third group of scholars[17] applies *distributive justice*[18] as their main standard for judging markets. From this viewpoint, a free market leads not only to higher productivity but also to income disparities, which, for social reasons, need to be corrected by the state. Redistribution policy is hence justified by ethical reasons.

If the goal of a society is to maximise benefits for the whole community, unintended outcomes can also result from *government failure*. In these cases, state intervention has a negative impact on public welfare. One of the reasons for such an outcome is a conflict between the public interest and the individual interests of the decision-makers. The theory of *public choice*[19] suggests that the decisions taken by democratically legitimised bodies have to be seen in the context of the interests of the people involved in the decision-making process. According to this theory, two concerns arise: first, individuals are likely to pursue their self-interests both in the political field and in economic markets; second, government regulations tend to be influenced by rent-seeking interests

[10] Smith (1976) 456.
[11] Perfect competition implies equal marginal benefits and equal marginal costs for every good in the market.
[12] Kirchgässner (1998) para 15.
[13] Sen (1997b) 94–95.
[14] For a survey of the economic theory of optimal intervention, see Petersmann (1991) 57–58.
[15] Watrin (1986) 6–11.
[16] Lastra (1992) 476–82; Cukierman, Kalaitzidakis, Summers and Webb (1993) 95–140.
[17] Watrin (1985) 140–41.
[18] For a comprehensive modern concept based on Rawls' theory of justice: Hinsch (2002).
[19] Frey (1984) 201–7.

in redistributing income for the benefit of regulated industries in exchange for the political support of the regulators.[20] It would therefore be naive to look at democratic institutions as impartial organs that act in the public interest.

All these orthodox approaches attempt to explain the choices of economic agents, their interactions with one another, and the results of these interactions, *within* the existing legal, constitutional and institutional structure of the society. Normative considerations enter through the efficiency criteria of theoretical welfare economics, and policy options are evaluated in terms of these criteria. Political decision-makers are then presented with a set of options from which to choose. In other words, non-trade concerns are considered under the aspect of efficiency and market enhancement.[21]

In contrast, constitutional economic analysis follows a different approach. In response to the shortcomings of public choice theory, it attempts to explain how different sets of legal, constitutional and institutional rules may influence or constrain the choices and activities of economic and political agents. It thus analyses and defines the framework within which the ordinary choices of economic and political options are made. Normative criteria are at the core of the analysis and are not merely a subcategory of efficiency-considerations. Constitutional economists therefore offer normative advice to political decision-makers in the process of, for example, constitutional change and establishing a "Constitution of liberty" that maximises the general welfare of citizens; in other words, they provide no advice for policy-makers on how to act within defined rules.[22]

One of the possible fields of application for constitutional economics and the reason for its inclusion in this section is the protection of human rights and labour rights by states. Ernst-Ulrich Petersmann has taken the lead, first in pointing out the similarities between economic and political markets with respect to consumer and citizen sovereignty paradigms and their underlying values,[23] and second—in a very controversial move[24]—by outlining possible scenarios for reconciling the two. We will return to this topic in the context of the linkage debate in chapter 3.

1.1.1.2. Protective versus Productive States

Where should the line for positive state measures be drawn? Although orthodox economic theories cannot answer this question, they nevertheless provide tools to assess the success of governmental policies and possible risks involved.[25] In

[20] Petersmann (2003) 52 with further references.
[21] Buchanan (1987) 585–588.
[22] *Ibid.*
[23] Petersmann (2003) 56–59.
[24] See the fierce debate between Petersmann and Alston: Petersmann (2002a), the challenge by Alston (2002) and comment by Howse (2002b) and the reply by Petersmann (2002b).
[25] Watrin (1985) 145.

the following section, I will refer to economic theories as orthodox economic theories, thus leaving aside for the moment the concept of constitutional economics introduced above.

Traditional legal philosophy views the state as a "shelter of last resort" that must accommodate the basic needs of its citizens. Typically, for economists the state and the market are alternative institutions, and which one prevails is a matter of choice. An important role is assigned to the state in improving the allocation of resources to the production of public goods.[26] Public goods are characterised by two qualities: "nonrivalry" and "nonexcludability". In contrast to private goods, they are consumed collectively, and the benefits for any single individual do not depend on the benefits enjoyed by others. Therefore, their consumption by the individual is not related to the quantities consumed by others (nonrivalry), as is the case with private goods, where the total consumption directly influences the supply. In addition, it is very difficult or impossible to prevent individuals from benefiting from a public good (nonexcludability). A typical example in the environmental context is clean air: everybody has access to it.

Because of the missing link between supply and demand and the high costs of excluding non-paying beneficiaries, it appears to make sense for an individual to avoid making any contribution to the production of public goods, relying instead on other members of the society to produce the public good. If this expectation is met, the "free rider" can benefit without costs. If every member of society follows this path, the working of the markets for these goods is disrupted and a classical prisoners' dilemma results. The role of the state then consists in establishing a consensus on the production of the public good. This can be either governmental provision of the public good, for which the costs of production are paid from general tax revenues, or private provision of the public good with governmental subsidisation.[27]

Which goods are public? There is consensus among economists that the protection of property is a prerequisite for the functioning of the market and thus a natural public good. The minimal conception of the state therefore means that the state has to implement effective mechanisms for protecting property. This economic concept of the protective state[28] (*Rechtsschutz-Staat*) with a focus on procedural rights differs from the legal "*Rechtsstaat*" with its broader goal of protecting not only procedural but also substantial individual rights.[29]

Proceeding beyond this minimalist approach raises several difficulties. Currently, most state expenditures are not dedicated to establishing and maintaining an efficient legal system but to social and other costs. In a *productive*

[26] The discussion of public goods is important in two respects: first, to define where state regulation is necessary and second—in the context of *global* public goods—to argue for international regulations instead of national laws.
[27] Cooter and Ulen (2004) 109.
[28] Buchanan (1975) 17–19, 95–98.
[29] We will see later that the World Bank, in its access to justice programme, relies on the economic concept. See chapter 2, section 2.2.4.1. below on the World Bank Articles of Agreement.

state (*Leistungsstaat*), several public and quasi-public goods (*meritorische Güter*) are offered. Examples include peace, environmental protection, monetary stability and state regulations.[30] In addition, a productive state is likely to provide private goods as well.[31]

In contrast to philosophy,[32] economic theories do not help us to choose which public goods should be provided by the state, but they do provide a method for assessing state efficiency and setting realistic goals.[33] In economic terms, the different public goods are on an equal footing; there is no hierarchy of values.[34] Working conditions are considered as public goods by economists to the extent that the same working conditions are shared by all workers in a firm and those conditions have a direct effect on both their well-being and their productivity.[35]

Decisions have to be made at three different levels. First, a constitutional system or framework (*Wirtschaftsverfassung*) must be chosen:[36] it can be a free market economy, a planned economy or a mixed model like the modern welfare state. The means of implementing the policy framework include competition policy, consumer protection and foreign trade policy. They are generally referred to as *Ordnungspolitik*. Second, the state can play an active role in the prevention of crises in the labour market, for instance by regulating the immigration of workers, with the goal of achieving full employment. These measures are known as *Ablaufpolitik*. *Strukturpolitik* aims at strengthening economically weak regions or sectors of the labour market. A common example is agricultural policy.

Finally, some governmental actions strive to redistribute income and resources (*Einkommens- und Verteilungspolitik*). The goal of re-establishing an equilibrium between social partners or between different segments of the population is achieved *inter alia* by providing, for example, minimum wages, compulsory social insurance and tax incentives.

1.1.1.3. Conclusions

The effects of globalisation on the labour market change the role for the state. As the president of the International Labour Conference 2001, Patricia A Sto Tomas, put it: "Globalisation, like golf, requires a handicapping system that allows the new players to catch up."[37]

[30] Buchanan (1975) 68–70.
[31] Eg postal services, public transport, motorways etc.
[32] Hinsch (2002) 31–49 and 169–94.
[33] See Drahos (2004) 322–29.
[34] Watrin (1985) 157–58. Or, as Lon L Fuller puts it, ". . . there seems to be implied some ultimate criterion that stands above books, food, clothing, and all the other things and services for which men may spend their money. The marginal utility economist cannot describe what this criterion is, though, unlike the moralist of aspiration, he has a word to cover his ignorance. That word is, of course, 'utility'." Fuller (1969) 17.
[35] Singh (2003) 122–25.
[36] Biaggini, Múller, Richli and Zimmerli (2005) 8–10.
[37] In her presidential address to the International Labour Conference, 89th session, 2001.

On the one hand, the state has to step in where markets are not able to protect fundamental values. On the other, a decentralised understanding of regulation[38] that involves a plurality of actors, a variety of legal and non-legal norms and the use of techniques that go beyond that of sovereign command by the state, is increasingly gaining importance. As a result, globalisation is about to end the old Westphalian system of sovereign nation states by challenging its basic principles.[39] As an alternative, a market-oriented approach is mainly advocated by industrialised countries.

It seems obvious however, that an unlimited free market is not sustainable for at least three reasons.[40] First, globalisation can widen the gap between winners and losers[41] to an extent that global security is potentially threatened.[42] The attacks on the World Trade Center on 11 September 2001 and other similar events have taught us that the stability of poor nations is a key element in maintaining world peace.[43] Second, market systems by definition are efficient only if there is competition. Given the lack of global antitrust rules, it is unlikely that competition will prevail without regulatory intervention. Thirdly, despite the discussion about deregulation, market systems must depend on the rule of law or they will tend to become mafia systems promoting a Darwinian system of survival of the fittest. The assumption that market systems will discipline themselves spontaneously has turned out to be overly optimistic, as demonstrated by situations in which the rule of law has not prevailed.[44]

1.1.2. Constitutional Principles

How do modern constitutions take economic insights into account and what institutional choices are made with respect to defining the criteria for state intervention in the labour market? The Swiss Constitution with its revision of 2000 provides a useful example because its development illustrates how economic

38 Black, J (2002) 2–10.

39 Valaskakis (2001) 64–66. According to Valaskakis (2001) at 49–52, the five principles of the old Westphalian Order are: 1) the primacy of sovereignty; 2) control over geographical territory; 3) national governments as the key players; 4) the emergence of a body of international law based on treaties between sovereign countries; and 5) war as a recognised instrument of international relations.

40 Valaskakis (2001) 65–66.

41 In economically advanced countries, the losers are unskilled labourers. See Bordo (2002) 28.

42 This concern was expressed most recently by a (controversial) resolution of the Commission on Human Rights: "Globalisation and its Impact on the Full Enjoyment of All Human Rights", Resolution 2001/32, UN Doc E/CN.4/RES/2001/32, 20 April 2001, adopted by roll-call vote of 37 votes to 15 with 1 abstention. For Asia-Pacific, see Hughes (2000) 14–17.

43 Discussions after the attacks on the World Trade Center on 11 September 2001 *inter alia* emphasised the relationship between poverty and terrorism. At the UN Conference on Financing for Development in Monterrey in March 2002, some countries called for a new "War on Poverty".

44 An example is the collapse of the rule of law in the former Soviet Union. The World Bank organised a conference on the rule of law in summer 2001: http://www4.worldbank.org/legal/?ljr_01/?index.html.

theory can be built step-by-step into a binding legal framework, thus making clear what questions need to be answered by policy-makers. In addition, lessons learned from the Swiss experience may serve as a basis for developing solutions at the global level.

1.1.2.1. *Laying the Foundation: The Swiss Constitutions of 1848 and 1874*

Two issues are of crucial importance in defining the constitutional legal framework for labour rights: social rights and economic freedom.

A) Social Rights The principle of social welfare was mentioned in early drafts of the Swiss Federal Constitution in 1832–33.[45] Ultimately, the first Federal Constitution of 1848 stated that the promotion of common welfare was one of the Confederation's main objectives.[46] The provision took up two of the goals of the French Revolution, *fraternité* and *égalité*, and attempted to distance the Constitution from the liberal protective state, the "*Nachtwächterstaat*". The revised Constitution of 1874, which was in force until 1999, contained the same provision (Article 2). In addition, Article 31bis para 1, which was incorporated in 1947, required the federal government to take the necessary measures to ensure the welfare and economic security of the people. Neither of these articles was considered legally enforceable or to have granted individual rights, but rather they were viewed as programmatic guidelines for state activities,[47] thus establishing a constitutional "social clause". In practical terms, the provisions on social insurance,[48] labour[49] and consumer protection[50] were the most important.[51]

Before 2000, the old Constitution contained no social rights, eg no right to governmental benefits, no right to work or to education.[52] Only in two cases did the Federal Supreme Court acknowledge enforceable unwritten social rights: the right to free legal assistance[53] (*unentgeltliche Rechtspflege*), which was essentially derived from due process, and the right to basic subsistence[54] (*Garantie der Existenzsicherung*) as a key factor in ensuring human dignity.

It must be noted that Switzerland has a tradition of being rather sceptical towards the introduction of new social rights in its Constitution. Several attempts

[45] For discussion on more far-reaching social rights see Kölz (1992b) 464–69, 522–25.

[46] Article 2 of the Federal Constitution of September 1848, reprinted (in German and French) in Kölz (1992a) 447. Meyer-Blaser and Gächter (2001) § 34, Rz 8.

[47] Aubert (1987a) Rz 28–35; Rhinow (1987) Rz 19–22.

[48] Articles 18 para 2, 22bis para 6, 34bis, 34ter para 1 lit. d, 34^{quater}, $34^{quinquies}$ para 2, 4 and Article 34^{novies}.

[49] Articles 34, 34ter, 56.

[50] Articles 31^{sexies}, $31^{septies}$, 34^{sexies}, $34^{septies}$, 64 and Article 69bis.

[51] Rhinow (2000) 170.

[52] Yet, the Constitution granted so-called "small social rights", which included the right to free elementary school classes (Article 27 para 2), the right to a decent funeral (Article 53 para 2) and the right to free military equipment (Article 18 para 3).

[53] BGE 122 I 203; 124 I 1; Kley-Struller (1995) 190–91; Müller, JP (1999) 542–53.

[54] BGE 121 I 367; 122 I 193; Kley-Struller (1996) 756–59; Müller, JP (1999) 166–80. For a comprehensive study see Gysin (1999).

failed to reach the necessary consent of the majority of the people and the cantons: namely, the right to work in 1894[55] and 1946,[56] the right to housing in 1970[57] and the right to education in 1973.[58] With respect to labour rights,[59] neither the proposed introduction of the 40-hour working week in 1976[60] and 1988,[61] nor the right to participation (*Mitbestimmung*) in 1976[62] and the extension of paid vacation time from four to five weeks in 1985[63] were approved.

B) Economic Freedom The counterpart to the guiding principles of social welfare in Article 2 and Article 31[bis] was the statement of economic freedom in Article 31. This provision was unique: no other country[64] has had a similarly broad yet explicit guarantee of the protection of economic activities in its constitution.[65] Apart from granting an individual right, this provision is also of institutional importance.[66] Its relevance lies in three different areas.[67]

First, the framers reacted to the nineteenth-century guild system, which restricted craftsmen from freely pursuing trade and commercial activities.[68] Human dignity, according to the framers, implied not only the freedom to choose one's own economic activity and be undisturbed by governmental intervention in its exercise but also access to different professions.

Second, the guarantee of economic freedom in the constitution also stood for a commitment to a market economy as opposed to a planned economy. In line with the liberal—negative or defensive—understanding of governmental responsibilities, Article 31 did not actively protect a system of free competition but required the state not to impede competition, thus seeking to maintain a neutral position or, in legal terms, to treat all competitors in the market alike.

Finally, in the face of differing economic regulations across the cantons, Article 31 aimed at establishing a free market for the entire territory of the confederation.[69] The importance of the concept of economic freedom was

55 Rejected by popular vote on 3 June 1894. BBl 1893 IV 369; 1894 II 354, 356, 358; 1894 III 89.
56 Rejected by popular vote on 8 December 1946. BBl 1946 II 773; 1947 I 454. AS 63 232.
57 Rejected by popular vote on 27 September 1970. BBl 1969 II 887; 1970 II 1628.
58 Rejected by popular vote on 4 March 1973. The majority of the people, but not the cantons, accepted the initiative. BBl 1972 I 375; 1973 I 1195.
59 For a historical overview, see Fazioli (1996) 9–11.
60 Rejected by popular vote on 5 December 1976. BBl 1975 II 2259; 1977 I 532, 1380.
61 Rejected by popular vote on 4 December 1988. BBl 1987 II 1017; 1989 I 230.
62 Rejected by popular vote on 21 March 1976. BBl 1973 II 237; 1976 II 660, 1048.
63 Rejected by popular vote on 10 March 1985. BBl 1982 III 201; 1985 I 1548.
64 The US Constitution protects economic liberties with the contracts clause in art I s 10, the takings clause in the Fifth Amendment and economic substantive due process in the Fifth and Fourteenth Amendments. Chemerinsky (1997) § 8.
65 Müller, JP (1999) 633. Biaggini (1996) 61–62 states that the combination of other fundamental rights often leads to a protection of economic freedom.
66 Rhinow, Schmid and Biaggini (1998) § 4 Rz 58–74; Müller, JP (1999) 637–43; Rhinow (1987) Rz 22.
67 Biaggini, Múller, Richli and Zimmerli (2005) 10–11.
68 Kölz (1992b) 589–94.
69 A similar approach can be found in the Constitution of the United States: the commerce clause in Article I section 8 clause 3 gives the power to regulate commerce among the states to the US Congress.

underlined by the fact that any restriction had to be based on the Constitution.[70] With regard to federalism, Article 31 para 2 was essential because it respected cantonal competence to regulate their own economic activities as long as such regulations complied with the *principle* of economic freedom. This provision responded to the fear that cantonal regulations might impede inter-cantonal trade.[71]

The priority granted to the principle of economic freedom was reflected in the fact that until 1911, cases involving this principle were adjudicated by the Federal Parliament and the Federal Council, whereas all other fundamental rights conflicts had been judged by the Federal Supreme Court since 1893.[72] In contrast to all other constitutional fundamental rights, which can be restricted if there is a sufficient legal basis and the restrictions are motivated by public interest and are proportional, restrictions of economic freedom follow a different approach.[73]

The Federal Supreme Court made it clear that not every public interest is capable of justifying a restriction on economic freedom. For example, measures that impede free competition in order to protect or give preferential treatment to certain commercial activities are unconstitutional.[74] In addition, measures that aim to establish a partially planned economy are not allowed.[75] The Federal Supreme Court and the majority of legal scholars[76] refer to these measures as being part of *economic* policy (*wirtschaftspolitisch*). The only constitutional measures are those that are motivated by *social* policy concerns (*sozialpolitische Massnahmen*),[77] are aimed at avoiding risk or danger to the public (*polizeiliche Massnahmen*)[78] or protect other non-economic public interests[79] such as the protection of the environment.

This narrow legal notion of economic policy creates a great deal of confusion because it differs from the economic concept. For economists, every governmental activity that influences the economy and accomplishes economic or social objectives is part of economic policy. In legal terms, however, complying

[70] Gygi and Richli (1997) 58.

[71] The US responded to this threat with the *dormant commerce clause*: according to this principle, state and local laws are unconstitutional if they place an undue burden on interstate commerce. The Supreme Court inferred this rule from the grant of power to Congress in Article I s 8 cl 3 of the US Constitution. *Pike v Bruce Church*, 397 USR 137 (1970) 142; *United States v Lopez*, 115 SCR 1624 (1995); Chemerinsky (1997) § 5.3; Regan (1995) 560–561; Regan (1986) 1091–1287. The recent decision of the US Supreme Court on the Burma/Myanmar sanctions (*Crosby v National Foreign Trade Council* 530 USR 366, 373 (2000)) did not touch on the dormant commerce clause but rejected the Massachusetts law on supremacy grounds. See Halberstam (2001b); and chapter 3 below, note 109 and accompanying text.

[72] Kälin (1994a), 4.

[73] Rhinow, Schmid and Biaggini (1998), §5 Rz 160–166.

[74] BGE 118 Ia 176.

[75] BGE 111 Ia 186.

[76] For an overview of the different opinions, see Biaggini (1996) 56–58.

[77] BGE 97 I 506.

[78] BGE 121 I 279, 282.

[79] BGE 102 Ia 104, 115. Rhinow, Schmid and Biaggini (1998) § 5 Rz 168–69.

with the principle of economic freedom means respecting the fundamental mechanisms of supply and demand in a free market economy.[80]

C) The State of Labour The old Swiss Constitution contained very few provisions that dealt explicitly with labour.[81] Several important labour rights were derived from the concept of economic freedom including the right to access the labour market and to choose[82] and pursue a profession,[83] the right to enter into a contract of employment and determine its contents,[84] the right to select staff members[85] and the right to choose the place of work.[86] All of these rights were of a procedural nature, in essence protecting the freedom of choice of contracting parties.

The Constitution of 1874 did strongly support *collective* labour rights such as the freedom to join unions,[87] which was ensured by the general freedom of association in Article 56. Since Confederation, the Federal Government has always recognised the importance of social peace between employers and workers and has therefore actively engaged in facilitating agreements. As a result, the government maintains a neutral position. If a consensus (*Gesamtarbeitsvertrag*) is reached by the parties in one sector of the economy, the government has the power to extend the obligations of the agreement to third parties (*Allgemeinverbindlicherklärung*).[88]

A third aspect of labour rights concerns the promotion of full employment as mentioned in Article 31^{quinquies} para 1 and 2. As such, it is part of the general policy to ensure stable economic development. Although these provisions granted no individual right to work, they were in compliance with the standards set by the European Social Charter.[89]

80 Rhinow (2000) 165. The treaty establishing the European Community contains a similar provision in Article 4(1):

> For the purposes set out in Article 2, the activities of the Member States and the Community shall include, as provided in this Treaty and in accordance with the timetable set out therein, the adoption of an economic policy which is based on the close coordination of Member States' economic policies, on the internal market and on the definition of common objectives, and conducted in accordance with the principle of an open market economy with free competition.

Although the notion of an open market economy is not very precise it reflects a common general understanding among the Member States of the European Union. See Biaggini (1996) 50–51.

81 For an overview, see Tschudi (1989).

82 BGE 105 Ia 67, 71; Tschudi (1989) 775.

83 BGE 109 Ia 116, 121–22.

84 BGE 106 Ib 125, 134–35; 80 I 155, 162.

85 BGE 122 I 44, 47; 114 Ia 307, 312.

86 BGE 119 Ia 374, 375.

87 Malinverni (1987) Rz 42–47.

88 Article 34ter para 1 lit c; Aubert (1987b) Rz 23–35.

89 Tschudi (1989) 776. As counterpart to the European Convention on Human Rights, the European Social Charter complements the political rights of the convention with social, economic and cultural rights and therefore has a function similar to the International Covenant on Economic, Social and Cultural Rights at the UN level. Switzerland signed the European Social Charter in 1976, yet due to the lack of consent in Parliament, it was never ratified. Today Switzerland fulfils all the requirements necessary for becoming a member. Bericht der Kommission für soziale Sicherheit und Gesundheit des Nationalrats zur parlamentarischen Genehmigung der Europäischen Sozialcharta vom 17 November 1995, BBl 1996 II 721 ff.

Formal protection of workers started at the end of the nineteenth century when the cantons initiated legislation to protect against the exploitative and hazardous forms of work that emerged during the industrial revolution. This legislation tended to emphasise the protection of children. With its law on maximum working hours of 1864, the canton of Glarus played a pioneering role worldwide.[90] In 1874, Article 34 para 1 gave the federal government the authority to legislate to protect factory workers. Despite being already very progressive for the times, this provision was supplemented by Article 34ter in 1908 and its revision in 1947, which extended the protection to workers in general.[91] With the Labour Act of 1964 (*Arbeitsgesetz*),[92] a comprehensive regime of worker protection norms was established.

Finally, after 1982 a new paragraph 2 of the general non-discrimination clause in Article 4 prohibited employment discrimination and specifically ensured gender equality in the workplace.[93] It was incorporated into Article 8 of the 2000 Constitution and is applicable to both governmental entities and private actors.

1.1.2.2. Attempts to Establish a Comprehensive Framework: the New Swiss Constitution of 1999

After several attempts to overhaul the Swiss Constitution failed,[94] in 1987 Parliament finally assigned to the Federal Council the task of revising the Constitution, but their mandate was limited to updating the text to the current state of law, thus preventing the introduction of any new principles or laws.[95]

The project lost some of its momentum in the following years due to the more urgent issue of Switzerland's integration into Europe. However, the situation changed when the majority of the cantons and the people rejected the accession to the European Economic Area on 6 December 1992. Internal reforms then returned to centre stage. Finally, in recognition of the need for adaptation to European law, Parliament decided that a new draft Constitution should be made available by 1998, the 150th anniversary of the Confederation.

The main goal of the revision was to bring the text of the Constitution in line with developments in the jurisprudence and society. During the parliamentary debate of the draft, the government strongly defended its narrow mandate as it had been formulated by Parliament itself in 1987. However, the draft tried to resolve some controversial issues by taking a clear position. This was especially necessary in order to gain the support of the cantons. In the proposal put forward by the Federal Council, the few innovations or clarifications were therefore limited to the relationship between the Federal Government and the cantons.

[90] Stolz (1968) 108.
[91] Tschudi (1989) 777–78.
[92] Bundesgesetz über die Arbeit in Industrie, Gewerbe und Handel vom 13 März 1964, SR 822.11.
[93] BBl 1978 II 1219; 1980 I 69, 1981 II 1266.
[94] For a critical review of the several attempts to reform the Constitution see Aubert (1991) 9–141; Eichenberger (1991) 143–273.
[95] Bundesbeschluss über die Totalrevision der Bundesverfassung vom 3 Juni 1987, BBl 1987 II 963.

During the parliamentary discussion, especially in the House of Representatives (*Nationalrat*), political issues became much more important than legal considerations. Following the concept of a "living constitution" that should reflect legal and social reality, Parliament included several new provisions for which there was widespread popular support. It became the job of several eminent legal scholars in the Senate (*Ständerat*) to ensure that the new Constitution would not only live up to political expectations but also comply with high legal standards.

The new Constitution follows a more systematic approach in defining rules and fundamental rights than the old one did, yet it still contains a provision protecting the *principle* of economic freedom. Article 27 delineates the fundamental right of economic freedom,[96] and a new section entitled *Economy* outlines the fundamental principles of economic policy:

> Article 94 *Principles of Economic Order*
>
> 1 The Confederation and the cantons shall respect the principle of economic freedom.
> 2 They shall safeguard the interests of the national economy and, together with the private sector of the economy, contribute to the welfare and economic security of the population.
> 3 Within the limits of their powers, they shall strive to create favourable conditions for the private sector of the economy.
> 4 Derogations from the principle of economic freedom, in particular measures against competition, shall be allowed only if foreseen by the Federal Constitution or based on cantonal monopolies.

Although the Constitution integrates developments in jurisprudence and legal theory into other areas, it fails to do so in relation to the principle of economic freedom. Unlike the Treaty establishing the European Community,[97] it makes no explicit statement of support for one particular economic system. In fact, with paragraph 4 (above), the new Constitution seems to perpetuate the old system by requiring a constitutional basis for any encroachment on economic freedom. However, the phrase "measures against competition" in paragraph 4 gives an unmistakable clue as to what will be considered a "derogation from the principle of economic freedom".[98] Taken in context with Article 27, Article 94 thereby implicitly contains a commitment to maintaining a market-oriented private economy.[99]

[96] Article 27 *Economic Freedom*

> 1 Economic Freedom is guaranteed.
> 2 It contains particularly the freedom to choose one's profession, and to enjoy free access to and free exercise of private economic activity.

[97] See note 81 above and accompanying text.

[98] The phrase "measures against competition" was introduced during the parliamentary debate on the request of the constitutional commission of the Senate. Rhinow (2000) 166; for a less critical view, see Vallender (1999) 681–82.

[99] Vallender (1999) 682–84.

In contrast to this rather tentative attempt to establish a more comprehensive and systematic economic framework within the Constitution, several new provisions break with tradition by mentioning social welfare and social rights. First, the preamble, which goes back to an earlier draft by the famous Swiss author Adolf Muschg,[100] states a clear commitment for the Confederation:

> We, the Swiss People and Cantons, . . . know . . . that the strength of a people is measured by the welfare of the weakest of its members. . . .

The preamble is followed by Article 2, which not only contains an established welfare clause in paragraph 2 but also seeks to ensure equal opportunities for all citizens[101] (paragraph 3). Neither of these provisions was mentioned in the original text by the Federal Council, but they were adopted during the parliamentary discussion.

Finally, a catalogue of social goals in Article 41 completes the new set of rules dealing with social justice. This catalogue was heavily debated during the political process. Article 33 of the governmental draft had pursued a narrow approach by stating that the social goals would not create individual rights and that any public support or service was subject to available means and only complementary to private responsibility and initiative. Parliament added the state's responsibility to provide protection against the economic consequences of old age, disability, illness, accidents, unemployment, maternity, orphanhood and widowhood.[102] By excluding only the derivation of direct subjective rights from social goals, it left the door open for the granting of unwritten individual rights that could be based on provisions other than the social goals clause.[103]

In addition to public obligations, the founders also stressed individual responsibility by stating that social security should still primarily rely on private initiative.[104] In fact, in doing so, the founders were applying the general concept of subsidiarity to the relationship between the state and its citizens. This notion of subsidiarity, which is now contained in the new Article 6, was already familiar in reference to the European Community[105] as well as to the old relationship

[100] The draft of 1977 (Bericht der Expertenkommission für die Vorbereitung einer Totalrevision der Bundesverfassung, Bern 1977,VE 77) contained a visionary preamble by Adolf Muschg, which led to heated discussions, partly because of its content and partly because of the political opinion of its author.

[101] Bearing in mind that the last of the cantons, Appenzell Inner Rhodes, granted the right to vote in cantonal affairs to women as late as 1990 following a decision by the Federal Supreme Court (BGE 116 Ia 359, 381–82), this provision is of particular importance because for the first time in Switzerland's constitutional history, female citizens are explicitly mentioned (*Bürgerinnen, citoyennes, cittadine*).

[102] Although not mentioned during the parliamentary debate, the "right to security in the event of unemployment, sickness, disability, widowhood, old age or other lack of livelihood in circumstances beyond one's control" is already contained in Article 25(1) of the Universal Declaration of Human Rights of 1948.

[103] Mader (1999) 699.

[104] Article 41(1) reads: "The Confederation and the Cantons shall strive to ensure that, *in addition to personal responsibility and private initiative* . . ." (emphasis added).

[105] Article 5 of the Constitution. See Breining-Kaufmann (1994) 457–58.

between the Confederation and the cantons.[106] In various other provisions as well,[107] Parliament added clauses to ensure that state obligations are not the primary means to pursue social goals, but that individual and private initiative should take the lead.[108]

The justiciability of socio-economic rights has been the subject of considerable jurisprudential and political debate in many countries. As we will see in section 1.2. below, the issue cannot be resolved without looking at constitutions in their international context, namely with regard to the Conventions of the International Labour Organisation[109] and the International Covenant on Social, Economic and Cultural Rights of 1966, which Switzerland ratified in 1992. Unlike many new democracies and developing countries,[110] the Swiss Parliament saw no need for any substantial reinforcement of socio-economic rights. This is in line with the policies of most industrialised nations, despite the fact that, for example, the number of the working poor in Switzerland increased significantly in the 1990s.[111]

1.1.2.3. Conclusions

The Swiss example illustrates how economic theory and political choices interact in defining the constitutional framework for labour rights. The constitutional concept of social rights to a large extent determines the legal nature of labour "standards" by framing them as either individual rights or social policy goals. Within the individual rights framework it is necessary to define whether labour rights are directly enforceable in court. In this respect, the international context is of importance since it may limit governmental discretion. This will be discussed in section 1.2. below.

There are several ways to accommodate general economic policy goals within a constitutional framework. One option lies in the definition of economic policy as a derivative of economic freedom. This is the approach chosen by the first Swiss Constitution. Such a statement can then be further developed into an institutional commitment to market economy. The Swiss example can serve as an illustration for both the orthodox and the constitutional economic approach. In partially relying on economic theory to clarify the meaning of the constitutional principle of economic freedom and thereby define the limits for state intervention

[106] Article 3 of the Constitution.

[107] Eg, in Article 12 *Right to Aid in Distress*.

[108] Rhinow (2000) 173.

[109] Müller, JP (1981) 292–99.

[110] The most recent example is South Africa. In order to eliminate apartheid, the South African Constitution contains several socio-economic rights. The Constitutional Court of South Africa in *Government of the Republic of South Africa v Grootboom* 11 BCLR 1169 (CC) (2000) [hereinafter *South Africa v Grootboom*] was the first high court in the world to come up with a solution for setting priorities in implementing socio-economic rights and thus ensuring protection without placing the court in an unacceptable managerial role.

[111] According to a recent study by the Federal Office of Statistics, in 1999 an estimated 250,000 people or 7.5% of the working population were living in households that were considered poor. Streuli and Bauer (2001); Pressemitteilung des Bundesamtes für Statistik, März 2001 Nr. 350-01022. For the different definitions of poverty, see OECD (2001b) Box 2.1 at 41.

in individuals' economic liberty, the government and courts have applied an *orthodox* economic approach. At the same time, however, the controversy surrounding the revision of the Constitution and in particular the inclusion of a new section entitled "*Economy*" belies a desire to apply economics at an earlier stage and at a higher level, in the very formulation of the constitutional framework; in other words, *constitutional* economics has also had a role to play. In sum, the provision that was finally adopted is somewhere in the middle since it refers to economic principles as a general foundation but neither overhauls the old concept completely, nor spells out what exactly these principles entail. Therefore, it still awaits clarification by the courts, which as we will see in the following chapter, will also have to consider the existing international legal framework when filling in constitutional gaps.

What, if anything, can be learned for global law from the Swiss example? The following points are worth mentioning and will be pursued in the following chapters of this book:

— The pioneering law protecting labour standards adopted by the canton (state) of Glarus was only enacted because workers participated directly in the law-making process.[112] The law thus illustrates the importance of democratic participation, a topic that will be further explored in the context of governance and legitimacy in chapter 4.

— Labour standards were at the core of early federal legislation because the need for consistency between the different state laws was recognised. Harmonisation was seen as the appropriate means to reach this objective. The same need for consistency appears at the global level and accordingly the same issues arise: is harmonisation the solution, and if so, to what extent? The discussion on the definition of core labour rights touches precisely on this issue. Therefore, the next section will examine existing international labour rights and current attempts to define a universally accepted, "harmonised" set of core labour standards.

1.2. INTERNATIONAL LABOUR RIGHTS

Labour rights as human rights have been enshrined in a wide array of international agreements and declarations:

United Nations (UN)

— Universal Declaration of Human Rights (1948)

— International Covenant on Economic, Social and Cultural Rights (1966)

— International Covenant on Civil and Political Rights (1966)

— Convention on the Elimination of all Forms of Discrimination against Women (1979)

— Convention on the Rights of the Child (1989)

[112] Stolz (1968).

International Labour Organization (ILO)
— Convention Concerning Forced or Compulsory Labour (1930) (No 29)
— Equal Remuneration Convention (1951) (No 100)
— Convention Concerning the Abolition of Forced Labour (1957) (No 105)
— Freedom of Association and Protection of the Rights to Organise Convention (1948) (No 87)
— Right to Organise and Collective Bargaining Convention (1949) (No 98)
— Discrimination (Employment and Occupation) Convention (1958) (No 111)
— Minimum Working Age Convention (1973) (No 138)
— Declaration on Fundamental Principles and Rights at Work (1998)
— Worst Forms of Child Labour Convention (1999) (No 182)

In this section we will look first at the international human rights instruments that have developed primarily under the aegis of the United Nations.

1.2.1. Human Rights Instruments

1.2.1.1. The Universal Declaration of Human Rights (1948)

The Universal Declaration of Human Rights extracts and summarises some of the principles that were set out in earlier ILO documents.[113] Probably the greatest innovation in the Universal Declaration, which served as a substitute for the missing bill of rights in the UN Charter, was the inclusion of economic, social and cultural rights.

The Declaration is a recommendation by the General Assembly and is thus not strictly legally binding.[114] However, most scholars believe that the Declaration elaborates on human rights that are to a large extent now recognised as *customary international law*.[115] If the labour rights protected by the Universal Declaration are considered norms of customary international law, they apply *erga omnes* and form obligations towards the international community as a whole. This does not imply however that they also form part of *ius cogens* and are therefore peremptory norms of international law.[116]

Initially, a single convention with more detailed provisions was intended to follow the Declaration. However, the Cold War ideologically split the world

[113] See Appendix A.1. for Arts 22–25.

[114] In the words of Eleanor Roosevelt, chairperson of the Commission on Human Rights, acting in her capacity as the principal representative of the US: "In giving our approval to the declaration today, it is of primary importance that we keep clearly in mind the basic character of the document. It is not a treaty; it is not an international agreement. It is not and does not purport to be a statement of law or of legal obligation. . . ." Quoted after Lauterpacht (1950) 398–99.

[115] "Legal Consequences for States of the Continued Presence of South Africa in Namibia (South West Africa) Notwithstanding Security Council Resolution 276 (1970)", ICJ Reports 1971, p 16, Separate Opinion of Justice Ammoun, at pp 76–79. Salcedo (1995) 922, 925. It is even argued that the UN Charter incorporates the Declaration thus giving it the status of a "quasi-treaty" obligation. Kokott (1998) 103–4.

[116] For a very clear analysis of the three different concepts, see Kokott (1998) 85–89.

and led to the drafting of two separate treaties: the International Covenant on Civil and Political Rights (ICCPR) and the International Covenant on Economic Social and Cultural Rights (ICESCR).[117] The covenants were adopted in 1966 after lengthy debates within the UN organs. It took another ten years for them to achieve the necessary number of ratifications and enter into force.[118] Until then, there was no other human rights instrument with such broad coverage as the Universal Declaration.

A) Article 22: Social Security The Universal Declaration contains several labour rights in Articles 22–25. Article 22 is an umbrella provision that lays the foundation with the right to social security and to the realisation of economic, social and cultural rights. The term social security was relatively new at the time and referred directly to the United States Social Security Act of 1935.[119] Still, as we have seen above,[120] many UN Member States had also already introduced social insurance policies.[121] In addition, the framers of the Declaration were part of a movement to expand welfare state provisions as part of the economic reconstruction after the Second World War.

Although it has been argued that social rights were included in the Declaration as a result of political pressure, namely by the former Soviet Union, the records of the Commission drafting the Declaration show that social rights were included right from the beginning. From the outset, the right to social security was defined in terms of insurance against unemployment, accident, disability, sickness and old age. Nevertheless, the inclusion of social rights remained controversial. In order to overcome the deadlock, René Cassin, the French delegate, was asked to prepare a new draft for the Drafting Committee.[122] During the subsequent discussion within the Committee, Cassin added a clause limiting the state's obligations "to the utmost of its possibilities". Following a proposal by the US delegation, the Committee finally came to an agreement, which was then submitted to the Commission.[123] In contrast to Cassin's draft, the participation of the beneficiaries was no longer required. In addition, the term "social security" now referred to situations in which an individual's livelihood might be at risk.

[117] See Appendix A.2. and A.3.
[118] Steiner and Alston (2000) 139.
[119] See above note 3.
[120] Above, section 1.1.1.
[121] For an overview, see Andreassen (1992) 322–29, 333.
[122] Cassin's draft of Article 22 read: "Every one has the right to social security. The state shall maintain effective arrangements for the prevention of unemployment and, with the participation of beneficiaries, shall provide for insurance against invalidity, illness, old age and all other involuntary and undeserved losses of livelihood. Mothers and children have the right to special regard, care and resources." E/CN.4/AC.1/W.R./Rev.1, p 7.
[123] This draft read: "Everyone has the right to social security. To the utmost of its possibilities, the State shall undertake measures for the promotion of full employment and for the security of the individual against unemployment, disability, old age and all other loss of livelihood for reasons beyond his control. Mothers and children have the right to special regard, care and resources." E./CN.4/21, p 80.

In the Commission, a general discussion on the necessity of an umbrella article to introduce the following social rights arose. While some delegations argued for a general provision, omitting the notion social security; some preferred to include the obligation of the State in the preamble or Article 2 of the Declaration; others saw no need for an umbrella article at all, given that there was no such provision for civil and political rights. A subcommittee was then charged with formulating an article that would take into account the different concerns, and eventually they came up with a very general provision. A particularly heated debate had taken place about the meaning of the term "social security" and whether it should be included in the article at all. The argument concerned whether a notion of social security that was different and much broader than the established definition provided by the ILO would create confusion. René Cassin, however, was firm in his belief that an umbrella article without reference to "the modern and widely accepted concept of social security" would not be understood by the people.

In the end, the Commission decided to avoid the concept of social security in Article 25 on the standard of living as it could indeed lead to misunderstanding, given the established "technical" definition of the term by the ILO. Following an initiative by the chairperson of the Commission, Eleanor Roosevelt, to overcome the ideological differences, the Commission finally agreed to start the umbrella Article 22 with a right to social security. However, no attempt was made to define the concept of social security. Not surprisingly, the debate was once again sparked in the General Assembly. This time the issue was whether the notion social security should be replaced by "social justice", which was already in the Constitution of the ILO and the most general term available. Ultimately, the Article proposed by the Commission was adopted with one amendment, substituting the words "set out below" with "indispensable for his dignity and the free development of his personality".[124]

B) Article 23: the Right to Work The framers of the Declaration were operating against the background of the interwar economic crises. Unemployment, in particular, was seen as one of the major reasons for the rise of the Nazi regime in Germany, and it has subsequently been considered a threat not only to individual welfare but also to democracy itself. Article 23 is therefore devoted to the labour-related aspects of economic freedom.

Article 23(1) grants what are often referred to as "classical labour rights",[125] including the right to work and the right to free choice of employment; it also provides safeguards such as the right to favourable conditions of work and the right to protection against unemployment. Based on the general principle of equality and human dignity as set out in Article 1, Article 23(2) prohibits discriminatory wages and affirms the right to equal pay for equal work. The Declaration does not limit itself to the formal aspect of equality but also

[124] Andreassen (1992) 343.
[125] For an overview, see Källström (1992) 357–77.

demands substantial rights: Article 23(3) requires remuneration to be "just and favourable", ie ensuring an existence worthy of human dignity. If the remuneration cannot guarantee this, it has to be supplemented by other means of social protection, which can be determined by individual states. Finally, Article 23(4) calls on the fundamental right to freedom of association and establishes right to form and join unions.[126]

The right to work principle includes several elements. First, it gives *every* person—not only citizens—the right to gain access to the labour market. Furthermore, individuals should be able to choose employment without interference from the government or other state authorities: forced work is thus rejected. Because access to the labour market is useless if working conditions are not fair, Article 23 states that the working environment must reach a certain standard. The same is true for wages and the protection against unemployment. The right to choose has no meaning if the person who uses it is unprotected against unemployment. Furthermore, the right to work is a prerequisite for the protection against discrimination and freedom of association.

The freedom to form unions was first stated in the ILO Constitution of 1919.[127] The importance of labour unions was also stressed in the ILO Declaration of Philadelphia in 1944.[128] After the Second World War in particular, unions were seen as a safeguard against dictatorship.

Unsurprisingly, the principle of just remuneration was one of the cornerstones of the ILO Constitution and had been enshrined in the ILO Convention No 26 of 1928.[129] Somewhat more surprisingly, the right to equal pay had already been acknowledged as a basic principle regulating labour conditions in all industrial communities in part XIII of the Treaty of Versailles.[130] However, the Depression of the 1930s meant that little was accomplished with respect to defining the contents of this right.

When it came to drafting the relevant article in the Universal Declaration, there was consensus that a right to work should be enshrined. However, the views about its contents differed. The main point in question was whether the right to work should be combined with an obligation for the individual to perform useful work for the society, thus adopting a humanistic approach in defining the meaning of work.[131] Such a provision had been established by the Constitution of the Weimar Republic.[132] The former socialist states strongly

[126] See Macklem (2005) 71.
[127] The first ILO Constitution was embodied in the Treaty of Versailles, Part XIII. See section 1.2.3.1 below.
[128] Paragraph III(e). See Introduction above, note 4 and accompanying text.
[129] Convention No 26 on Minimum Wage-Fixing Machinery.
[130] Article XXIII of the Treaty, above note 127, states that Members ". . . will endeavour to secure and maintain fair and humane conditions of labour for men, women, and children, both in their own countries and in all countries to which their commercial and industrial relations extend, and for that purpose will establish and maintain the necessary International Organisation".
[131] See discussion in the Introduction above, section I.1.1.
[132] Article 163.

supported a broad notion of public goods[133] as a provision that would emphasise an obligation of the state to use all its power to create work for everybody. Yet, for formal reasons the proposal was rejected.[134] The majority of the Drafting Committee argued that Article 23 should be confined to protection against unemployment for working people, while Article 25 would deal with social benefits in the event of general unemployment.

C) Article 24: Working Conditions Article 24 addresses working conditions. The need for rest and leisure had long been acknowledged by the ILO and was not controversial at the time of the Universal Declaration. The concept of "rest" involves the limitation of working hours and was intended to guarantee a real cessation of activity, giving individuals the opportunity to regain strength. Separate and distinct from rest,[135] "leisure" should allow individuals to cultivate the mind and personal interests. This distinction reflects the broad notion of work applied by the ILO.[136]

Overall, Article 24 was designed to tackle three problems: weekly rest, limitation of working hours and holidays with pay. The right to weekly rest was universally accepted and is one of the less controversial labour rights. In many cultures, it stems from religious traditions.[137] The right to periodic holidays with pay is limited to persons having paid work. This is the reason why the framers explicitly mentioned the limitation of working hours.[138]

Debates arose around the limitation of working hours and the provision of paid holidays. As a result, only a few of the ILO conventions limiting working hours have ever entered into force. However, more progress was made with respect to paid holidays. The vast majority of states today have legislation on paid holidays, and the duration has been substantially prolonged over the years.

D) Article 25: Standard of Living The right to an adequate standard of living is at the core of social rights. In order to enjoy social rights, some economic rights such as the aforementioned right to work and work-related rights (Articles 23 and 24) and the right to social security[139] are necessary.

Article 25 of the Universal Declaration of Human Rights was inspired by Franklin D Roosevelt's famous "Four Freedom Address" in 1940,[140] which

133 See section 1.1.1.2. above.
134 A/C3/SR 140, p 11.
135 See Introduction, section I.1.1.
136 See Introduction, note 26 and accompanying text.
137 Melander (1992) 381.
138 Melander (1992) 380.
139 Eide (1998) 122.
140 Eighth Annual Message to Congress, 6 January 1940, in: Roosevelt (1940) 672; Hunt (1995) 194–200.

included the freedom from want.[141] In 1942, following the Four Freedom Address, the American Law Institute prepared a proposal for an International Bill of Rights. This proposal, although not adopted at the founding conference of the UN in San Francisco in 1945, had a major influence on the first draft of the Universal Declaration prepared by the Secretariat of the UN Human Rights Division. As mentioned above,[142] the inclusion of the term social security was controversial. In the end, elements of the drafts for Articles 22 and 25 were combined. This is why, in paragraph 1 of Article 25 the final clause "and the right to security in the event of unemployment . . ." was added.[143] Thus to some extent, Article 25 is a further elaboration of Article 22.

Notably, there was no significant controversy about the adoption of Article 25.[144] The difficulties arose years later and will be discussed in the following sections in the context of the International Human Rights Covenants.

1.2.1.2. *International Covenant on Economic, Social and Cultural Rights (1966)*

After the adoption of the Universal Declaration in 1948, the next step was to translate the rights it recognised in Articles 22–28 into binding treaty obligations.[145] It took almost twenty years for the International Covenant on Economic, Social and Cultural Rights (ICESCR) and the International Covenant on Civil and Political Rights (ICCPR) to be adopted in 1966.[146] The main reason for the delay was the Cold War, which not only slowed down the work on the International Covenants but also stalemated inventive proposals such as the establishment of a United Nations High Commissioner for Human Rights.[147]

[141] Roosevelt (1940) 672; Hunt (1995) 200:

> [. . .] there is nothing mysterious about the foundations of a healthy and strong democracy. The basic things expected by our people of their political and economic systems are simple. They are:
>
> Equality of opportunity for youth and for others.
>
> Jobs for those who can work.
>
> Security for those who need it.
>
> The ending of special privilege for the few.
>
> The preservation of civil liberties for all.
>
> The enjoyment of the fruits of scientific progress in a wider and constantly rising standard of living.
>
> [. . .]
>
> The third is freedom from want—which, translated into world terms, means economic understandings which will secure to every nation a healthy peacetime life for its inhabitants—everywhere in the world.

[142] See section 1.2.2.1. above.

[143] Eide (1992) 392.

[144] *Ibid*, 385.

[145] Steiner and Alston (2000) 139.

[146] See Appendix A.2. for text of ICESCR Arts 6–10.

[147] Van Boven (1999) 10–11; Freeman (1999) 32.

Whereas the Commission on Human Rights had been working on a single draft covenant dealing with both political and socio-economic rights between 1949 and 1951, in 1951 the General Assembly decided to draft two separate covenants. The main argument for having two covenants was that civil and political rights were more clearly enforceable or justiciable, while economic, social and cultural rights were not or might not be. In addition, it was argued that the former were immediately applicable, while the latter were to be progressively implemented. Finally, civil and political rights were considered rights "against" the state, that is, against unlawful and unjust actions on the part of the state, while economic and social and cultural rights were rights that the state would have to take positive action to promote.[148]

Over the years, the reporting procedures, which are the main tools for monitoring the compliance with the Covenants, have been broadened in scope. The Committee on Economic, Social and Cultural Rights has made clear that states have an obligation to "respect, protect and fulfil" the provisions of the ICESCR.[149] The obligation to "respect" requires state parties not to take any measures that result in denying individuals access to the rights guaranteed by the Covenant. The obligation to "protect" requires measures by the state to ensure that enterprises or private individuals do not prevent individuals from exercising their rights. Finally, the obligation to "fulfil" means the state must positively engage in activities intended to facilitate people's access to and utilisation of resources and the means to enjoy their rights under the Covenant. Whenever an individual or a group is unable to exercise or gain access to their rights for reasons beyond their control, the state must actively step in and provide that right directly.[150]

A) Article 6: the Right to Work Articles 6–9 of the ICESCR address two types of labour rights: labour rights that are substantial provisions by guaranteeing a concrete result, eg wages; and labour rights that attempt to empower and are more process-based.[151]

Article 6 grants the right to work. The initial proposals fell into three main groups[152] according to three different concepts of what domestic labour market policy entails.[153] The socialist states proposed a right to work that included the

148 Annotations on the Text of the Draft International Covenants on Human Rights, UN Doc A/2929 (1955) paras 8–11.

149 CESCR, General Comment No 14 (2000), UN Doc E/C.12/2000/4 paras 30–33; CESCR, General Comment No 12 (1999), UN Doc E/C.12/1999/5 para 15. For a general overview on the nature of states parties obligations under the ICESCR, see Alston and Quinn (1987) 165–81.

150 For the conceptual framework see Breining-Kaufmann (2005) 96–107.

151 See para 7 of the Maastricht Guidelines for the distinction between obligations to conduct and to result. *Maastricht Guidelines on Violations of Economic, Social and Cultural Rights*, Maastricht, 22–26 January 1997, para 19, available at http://heiwww.unige.ch/humanrts/instree/Maastrichtguidelines_.html [hereinafter Maastricht Guidelines]. See also note 29 above and accompanying text.

152 For an excellent overview, see Craven (1998) 195–96.

153 See section 1.1.1.2. above.

obligation of the state to ensure full employment or eliminate unemployment.[154] By contrast, Western states supported a provision that required states to "promote conditions" under which the right to work might be realised.[155] A third opinion was that the article should include a bold statement of the right to work while deferring a decision on whether the obligation should be progressive until the adoption of a general clause.[156] It soon became clear that most countries would not accept an obligation to guarantee a right to work in the sense of the first proposal. This was mainly because they feared that such a guarantee would commit states to a centralised system of government and require that all labour be under the direct control of the state.[157] Because the implementation of the right to work in many countries depended on their particular stage of economic development, it was generally considered that such a right could only be achieved progressively.

Article 2(1) of the Covenant provides for the progressive realisation of the rights recognised in the Covenant by taking into account available resources, so it was logical for Article 6 to encapsulate the principle that states recognise the right to work, instead of guaranteeing it. The idea that the state should provide a job for every person who is available for and willing to work was thus clearly rejected.[158] Accordingly, when reviewing the reports on the implementation of the Covenant, the Committee on Economic, Social and Cultural Rights required member states to *ensure* rather than *guarantee* that there is "work for all who are available for and seeking work". On several occasions the Committee made clear that the right to work could be implemented only if work was available.[159]

Despite this limitation, Article 6 still goes further than the Universal Declaration, because it not only ensures free access to the labour market but also aims at levelling the playing field by providing the basic conditions for an efficiently functioning labour market, such as vocational guidance, employment services and guidelines to promote full employment.

There was controversy about whether Article 6 should include any reference to the implementation process at all. It was argued that it would be better to state the principle of the right to work in general terms, leaving the specifics of implementation to the ILO. It was also argued that inserting specific implementation clauses into some articles and not into others would be illogical. On the other hand, most states felt that in order for the Covenant to go beyond the

154 USSR proposal, in: UN Doc E./CN.4/AC.14/2 at 3 (1951).

155 These were the proposals by the USA, Denmark and Egypt. UN Doc E./CN.4/AC.14/2 at 3 (1951).

156 Proposal by Yugoslavia, in: UN Doc E./CN.4/AC.14/2 at 3 (1951).

157 This argument was namely put forward by Eleanor Roosevelt: ". . . it was difficult to see how democratic States could guarantee absolutely and by their own action the right to work to all persons without becoming totalitarian States . . ." UN Doc E./CN.4/SR.275 at 11 (1952).

158 Craven (1998) 196, 203–4.

159 "Revised Guidelines Regarding the Form and Content of Reports to be Submitted by States Parties under Arts 16 and 17 of the International Covenant on Economic, Social, and Cultural Rights", UN Doc E/1991/1, 17 June 1991, Annex [Hereinafter "Reporting Guidelines"] at Article 6(2)(b).

Universal Declaration, it was necessary to include implementation details that went further than those found in Article 2.[160] However, in the case of full employment, there was a mixed approach. Although full employment must be seen as a method of implementing the right to work, it was also presented as a goal in its own right. In order to make sure that no trade-offs between the right to work and other civil and political rights were allowed, the clause "under conditions safeguarding fundamental political and economic freedoms to the individual" was included in Article 6(2).[161]

In the work of the Committee on Economic, Social and Cultural Rights, the term "unemployment" is difficult to interpret. While economists differentiate between frictional, cyclical and structural unemployment and thus do not equate full employment with total absence of unemployment, the legal discussion overlooks these important differences. Frictional unemployment reflects the number of people who are between jobs and is therefore much more a question of mobility than one of inadequate labour markets. Cyclical unemployment is usually the result of a deficiency in demand for labour. Structural unemployment, which increased sharply in OECD countries in the 1990s and was to become an immense problem in Europe,[162] results from imperfections in the labour market, such as a mismatch between training and demand for labour.[163] Even with unemployment rates above zero per cent there can still be full employment from an economic point of view, depending on the circumstances in a particular country.[164]

The formulation in Article 6 permits these economic facts to be taken into account: states are not required to achieve full employment but must establish policies and techniques that *aim* at full employment.[165] According to the Committee's guidelines, states are thus expected to offer some form of explanation for their current level of unemployment and further information on the nature of the unemployment. In addition, detailed information is requested with respect to different categories of workers, such as women, young persons, older workers and disabled workers.[166] This requirement is in line with what the OECD and ILO expect from their member countries.

However, the Committee is still struggling with the definition of unemployment, which has been particularly problematic for developing countries,[167]

[160] Craven (1998) 200.

[161] Craven (1998) 202–3; Källström (1992) 362.

[162] See OECD (1998) Table 1; OECD (2001b) Table 1.3.

[163] The distinction between cyclical and structural unemployment is important for policy purposes. The structural unemployment rate or—in economic terms—non-accelerating inflation rate of unemployment (NAIRU) cannot be reduced by macroeconomic policy without causing wage growth and thus inflation to increase. IMF, World Economic Outlook 1999, at 90.

[164] Craven (1998) 206.

[165] For an economic assessment of active labour market policies, see Martin (1998) paras 16–65.

[166] Reporting Guidelines, above note 159, at Article 6(2)(a).

[167] OECD countries usually submit the statistics they have already established for the OECD country exams. An example of statistical difficulties can be found in OECD (2001b) Box 1.1.

where many members of the population work in the informal sector.[168] So far, the Committee has neither determined a clear statistical indicator nor set a ceiling above which unemployment rates would be unacceptable.

Together with Article 2(2), Article 6 prohibits discrimination with respect to access to employment. The Committee has adopted the ILO definition of discrimination and is thus especially concerned with:

> distinctions, exclusions, restrictions, or preferences, be it in law or in administrative practices or in practical relationships, between persons or groups of persons, made on the basis of race, colour, sex, religion, political opinion, nationality, or social origin, which have the effect of nullifying or impairing the recognition, enjoyment, or exercise of equality of opportunity or treatment in employment or occupation.[169]

In a way that is similar to the "Bona Fide Occupational Qualification" in US employment discrimination law,[170] the Committee, as well as the ILO, accepts that employers must make distinctions between potential employees based on the particular requirements of a job. However, the Committee is especially critical when it comes to restrictions based on political affiliation. It made clear that "... Discrimination in employment on the ground of political opinion should be explicitly prohibited by law."[171]

Another important issue is the treatment of aliens. The Covenant in Article 2(3) allows for the differential treatment of non-nationals in the case of developing countries. It could thus be argued that restrictions for non-nationals in developed countries are implicitly prohibited. The United Kingdom made a specific reservation upon ratification to interpret Article 6 as not precluding the imposition of restrictions based on birth or residence qualifications. France also made a declaration that Article 6 is not to be interpreted as derogating from provisions governing the access of aliens to employment. While the Committee has not yet specifically dealt with the question of immigration policies, Article 4 might well play a role in determining which restrictions are allowed.[172] According to Article 4, states are required to show that any restrictions they impose on the employment opportunities of foreign workers are determined by law and are solely for the purpose of promoting the general welfare in a democratic society.

Although implementation of Article 6 can happen progressively, the prohibition of discrimination has to be implemented immediately—as is the case with Article 2(2).[173] However, legislation is not enough to satisfy this obligation. The

[168] For discussion of informal sectors of the economy, see Introduction, section I.1.2.
[169] Reporting Guidelines, note 159 above, at para 3(a) to Article 6.
[170] *Dothard v Rawlinson* 433 USR 321 (1977); *International Union UAW v Johnson Controls Inc* 499 USR 187 (1991).
[171] Concluding observations on report of Germany, E/C.12/1993/4 at 2, para 8.
[172] Craven (1998) 213–14.
[173] This is confirmed by the drafting history, the "Limburg Principles on the Implementation of the International Covenant on Economic, Social and Cultural Rights", UN. Doc E./CN.4/1987/17, Annex, reprinted in (1987) 9 HRQ 122–35, at para 35, and the practice of the Committee; Craven (1998) 181, 215.

Committee requires states to take appropriate action to ensure the observance of the principles of non-discrimination with respect to employment and vocational guidance under private control.[174]

Finally, Article 6 also prohibits forced labour by providing for the right to choose employment. Until recently, the Committee did not deal specifically with forced labour, because there is an explicit prohibition of forced labour in Article 8 of the ICCPR.

B) Article 7: Just and Favourable Conditions of Work Article 7 outlines just and favourable conditions of work. Among these, the principle of equal pay has undergone significant change since its formulation in the Universal Declaration. It no longer requires equal pay for equal work but equal remuneration for work of equal value. This change reflects the principle of equal remuneration as established by the ILO Convention No 100 on Equal Remuneration (1951). Remuneration as defined by the ILO includes all work-related benefits, not just the pay cheque. Although the Committee has concentrated on the issue of wages and has thus so far not recognised this difference,[175] the new provision is still far broader than that of the Universal Declaration: it not only protects against dual pay scales but also aims at preventing indirect wage discrimination, which is prevalent in typically female occupations that have lower pay and lower prestige despite requiring high levels of skills. It is up to the states to set their own standards for remuneration that allows a decent standard of living. The Committee requires that the minimum wage should at least be sufficient to fulfil the "basic needs" of the worker.[176]

Despite the broadening of the concept of remuneration, in practice the Committee has been concerned mostly with minimum wages. While opinions within the Committee vary as to whether a compulsory minimum wage should be the primary means of ensuring equitable remuneration and on the extent to which worker participation in determining the standards is required, there is a consensus that sufficient enforcement of minimum wages is most important. It is not clear whether the Committee follows the approach adopted by the ILO in taking into account not only the needs of the workers and their families, but also other economic factors such as levels of productivity and the desirability of maintaining high levels of employment. In its Reporting Guidelines, the Committee refers to economic factors in a very general way.[177] It is therefore not yet clear whether economic considerations justify minimum wages below the level that would provide for basic needs.[178]

[174] For example Simma, E/C.12/1989/SR.8 at 8, para 46.

[175] Craven (1998) 233–34.

[176] The Committee intervened in the case of Kenya: Concluding observations on report of Kenya, E/C.12/1993/6 at 3, para 12.

[177] "Reporting Guidelines", note 159 above.

[178] Craven (1998) 236.

Overall, Article 7 lacks the precision of other international instruments such as the ILO Conventions and the European Social Charter.[179] Difficulties arise from the fact that the right to just and favourable working conditions mainly depends on the relationship between private individuals. In most countries, working conditions are the subject of private employment contracts and collective agreements. Effective implementation of the right stipulated in Article 7 depends heavily upon its horizontal application. As a result, the legal regulation of individual states tends to focus on defining minimal thresholds and providing enforcement mechanisms.

C) Article 8: the Right to Form and Join Trade Unions Article 8 has been very controversial from the beginning. First, it was debated whether the right to form unions should be included at all in the ICESCR, given that the freedom of association is already in the ICCPR. Second, it was argued that because this right would only relate to a special group of persons and not to everyone, the right to form and join trade unions is not technically a human right. Article 8 was finally adopted after significant compromise, and accordingly, coherence is not one of its biggest merits.

Article 8 starts with the definition of states' obligation. Because the right to join and form trade unions is an integral part of the freedom of association found in Article 22 of the ICCPR, it is not subject to progressive realisation but must be implemented immediately. This is the reason why Article 8 requires the states to *ensure* the right and not merely to *recognise* it. The restriction of Article 2(1) therefore does not apply. As a result, Article 8 is self-executing and can be invoked in courts.[180]

The reference to the ILO Convention No 87 in Article 8(3) is important because the ILO Convention only allows limitations on the rights of members of the armed forces and the police, but unlike Article 8 not on the members of the government administration. A state that imposes wholesale restrictions on the ability of public servants to join or form trade unions would therefore be in violation of not only the ILO Convention but also the Covenant.[181]

Article 8 is a hybrid provision, granting individual and collective rights at the same time. As such, it also protects trade unions from state interference. Of particular importance is Article 8(1)(c), which was intended to protect the right of trade unions to bargain collectively.[182] By using the term "promote" in its reports, the Committee has made clear that it does not expect states to guarantee the right to bargain collectively to every trade union. It is acceptable to limit the right to consultation and negotiation in the collective bargaining process to the "most representative" union, yet this requirement must not impede the right of trade unions to participate freely in collective bargaining processes, irrespec-

[179] See, eg, Articles 2 and 3 of the European Social Charter.
[180] Künzli and Kälin (1997) 123.
[181] Craven (1998) 263.
[182] Craven (1998) 256.

tive of their size.[183] Furthermore, the Covenant does not require states to ratify the relevant ILO Convention No 98 on the Right to Organize and Collective Bargaining of 1949.

Unlike other international human rights instruments, Article 8(1)(d) explicitly guarantees the right to strike. Even though the right to strike is usually exercised in a collective way by trade unions, it is framed as an individual right in the Covenant. As a result, the provision also covers the protection of the worker in case of a dismissal based on the exercise of his or her right to strike.[184]

According to Article 8(1)(a), restrictions on the right to join and form trade unions should be

> . . . prescribed by law and [. . .] necessary in a democratic society in the interests of national security or public order or for the protection of the rights and freedoms of others.

These requirements correspond with the relevant rules found in Article 22 of the ICCPR and the jurisprudence of the European Court of Human Rights.[185]

D) Article 9: the Right to Social Security Despite its importance, Article 9 is the shortest article in the ICESCR. The ILO had lobbied successfully for a general formulation, leaving as much power as possible within the specialised agencies to design the precise and detailed provisions necessary for effective implementation.[186]

E) Article 10: Child Labour Under Article 10's general aim to protect the family, Article 10(3) contains a prohibition on social and economic exploitation of children and more specifically prohibits the employment of children in work that is hazardous to their health, morals or development. In addition, states are required to set minimum age limits for paid child labour. The norm is very general and has served as the basis for the more elaborate provisions in the Convention on the Rights of the Child.[187] However, Article 10 does not mention the word "right"; thus no individual and enforceable rights can be derived from paragraphs 1 and 2. With regard to paragraph 3, the Committee held that it further develops the general anti-discrimination provision in Article 2(2) and must therefore be implemented immediately.[188]

183 E/CN.12/1/Add.72 para 29. See also Macklem (2005) 71–72.
184 In a similar sense the Swiss Supreme Court, BGE 125 III 277, 283–85: the participation in a lawful strike is not considered a breach of contract of employment, regardless whether the worker concerned is a member of the union or not.
185 See eg *Sunday Times v United Kingdom*, European Court of Human Rights, Series A, vol 30, judgment of 26 April 1979, p 30, para 49.
186 UN Doc A/2929 (1955) at 24–25.
187 See section 1.2.2.5. below.
188 CESCR, The nature of States parties obligations (Art 2(1) of the Covenant) (Fifth session, 1990, contained in Document E/1991/23), General Comment No 3, para 5.

1.2.1.3. International Covenant on Civil and Political Rights (1966)

In contrast to the ICESCR, the ICCPR follows a more traditional approach and grants rights as civil liberties.[189] Article 2(1) requires states to *respect and ensure* the rights of the Covenant. While the obligation to respect indicates the negative character of civil and political rights and thus obligates states to refrain from interfering with these rights, the obligation to ensure is institutional and positive in character. State parties are also required to take positive steps to give effect to the rights.[190] Although this obligation depends on the content of a given right, some general principles are applicable. Most importantly, such a positive duty entails enacting laws to implement the obligations under Article 2(2) and to providing effective remedies under Article 2(3).[191] In addition, Article 2 makes clear that the rights in the Covenant have to be implemented immediately. Under Swiss law they are—with the exception of the right to self-determination in Article 1—self-executing.[192]

With respect to labour rights, the ICCPR contains both substantive and process-based rights. The most important provisions are the prohibition on slavery and forced labour in Article 8 and the freedom of association and trade unions in Article 22.

A) Article 8: Prohibition of Slavery and Forced Labour The prohibition of slavery might at first glance seem obsolete nowadays, but unfortunately, new forms of slavery are increasing due to international migration of workers, sex tourism in developing countries and drug trafficking.[193] Because it is difficult to draw the line between slavery and slavery-like practices, Article 8 also contains a prohibition on servitude and forced labour.[194] In a labour-related context, where formal slavery has become rare, it is the prohibition of servitude and forced labour are most relevant.

The term "servitude" in Article 8(2) refers to slavery-like practices and, with respect to work, includes all forms of traffic in women and children, child labour or prostitution. It is important to note that the notion of servitude implies that the victims not only are economically exploited but may also be

[189] See Appendix A.3. for text of ICCPR Arts 8 and 22.

[190] See Breining-Kaufmann (2005) 101–2.

[191] Nowak (2005) paras 18–19 on Article 2.

[192] If the treaty does not provide an answer as to whether a provision is self-executing, the solution must be sought in domestic law. The criterion is then which organ is most capable of interpreting international law: Müller, G (2001) § 70 Rz 39; Wüger (2001) 105–9. The Swiss Supreme Court confirmed the "constitutional content" of the ICCPR and thus its immediate applicability in BGE 120 Ia 247, 255; 125 I 21, 34.

[193] See the report by the ILO: ILO (2005); Nowak (1993) para 2 on Article 8.

[194] The Covenant does not define the term slavery. A generally accepted definition can be found in Article 1 of the Slavery Convention of 1926, League of Nations Treaty Series (UNTS), vol 60, 253: Slavery is "the status or condition of a person over whom any or all of the powers attaching to the right of ownership are exercised." The European Court of Human Rights also applies this definition: *Van Droogenbroeck v Belgium*, European Court of Human Rights, Series A, vol 50, p 50 at paras 32–33; Frowein and Peukert (1996) 59–61.

very dependent—for whatever reason—on other individuals.[195] A recent example was the El Monte factory in Los Angeles, where until 1995 Thai women who had illegally immigrated—all indentured to their employer—were forced to work under slavery-like conditions.[196]

Article 8(3) prohibits all forms of forced labour.[197] It prohibits the state from compelling the individual to work. However, in contrast to slavery and slavery-like practices, the prohibition of forced or compulsory labour recognises permissible exceptions and derogations. The key criterion for forced labour is the element of involuntariness. Article 2(1) of ILO Convention No 29 defines forced or compulsory labour as

> all work or service which is extracted from any person under the menace of any penalty and for which the said person has not offered himself voluntarily.

This broad notion of compulsory or forced labour as used in the Covenant does not require the labour to be unjust, oppressive or particularly harsh, unlike the European Charter on Human Rights.[198]

Both the prohibition of forced or compulsory labour and the prohibition of slavery have a horizontal effect; they thus require states to impose respective legal obligations on private actors, such as multinational enterprises.[199] They do not hold private actors directly responsible; in other words, there is no *Drittwirkung*. States are required to take appropriate measures to ensure the realisation of these rights by adopting laws and establishing effective procedures to enforce them. In contrast to the prohibition of slavery and servitude, there are several exceptions to the prohibition of forced work in Article 8(3)(b) and (c). The relevant ILO Conventions No 29 and 105 can be drawn on to interpret these exceptions.

In 2001, the Commission on Human Rights initiated a special fact-finding mission to Burma/Myanmar to investigate in particular the situation relating to possible forced labour and the compliance with the respective ILO convention.[200]

[195] Nowak (2005) para 13 on Article 8.

[196] The Smithsonian Institution documented the case in 1998 in an exhibition at the National Museum of American History. Liebhold and Rubenstein (1998) 4–25. This exhibition is also documented at http://americanhistory.si.edu/sweatshops/elmonte/elmonte.htm. For a summary of this case and its context in the fashion industry, see Schoenberger (2000) 38–47 and 48–76.

[197] A generally accepted definition of forced or compulsory labour can be found in ILO Convention No 29 on Forced Labour (1930) and ILO Convention No 105 on the Abolition of Forced Labour (1957).

[198] Nowak (2005) para 17 on Article 8.

[199] Nowak argues that the prohibition of forced labour is mainly directed at states while the prohibition of slavery primarily has a horizontal effect: Nowak (2005) paras 6 and 18 on Article 8 and para 20 on Article 2.

[200] "Situation of Human Rights in Myanmar," Commission on Human Rights resolution 2001/15, 18 April 2001, UN Doc E/CN.4/RES/2001/15; Reports of the Special Rapporteur of the Commission on Human Rights on the situation of human rights in Myanmar, UN Doc A56/312 of 20 August 2001; UN Doc E./CN.4/2002/45 of 10 January 2002; UN Doc E/CN.4/2003/41 of 27 December 2002; UN Doc A/58/219 of 5 August 2003; UN Doc E/CN.4/2004/33, 5 January 2004; "Resolution on the Situation of Human Rights in Myanmar Adopted by the General Assembly", A/Res/56/231, 28 February 2002. See also Maupain (2005b) 103–4.

B) Article 22: Freedom of Association and Trade Unions Article 22 is unique in several respects: unlike the Universal Declaration and the European Convention on Human Rights, it treats the freedom of association separately from the closely related freedom of assembly. In addition, the specific saving clause in Article 22(3) in favour of the ILO Convention No 87 is unique in the whole Covenant.

The freedom of association and trade unions was integrated in the ICCPR to underline its threefold character: it is not only an *economic* right that protects the freedom of trade unions, but also a *political* and *civil* right. As such, it grants protection against state and private interference when an individual wishes to associate with others. Because political interests can only be nourished in community with others, it is indispensable for the functioning of a democratic society. This is the reason why the freedom of association and trade unions can be found in both covenants. In particular, it was feared that the failure to include this freedom in the ICCPR might create the impression that it was not a civil right.[201]

What are the differences between the two provisions in the ICCPR and the ICESCR? Article 22 of the ICCPR is broader with respect to the interests that can be promoted by trade unions. While the ICESCR limits the freedom of trade unions to organisations for the *promotion and protection of economic and social interests*, the ICCPR refers to the general interests of everyone ("his interests"). With this formulation, the framers underlined the fact that trade unions often fight for the civil rights of their members.[202]

In contrast to Article 8 of the ICESCR, Article 22 of the ICCPR does not mention the right to strike. A majority of the Human Rights Committee initially concluded that the fact that it was expressly adopted in the ICESCR but not mentioned in the original draft for a single human rights covenant meant that it was not covered by Article 22.[203] A minority came to the contrary conclusions by stressing that there was no apparent reason "to interpret article 22 in a manner different from the ILO when addressing a comparable consideration."[204]

With regard to the safeguard clause in Article 22(3), which calls for an interpretation of Article 22 in line with ILO Convention No 87, the minority opinion seems difficult to refute. Following widespread criticism, the Committee reversed its decision and now recognises a right to strike based on Article 22.[205]

201 Nowak (2005) paras 3 and 12 on Article 22.

202 The idea is an early version of the more elaborate concept of *Verbandsbeschwerde* in Swiss law, which gives associations—under certain conditions—the right to represent the interests of their members in court. Kälin (1994a) 268.

203 Decision of the Human Rights Committee under the Optional Protocol to the ICCPR, *Alberta Union v Canada*, 18 July 1986, Communication No 118/1982, paras 6.3–6.5.

204 Individual opinion in *Alberta Union v Canada*, above note 203, para 7. The minority opinion was strongly supported by Leary (1996) 22.

205 CCPR/C/79/Add.73. See also Macklem (2005) 72–73.

1.2.1.4. *Convention on the Elimination of all Forms of Discrimination against Women (1979)*

The Convention on the Elimination of all Forms of Discrimination against Women (CEDAW) (1979) was an elaboration of the principle of non-discrimination on the basis of sex.[206] By focusing on gender equality, the provisions of the CEDAW are much more specific than related norms in other human rights treaties. An Optional Protocol that entered into force on 22 December 2000 provides the possibility for the CEDAW Committee to receive complaints from individuals and groups,[207] thus filling one of the major gaps in the Convention.[208]

The Convention contains a broader definition of discrimination than that contained in the earlier treaties, covering both equality of opportunity (formal equality) and equality of outcome (*de facto* equality).[209] Discrimination is defined as

> . . . any distinction, exclusion or restriction made on the basis of sex which has the effect or purpose of impairing or nullifying the recognition, enjoyment or exercise by women, irrespective of their marital status, on a basis of equality of men and women, of human rights and fundamental freedoms in the political, economic, social, cultural, civil or any other field.[210]

The Convention attempts to overcome not only the divide between civil and political rights on the one hand and economic and social rights but also the traditional public/private dichotomy observed in international law.[211]

A) Article 11: Non-discrimination in Employment With regard to labour rights, Article 11 sets out a comprehensive right to non-discrimination in employment.[212] Elaborating on the broad notion of discrimination contained in Article 1, Article 11(1) requires states parties to take all appropriate measures to eliminate discrimination in order to ensure the enumerated rights related to employment. The catalogue of rights contains the right to work; the right to the same employment opportunities, including the application of the same criteria for selection in matters of employment; the right to free choice of profession and employment; the right to promotion; the right to equal remuneration; the right to social security; and the right to protection of health and safe working conditions. Unlike other UN human rights treaties, the Convention does not stop at

[206] Charlesworth (1998) 785.

[207] Article 2 of the Optional Protocol to the Convention on the Elimination of Discrimination against Women, adopted by General Assembly resolution A/54/4 on 6 October 1999 and entered into force on 22 December 2000. For full text of Arts 2 and 3 of the Optional Protocol, see Appendix A.6.

[208] Charlesworth (1998) 786.

[209] Charlesworth and Chinkin (2000) 217.

[210] Article 1 CEDAW.

[211] For example Articles 2(e) and 16 CEDAW; Müller, JP (1999) 454; Chinkin (1999) 387–95.

[212] See Appendix A.4. for full text of Art 11 CEDAW.

stating general principles but also mentions the practices that often cause the most insurmountable barriers in the real world, such as discriminatory promotion policies or unequal training opportunities. If one looks at the cases that have been brought before national courts[213] and before the ECJ[214] and the ECtHR[215] concerning gender discrimination in employment, the vast majority refer to issues that are covered by Article 11.

Although Article 11 is not self-executing, it has proven to be a source of inspiration for many national laws. With a broader ratification of the Optional Protocol, there is reason to hope that it will become even more influential and effective in the future.

1.2.1.5. Convention on the Rights of the Child (1989)

Exploitation of children takes many forms and is usually the result of a breach of several fundamental rights. The need to protect children from exploitation due to their vulnerability and immaturity was reflected in the Declaration on the Rights of the Child, which was adopted by the General Assembly of the League of Nations in 1924[216] and expanded by the UN in 1948 and 1959.[217] The Declaration affirmed (in its 1959 version) the need to protect children against all forms of exploitation.

The Convention on the Rights of the Child was adopted in 1989 and has been almost universally ratified.[218] It applies to every human being under the age of 18, unless under the law applicable to the child, maturity is attained earlier.[219] The Convention further develops the concept of the Declaration by incorporating a general prohibition against all forms of exploitation and by granting the child a right to be protected against economic exploitation. This is an important

[213] Leading cases for Switzerland: BGE 117 Ia 262; 120 Ia 95; 124 II 409; with explicit reference to CEDAW: BGE 125 I 21; For the US: *Price Waterhouse v Hopkins* 490 USR 228 (1989); *County of Washington v Gunther* 452 USR 161 (1981).

[214] Case 43/75 *Defrenne II v Société anonyme belge de navigation aérienne Sabena* [1976] ECR 455; Case C-450/93 *Kalanke v Freie Hansestadt Bremen* [1995] ECR I-3051, modified in Case C-409/95 *Marschall v Nordrhein-Westfalen* [1997] ECR I-6303; Case C-309/97 *Angestelltenbetriebsrat v Wiener Gebietskrankenkasse* [1999] ECR I-2865; Case C-158/97 *Normenkontrollverfahren auf Antrag von Badeck et al* [2000] ECR I-5539; Case C-220/02 *Oesterreichischer Gewerkschaftsbund, Gewerkschaft der Privatangestellten v Wirtschaftskammer Oesterreich*, Judgment of the ECJ, 8 June 2004.

[215] Case 108/1995/614/702 *Van Raalte v The Netherlands*, Judgment of 21 February 1997, ECtHR Reports 1997 I 173. Case 37112/97, *Fogarty v The United Kingdom*, Judgment of 21 November 2001, ECtHR Reports 2001 XI 157.

[216] Principle 2.

[217] Principle 9 of the Declaration on the Rights of the Child, adopted by the UN General Assembly on 20 November 1959, Resolution 1386 (XIV).

[218] The Convention entered into force in record time on 2 September 1990. With the exception of the US and Somalia, all countries have ratified the Convention. With 191 ratifications, it covers 97% of the world's children. See Fallon and Tzannatos (1998) 6. See Appendix A.5. for text of Arts 32 and 35.

[219] Article 1.

difference from other provisions in the Convention, which emphasise the duty of the state to protect the child without providing an explicit individual right.[220]

A) Article 32: Minimum Age and Working Conditions Not all types of child labour are considered exploitation under the Convention.[221] Article 32 refines the definition that is already contained in Article 10(3) ICESCR[222] by declaring child labour exploitative when it threatens the physical, mental, emotional or social development of the child. It is therefore not work per se that is the focus of the Convention but its abuse.[223]

As for the minimum age, Article 32 does not raise the existing international standards. Yet, by including *any* work—including domestic and agricultural work—that is likely to be hazardous or to interfere with the child's development, the field of application is broader than in the relevant ILO Conventions and other international instruments.[224] Parties to the Convention are required to protect children from economic exploitation within their jurisdiction even when the exploitation occurs in an economic sector that the state has excluded from the ambit of ILO Convention No 138.[225]

While Article 32 is an improvement in that it requires states to provide for the appropriate regulation of the hours and conditions of employment together with appropriate sanctions and penalties, it is weakened by the absence of any indication as to the content of the conditions and the limitations on hours. The only requirement is that they should not amount to economic exploitation.[226] These details can however be found in the relevant ILO instruments.[227]

B) Article 35: Prohibition of Forced Labour and Slavery Article 35 calls on countries to take measures to prevent the abduction, sale or trafficking of children for any purpose or in any form. Of particular relevance for children are debt bondage and specific aspects of child trafficking. The significance of Article 35 lies in its provisions on sale and trafficking, as it fills gaps that existed before the adoption of the Convention. For the first time, it provides a sufficiently binding and broad framework for the potential effective control of the international trafficking of children.

The sale and trafficking of children occur in relation to three different but overlapping practices: inter-country adoption, forced labour and sexual exploitation. The first was one of the main reasons for the incorporation of

[220] For example Article 34 on sexual abuse.

[221] Child labour can be divided into five categories: domestic, non-domestic, non-monetary, bonded labour, wage labour and marginal economic activity. It extends to paid employment, piecework at home and unpaid work within the family. Van Bueren (1995) 264.

[222] See section 1.2.2.2.*E)* above.

[223] Van Bueren (1995) 264; Detrick (1999) 564–67.

[224] See section 1.2.2. below.

[225] Committee on the Rights of the Child, "General Guidelines for Periodic Reports", 20 November 1996, UN Doc CRC/C/58 para 152; Van Bueren (1995) 269.

[226] Article 32(2)(b) and (c); Van Bueren (1995) 271; Detrick (1999) 570.

[227] Minimum Age Recommendation (No 146) para 12(1).

Article 35 into the Convention. Article 35 covers all forms of trafficking and sales, whether within one state or across borders. Sometimes adoption is used as a cover for economic exploitation, thus making the application of a single-issue treaty difficult.[228] The adoption of the all-embracing Article 35 was therefore a milestone in the prosecution of trafficking. It has already been applied in Romania[229] and Albania.[230] After an increase in international adoptions that was seen as national tragedies and in light of the Convention, both countries amended their adoption laws.

1.2.1.6. Recent Developments: Protocols on Trafficking

In the context of the fight against transnational crime, the UN adopted a *Protocol to Prevent, Suppress and Punish Trafficking in Persons, especially Women and Children* in November 2000.[231] The Protocol supplements the UN Convention against Transnational Organized Crime.[232] The last decade has seen an explosion in the number of persons trafficked across national borders and between continents and then forced into activities including sweatshops, domestic service and prostitution. This is often a form of contemporary bondage, where the persons involved have to pay off the expenses advanced to them for their illegal transport and immigration.[233] The Protocol is the first UN document to provide a legal definition of trafficking:

> . . . the recruitment, transportation, transfer, harbouring or receipt of persons, by means of the threat or use of force or other forms of coercion, of abduction, of fraud, of deception of the abuse of power or of position of vulnerability or of the giving or receiving of payments or benefits to achieve the consent of a person having control over another person, for the purpose of exploitation.[234]

The Protocol specifies that exploitation includes, among other things, forced labour or services, slavery or practices similar to slavery or servitude. It is important, and different from the existing regulations on forced labour, that consent by an adult victim of trafficking shall be irrelevant when any of the means included in the definition have been used. Because the problem of trafficking exceeds the capacity of labour authorities, the UN now calls for international co-operation and cross-border efforts to prosecute the criminals involved.

228 Van Bueren (1995) 280.
229 "Report of a Group of Experts on the Implementation of the Convention on the Rights of the Child Regarding Inter-country Adoption", 1991.
230 Van Bueren (1995) 282.
231 Adopted on 15 November 2000 by General Assembly Resolution 55/25. Text in UN Doc A/55/383. The Protocol entered into force on 25 December 2003.
232 Adopted on 15 November 2000 by General Assembly Resolution 55/25. Text in UN Doc A/55/383. The Convention entered into force on 28 September 2003.
233 ILO (2001a) para 35.
234 Article 3(a).

Similarly, the Convention on the Rights of the Child was supplemented by the *Optional Protocol on the Sale of Children, Child Prostitution and Child Pornography.*[235] It specifically addresses the sale of children for forced labour in Article 3(1)(a)(i)c.

1.2.2. ILO Regulations

1.2.2.1. The Constitutional Structure of the ILO

At the end of the First World War there was a need for international regulation of labour conditions for three major reasons. First, increasing the level of labour standards was considered a humanitarian issue. Second, there was a broad consensus that industrial peace and international peace were closely related, and there was considerable fear of social disorder. Third, the parties at the table in Versailles were convinced that if social protection was not increased, world peace would be severely threatened by countries that undermined labour standards and promoted social dumping.[236]

Establishing international labour standards thus became the primary objective for the founders of the ILO. The original Constitution, drafted by the Commission on International Labour Legislation at the 1919 Peace Conference and embodied in the Treaty of Versailles, identified a series of existing labour conditions that involved such injustice and hardship as to threaten world peace. It affirmed that the failure of any nation to adopt humane conditions of labour constituted an obstacle for other nations desiring to improve conditions in their own countries. Peace required social justice. The ILO was established as a permanent organisation to address these problems. The Constitution did not attempt to impose substantial obligations on Member States but set up an institutional framework for the definition of precise standards and enforcement measures.

In light of recent developments, it is not surprising that the ILO, from the outset, put so much emphasis on standard setting. Standards are a tool for resolving conflicts between different interest groups through policy and legislation. Labour standards set a minimum threshold, ensuring that workers are not totally at the mercy of their employers. However, the role of labour standards in a globalised economy has become very controversial, with some governments arguing that they deprive countries of their competitive advantage, especially developing countries.[237] This controversy will be discussed later in chapter 3.

[235] Adopted and opened for signature, ratification and accession by General Assembly resolution A/RES/54/263 of 25 May 2000. The Protocol entered into force on 18 January 2002.

[236] O'Higgins (2002) 56. In fact, the discussion was very similar to the current debate on the relation between poverty and terrorism. See note 43 above.

[237] Samson and Schindler (1999) 185–86.

As of 1 October 2005, the existing body of ILO standards consists of 157 conventions[238] and 175 recommendations.[239] In addition, since 1919 the International Labour Conference (ILC) has adopted four declarations, the most recent in June 1998. While the conventions are legally binding treaties governed by international law, recommendations are designed to provide guidance in matters of policy, legislation and practice and are used when a "subject, or aspect of it, dealt with is not considered suitable or appropriate at that time for a Convention."[240] Because of their nature, recommendations are not open for ratification.[241]

The ILO is the only international organisation with a *tripartite* approach. At the International Labour Conference each Member State is represented by a delegation comprising two government representatives, one representative for workers and one representative for employers.[242] A similar rule applies to the executive organ, the Governing Body: half the members represent governments, one-quarter employers and one-quarter workers.[243] Conventions and Recommendations need to be adopted by the International Labour Conference in order to become binding.[244] Because of this parliamentary process, in which non-governmental representatives also take part, ILO conventions may not be ratified subject to reservations.[245] After their adoption, ILO conventions have no immediate binding effect unless they are ratified by a Member State. However, Member States are obligated to bring all conventions and recommendations before the authorities that are competent to enact legislation or take other appropriate measures to implement them within 18 months.[246]

With regard to the four declarations adopted by the International Labour Conference, it must be noted that with the exception of the Declaration of Philadelphia in 1944,[247] which became part of the Constitution of the ILO, they are not legally binding but rather promotional in nature.

238 Of the 185 conventions, Nos 4, 15, 20, 21, 28, 31, 34–40, 43, 46, 48–51, 60, 61, 64–67, 86, 91 and 104 have been withdrawn.

239 Of the 195 recommendations, Nos 1, 5, 11, 15, 37–39, 42, 45, 50, 51, 54, 56, 59, 63–66, 72 and 73 have been withdrawn.

240 Article 19(1)(b) of the ILO Constitution of 1944. For a detailed analysis, see Maupain (2000).

241 Bartolomei de la Cruz, von Potobsky and Swepston (1996) 20.

242 Article 3(1) ILO Constitution. Bartolomei de la Cruz, von Potobsky and Swepston (1996) 9–11.

243 Article 7(1) ILO Constitution.

244 The supervision of standards and of the Director-General lies also within the competence of the International Labour Conference. The International Labour Office is the permanent secretariat of the ILO.

245 Samson and Schindler (1999) 194; Leary (2003) 183. See the memorandum prepared by the ILO at the request of the International Court of Justice in the Genocide Case: "ICJ Pleadings, Reservations to the Convention on the Prevention and Punishment of the Crime of Genocide", pp 216–82, also quoted in The International Labour Code 1951, ILO, vol I, pp xcix–ciii. For a summary of the different views on the legal nature of ILO Conventions, see Bartolomei de la Cruz, von Potobsky and Swepston (1996) 21–24.

246 Article 19(5)(b) ILO Constitution.

247 See Introduction above, note 4. The International Labour Office moved to Montreal during the Second World War in order to be able to continue its work away from the main hostilities. Sohn (1999) 601.

The Declaration of Philadelphia is a fundamental statement of the specificity of labour in a commercial context, declaring that labour is not a commodity. The origins of this basic proposition go back to the Irish economist John Kells Ingram, who used the phrase in an address to the British Trades Union Congress meeting in 1880.[248] The idea was then taken up by the American Samuel Gompers and the Irishman Edward J Phelan during the negotiations of the Treaty of Versailles and resulted in Article 427 of the treaty, which states that "labour should not be regarded merely as a commodity or article of commerce." The word "merely" was added because of British insistence and was seen by Gompers as a major defeat.

The Philadelphia Declaration finally resolved the issue with its clear statement that labour is not a commodity. As such, the sentence represents one of the fundamental principles of international labour law. What Ingram had in mind was that the pricing of labour cannot be left solely to market forces but that wages have to allow for a decent standard of living for the workers and their families. In addition, it also means that a worker cannot be transferred from one employer to another without that worker's consent. Furthermore, the ILO based its efforts to outlaw fee-charging employment agencies on the principle that labour is not a commodity.[249] The concept was *inter alia* taken up by Article 23(3) of the Universal Declaration of Human Rights and by Article 4 of the European Social Charter.

Another key element of the ILO constitution is the acknowledgment of the relationship between poverty and peace. As early as 1944, the Philadelphia Declaration explicitly pointed out the danger that lies in the inequality between different nations:

> Article I
>
> (c) Poverty anywhere constitutes a danger to prosperity everywhere.

Remarkable and very innovative for the time is Article II(d),[250] which requires the ILO to integrate itself in *all* international economic and financial policies and measures. In other words, this is a clear statement for *mainstreaming*. This early development is important and partially set the stage for recent debates about the role of the ILO in a global economy.[251]

The Philadelphia Declaration prefigured by a few years certain parts of the Universal Declaration of Human Rights. Two other declarations concerned the

[248] For a detailed account of the history of this provision, see O'Higgins (1997) 225–34.

[249] O'Higgins (1997) 230–31.

[250] Article II

> Believing that experience has fully demonstrated the truth of the statement in the Constitution of the International Labour Organization that lasting peace can be established only if it is based on social justice, the Conference affirms that . . .
>
> (d) it is a responsibility of the International Labour Organization to examine and consider all international economic and financial policies and measures in the light of this fundamental objective . . .

[251] Samson and Schindler (1999) 188–89.

ILO's policy against Apartheid and principles on Multinational Enterprises.[252] The most recent Declaration on Fundamental Principles and Rights at Work will be dealt with below in section 1.2.3.3.

The ILO has three main means of action. The first as we have just seen is the setting of labour standards. Less well known but of increasing significance is technical co-operation. Due to the integration process in Europe, the European Union is taking over some of the broader ILO functions for its Member States.[253] As a result, the ILO—although not altogether pleased with the development in Europe—has an increased capacity for providing technical assistance to developing countries. Technical assistance has thus become an important means of implementing labour standards and, as the case of Burma/Myanmar shows, has started to include elements of conditionality.[254]

Finally, the ILO's third major course of action worldwide is taking the lead in research and studies in the context of labour.

1.2.2.2. Fundamental Conventions

For years, the ILO has referred to the seven above-mentioned conventions (Nos 87, 98, 29, 105, 138, 100, 111)[255] as protecting the basic human rights of workers, a classification that has been adopted by scholars and ILO experts ever since it was first mentioned by Wilfried C Jenks in 1963.[256] Convention No 182 banning the worst forms of child labour, which entered into force in November 2000, is set to become the eighth fundamental convention.

Because no reservations can be made upon ratification, flexibility is built into the conventions.[257] Sometimes conventions are divided into different parts, and governments can choose the parts they want to ratify.[258] Some conventions leave room for temporarily lower standards[259] or for the exclusion of special persons or undertakings.[260]

The conventions that are considered human rights treaties[261] refer to four different subjects: the abolition of forced labour, the freedom of association and collective bargaining, discrimination in the workplace and the elimination of child labour. Although the International Labour Conference plays an important

252 "Declaration concerning Action against Apartheid in South Africa of 1964 supplemented in 1988 and 1991"; "Tripartite Declaration of Principles concerning Multinational Enterprises and Social Policy of 1977".

253 With respect to collective labour rights see Davies (2005) 190–92.

254 For the Burma/Myanmar case, see section 1.2.2.2.B below.

255 See the list on p 26 above. For the text of relevant provision in these conventions, see the Appendix to this book.

256 Jenks (1963) 103.

257 Valticos and von Potobsky (1995) paras 96–105.

258 Eg Article 2(a)(ii) Social Security (Minimum Standards) Convention, 1952 (No 102).

259 Eg Article 3 Convention No 102. See note 258 above, Article 2(1) Convention No 121.

260 Eg Article 5 Night Work (Women) Convention No 41 and Article 11(3) Night Work (Women) Convention No 89.

261 Cleveland (2003) 137–38.

role in establishing rules, the only official competence for an authorised interpretation of the provisions of a convention lies with the International Court of Justice.[262] However, the court has decided only one case, which was of a very technical nature.[263] In practice, the comments of the supervisory organs are of more importance, as are the interpretations offered by the International Labour Office to Member States on request. The influence of the ILO supervisory bodies in fact extends far beyond the ILO itself: the organs of the UN tend to rely on ILO case law when interpreting labour rights.[264]

Like the UN Covenants, the enforcement of ILO conventions relies heavily on reports that are submitted, together with the comments of the social partners, to the "Committee of Experts on the Application of Conventions and Recommendations".[265] Unlike the other organs of the ILO, the Committee of Experts is not a tripartite organ but instead consists of lawyers who are supposed to act as independent experts. The comments by the Committee can be observations on non-compliance, which are published, or direct requests to the government concerned, which are not to be published.[266] Because of the "diplomatic" character of the ILO, observations are seen as a means to mobilise governments into overcoming failures in compliance. In addition to these individual comments, the Committee of Experts undertakes a general study of one particular subject every year. For this purpose, reports are requested from all countries, regardless of whether or not they have ratified the relevant conventions.

A) Forced Labour (Convention Nos 29 and 105) The classic legal definition of forced or compulsory labour can be found in Article 2(1) of the first ILO Convention on the subject, the Forced Labour Convention (No 29) (1930):

> The term "forced or compulsory labour" shall mean all work or service which is exacted from any person under the menace of any penalty and for which the said person has not offered himself voluntarily.

Although this legal definition has not changed, the context of forced and compulsory labour is evolving over time.[267] In 1926, the League of Nations' Slavery Convention was adopted. This convention prohibited all aspects of the slave trade. In addition, contracting parties were required to take all necessary measures to prevent forced or compulsory labour from developing into slave trade-like conditions. At the request of the League of Nations, the ILO drafted a set of regulations, which finally led to the adoption of Convention No 29 in 1930. The main issues of concern were the exaction of forced and compulsory labour from native populations during the colonial period.

262 Art 37(1) of the ILO Constitution.
263 "Opinion on the Competence of the ILO in Regard to International Regulation of the Conditions of Labour of Persons Employed in Agriculture" 1922 PCIJ, Series B, No 2, p 39.
264 See p 35 above.
265 Articles 19, 22 and 35 of the ILO Constitution.
266 Valticos and von Potobsky (1995) paras 658–62.
267 For an overview of the evolving faces of forced labour, see ILO (2001a) paras 19–40. The following paragraphs draw on this analysis. See also ILO (2005).

The second major period of standard-setting activity came at the end of the colonial era, during the 1950s, and was motivated by growing concern over the use of forced labour for political purposes. In addition, the world had witnessed forced labour on a massive scale during the inter-war period and the Second World War. These experiences inspired the inclusion of the prohibition of forced labour in the Declaration of Philadelphia and the Universal Declaration on Human Rights. Millions of people were being held in labour camps for political reasons by the 1950s. In this context, the UN adopted its 1956 Supplementary Convention on the Abolition of Slavery, the Slave Trade and Institutions and Practices similar to Slavery. Only a year later, the ILO adopted its Abolition of Forced Labour Convention (No 105). Article 1 of this Convention supplements the earlier instrument by calling for the immediate and complete abolition of any form of forced labour in five specified cases:

a. as a means of political coercion or education or as a punishment for holding or expressing political views or views ideologically opposed to the established political, social or economic system;
b. as a method of mobilizing and using labour for purposes of economic development;
c. as a means of labour discipline;
d. as a punishment for having participated in strikes;
e. as a means of racial, social, national or religious discrimination.

The prohibition of slavery and slavery-like practices are peremptory norms of international law *(ius cogens)* and thus binding on the international community as a whole.[268] This is probably why the ILO Conventions Nos 29 and 105 attracted a large degree of international acceptance and are the most highly ratified of the fundamental Conventions (168 ratifications for Convention No 29 and 165 for Convention No 105).[269]

At the time that these ILO Conventions were adopted, states were seen as key actors. However, the conventions include references to non-state actors and hold states responsible for forced labour, even if private individuals or enterprises exact it;[270] they thus impose horizontal obligations on the state.[271] The state remains responsible if forced labour is not prevented or punished. While this represented a shift in ideology at the time the conventions were drafted, recent developments in international law provide further support for such an

[268] *Barcelona Traction, Light and Power Co Ltd (Second Phase) (Belgium v Spain)*, ICJ Reports 1970, 3, 32 and 304 (5 Feb), separate opinion by Justice Ammoun. See also Article 53, Vienna Convention on the Law of Treaties (1969).

[269] As of October 2005.

[270] Article 5(1) of Convention No 29 reads:

> No concession granted to private individuals, companies or associations shall involve any form of forced or compulsory labour for the production or the collection of products which such private individuals, companies or associations utilize or in which they trade.

[271] See note 199 above and accompanying text.

approach.[272] Modern policies like the one adopted by the International Finance Corporation (IFC) follow this ILO approach.[273]

Today, the increasing amount of trafficking is a major concern for the ILO in the context of forced labour.[274]

B) Enforcing Convention No 29: The Case of Burma/Myanmar In 1996, a complaint was presented under Article 26 of the ILO Constitution against the government of Burma/Myanmar for non-observance of the Forced Labour Convention (No 29).[275] The ILO Governing Body appointed a Commission of Inquiry to visit Burma/Myanmar, and the findings and recommendations of the Commission were communicated to the government of Burma/Myanmar in July 1998. However, no substantial steps were taken by Burma/Myanmar, and in June 2000 the International Labour Conference invoked, for the first time in ILO history, Article 33 of the Constitution, calling upon the government of Burma/Myanmar to take concrete action to implement the recommendations of the Commission of Inquiry.[276] Because the conditions set up in the Resolution had not been met by November 2000, the Governing Body, at its 279th session, stated that paragraph 1 of the Resolution[277] would now take effect:

> The International Labour Conference . . .
>
> 1. Approves in principle, subject to the conditions stated in paragraph 2 below, the actions recommended by the Governing Body, namely:
>
> (a) to decide that the question of the implementation of the Commission of Inquiry's recommendations and of the application of Convention No 29 by Myanmar should be discussed at future sessions of the International Labour Conference, at a sitting of the Committee on the Application of Standards specially set aside for the purpose, so long as this Member has not been shown to have fulfilled its obligations;
> (b) to recommend to the Organization's constituents as a whole—governments, employers and workers—that they: (i) review, in the light of the conclusions of the Commission of Inquiry, the relations that they may have with the Member State

[272] United States Diplomatic and Consular Staff in Teheran, ICJ Reports 1980, pp 3, 30–37 at paras 61–79; See also Articles 4–8 of the ILC Draft on State Responsibility: International Law Commission, State Responsibility, Draft Articles adopted by the International Law Commission at its fifty-third session, UN Doc A/CN.4/L.602 Rev.1 [Hereinafter ILC, Draft State Responsibility]. Report of the International Law Commission on the work of its fifty-third session, 23 April–1 June and 2 July–10 August 2001, GA OR 56th sess, Supp No 10 (A/56/10), Commentary to Chapter II, Introduction. On 12 December 2001, the General Assembly "took note" of the draft, thus staying neutral with regard to its content: UN Doc A/RES/56/83, 28 January 2002.

[273] See chapter 2 below, note 142 and accompanying text.

[274] ILO (2001a) 47–57, 100.

[275] For a comprehensive account see Maupain (2005b) 94–123.

[276] Resolution concerning the measures recommended by the Governing Body under article 33 of the ILO Constitution on the subject of Myanmar, adopted by the International Labour Conference at its 88th Session on 14 June 2000, Provisional Record, 6–4, p 21.

[277] See *ibid*.

concerned and take appropriate measures to ensure that the said Member cannot take advantage of such relations to perpetuate or extend the system of forced or compulsory labour referred to by the Commission of Inquiry, and to contribute as far as possible to the implementation of its recommendations; and (ii) report back in due course and at appropriate intervals to the Governing Body;

(c) as regards international organisations, to invite the Director-General: (i) to inform the international organisations referred to in article 12, paragraph 1, of the Constitution of the Member's failure to comply; (ii) to call on the relevant bodies of these organisations to reconsider, within their terms of reference and in the light of the conclusions of the Commission of Inquiry, any cooperation they may be engaged in with the Member concerned and, if appropriate, to cease as soon as possible any activity that could have the effect of directly or indirectly abetting the practice of forced or compulsory labour;

(d) regarding the UN specifically, to invite the Director-General to request the Economic and Social Council (ECOSOC) to place an item on the agenda of its July 2001 session concerning the failure of Myanmar to implement the recommendations contained in the report of the Commission of Inquiry and seeking the adoption of recommendations directed by ECOSOC or by the General Assembly, or by both, to governments and to other specialized agencies and including requests similar to those proposed in paragraphs (b) and (c) above;

(e) to invite the Director-General to submit to the Governing Body, in the appropriate manner and at suitable intervals, a periodic report on the outcome of the measures set out in paragraphs (c) and (d) above, and to inform the international organisations concerned of any developments in the implementation by Myanmar of the recommendations of the Commission of Inquiry.

The ILO then suspended technical co-operation and assistance to Burma/Myanmar except that directly related to the immediate implementation of the recommendations of the Commission of Inquiry. In a meeting in March 2001, the Burma/Myanmar authorities agreed to discuss modalities for an objective assessment of the progress it claimed to have made. In May 2001 an "Understanding on an ILO Objective Assessment"[278] was reached, and a high-level team was sent to Burma/Myanmar to carry out "an objective assessment of the practical implementation and actual impact of the framework of legislative, executive and administrative measures taken by the authorities" in September 2001.[279]

After careful examination of the report, the Governing Body noted that the new legislation in Burma/Myanmar had very limited impact and concluded that permanent ILO representation should be put in place in Burma/Myanmar as soon as possible.[280] For this purpose, another technical co-operation mission

278 ILO, GB 282.4/Appendices, Appendix I.

279 ILO, "Developments concerning the Question of the Observance by the Government of Myanmar of the Forced Labour Convention (No 29)", Report of the High-Level Team, November 2001, GB.282/4, paras 7–8.

280 ILO, "Conclusions concerning the Question of the Observance by the Government of Myanmar of the Forced Labour Convention (No 29)", Adopted after examination of the report of the High-Level Team, GB 282/4/2, November 2001.

was sent to Burma/Myanmar in February 2002.[281] The ILO delegation discussed the possibilities of permanent ILO representation in Burma/Myanmar and the establishment of an ombudsperson for victims of forced labour. Despite the efforts of the ILO team, the Burma/Myanmar authorities remained very sceptical and only agreed to having a liaison officer rather than the proposed permanent mission. No substantial progress was made with regard to the ombudsperson.

Following the return of the mission to Geneva, the Government of Burma/Myanmar expressed its willingness to discuss the issue further and sent a delegation to Geneva. Subsequent to—in the words of the ILO—"extended and sometimes difficult negotiations", an understanding on the appointment of an ILO Liaison Officer in Burma/Myanmar was finally reached.[282] The tasks of the Liaison Officer proved to be difficult: while the situation with respect to forced labour improved somewhat in the central parts of Burma/Myanmar, no progress could be reported in border areas.[283] The special rapporteur of the UN Commission on Human Rights, Paulo Sergio Pinheiro, reached the same conclusions.[284]

The interpretation of Article 33 of the Constitution led to considerable debate within the ILO.[285] While it is clear that measures can entail neither expulsion from the Organisation nor suspension of a member's voting rights,[286] there is controversy as to how far the Governing Body can go in inviting other international organisations or Member States to take sanctions. The Association of Southeast Asian Nations (ASEAN)[287] took a firm stand at the International Labour Conference in urging the ILO not to end the dialogue with Burma/Myanmar nor to force it out of the ILO.[288]

Following the ILO Resolution several member countries took measures against Burma/Myanmar.[289] However, although these measures were presented to the ILO as a follow-up to the Resolution, in most cases they had taken place because of other developments. For example, in the case of Switzerland a federal ordinance was issued on 2 October 2000 imposing an arms embargo and

[281] ILO, "Developments concerning the Question of the Observance by the Government of Myanmar of the Forced Labour Convention (No 29)", Report of the ILO technical cooperation mission to Myanmar (19–25 February 2002), GB 283/5/2, March 2002.

[282] ILO, "Developments concerning the Question of the Observance by the Government of Myanmar of the Forced Labour Convention (No 29)", Further developments following the return of the ILO technical cooperation mission, GB 283/5/3, March 2002.

[283] ILO, "Developments concerning the Question of the Observance by the Government of Myanmar of the Forced Labour Convention (No 29)", GB 289/8, March 2004.

[284] "Situation of Human Rights in Myanmar", Report of the Special Rapporteur, transmitted to the members of the General Assembly by the Secretary-General, UN Doc A/58/219, 5 August 2003.

[285] Maupain (2005b) 115–20.

[286] International Labour Conference, 88th Session, Measures recommended by the Governing Body under article 33 of the Constitution, Provisional Record of Proceedings No 4, p 4/5, para 12.

[287] ASEAN accepted Myanmar as a member only after considerable debate. http://www.aseansec.org.

[288] See for example the statement of Mr Mishra, representing the government of India, Reports of the proceedings, note 286 above, 4/10–4/11.

[289] See the list in GB 280/6 at paras 13–21.

prohibiting the export of equipment that could be used for the purposes of internal repression[290] due to the lack of progress in democratisation in Burma/Myanmar and to systematic violation of human rights (including workers' rights). Still, this measure was the autonomous implementation by Switzerland of regulations similar to those adopted by the EU. Reports to the Swiss Parliament mention only the measures taken by the EU as a motivation; nothing is said about the ILO.[291]

The controversy about Burma/Myanmar and the debate about the interpretation of Article 33 of the ILO Constitution bring into sharp relief the tenuousness of the ILO's credibility and authority. If the ILO fails to fulfil its mandate as the key organisation for labour rights, labour issues are likely to be dealt with only on a national basis.[292]

C) Freedom of Association and Collective Bargaining (Convention Nos 87 and 98) Two significant events concerning human rights took place in 1948: the first was the adoption by the ILO of the Freedom of Association and Protection of the Right to Organise Convention (No 87); the second was the adoption by the UN of the Universal Declaration of Human Rights just a few months later. The main difference between Convention No 87 and the Universal Declaration of Human Rights (and other UN Covenants) is that the Convention refers explicitly to both employers' and workers' organisations.[293]

When the ILO incorporated the Declaration of Philadelphia into its Constitution in 1946,[294] freedom of association was reaffirmed as one of the organisation's fundamental principles.[295] Two years later, however, the adop-

[290] Verordnung über Massnahmen gegen Myanmar, AS 2000, 2648.

[291] Bericht zur Aussenwirtschaftspolitik 2000 sowie Botschaften zu Wirtschaftsvereinbarungen, BBl 2000, at 905; Botschaft zu einem Bundesgesetz über die Durchsetzung von internationalen Sanktionen, BBl 2000 1433 [hereinafter Botschaft EmbG] at 1445.

[292] It has been argued that other organisations such as the WTO could step in. With a view to recent developments as expressed in the Singapore Declaration, this seems rather unlikely. See the statements of Mr Warrington, representing the government of the United Kingdom in: Provisional Record of proceedings, note 286 above, p 4/9; and Mr Brett, representing the Workers, United Kingdom, Provisional Record of Proceedings, p 4/12. Maupain (2005b), 107–14.

[293] Trade unions played an important role in the creation of the institutional framework for the ILO: the Peace Conference after the First World War, for the first time in history, had created a tripartite institution. For the first time, delegations to a peace conference included representatives of employers' organisations and trade unions. The first chairman of the Commission on International Labour Legislation, which elaborated the draft Constitution of the ILO, was Samuel Gompers, President of the American Federation of Labor. Dunning (1998) 154–55. Furthermore, because union members played a crucial role in the drafting of Convention No 87, its articles are not only clear and concise, but also easily understandable.

[294] Declaration Concerning the Aims and Purpose of the International Labour Organization, adopted at the 26th General Conference of the ILO in Philadelphia on 10 May 1944 as an Annex to the ILO Constitution, para II(a) [hereinafter Philadelphia Declaration], available at http://www.ilo.org/public/english/overview/iloconst.htm. See Introduction above, note 4.

[295] Swepston (1998) 170–71. Previously, the only instruments, which really amounted to what are called human rights treaties today, were the Slavery Convention adopted by the League of Nations in 1926 and the Forced Labour Convention (No 29) adopted by the ILO in 1930.

tion of the Freedom of Association Convention proved nevertheless to be very difficult.[296]

Membership in the ILO requires formal acceptance of the obligations contained in its Constitution, which includes a clear affirmation of the principle of freedom of association.[297] As a result, member countries must respect the principle of freedom of association whether or not they have ratified Convention No 87.[298] The Committee on Freedom of Association (CFA), which was created by the Governing Body of the ILO in 1951, may thus examine complaints on the subject of freedom of association in all member countries. If a country has indeed ratified Convention No 87, the CFA, after examining the case, will submit the complaint to the Commission of Freedom of Association for follow-up.[299] In all other cases, the CFA itself follows up the effect given to complaints.

Convention No 87 translates the principle of freedom of association into specific rights capable of enforcement in law and applicable in practice.[300] With regard to individual rights, the supervisory bodies deal in particular with Article 2, which stipulates the right to establish organisations without previous authorisation and the right of workers and employers to establish and join organisations of their own choosing.[301] Of particular importance for the individual are several civil rights that, in the view of the supervisory bodies, are a prerequisite for the freedom of association, namely the rights to personal security, freedom of opinion and expression, freedom of assembly and protection of trade union premises.[302]

Article 3 introduces the collective rights of organisations of employers and workers, starting with their internal autonomy. It continues with their right to exercise their mandate without state interference. Unlike the ICESCR, Convention No 87 does not mention the right to strike. Nevertheless, the ILO's supervisory bodies have had to deal with this question more often than any other subject in labour relations. As a general rule, the right to strike is considered an "intrinsic corollary of the right of association protected by Convention No 87".[303]

Because the right to strike rests on Articles 3 and 10 of the Convention, which deal with collective rights, the CFA has stated that the right to call a strike is the

296 For a detailed description of the adopting process, see Dunning (1998) 156–63.

297 The preamble of the Constitution affirms the principle of freedom of association, and Article I(b) of the Declaration of Philadelphia, which is incorporated into the Constitution, names the freedom of expression and the freedom of association as essential principles to sustained progress.

298 So far 144 countries have ratified Convention No 87.

299 If a government has not ratified the Convention, the Commission can only become active if the government against which a complaint has been filed agrees to the examination. The Commission was created in 1950 following discussion with ECOSOC. See ILO (1996) Annex 1.

300 Dunning (1998) 163.

301 Swepston (1998) 181–84 with further references.

302 For a detailed list, see Swepston (1998) 176–81. For an analysis of recent cases, see Macklem (2005) 65–68.

303 ILO (1994) para 179.

sole preserve of trade union organisations.[304] However, it is acceptable under the Convention to prohibit strikes by certain categories of workers, especially those who are providing essential services.

From a national government's point of view, the purpose of protected activities is of special importance. In the original ILO Constitution, the freedom of association was explicitly restricted to "all lawful purposes". When a similar provision was included in the preamble of the draft for Convention No 87, it was rejected not only by workers but also by some governments. The argument was that it seemed unacceptable to make the international right of freedom of association subject to national legislation. After lengthy debate, the final wording of Article 8 reads:

> 1. In exercising the rights provided in this Convention workers and employers and their respective organisations, like other persons or organised collectivities, shall respect the right of the land.
> 2. The law of the land shall not be such as to impair, nor shall it be so applied as to impair, the guarantees provided for in this Convention.

One of the major tasks of the ILO has been to advance collective bargaining throughout the world. This task was laid down in the Declaration of Philadelphia in 1944 and embodied in the Right to Organise and Collective Bargaining Convention (No 98) of 1949, which has been ratified by 154 countries as of October 2005. Today, however, the importance of collective bargaining has changed due to several recent developments. On the one hand, the growing informal sector has limited the scope of collective bargaining,[305] and collective bargaining has lost some of its room for manoeuvre and contractual freedom as a result of the growing influence on national economic policy wielded by international organisations such as the Bretton Woods Institutions (BWIs).[306] On the other hand, the increasingly tough competition brought about by technological innovation and globalisation has reduced the importance of sectoral agreements in many countries and at the same time enhanced collective bargaining at the enterprise level.[307]

304 ILO (1996) para 477.

305 For discussion of the informal sector, see Introduction, section I.1.2. above.

306 The CFA acknowledges that there are cases where economic stabilisation or structural adjustment policies are necessary and wage rates cannot be fixed freely by means of collective bargaining for "imperative reasons of national economic interest." However, "these restrictions should be applied as an exceptional measure and only to the extent necessary, should not exceed a reasonable period and should be accompanied by adequate safeguards to protect effectively the standard of living of the workers concerned, in particular those who are likely to be the most affected." ILO (1994) para 260.

307 An example is the Swiss banking industry where the country-wide collective bargaining rounds between unions and employers' organisations were replaced by negotiations at the enterprise level in 1995. As a result, employees' representatives meet with a management delegation and discuss salary increases for the following year. While this new system allows for tailor-made solutions for each enterprise, it has also led to a significant loss in transparency, making wage comparisons more difficult. In addition, many employees' delegations have found themselves faced with a rather daunting task and now require training in negotiating skills as well as

Article 4 of Convention No 98 focuses on terms and conditions of work and employment and on the regulation of the relations between employers and workers and their respective organisations. The supervisory bodies apply a broad concept to working conditions. Apart from the traditional working conditions such as working time, overtime, rest periods, wages etc they also cover "certain matters which are normally included in conditions of employment" such as promotion, transfer, dismissal without notice and assignment of jobs.[308] This trend is very much in line with the recent developments in industrialised countries, where collective bargaining procedures are used to address a broad spectrum of entrepreneurial problems such as downsizing[309] or the adaptation of working hours to the production process.[310]

In light of the ongoing discussion about the privatisation of public enterprises, the question of whether the right to collective bargaining also applies to civil servants and public enterprises has become of crucial importance for governments. Article 5 of Convention No 98 allows the exclusion of only the armed forces, the police and public servants engaged in the administration of the state. The latter category leaves room for interpretation. The CFA held that matters that "clearly appertain primarily or essentially to the management and operation of government business" can be regarded as outside the scope of negotiation. According to the CFA, the Convention's coverage includes *inter alia* personnel in national undertakings and public bodies, the staff of national radio and television services, teaching personnel and employees of the postal and telecommunication services.[311]

The right of trade unions to organise, to run their own affairs and to bargain collectively has increasingly been recognised, although in many countries, workers' organisations still have many obstacles before them. Recent problems include anti-union discrimination, exclusion of some categories of workers or certain economic sectors from the coverage of the right to bargain, governmental intervention in collective bargaining and restrictions on the right to negotiate.[312]

economics. This has led the employers' organisation and the unions to organise joint seminars in which these skills are taught.

308 ILO (1994) para 250, including footnote 17. Gernigon, Odero and Guido (2000) 39.

309 See for example the Swiss Federal Worker Participation Act of 1993 (Bundesgesetz über die Information und Mitsprache der Arbeitnehmerinnen und Arbeitnehmer in den Betrieben, SR 822.14). According to its Article 10, workers' representatives have *inter alia* participation rights in the case of collective dismissals.

310 See the creative flexible working scheme "5000 mal 5000" developed by Volkswagen in collaboration with unions to avoid dismissals. The goal of the model was to re-integrate unemployed workers by combining training with wages that allowed for competitive pricing of the manufactured products. Verhandlungsergebnis zwischen den Verhandlungskommissionen der Volkswagen AG und der Auto 5000 GmbH einerseits und der Industriegewerkschaft Metall, Bezirksleitung Hannover, andrerseits vom 28. August 2001.

311 ILO (1996) paras 597–603. See also Macklem (2005) 67–68.

312 Bartolomei de la Cruz, von Potobsky and Swepston (1996) 224–29.

D) Equal Remuneration and Discrimination (Convention Nos 100 and 111)
Several developments contributed to the creation of ILO Convention No 100 on Equal Remuneration in 1951 and Convention No 111 on Discrimination (Employment and Occupation) in 1958. The World Wars had involved the civilian population like no other conflicts before, bringing a massive influx of women into industry, particularly war industries, to replace the men who had been called to fight. As a result, women had not only demonstrated that they could do the work, but also claimed that this fact should be reflected in their pay. The principle of equality between men and women was included in the UN Charter, and more specifically, the Universal Declaration of Human Rights in Article 23(2) contained the principle of equal pay for equal work.[313] Therefore, by the late 1940s the ILO believed that the time was ripe for a specific instrument in this area. Finally, an invitation by the ECOSOC to "proceed as rapidly as possible, with the further consideration of this subject and to report to the Council on the action which it has taken" led to a decision by the ILO Governing Body in December 1948 to include the subject of equal remuneration on the agenda of the ILO Conference. This resulted in the adoption of Convention No 100.[314]
The post-War decolonisation movement, together with the civil rights discussion in the US, gave rise to the notion of racial equality as a basic principle of international relations. For the ILO it led to an expansion of the regulation concerning equality in a more general sense. Again, the ECOSOC initiated the process by inviting the ILO to undertake a study on the question of discrimination in employment and occupation. The Governing Body acted upon this invitation and included the question on the agenda of the 1955 Conference. The groundwork for Convention No 111 had been laid by the Declaration of Philadelphia of 1944, which stated:

> . . . all human beings, irrespective of race, creed or sex, have the right to pursue their material well-being and their spiritual development in conditions of freedom and dignity, of economic security and equal opportunity . . .[315]

Convention No 111 was adopted in 1958 and has been ratified by 163 countries as of October 2005. It reflects the "pervasive concern of the ILO with equality as a fundamental condition of human dignity and social justice".[316]

Convention No 100 is often considered "promotional" in character. It obligates the ratifying states to do what they can, in good faith, to ensure the application of the principle of equal remuneration, but it does not require them to guarantee its effective and general application (Article 2). This means that states are required to guarantee the effective application only in cases where

[313] See section 1.2.2.1. above regarding Article 23(2) of the Universal Declaration of Human Rights. In addition, a number of countries have incorporated the principle of equal remuneration in their constitutions; the first of these was Mexico in 1917.
[314] Bartolomei de la Cruz, von Potobsky and Swepston (1996) 234–35.
[315] Para II(a).
[316] Bartolomei de la Cruz, von Potobsky and Swepston (1996) 236–37.

they have a direct influence, for example, in government employment. With regard to sectors where the state has no direct enforcement authority, for instance, when wages are determined by collective bargaining agreements, the Convention requires the state *to promote* the application of the principle. The state thus has an obligation to *guarantee* the application of the principle in the following situations: when the state is the employer, or in some other manner controls the undertakings; when the state intervenes in the wage-fixing process, principally when wage rates are controlled by the public authorities or their regulation is obligatory; and when there is legislation related to equality of treatment in remuneration. According to the Committee of Experts, the obligation to *promote* is imposed in cases in which "the state is not in a position to ensure the application of the principle of equal remuneration."[317] Convention No 100 is thus a good example of the ILO's flexible approach.[318]

The measures required from a government depend on the methods already in operation for determining wages or remuneration. Therefore, the Convention does not favour any particular method of evaluation. However, practice has shown that many countries use the analytical job evaluation methodology[319] and that there is a growing consensus that this is the most practicable method of ensuring the application of the principle of equal remuneration in practice. The Committee's main concern is that when undertaking such evaluations the utmost care is taken in identifying those jobs commonly regarded as being carried out by women, so that the degree of subjectivity and gender bias is minimised.[320]

With 162 ratifications out of the total membership of 178,[321] Convention No 100 is one of the most highly ratified ILO Conventions. However, the implementation of this convention has proven to be anything but simple. Nevertheless, progress has been made, and the Committee of Experts was able to note in 2001:

> In this 50th anniversary year of the Convention, the Committee can note with interest the indications that some governments and social partners are focusing on the issue of equal pay as a matter of priority. In hoping for greater implementation of the Convention, the Committee must conclude by welcoming the progress that has been achieved in the application of the principle of equal remuneration between men and women and the leading role that Convention No 100 has played during these 50 years.[322]

[317] ILO (1986) paras 25–28, 29.

[318] See note 257 above and accompanying text.

[319] This method is very common in Switzerland and applied by courts when determining which jobs are equal. BGE 124 II 409 E. 10d; 125 II 385 E. 4b; 125 I 71 E. 3a–b). Decision of the Administrative Court Zurich (Verwaltungsgericht Zürich), 22 January 2001, VK 1996.00011. For a new analytical method see the decision by the Federal Supreme Court of 22 December 2003: BGE 130 III 145.

[320] ILO, "General Report of the Committee of Experts on the Application of Conventions and Recommendations", 2001, para 43.

[321] As of October 2005.

[322] ILO, "General Report of the Committee of Experts on the Application of Conventions and Recommendations", 2001, para 50. For an overview of recent issues see paras 36–49 of the "General Report".

Convention No 111 and its accompanying Recommendation No 111 were considered progressive at the time of their adoption because they apply an effects test in defining discrimination, thereby encompassing both direct and indirect discrimination. In addition, they do not require proof of discriminatory purpose.[323] According to Article 1(1)(a) of Convention No 111, discrimination includes:

> Any distinction, exclusion or preference made on the basis of race, color, sex, religion, political opinion, national extraction or social origin, which has the effect of nullifying or impairing equality of opportunity or treatment in employment or occupation.

The definition thus contains three elements:

1. a factual element (the existence of a distinction, an exclusion or preference originating in an act or omission) that constitutes a difference in treatment;
2. a ground on which the difference of treatment is based; and
3. the objective result of this difference in treatment (the nullification or impairment of equality of opportunity or treatment).[324]

The basic concept of discrimination underlying the Convention is *group discrimination*. The drafters believed that the individual would act as an "attorney general" in the interest of others. While this approach was not well accepted in Western Europe at the time, similar initiatives have recently been adopted by the European Union.[325]

States are required to adopt the elimination of discrimination as an objective on the grounds listed in the Convention. This principle is developed in Article 3, which refers to the measures laid down to ensure the application of the principle of equality.[326] With regard to remuneration, which is outlined in more detail in Recommendation No 111 paragraph 2(b)(v), the Committee of Experts stated that the value of work must not be assessed by race, sex etc but by the amount of effort that the individual brings to the product regardless of its market value. This approach is similar to the conception of value put forward by John Locke and Karl Marx and not surprisingly is highly controversial.

E) Child Labour (Convention Nos 138 and 182) Industrialisation brought about a growing public concern with child labour, which led to several national regulations at the end of the nineteenth century. When the ILO was established,

[323] ILO (2003) p 16 Box 2.1 and paras 56–66. The US Supreme Court requires a discriminatory purpose in addition to discriminatory effect for a facially neutral provision to violate the Fourteenth Amendment of the US Constitution: *Washington v Davis* 426 USR 229 (1976); *Personnel Administrator of Massachusetts v Feeney* 442 USR 256 (1979). No such purpose is required under Article 141 of the Treaty Establishing the European Community: Case C-167/97 *Regina v Secretary of State for Employment* [1999] ECR I-623.

[324] See ILO (1986) para 23.

[325] European Union Council Directive 2000/78/EC of 27 November 2000, establishing a general framework for equal treatment in employment and occupation, OJ L 303/16.

[326] Bartolomei de la Cruz, von Potobsky and Swepston (1996) 258.

the protection of children and young workers was considered one of its main tasks. The conventions adopted aim to protect children and young workers in three major ways: they set a minimum age for admission to employment, night work and medical examination.[327] Over the years, ten different conventions have been adopted that dealt with the minimum age for admission to employment, covering various fields of activity. In 1973 the various instruments were consolidated in a single convention, the Minimum Working Age Convention (No 138).

Convention No 138 applies a different approach from its predecessors in combining broader coverage with greater adaptability to national situations.[328] Article 1 requires ratifying states to pursue national policy that is designed to ensure the effective abolition of child labour and to increase progressively the minimum age for admission to employment or work at a level consistent with the fullest physical and mental development of young persons.[329] The Convention leaves the specification of a minimum age to the ratifying states. However, it states that the minimum age should not be less than the age of completion of compulsory schooling and, in any case, should not be less than 15 years—or 14 years as an initial step for developing countries.[330] Exceptions are possible for "light" work; for "hazardous" work, the minimum age is set at 18 years, regardless of a country's level of development.[331]

By 1997, Convention No 138 had attracted less than a third of the number of ratifications obtained by the 1989 United Nations Convention on the Rights of the Child. In particular, no Asian country except Nepal had ratified it, although Asia at the time accounted for some 60 per cent of child labour worldwide. While there is an emerging consensus that exploitative child labour is morally unacceptable, the translation into legal terms has proved to be difficult.[332] The Director of the ILO summarised the situation at the Amsterdam Conference on Child Labour in February 1997:

> Convention No 138 is one of the basic ILO instruments . . . and remains one of the essential pillars of a coherent policy to combat child labour at the national level. But experience has shown that this convention raises problems for some States which find it too complex to apply in detail and which therefore hesitate in ratifying it. It thus seems necessary to draw up a new instrument which is expressly directed against the extreme forms of child labour. This new Convention would supplement and not replace Convention No 138.[333]

[327] Valticos and von Potobsky (1995) para 507.
[328] Lansky (1997) 235.
[329] Valticos and von Potobsky (1995) para 517.
[330] Article 2.
[331] Article 3(1).
[332] For a more detailed discussion, see Van Bueren (1995) 265–68. As of October 2005, 141 countries have ratified Convention No 138.
[333] Quoted in Lansky (1997) 244.

The issue of child labour and the adoption of a new international labour standard were subsequently put on the agenda for the International Labour Conference in 1998.

After intensive discussion about the definition of intolerable child labour,[334] agreement was finally reached by introducing the term "worst forms of child labour". According to Article 3 of the new convention, this notion comprises all forms of slavery, child prostitution, the use of children for illicit activities and work that is likely to harm the health, safety or morals of children. The Convention applies a very pragmatic approach, not only by focusing on the worst forms of child labour, but also by emphasising the importance of providing education (Article 7(2)).[335] The Worst Forms of Child Labour Convention (No 182) together with the Recommendation Concerning the Prohibition and Immediate Action for the Elimination of the Worst Forms of Child Labour (No 190) were adopted on 17 June 1999. As of October 2005, the Convention had received 156 ratifications—the fastest ratification pace in the history of the ILO.

Convention No 182 reflects an increasingly common trend in international human rights law: a focus on *extreme* conditions or *basic* rights in order to facilitate an international consensus. Another example in this context is the focus on extreme poverty within the UN bodies.[336]

Recommendation 190 tries to compensate for the vague language in the Convention. Although not legally binding, the Recommendation is much more specific and fills in the gaps left open by the Convention. As such, it not only serves as a means for interpretation of the Convention but also clarifies the meaning of implementation and enforcement. Very much in line with the work of the International Law Commission on state responsibility,[337] paragraph 12 defines which forms of child labour should be considered criminal offences by the States. Paragraph 15(d) goes even further by suggesting an extraterritorial effect of the Convention:

> 15. Other measures aimed at the prohibition and elimination of the worst forms of child labour might include the following:
>
> . . . (d) providing for the prosecution in their own country of the Member's nationals who commit offences under its national provisions for the prohibition and immediate elimination of the worst forms of child labour even when these offences are committed in another country.

This example illustrates the pragmatic approach of the ILO in designing legally binding instruments with a limited scope but a realistic chance of being ratified

[334] Lansky (1997) 245–48.

[335] The lack of appropriate educational facilities is one of the causes of the persistence of child labour. Practical evidence shows that the elimination of child labour can force the affected children into crime and prostitution if no alternatives to the loss of the job are provided. See CUTS (1999).

[336] See chapter 2, section 2.2.6. below, note 275 and accompanying text.

[337] See note 272 above.

by many member countries and leaving the more specific issues to the non-binding instruments.

In sum, under Conventions No 138 and 182 three forms of child labour are to be abolished: first, labour that is performed by a child who is *under the minimum age* specified for that kind of work; second, labour that jeopardises the well-being of a child (known as *hazardous* work); finally, forms of child labour that are internationally defined as the *worst forms*, including slavery, trafficking, debt bondage and other forms of forced labour, forced use of children in armed conflict, prostitution and pornography, and illicit activities.[338]

As mentioned earlier,[339] the ILO has been especially concerned with the increasing cases of trafficking. Initial small-scale studies that were undertaken in the context of forced labour have show that children are among those most affected by trafficking, especially in Asia. Although, for example, in South-East Asia the number of girls trafficked for prostitution by force is decreasing, more are being persuaded to enter prostitution voluntarily, in part because of their ignorance of the precise nature, dangers and stigmas attached to this activity. Particularly alarming are surveys from Thailand, where coercion, deception and the selling of minors occur most commonly in cases of direct recruitment from villages. Research from poor villages in Nepal found that fathers and other relatives might be so desperate as to sell children to intermediaries. In Africa, boys are mainly trafficked for work on plantations and girls as domestic servants, but street trade, catering and prostitution also occur. Trafficking in children is not limited to the developing world, but also occurs in industrialised countries.[340] A recent report estimates the number of women and children trafficked into the US at 50,000 annually.[341]

1.2.2.3. The ILO Declaration on Fundamental Principles and Rights at Work (1998)

The ILO Declaration on Fundamental Principles and Rights at Work of June 1998[342] is at the centre of not only the ongoing debate about the concept of core labour rights but also the highly controversial discussion on the transformation of the International Labour Regime and the linkage of trade and labour rights.[343]

[338] ILO (2002) para 26 and Box. 2.
[339] See note 274 above and accompanying text.
[340] ILO (2001a) paras 152–66; ILO (2005) Figure 1.1. at p 10 and paras 223–36.
[341] US Department of State, Victims of Trafficking and Violence Protection Act of 2000—Trafficking in Persons Report, July 2001.
[342] Adopted by the International Labour Conference, 86th Session, 18 June 1998. See ILC, Record of Proceedings, Nos 20 and 22 (86th Session, Geneva, 1998), available at http://www.ilo.org [hereinafter ILO Declaration]. For an extensive account of its genesis, see Alston (2004) 462–70. For the full text, see Appendix A.15 of this book.
[343] See the recent debate between Alston, Langille and Maupain: Alston (2004) 457–521; replies by Langille (2005) 409–37 and Maupain (2005a) 439–65; rejoinder by Alston (2005a) 467–80.

The genesis of the Declaration can be traced to discussions and debates during the 75th anniversary of the ILO in 1994, the Programme of Action adopted by the World Summit for Social Development in Copenhagen in 1995[344] and to the WTO Ministerial Meeting in Singapore in 1996.

A first attempt to link trade and labour rights was undertaken in the Havana Charter for an International Trade Organisation in 1948. Its Article 7 stated:

> . . . the members recognize that [. . .] all countries have a common interest in the achievement and maintenance of fair labour standards related to productivity, and thus in the improvement of wages and working conditions as productivity may permit. The members recognize that unfair labour conditions, particularly in production for export, create difficulties in international trade, and accordingly, each Member shall take whatever action may be appropriate and feasible to eliminate such conditions within its territory.[345]

The Havana Charter, and the permanent International Trade Organisation that it would have created, never came into force. Instead, multilateral trade was addressed through a contract, the General Agreement on Tariffs and Trade (GATT). A proposal put forward by the US to include an informal social clause in the sense of the Havana Charter, which would have required Member States to consult with the ILO in cases that dealt with labour standards, found no support from other contracting parties.[346]

With the creation of the WTO, the debate over a social clause emerged once again.[347] However, the Uruguay Round closed in 1994 with the Marrakesh Declaration and the refusal to set up a committee within the WTO to study the link between labour standards and trade. Later, an agreement was reached to discuss trade and labour standards at the first ministerial conference of the WTO in Singapore in 1996. But the debate was over almost before it started. Before the conference began, the then-Director-General of the WTO, Renato Ruggiero, issued a statement about a possible consensus on four key points:[348]

1. All WTO member nations oppose abusive work place practice, through their approval of the United Nations Universal Declaration of Human Rights.
2. The International Labour Organization holds primary responsibility for labour issues.
3. Trade sanctions should not be used to deal with disputes over labour standards.
4. Member States agree that the comparative advantage of low-wage countries should not be compromised.

[344] "Final Copenhagen Declaration and the Program of Action", Report of the World Summit for Social Development, Copenhagen 6–12 March 1995, UN Doc A./CONF./166/9.

[345] "Final Act and Related Documents", United Nations Conference on trade and Employment, Cuba, 21 November 1947 to 24 March 1948, UN Doc ICITO/1/4(1948).

[346] The proposal is quoted in Blackett (1999) note 14.

[347] For a detailed analysis of the events, see Blackett (1999) 43–47.

[348] WTO Press Brief, "Trade and Labour Standards", December 1996.

Unlike the World Bank and the IMF, the ILO does not have full observer status at the WTO. Notably, the Director-General of the ILO was originally invited to address the ministers at the Singapore Conference, but several developing countries opposed his invitation, and it was withdrawn.[349] The conference then proceeded very much in accordance with the key points outlined by Ruggiero and ended with the proclamation of the Singapore Declaration.[350] Its paragraph 4 reads:

> We renew our commitment to the observance of internationally recognised core labour standards. The International Labour Organization (ILO) is the competent body to set and deal with these standards, and we affirm our support for its work in promoting them. We believe that economic growth and development fostered by increased trade and further trade liberalization contribute to the promotion of these standards. We reject the use of labour standards for protectionist purposes, and agree that the comparative advantage of countries, particularly low-wage developing countries, must in no way be put into question. In this regard, we note that the WTO and ILO Secretariats will continue their existing collaboration.

As a result, the labour mandate was sent back to the ILO. Yet, at the same time, the WTO and the BWIs were signing agreements to enhance their co-operation.[351] The WTO members confirmed this arrangement at the Ministerial Conference in Doha in 2001.[352]

In parallel with the WTO, the UN addressed the social dimension of development and globalisation at the 1995 World Summit for Social Development in Copenhagen. Paragraph 54 of the Copenhagen Programme of Action stated:

> Governments should enhance the quality of work and employment by:
>
> (a) Observing and fully implementing the human rights obligations that they have assumed;
>
> (b) Safeguarding and promoting respect for basic workers' rights, including the prohibition of forced labour and child labour, freedom of association and the right to organize and bargain collectively, equal remuneration for men and women for work of equal value, and non-discrimination in employment, and fully implementing the conventions of the International Labour Organization in the case of States party to those conventions and taking into account the principles embodied in those conventions in the case of those countries that are not States party to thus achieve truly sustained economic growth and sustainable development;

349 Blackett (1999) 44.

350 WTO, "Singapore Ministerial Declaration", adopted on 13 December 1996, WT/MIN (96)/DEC, Doc No 96-5316 [hereinafter "Singapore Declaration"].

351 Agreements between the WTO, the IMF and the World Bank, signed on 9 December 1996. Text in WT/GC/W/43 Annex I (WTO/IMF Agreement) and Annex II (WTO/World Bank Agreement).

352 WTO, Doha Ministerial Declaration, adopted on 14 November 2001, WT/MIN(01)/DEC/W/1, para 8: "We reaffirm our declaration made at the Singapore Ministerial Conference regarding internationally recognised core labour standards. We take note of work under way in the International Labour Organization (ILO) on the social dimension of globalisation."

(c) Strongly considering ratification and full implementation of ILO conventions in these areas, as well as those relating to the employment rights of minors, women youth, persons with disabilities and indigenous people;
(d) Using existing international labour standards to guide the formulation of national labour legislation and policies;
(e) Promoting the role of the ILO, particularly as regards improving the level of employment and the quality of work.

The Copenhagen Programme of Action thus implies that in the context of a globalised economy there are rights so fundamental that they must be respected, regardless of ratification and formal legal obligations.[353] These rights, as enumerated in paragraph 54(b), correspond to the core human rights conventions of the ILO as described above.[354]

By the mid 1990s, there was thus enough evidence for a broad international consensus-building on the content of a set of core labour issues in accordance with the aforementioned ILO practice. The Copenhagen World Summit for Social Development in 1995, the OECD reports "Trade, Employment and Labour Standards" (1996)[355] and "International Trade and Core Labour Standards"(2000),[356] as well as the WTO Singapore Ministerial Declaration adopted on 13 December 1996, all refer explicitly to the core labour standards as defined by the ILO.

In addition, there were signs of a developing conception of these core issues as labour *rights* and not as labour *standards*. This development is important for several reasons. First, it shifts the emphasis from economic efficiency to fundamental human rights. Second, a rights-based approach underlines the importance of fair contracting process and does not attempt to define universal common outcomes, which would be impossible.[357] Therefore, the focus is on process, rather than on results.[358]

In contrast to substantive labour law, which defines binding standards for the contracting parties, such as maximum working hours or minimal wages, procedural labour rights aim to foster self-determination by essentially granting freedom of contract and thus freedom of choice.[359] Rather than standards (outcomes) or contract provisions, the Declaration focuses on process rights. Moreover, rights-based reasoning is also increasingly applied by the UN in establishing practical polices. It implies that the core labour rights exist *prior* (rather than posterior) to legal recognition. New regulations are not necessarily

[353] Samson and Schindler (1999) 189.
[354] In addition, paragraph 44 called for the protection of "the basic rights, health and safety of workers and the progressive improvement of overall working conditions" with regard to small enterprises and the informal sector. Paragraph 47 refers to the basic rights of workers as defined by the relevant ILO and other international instruments.
[355] OECD (1996a) at 10.
[356] OECD (2000) at 17–18.
[357] Bellace (2001) 272; Langille (1999) 241–42.
[358] McCrudden and Davies (2000) 51–52. See also note 29 above and accompanying text.
[359] Langille (2005) 429; Hepple (2005) 59.

the only means to protect these rights. They can also be helped by other developments, such as the creation of new institutions.[360]

After a period of uncertainty about its role on the international stage in the 1990s—some authors have called it an identity crisis[361]—the ILO found itself in a perplexing situation. On the one hand, the resurrection of social justice as an issue in political and economic debates and the recognition of the ILO as the leading organisation for dealing with labour rights were reassuring. On the other hand, the WTO had rejected labour rights as fit subject matter for its debate and—despite the glorifying words used in Singapore—had dismissed the ILO as marginal in the elaboration of standard rules for international trade.

As a consequence, the ILO decided to capitalise on the overwhelming reaffirmation of faith in the official texts by focusing again on compliance with core labour rights. A campaign was launched to increase the number of ratifications of the fundamental conventions. In addition, a new approach emerged, which obligated all Member States, by virtue of their acceptance of the Constitution and hence the objectives and principles of the ILO, to respect fundamental labour rights even in the absence of ratification of the relevant conventions.[362]

As part of this new approach, the ILO Declaration on Fundamental Principles and Rights at Work was adopted on 18 June 1996 and defines the freedom of association and the effective recognition of the right to collective bargaining, the elimination of all forms of forced or compulsory labour, the effective abolition of child labour and the elimination of discrimination in respect of employment and occupation (Conventions No 87, 98, 29, 105, 138, 100, 111) as core labour rights.[363] It declares them applicable to all Member States regardless of whether they have ratified the respective conventions.[364] On a critical note it must be pointed out, however, that in contrast to the human rights framework developed by the competent UN organs, social labour rights such as health and safety standards are not included in the core set—leaving open a whole field that is of crucial importance for workers.[365]

[360] Sen (2000) 123.

[361] Langille (1999) 231–37; D'Antona (2002) 32–33, who talks about an identity crisis of labour law in general.

[362] ILO (1997) II.D.

[363] For the ILO definition of core labour standards, see Langille (1999) 238; Leary (2003) 185–86. The Declaration was adopted by 273 against zero votes with 43 abstentions. The quorum was 264, which means the Declaration survived by nine votes. The opposition to the Declaration was led by the Government of Egypt and included representatives from a number of Gulf States, a number of Asian and several Latin American countries. Nineteen of the abstaining governments had not ratified all the fundamental conventions and were therefore subject to the follow-up procedures of the Declaration. The countries were: Egypt, Indonesia, Bahrain, Kuwait, Lebanon, Malaysia, Mauritania, Mexico, Burma/Myanmar, Peru, Qatar, Saudi Arabia, Singapore, Syrian Arab Republic, United Arab Emirates, Viet Nam, Oman, Pakistan and Sudan. ILO, *Review of Annual Reports Under the Follow-up to the ILO Declaration o the Fundamental Principles and Rights at Work*, "Part I: Introduction by the ILO Declaration Expert-Advisers to the Compilation of Annual Reports", GB 277/3/1, Geneva, March 2000, para 42.

[364] Paragraph 2 of the Declaration.

[365] Alston (2004) 486–87.

Although the ILO Declaration has no direct legal effect on the member countries and is not legally enforceable, it nevertheless represents a milestone in the emerging international consensus about the content of a set of core labour rights.[366] While the objectives of the ILO Declaration were not controversial, low-wage developing countries remain fearful that industrialised nations might link labour standards with trade policy and thus deprive them of their competitive advantage.[367] This is the reason why paragraph 5 of the Declaration explicitly states:

> . . . that labour standards should not be used for protectionist trade purposes, and that nothing in this Declaration and its follow-up shall be invoked or otherwise used for such purposes; in addition, the comparative advantage of any country should in no way be called into question by this Declaration and its follow-up.

This provision is in line with paragraph 4 of the WTO Singapore Ministerial Declaration[368] and represents a considerable shift since the Philadelphia Declaration of 1944, which emphasised the equality of free trade and labour rights and the need for the integration of free trade into labour standards.[369] Now, it is the protection of free trade that has priority.

In other words, the ILO has abandoned its concept of purity, which was its compass in the past, in favour of a pragmatic approach that is more likely to be effective. It has thus given up high standards in order to win effectiveness. This is not *a priori* a bad plan, but as it stands, there is no acknowledgement of a crucial point: not only can labour rights be abused for protectionist reasons, but the argument of comparative advantage may also be perverted to justify violations of core labour rights. The ILO has failed to take a stand for this side of the problem.[370]

Although the ILO Declaration[371] does not have the same legal binding force as ILO recommendations and conventions, it reflects a broad consensus on minimum labour rights:

> The four core labour rights are basic and sound in affirming a deep and profound respect for human beings as ends in themselves (and not commodities, to use the ILO language) with an equal right to concern for their well-being, and respect for their ability and need to exercise personal autonomy in leading fully developed lives.[372]

366 For a very critical account in this respect, see Alston (2004) 509–10.

367 A recent example for linking trade policy and labour standards is the Communication from the Commission to the Council, the European Parliament and the Economic and Social Committee Promoting Core Labour Standards and Improving Social Governance in the Context of Globalisation, 18 July 2001, COM (2001) 416 final.

368 "4. . . . We reject the use of labour standards for protectionist purposes, and agree that the comparative advantage of countries, particularly low-wage developing countries, must in no way be put into question."

369 See Introduction, section I.1.1., note 4 and accompanying text; see also note 247 above.

370 See Langille (1999) 251, who suggests that para 5 should have read: "Stresses that arguments in favour of trade liberalization and against protectionism should not be used for the purpose of avoiding respect for core labour rights. In addition this Declaration and its follow-up should in no way be called into question by references to, or arguments from 'comparative advantage'."

371 Note 342 above.

372 Langille (1999) 253.

According to its special character, the follow-up cannot substitute for the regular supervisory procedures of the ILO.[373] As outlined in the Annex to the Declaration:

> The follow-up is to be promotional, meaningful and effective. Its purpose is to encourage the efforts made by Member States to promote the fundamental principles and rights at work and to permit technical cooperation needs to be identified.[374]

There are two main tools: an annual report on situations in countries where the core Conventions on the four fundamental rights have not been ratified; and each year a global report which will give an overview of the situation concerning one of these rights for all countries. (See Figure 1.1.)

The first global report was in 2000 and addressed freedom of association.[376] The reports of the following three years, which focused on forced labour,[377] child labour[378] and discrimination[379] respectively, completed the first set. In 2004 the second cycle started with a report on Organizing for Social Justice,[380] followed by the 2005 study on a Global Alliance against Forced Labour and the 2006 report on the End of Child Labor Within Reach.[381] The reporting process is based on Article 19(5) of the Constitution, which gives the ILO the authority to request information from non-ratifying countries, and as a result, countries that have not adopted the Declaration have submitted contributing reports along with the governments that have. The reports provide excellent summaries of the law and practice with respect to core labour rights internationally.

While the monitoring process is purely promotional and thus does not include sanctions, the number of ratifications of the eight ILO fundamental conventions has significantly increased since the adoption of the Declaration. Comments by ratifying governments indicate that the Declaration played an important role in this development.[382] Nevertheless, more detailed empirical studies are necessary to verify this argument.[383]

The traditional sources of international law are insufficient to accommodate the concept of core labour rights. According to Article 38 of the Statute of the International Court of Justice, there are four recognised sources of international

[373] For an overview of the follow-up, see Tapiola (2000) 13–14.

[374] ILO, *Review of Annual Reports under the Follow-up to the ILO Declaration on Fundamental Principles and Rights at Work*, "Part I: Introduction by the ILO Declaration Expert-Advisers to the Compilation of Annual Reports", March 2001, GB.280/3/1 [hereinafter Review 2001], para 5.

[375] ILO, *Review of Annual Reports under the Follow-up of the ILO Declaration on Fundamental Principles and Rights at Work*, Governing Body, 289th Session, March 2004, GB.289/4 (& Corr 1 and 2) Annex 1.

[376] ILO (2000a) Report I (B).

[377] ILO (2001a).

[378] ILO (2002).

[379] ILO (2003).

[380] ILO (2004a).

[381] ILO (2005); ILO (2006).

[382] Maupain (2005a) 455.

[383] Alston (2005a) 479.

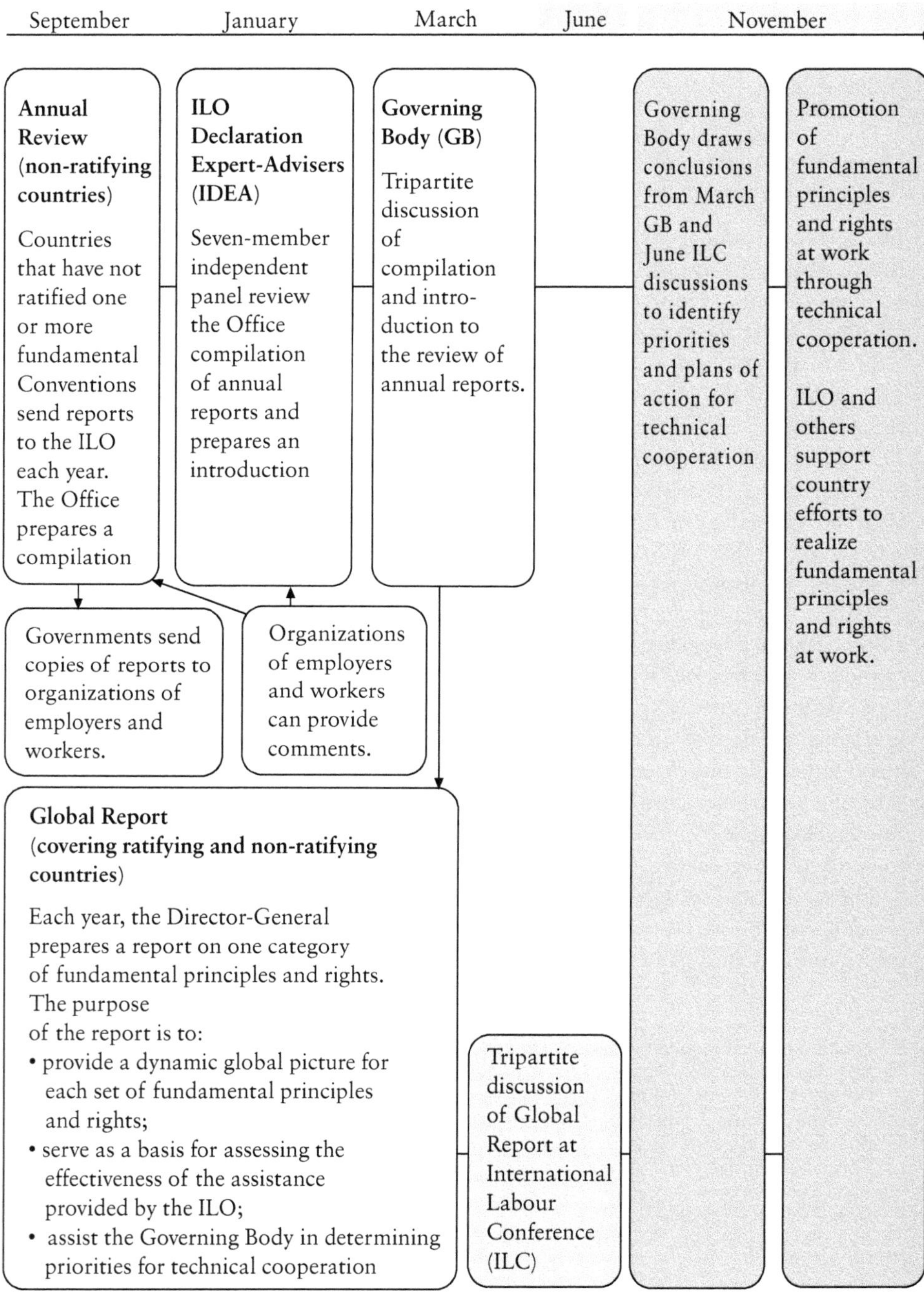

Figure 1.1. *Follow-up to the Declaration*

law: international agreements or conventions; custom; general principles of law common to the major legal systems of the world; and the judicial decisions and teachings of distinguished scholars. In the context of labour rights, the first three sources are of particular interest. The conventions mentioned above undoubtedly create legal obligations for the states that ratify them, and include detailed supervisory mechanisms. But do they also bind other states? There is a broad debate going on about which labour rights can be considered customary international law or even *ius cogens*. As mentioned above, the labour rights contained in the Universal Declaration on Human Rights are considered customary international law. Did the ILO Declaration further develop this concept? In order for the rights and obligations included in the Declaration to be considered customary international law, a broadly consistent state practice as well as the *opinio iuris* that such practice is required by international law needs to be established. So far, no comprehensive study has been undertaken in this regard.[384]

Although the ILO Declaration was politically controversial at the time of its adoption, most of the 19 abstaining governments[385] that are subject to the special implementation procedures have co-operated in the implementation of the Declaration through the—admittedly weak—ILO reporting procedures,[386] thus further underlining the consensus in the international community about core labour rights.

In terms of substance, there are several reasons for focusing on basic or core labour rights. First, the ILO takes up an approach which was originally developed in international human rights law to overcome difficulties in defining which human rights violations should be of international concern and thus be outside the protected *domaine réservé* of the state. In 1967, the United Nations Economic and Social Council (ECOSOC) passed Resolution 1235, drawing the line at gross and systematic violations of human rights.[387] This concept was taken up by scholars and the ICJ, and was further developed to define some human rights as being so basic or essential that they are considered obligations *erga omnes*[388] or even *ius cogens*.[389] When applied to labour rights, this concept

[384] Such a project would entail research that is similar to the recently published study on customary international humanitarian law: Henckaerts and Doswalt-Beck (2005).

[385] See note 363 above for the countries that have abstained.

[386] ILO, *Review of Annual Reports under the Follow-up to the ILO Declaration on the Fundamental Principles and Rights at Work*, "Introduction by the ILO Declaration Expert-Advisers to the Compilation of Annual Reports", GB 289/4 (& Corr 1 and 2), Geneva, March 2004, paras 16, 19–23 and Table 1. Of the 19 abstaining governments (note 363 above), five (Egypt, Indonesia, Mauritania, Mexico and the Syrian Arab Republic) have meanwhile ratified all the seven fundamental conventions mentioned in the Declaration. All others supplied one or more reports under the follow-up procedures. Overall, up to 2004, the reporting rate increased from 56 to 63 per cent. Also, the number of countries that have ratified all the fundamental conventions increased, thus reducing the number of governments obliged to submit a report under the follow-up of the Declaration. Ibid, paras 22–23.

[387] ECOSOC Resolution 1235 (XLII), 6 July 1967, confirmed later by Resolution 1503 (XLVIII), 27 May 1970.

means that the core labour rights are considered the basis of any human activity in the workplace. They are therefore binding for all ILO members, and given the large number of ILO Member States, they come close to being obligations *erga omnes*. In the ILO's own words:

> fundamental rights are not fundamental because the Declaration says so; the Declaration says that they are fundamental because they are.[390]

A second important issue is the distinction between the obligations imposed on Member States by the ILO Declaration and those imposed by the fundamental conventions. While from a formal point of view the Declaration per se is not legally binding, it attempts to compensate for this by declaring core labour rights binding for all Member States regardless of whether they have ratified the respective conventions. The ILO thus extended the approach of the ILO Constitution, which requires every member to respect freedom of association and to comply with specific reporting procedures regarding *all* core labour rights.[391] In contrast to freedom of association, there is no legal foundation in the ILO Constitution for extending the reporting procedures for all core labour rights to all Member States.[392]

This raises the question of how the Declaration and the fundamental conventions relate to one another. During the drafting of the Declaration, it was emphasised that the Declaration would not establish new *legal* obligations on Member States but reflect *policy* obligations that members incur by virtue of their ILO membership. In addition, Member States insisted that the principles and rights of the Declaration only encompass the *essence*, that is, the goals, objectives and aims of the fundamental conventions, not the detailed legal obligations that come with ratification.[393] The problem with this approach is that the content of the principles remains vague and their relationship with the

[388] *Barcelona Traction, Light & Power Co Ltd*, ICJ Reports 1970, at 3, paras 33–34; *Case Concerning East Timor (Portugal v Australia)*, ICJ Reports 1995, 90, 102.

[389] Article 53 VCLT defines *ius cogens*: "A peremptory norm of general international law is a norm accepted and recognised by the international community of States as a whole as a norm from which no derogation is permitted and which can be modified only by a subsequent norm of general international law having the same character." Simma and Alston (1992), 82, 94. Both, the concept of obligations *erga omnes* and *ius cogens* are intended to protect basic moral values and the common interests of states. While the classical examples for both concepts largely coincide, the methodology behind them is different: Article 53 applies a "test" approach by relying on the recognition by the international community, the fact that no derogation is permitted and that modifications are only possible by a subsequent norm of general international law that has the same character, thus is peremptory. In contrast, the ICJ chose a "value based" approach for defining obligations *erga omnes*. Ragazzi (1997), 72.

[390] International Labour Conference, 86th Session, Geneva 1989, Report VII.

[391] See note 297 above and accompanying text.

[392] Given the promotional nature of the Declaration, such an argument is however unlikely to make any practical difference. Hepple (2005) 59

[393] "Report of the Committee on the Declaration of Principles: Submission, Discussion and Adoption", International Labour Conference, 86th Session, Geneva, June 1998, Remarks by Mr Potter. Available at http://www.ilo.org/?public/?english/?standards/?relm/?ilc/?ilc86/?com-decd.htm. See also Coxson (1999) 496–98. Alston is heavily critical of this approach: Alston (2004) 490–95.

fundamental conventions unclear. The rights and values enshrined in the Declaration are indeed important, and in the words of François Maupain,

> the Declaration is like "the wisdom tooth" of the Constitution, which was already there but finally pierced through the gum in its maturity . . .[394]

But nonetheless, the normative content of the Declaration still needs to be developed further.[395]

From a conceptual point of view, the approach chosen by the ILO reflects the fact that there is no hierarchy of positive norms in international law: all we have are treaties. Unlike domestic constitutional law, current international law cannot accommodate the need for written binding rules below the treaty level. While the Declaration attempts to solve this dilemma by referring to principles, it does not allocate the task of giving concrete content to them.[396] This is of particular relevance not only to governments but even more so to non-state actors who are not formally addressed by the Declaration.

In sum, the ILO Declaration constitutes an emergent form of legally binding rules that reflects the need for transnational legislation based on consensus and applicable across different cultures. Its relevance will become more striking when we look at how it interacts with other legal regimes in chapters 2 and 3.

1.2.2.4. Other ILO Initiatives

The Declaration on Fundamental Principles and Rights at Work marked the beginning of an overarching ILO campaign to promote core labour rights. One activity comprised the revision and integration of existing standards.[397] In a third, more important step, the ILO launched an initiative in 1999 to achieve decent work for all,[398] focusing on four strategic objectives: standards and fundamental principles and rights at work; employment; social protection; and social dialogue, with gender and development as cross-cutting priority themes.[399] The Decent Work initiative puts labour rights in a broader context:

> The comprehensive view of society that informs the approach adopted in the ILO vision of decent work [. . .] provides a more promising understanding of the needs of institutions and policies in pursuit of the rights and interests of working people. It is not adequate to concentrate only on labour legislation since people do not live and work in a compartmentalized environment. The linkages between economic, political and social actions can be critical to the realization of rights and to the pursuit of the

394 Maupain (2005b) 444.
395 Similarly, see Hepple (2005) 59–62.
396 Similarly, see Alston (2005a) 476.
397 See Hepple (2005) 63.
398 ILO (1999b) 5: "The primary goal of the ILO today is to promote opportunities for women and men to obtain decent and productive work, in conditions of freedom, equity, security and human dignity."
399 For the implementation of the Decent Work initiative, see ILO (2001b).

broad objectives of decent work and adequate living for working people.[400]

The fourth and most recent ILO initiative was the establishment of the World Commission on the Social Dimension of Globalization in February 2002. It presented its final report, entitled "A Fair Globalization: Creating Opportunities for All", on 24 February 2004.[401] The report calls for more policy autonomy in developing countries with respect to global rules on trade and finance. Respect for core labour standards should be strengthened, especially in export processing zones. The report also calls on all international institutions to promote core labour standards within their respective mandates.

1.2.3. Excursus: Cultural Relativism and the "Asian Values" Debate

Are core labour rights universal? In the early 1990s a new challenge to human rights including labour rights emerged. While state sovereignty was the main argument against universal human rights during the cold war, the new debate focuses on culture. The strongest opposition to universal labour standards comes from Asian political leaders such as Lee Kuan Yew, Singapore's former prime minister, and Malaysia's former Prime Minister Mohamed Mahatir. They argue that "Asian values" prevent the establishment of a universal set of core labour rights by applying different cultural standards to basic human rights, eg regarding freedom as less important than in the West. Given this difference of value systems—the argument runs—Asia must be faithful to its own system of philosophical and political priorities. Proponents of Asian values state that Western states apply a double standard in criticising the human rights standards of Asian countries, and that in any event, there are more important priorities and that human rights can only be understood in their cultural context.[402] Proponents of the "Asian values" line of reasoning combine elements from the debate about women's and indigenous peoples' rights by using culture as both an argument against a certain type of human rights and an asset that must be protected by international law.[403]

The concept of "Asian values" with regard to human rights was reflected in the so-called "Bangkok Declaration", a preparatory report of Asian countries to the 1993 Vienna World Conference on Human Rights.[404] In the context of labour rights, adopting "Asian values" leads to a significant weakening of universal standards. Proponents of the Bangkok Declaration suggest that it is

400 Sen (2000) 127.

401 First conclusions for the role of the ILO in this process were drawn at the 92nd session of the International Labour Conference: ILO (2004a) 49–55.

402 Engle (2000) 314; Mehmet, Mendes and Sinding (1998b) 170–93.

403 Engle (2000) 312.

404 "Report of the Regional Meeting for Asia of the World Conference on Human Rights", UN Doc A./Conf. 157/PC/59 (1993) para 8 [hereinafter Bangkok Declaration]. For a detailed analysis, see Otto (1997) 7–12.

premature to begin thinking about civil and political rights before a certain stage of development is reached, as "poverty is one of the major obstacles that hinder the full enjoyment of human rights".[405] This would imply that universal labour rights apply only where their positive impact on reducing poverty can be proven. On the other hand, the assertion of "Asian values" also prohibits the imposition of conditionalities based on (other) human rights and requires that responsibility for economic development is left in the hands of the Asian states.[406]

As Amartya Sen and others have shown, the theory of "Asian values" is clearly flawed in several aspects.[407] First, there is empirical evidence for the positive role of human rights in the prevention of economic and social disasters generally. Second, tolerance and freedom are substantial and important components of the diverse Asian traditions. Moreover, there is no such thing as a general Asian culture or value system. Finally, the notion of human rights does not build on citizenship or local legislation but on our shared humanity. As a contrasting case in point, the Bangkok NGO Declaration on Human Rights[408] stresses in its very first paragraph that human rights are universal. Indeed, the claim for Asian values appears to be more a reflection of local political power than a coherent system of values.[409]

While states should be free to choose the means to implement labour rights according to their own cultural and political settings, the violation of these rights is a challenge for the entire international community.[410] It is this understanding that is reflected in Section I, paragraph 5 of the World Conference on Human Rights Vienna Declaration and Programme of Action of 1993.[411]

1.2.4. Conclusions

The historical development of core labour rights shows that they do not have a monocausal background but are rather the result of attempts to reconcile conflicting interests. In addition, the concerns of domestic legislators cause dif-

[405] Bangkok Declaration, note 404 above, para 19.
[406] Engle (2000) 313.
[407] Sen (1997a) 33; Sen (1999) 227; Ghai (1995) 5.
[408] Available at http://www.hr-alliance.org/aphr-ft/bangkok.htm.
[409] Chinkin (2001).
[410] As Louis Henkin noted more than 20 years ago,

> Legitimate claims of cultural pluralism and of some measure of ethical relativism must not be allowed to dilute essential values and reduce them to matters of opinion or taste. Cultural differences and traditions may explain, even justify, different ways of giving expression to the values accepted by all in the international human rights documents; they cannot explain or justify barbarism and repression.

Henkin (1978) at 129. See also Tomuschat (1981) 609.
[411] United Nations, World Conference on Human Rights, Vienna Declaration and Programme of Action, A/CONF.157/23, 12 July 1993.

ficulties at the international negotiating table and have resulted in a variety of legislative methods for implementing core labour rights.

Although several attempts have been made to include substantive labour rights provisions such as minimum wages in international instruments, the consensus on core labour rights encompasses only process-oriented rights and does not include social labour rights. Even at the domestic level, substantive labour rights are often only framed as social goals or objectives.

In order to grasp the content of core labour rights, the different legal instruments must be seen in context and interpreted consistently. Figure 1.2. summarises the current situation.

Figure 1.2. *Core Labour Rights in International Law*

Legal instrument	Abolition of forced labour	Freedom of association and collective bargaining	Non-discrimination	Abolition of child labour
Universal Declaration	Art 23 Right to choose employment	Art 23 (4) Freedom to form and join unions	Art 23 (2) • No discriminatory wages • Equal pay for equal work	
ICESCR	Art 6 • Right to choose employment • Progressive realisation	Art 8 • Right to form and join trade unions • Immediate realisation • Protects individuals and trade unions from state interference Art 8 (1) (c) • Right of trade unions to bargain collectively • States must "promote" right Art 8 (1)(d) • Right to strike	Art 6, Art 2 (3) • Access to employment Immediate, not , progressive implement -ation Art 7 • Equal remuneration for work of equal value • Minimum wages for fulfilling basic needs	Art 10 (3) • Protection from economic exploitation • No employment in work harmful to morals or health • No hazardous work • States should set age limits for paid employment
ICCPR	Art 8 • Prohibition of slavery and slavery-like practices • Prohibition of forced labour. Key criterion: involuntariness • Immediate implementation	Art 22 • Freedom of association and trade unions • Safeguard clause in 22(3): ILO Convention No 87 • Protects general interests of everyone • Immediate implement-ation		

Legal instrument	**Abolition of forced labour and collective bargaining**	**Freedom of association**	**Non-discrimination**	**Abolition of child labour**
Convention on the Rights of the Child	Art 35 Measures to prevent trafficking and sale of children regardless of purpose			Art 32 (1) • Protection from economic exploitation • Protection from work that is a threat to health or development of the child Art 32 (2) States are required to take concrete measures with regard to • minimum age • working conditions, including working hours • penalties and sanctions in case of violation Art 35 Measures to prevent trafficking, sale of children regardless of purpose

ILO Forced Labour Conventions (Nos 29 and 105)	*Convention No 29* Art 1 Abolition of forced labour: • Involuntary • Threat of penalty *Convention No 105* Art 1 • Abolition of any form of forced labour: • for political coercion or education • for economic development • as labour discipline • as punishment for participating in strikes • as means of racial, social, national or religious discrimination			
ILO Conventions on Freedom of Association and Collective Bargaining (Nos 87 and 98)		*Convention No 87* Art 2 Right of workers and employers to establish and join organisations Art 3 Rights of organisations of employers and workers: • internal autonomy • exercise their mandate without state interference • Right of unions to strike (not mentioned but intrinsic to right of association)		

Legal instrument	Abolition of forced labour	Freedom of association and collective bargaining	Non-discrimination	Abolition of child labour
		Convention No 98 Art 4 States must encourage and promote collective bargaining on termsand conditions of employment. Art 6 Exceptions: armed forces, police and public servants engaged in administration of the State.		
ILO Convention on Equal Remuneration and on Discrimination (Nos 100 and 111)			*Convention No 100* Art 2 States are required: • to promote equal remuneration • to ensure application where possible States are obliged to guarantee equal remuneration: • when state is employer • when state intervenes in wage-fixing process • in legislation on equal remuneration	

			State must promote principle insituation where it cannot ensure its application. *Convention No 111* Art 3 • incorporation of principle of non-discrimination • effects test	
ILO Conventions on Child Labour (Nos 138 and 182) and Recommendation No 190				*Convention No 138* Art 2 Minimum age • not less than age of completion of compulsory schooling and in any case not less than 15 years (14 yrs for developing nations. • for hazardous work is 18 years. *Convention No 182* Art 3 Prohibition of worst forms of child labour: • slavery • child prostitution • use of children for illicit work activities • work that is likely to harm health, safety or morals

Legal instrument	**Abolition of forced labour**	**Freedom of association and collective bargaining**	**Non-discrimination**	**Abolition of child labour**
				Art 7 (2) (c) States must ensure access to free basic education *Recommendation 190* Para 12 Defines slavery, use of children for prostitution and illicit activities as criminal offences by the states Para 15 (d) Extraterritorial effect of the Convention

2

International Economic Organisations and Core Labour Rights: Conflicting Interests

> And above all, I have learned about a common humanity. People in poverty want for their children what we in this hall want for ours: education, good health, security, and opportunity. They want voice. They do not want charity. They want a chance to make a better life for themselves. They want respect for their human rights.
>
> James D Wolfensohn, Former President of the World Bank Group[1]

AS CHAPTER 1 has demonstrated, the concept of core labour rights raises difficult legal and political questions: In addition to the legal obligations resulting from constitutional rules and international treaties, states are faced with the increasing influence of international organisations on the formulation of their domestic economic and social policy. This influence rarely emanates from "hard" legal stipulations but from obligations implicit to the membership of these organisations.

In an ideal world, these obligations would complement each other and enhance labour rights. However, in reality, conflicts occur. This chapter will first look at the theoretical framework within which international organisations operate and then discuss the practical examples of the Bretton Woods Institutions (BWIs), the World Trade Organization (WTO) and the Organisation for Economic Co-operation and Development (OECD).

2.1. DIFFERENT APPROACHES TO LABOUR RIGHTS: ECONOMIC NECESSITY, MAINSTREAMING AND CONSTITUTIONALISM

2.1.1. Economic Rationales to Approach Labour Issues

From a utilitarian point of view, the violation of core labour rights should be addressed only if the compliance with these rights leads to a better economic

[1] "Building an Equitable World", Address to the Board of Governors at the Annual Meeting of the International Monetary Fund and the World Bank Group, Prague, 26 September 2000.

result. But what does a better result mean? Increased productivity or higher profits for the stakeholders?[2] In considering this question, we must first examine the larger ongoing economic debate.[3] While debate in this area is obviously extensive, the major economic arguments in favour of harmonised international core labour standards can be classified into four groups and summarised as follows:[4]

— *International market failures*: International market failures require joint action by governments.
— *Unfair competition (social dumping)*: Countries with low labour standards have an unfair competitive advantage in international trade.
— *Race to the bottom*: Unfair competition will cause a "race to the bottom" as countries attempt to attract capital and investments by lowering their labour standards and thus reducing the cost of production.
— *Welfare of workers in developing countries*: The standard of living in developing countries will benefit from higher labour standards.

Harmonising labour standards also raises concerns among developing countries, who often suspect that industrialised countries impose higher labour standards on them for protectionist reasons. However, the surest way to improve labour standards is economic growth, which is facilitated by international trade. Industrialised nations on the other hand must acknowledge that violation of core labour standards is definitely not the main advantage that developing countries have when it comes to the production of labour-intensive goods. Economic theory has established that low labour standards are not directly related to competitive advantage.[5] Yet, trade pressures associated with a country's WTO market access commitments could cause it to delay the introduction or enforcement of stricter labour standards.[6] Economic theory suggests that races to the bottom typically rely on restrictions on policy instruments such as the impossibility of raising tariffs under WTO law.[7]

As Stephen Golub has noted, it is difficult if not impossible to separate the economic and moral dimensions of a harmonised set of core labour standards.[8] In his view, international compliance with core labour standards can be best defended as a way of increasing the legitimacy of a liberal international trading system, as well as being desirable in itself.

Nonetheless, the economic evidence varies for each of the different core labour rights.[9] For example, it can be safely said that in the long term child

[2] Basu (2001) 62–66.
[3] For an excellent analysis, see Singh (2003) 116–35.
[4] Golub (1997) 19–22; for a historical overview, see Engerman (2003) 58–59, 61–62.
[5] Singh (2003) 141–44; Bagwell and Staiger (2002) 140.
[6] Bagwell and Staiger (2001b) 4.
[7] Singh (2003) 47–52.
[8] Golub (1997) 19.
[9] For an overview and discussion of the different economic arguments, see Morici and Schulz (2001) 39.

labour, forced labour and discrimination in employment have a negative effect on growth, but this is less clear for freedom of association and the right to collective bargaining. The effects of restrictions on the freedom of association and collective bargaining depend on whether labour markets are competitive or employers enjoy some measure of monopoly power.

In competitive labour markets the long-term effects are ambiguous: restrictions on freedom of association and collective bargaining may have either negative or positive effects on resource allocation, investment and growth. On the one hand, they inhibit workers from organising, which makes them an easier target for exploitation, thus impairing other core labour rights. On the other hand, there has been extensive discussion about the role of unions and the fact that collective bargaining can lead to wages that are above market price in a particular sector.[10] As a result, employment, investment and growth might be negatively affected. However, in 1996 an OECD study came up with a very strong argument: it noted that the above-mentioned negative effects on efficiency can be outweighed by the favourable impact of freedom of association on workers' motivation and productivity.[11] The findings of the 1996 study were confirmed in an update four years later.[12] If this is the case, then denying workers access to unions and collective bargaining may have an overall negative impact on development and long-term growth after all.

The situation is clearer in monopsonistic labour markets, ie markets that are not perfectly competitive and where a single or a few firms dominate employment.[13] Under such conditions, employers can maximise their profits by setting employment and wage rates according to the marginal costs, in other words below the level that would prevail under competitive conditions.[14] The result is a misallocation of resources and lower GDP.[15] The optimal policy response is to increase competition in the demand for labour, to subsidise employment in this sector, or alternatively, to allow workers to organise and bargain. If the collective bargaining process results in a fixed wage that is closer to the competitive wage than the monopsony wage and in an employment rate that is closer to the equilibrium, the distortions in the economy would be reduced and collective bargaining would lead to a more efficient allocation of resources, more exports, and higher GDP. In fact, Pareto efficiency might be restored. In this case, denying workers the right to bargain collectively would by contrast perpetuate the distortions in the labour market.[16] However, if unions decide to bargain only

[10] Maskus (1997) 30.

[11] OECD (1996a) at 222. For an overview of the different arguments, see Maskus (1997) 38.

[12] OECD (2000) at 26.

[13] Monopsony can be natural in a small market in which there are limited numbers of employers, or it can be supported by governmental barriers to the entry of other employers in the labour market. Monopsony can also arise if a national or local government decides to limit entry and exit of workers from a particular regional labour market and also requires natural or legislated limitations on international labour migration. See Maskus (1997) 31.

[14] For a detailed description, see *ibid*, 32; Singh (2003) 125–26.

[15] For a detailed explanation of this argument, see Morici and Schulz (2001) 47–48.

[16] Maskus (1997) 6.

over a higher wage and the employment rate remains the same, efficiency would not be improved. The same is true if unions go for higher employment levels and lower wage rates.

In summary, economic evidence suggests that core labour standards can in principle enhance the efficient operation of labour markets and thus increase the level of productivity and GDP.[17] While this is generally the case for the prohibition of exploitative forms of child labour, forced labour and discrimination, the evidence in the case of freedom of association and collective bargaining is more ambiguous, suggesting that the positive effects depend on underlying national economic frameworks and structures.

2.1.2. The Concept of Mainstreaming

2.1.2.1. Background

Instead of focusing on economic effects, mainstreaming puts the emphasis on rights. Could labour rights be included on a routine basis into the activities of the Bretton Woods Institutions? What exactly would a concept of mainstreaming labour rights imply?

The concept of mainstreaming was introduced to international financial institutions in the (limited) context of gender equality after the Fourth International Conference on Women in Beijing in 1995.[18] Given that mainstreaming has been accepted by both the International Monetary Fund (IMF) and the World Bank in this context, the question arises why mainstreaming labour rights seems to encounter so much resistance.

Generally speaking, mainstreaming human rights means re-organising, improving and evaluating policy processes so that the actors who are normally involved in policy-making incorporate a human rights perspective into their work at all levels and at all stages.[19] One of the most recent examples is the inclusion of a mainstreaming policy in the implementation of the Human Rights Act in the United Kingdom, which included inter alia the establishment of a specialised monitoring body, the training of judges and a systematic review of any proposed legislation with respect to its compliance with human rights.[20] Legally speaking, mainstreaming gender equality involves the incorporation of equal opportunity issues and non-discrimination into all actions, programmes and policies from the outset.[21] To put it succinctly, mainstreaming does not discuss the objectives of fostering eg, gender equality, but rather provides tools and methods to do so in practice. It is therefore empowering by nature.

[17] OECD (2001a) 31–34.
[18] Murphy (1997) 17; Council of Europe (1998) 17.
[19] McCrudden (2005) 9.
[20] For a detailed discussion, see *ibid*, 10.
[21] Rees (1998) 3.

This basic assumption aside, there are two different approaches to mainstreaming. The first is a proactive approach that involves new legislative action, as has been applied in Northern Ireland. This course of action takes gender issues far beyond traditional equal treatment and positive action approaches by requiring that "equality be seen as an integral part of all public policy making and implementation".[22] The alternative is a more process-oriented approach that underlines the need to use existing mechanisms for protecting rights and promoting sociologically desirable diversity in response to the weaknesses of positive action.[23] From this point of view, the concept of mainstreaming is much more about transforming existing institutions than about concrete positive action or positive discrimination, of which affirmative action programmes could be cited as an example.

Examples of mainstreaming can be found in the corporate world, where companies use mission statements to incorporate basic values into their daily business activities. The Trading Charter of The Body Shop (1994), for example, refers explicitly to the Universal Declaration of Human Rights.[24] Stringent codes of conduct can, if clearly formulated and enforced, serve as a tool to mainstream labour rights in private enterprises' activities.[25]

Outside the gender context, the United Nations Children's Fund (UNICEF) has applied the concept of mainstreaming by basing all of its activities on the 1989 Convention on the Right of the Child, which now serves as UNICEF's charter. Given the legally binding character of the Convention, UNICEF's decision to treat it like a constitution is a significant move. While this approach is widely accepted by the international community with respect to children's rights, however, the situation is different when it comes to development. Similar attempts undertaken by the United Nations Development Programme (UNDP) have not received an overwhelmingly positive response so far.

At the national level, an interesting example can be found in Switzerland. In 1993, the Swiss Parliament decided that every future proposal for federal legislation[26] must include a section on the compatibility of the proposed regulation with existing European law.[27] Bearing in mind that, until very recently, every

[22] McCrudden (1999a) 1699.

[23] See Byrnes (1997) 383.

[24] The Body Shop, for example, in its Trading Charter (1994) refers explicitly to the Universal Declaration of Human Rights. Available at http://www.thebodyshop.com. For text of Arts 22–25 of the Universal Declaration, see Appendix A.1.

[25] Mainstreaming human rights into business activities is suggested *inter alia* by the UN Global Compact (see chapter 3, section 3.1.2.1. below) and by the new UN Norms on the responsibilities of transnational corporations and other business enterprises with regard to human rights, UN Doc E/CN.4/Sub.2/2003/12/Rev.2, 26 August 2003, para 15.

[26] In the normal legislation process, proposals for new laws or amendments of existing regulations are submitted to Parliament, accompanied by a government message, explaining the reasoning behind the proposed law, its impacts on financial and human resources, the accordance with the current legislative planning process, the relations to existing European law and finally compatibility with the Federal Constitution.

[27] *Botschaft über das Folgeprogramm nach der Ablehnung des EWR-Abkommens vom 24. Februar 1993*, BBl 1993 I 805 ff, at 823.

attempt to attach Switzerland to the European Community, let alone formally integrate it, had failed, the Government's approach was a risky undertaking. However, the effect was immensely positive. Compatibility with European law has become a standing item on the agenda of the legislator.[28] In cases where the government suggests *not* complying with European standards, the reasons have to be carefully explained. Overall, the result of the new approach has been a broad incorporation of European legal standards into legislation.[29]

2.1.2.2. Mainstreaming Labour Rights?

Given these examples and practical experiences, how could core labour rights be mainstreamed into the activities of international economic organisations such as the Bretton Woods Institutions and the WTO? Taking the BWIs as an illustrative example, several requirements would need to be fulfilled: consensus, legitimacy, responsibility and accountability.

A) Consensus First, a consensus on what core labour rights are has to be established. As mentioned above, the ILO Declaration on Fundamental Principles and Rights at Work (1998) represents a very broad if not universal consensus on what core labour rights are.[30] Although the Declaration, as we have seen, is not strictly legally binding, the vast majority of ILO Member States have reaffirmed their commitment to its standards not only by verbal statements but also by participating in the monitoring process.[31]

B) Legal Basis or the Question of Legitimacy Second, an international organisation that attempts to apply a concept of mainstreaming needs a legal basis for doing so.[32] The legitimacy to do so can stem either from already existing legal obligations such as international human rights treaties, the aforementioned ILO Conventions or a clear mandate from the member countries. In addition, customary international law could serve as a legal basis.

The idea that at least some human rights form part of customary international law or *ius cogens* and create legal obligations *erga omnes*, is rapidly gaining ground among scholars and was also reflected in Article 40 of the first draft of the International Law Commission (ILC) articles on state responsibility, where it was stated that all states are injured by violations of human rights.[33] When the new Commission took office in 1999, it started reviewing the draft and reintroduced the distinction between injured and non-injured states. However, the new Article

28 Thürer (1993) 91–94.

29 Of course, the fact that Switzerland is following a monistic tradition and that both the European and the Swiss legal orders are based on a common system of values has facilitated the process.

30 See chapter 1, section 1.2.2.3. above, particularly note 390 and accompanying text. For text of the ILO Declaration, see Appendix A.15.

31 See chapter 1, section 1.2.2.3. above.

32 McCrudden (1999a) at 1772. For the WTO, see also Howse and Mutua (2000).

33 Report of the International Law Commission on the work of its forty-eighth session, 6 May–26 July 1996, Draft Articles on State Responsibility, Art 40(2)(e)iii.

48(1)(b) still holds states accountable and responsible for the breach of obligations that are owed to the international community as a whole, which includes obligations *erga omnes* and in particular human rights obligations.[34]

Of particular interest for the lending activities of the Bretton Woods Institutions is Article 16 of the ILC draft, which holds a state responsible for aiding or assisting another state in the commission of an internationally wrongful act.[35] While it is very difficult to prove the causality between aid and the commission of an internationally wrongful act in practice, an obligation for states and international organisations to examine the impact of their aid and assistance programmes on human rights in the form of a *human rights audit* may be drawn from this provision.

As we have seen, there is a strong legal basis for core labour rights, with the ILO Declaration on Fundamental Principles and Rights at Work leading the way.[36] While the Declaration itself has to be considered *soft law,* there is evidence that core labour rights can be considered as binding legal obligations *erga omnes.*[37] However, the process of mainstreaming itself and all the activities that this involves, are not mentioned in legally binding documents. It cannot be emphasised enough how crucial a strong legally binding commitment to mainstreaming is: to make it effective, international organisations must formally include mainstreaming labour standards not only in operational directives, but also in their (social) policy strategies.

C) Responsibility and Accountability Mainstreaming may sound harmless, but it can lead to quite dramatic changes in administrative and governmental decision-making processes. Given the variety of cultures represented in international organisations such as the Bretton Woods Institutions and the WTO, tensions and conflicts in applying mainstreaming are likely to occur. To make it work in practice, clearly delineated responsibilities are therefore necessary.[38] If the responsibility for mainstreaming core labour rights were left for instance to the different projects within the Bretton Woods Institutions, these rights would be unlikely to be applied in a consistent manner. In any event, the need for coordination with the relevant ILO bodies requires a centralised unit that can be a contact point for all labour rights issues. The World Bank has already led the way with its gender equality and Global Child Labor Programs. It is easy to imagine establishing a special labour rights or even a human rights unit within the Bank's Human Development Network.

34 International Law Commission, Draft Articles on State Responsibility, adopted by the ILC at its fifty-third session, UN Doc A/CN.4/L.602 Rev.1 [Hereinafter ILC, Draft State Responsibility], Commentary on Article 48(8)–(10). See chapter 1 above, note 272.

35 International Law Commission, *ibid*, Commentary on Article 16, at pp 150–55. The implications of this standard of "aiding and abetting" have been clarified by the ICTY in *Prosecutor v Furundzija*, IT-95-17/1-T, 10 December 1998, reprinted in 38 ILM 317 (1999).

36 For discussion of the ILO Declaration, see chapter 1, section 1.2.2.3. above.

37 See chapter 1, section 1.2.2.3, note 390 and accompanying text.

38 This is one of the many lessons learned from the experience in Northern Ireland. See McCrudden (1999a) 1772.

Moreover, mainstreaming will not reach its goals without clear rules of accountability. Most international organisations now include paragraphs on gender equality in their annual reports. This approach is hardly sufficient to fulfil the expectations of citizens and member countries of obtaining an objective evaluation of mainstreaming activities.[39] The World Bank already has a mechanism for review in the form of the Inspection panel.[40] As will be discussed later, only groups, not individuals, can bring claims before the panel. And although the panel is independent, the Board of Executive Directors decides on a case-by-case basis whether an investigation should take place. These two shortcomings must be reviewed if the panel is to play a role in the accountability process.

At the domestic level, a similar approach has been adopted by several countries that have revised their constitutions and introduced so-called "social goals", which are used as important guidelines for all state activities but do not grant justiciable rights to individuals.[41]

2.1.3. Constitutionalism as a Process

With globalisation becoming increasingly important,[42] the role of the nation-state has significantly changed: markets are to some extent replacing national boundaries and reshaping the spheres of influence for national regulations.[43] The cross-border activities of international organisations affect individuals much more than they did a decade ago. In fact, in many circumstances, international organisations perform functions that were previously undertaken by states, thus becoming quasi-governmental organisations. Because of this tendency, the pressure by citizens and non-governmental organisations (NGOs) for international organisations to become more open and transparent has increased.[44] At the legal level, some scholars argue that international organisations have to be constitutionalised, while others see this as a step too far, especially with respect to the WTO.[45] The following sections will look at the definition of constitutionalism and address the question of what constitutionalising the major international organisations would imply for core labour rights.

[39] Interestingly, accountability is not mentioned in a visionary document "What the Bank Would Look Like if Gender were Mainstreamed: The Views of Gender Practitioners" quoted in Murphy (1997) 46.

[40] See section 2.2.3.1.D below.

[41] Eg, Article 41 of the new Swiss Constitution, SR 101; English translation available at http://www.swissemb.org/legal/html/constitution.html.

[42] See Introduction, section I.2. above.

[43] Strange (1998) 82.

[44] Bradlow (2001) 9–36.

[45] For ongoing discussion on this topic, see: Alston (2002) 815–44; Petersmann (2002a); Petersmann (2002b); Howse (2002b) 651–59; Jackson (1998) 101–5; Jackson (2003) 794–800; Petersmann (1997) 57–65; Weiler (1991) 2403; Cottier (2000) 220–22; Howse and Nicolaidis (2001) 227–52; Cass (2001) 39–75; Krajewski (2001) 120 and 252; Charnovitz (2002a) 306; Gerstenberg (2002) 188–91; Cottier and Hertig (2003) 270–75. For a summary of the current discussion about the WTO, see Duvigneau (2001) 297–306.

While always serving the causes of liberty and peace through governance,[46] a comprehensive theory of constitutionalism must reflect the environment within which a society operates.[47] The idea of constitutionalism can be traced back to the writings of Immanuel Kant,[48] who developed Jean-Jacques Rousseau's concept of the social contract and overcame the lack of peoples' rights in Thomas Hobbes' theory by setting up for the first time a conceptual framework of constitutionalism as limited government under the rule of law.[49] His theory has played a significant role for many national constitutions.

Classic constitutionalism draws on the Kantian categorical imperative and is based on the Westphalian notion of the nation state.[50] National (constitutional) law is seen as a tool for implementing a society's purpose and realising its constitutional idea; it has both formal[51] and substantial[52] limits. In contrast, international law is understood as a law of co-existence—as opposed to a law of co-operation[53]—among sovereign nation states; in other words, it is a "constitution-free zone" or "unsociety".[54]

With the emergence of new players such as NGOs and the changing role of nation states in an increasingly globalised environment, the notion of constitutionalism has changed dramatically. The ongoing discussion about constitutionalising international organisations aims to overcome the traditional dichotomy between national and international law. Constitutionalisation in this context focuses on the *process* of integrating constitutional ideas into international institutions.[55] It is not a static method of observing what is "out there" in the constitutional landscape but a highly reflexive process.[56]

Because of its close relationship to the nation state and to the core values of a society, constitutionalism comes in many shapes and forms.[57] This variety, together with conceptual differences between common law and civil law,[58] different understandings about the relevance of international law[59] and the fact that some authors focus on existing positive law and *real* constitutions[60] rather

[46] Müller, JP (1997) 57–66.
[47] Allott (2002) 12.30–12.32, argues that the various forms of constitutionalism are all based on at least one of four general theoretical concepts: divine order, the sovereignty of law, natural cosmic order and natural social order.
[48] Kant (1982) *Die Metaphysik der Sitten, Werkausgabe.*
[49] Petersmann (1998) 6.
[50] Hobe (2002) 657–59.
[51] An example is the majority requirements for changing the Constitution.
[52] An example is the (inherent) principle that fundamental rights must not be abolished even by majority decisions.
[53] This distinction goes back to Friedmann, W (1964) 60–63.
[54] Allott (2002) 10.12.
[55] Biaggini (2000) 469.
[56] Walker (2001) 39; Weiler (1999) 223.
[57] Cass (2005) 28–57.
[58] Stoner (2003) 154–64.
[59] For the recent controversy in the United States, see Amann (2004) 597–610.
[60] Such as for example Alston (2002).

than on *idealistic* and philosophical approaches,[61] accounts for much of the ongoing heated scholarly debate.

Despite the variety of opinions on and formulations of constitutionalism, five key principles emerge: the rule of law, separation of powers, fundamental rights, democratic participation and social justice.[62] As Figure 2.1. illustrates, these principles encompass both procedural and material elements, resulting in a comprehensive notion of constitutionalism.

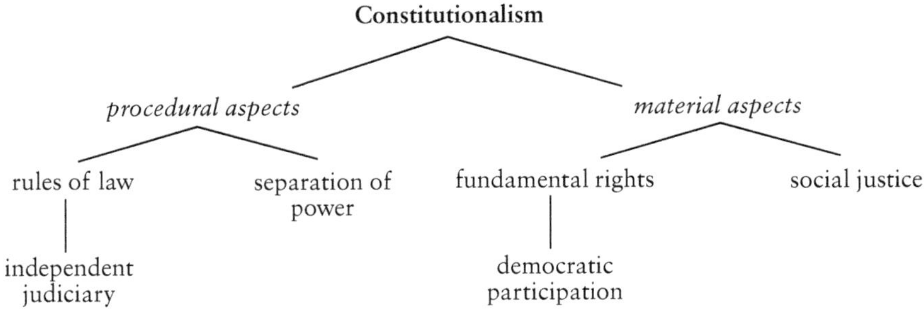

Figure 2.1. *The Five Key Principles of Constitutionalism*

2.1.3.1. *Rule of Law*

"Law is reasoning from commitment."[64] The rule of law is commonly defined in procedural terms as a well-ordered legal system under an independent judiciary.[65] It aims at preventing the establishment of arbitrary power. As a result, the law also binds the lawmaker. Laws must be clear and precise in their formulation, allowing citizens to understand what effect they will have on their personal freedom.[66] The rule of law also implies what is commonly referred to as "necessity and proportionality of governmental restraints". The concept of personal freedom that underlies the idea of constitutionalism forces governments to refrain from interference with citizens' liberties unless there is a compelling public interest.

Applied to the example of international economic institutions such as the Bretton Woods Institutions or the OECD, it becomes obvious that these institutions rarely address the relationship between government and citizens directly. For instance, making labour markets more flexible and efficient often entails

[61] Like Petersmann (2002a).
[62] Petersmann (1996) 426.
[63] This figure draws from Haller and Kölz (2004) 130.
[64] Black, Ch (1999) 5.
[65] Other than the concept of "*Rechtsstaat*", the common law tradition understands the law as less static and more focused on procedure. As a result, supremacy of the law means that the law should be further developed by its own force and not be motivated by non-related considerations. Stoner (2003) 19–20, 80–81.
[66] Stein (2001) at 493–94.

abandoning protective governmental measures, such as limited market access for migrant workers. In the area of monetary policy, the IMF as a rule requires the liberalisation of capital markets, thus obliging borrowing countries to abandon market and currency restrictions. These actions are motivated less by a desire to guarantee individual freedom than a wish to accomplish economic objectives, and the effects the actions will have on individual citizens is often glossed over.

As to the independent judiciary, several economic institutions have created independent supervisory bodies: for example, the World Bank has established an independent panel to supervise the Bank's compliance with its own policies.[67] The IMF has no comparable surveillance body but has established a new Independent Evaluation Office (EVO).[68] With its rule-based dispute settlement system, the WTO is the first international economic institution to have a court-like supervisory body.[69]

The Bretton Woods Institutions lack a constitutional framework that is directly applicable to the Member States or even their citizens. Member State compliance with detailed economic programmes is clearly the emphasis, not the observance of abstract legal rules. A case in point, funding by the Bretton Wood Institutions can bypass the decision-making process of national parliaments—a process that is crucial to democratic governance.[70]

2.1.3.2. *Separation of Powers*

The reorganisation of the international community that took place after the Second World War deliberately entailed the creation of different forums for different policies, such as the ILO for labour issues, the Bretton Woods Institutions for monetary policy and the GATT for international trade. The idea was to accumulate as much expertise as possible in each organisation but also to avoid the risk of a political blockage, which might occur if one body were invested with the responsibility of dealing with all the urgent post-war questions. While in theory it is possible to interpret this set-up as a system of checks and balances,

[67] See section 2.2.3.1.D below.

[68] The director for the EVO was named on 27 April 2001. For additional information, see IMF, "Making the IMF's Independent Evaluation Office (EVO) Operational: A Background Paper", 7 August 2000, available at http://www.imf.org/external/np/eval/evo/2000/Eng/evo.htm.

[69] Ehlermann (2002) 606.

[70] This was the case with the IMF's loans to the former Soviet Union: The International Financial Institution Advisory Commission, "Report to the Congress of the United States on the future roles of seven international financial institutions", Washington DC 2000 [hereinafter "Meltzer Report"], chapter 2. See also the response by James D Wolfensohn, "A Misreading of the Positive Role of the World Bank", *International Herald Tribune*, 14 March 2000. The argument was also raised during the recent review of the Poverty Reduction Strategy Paper (PRSP) Approach. The EU and other stakeholders expressed their concern about the limited role of national parliaments in the preparation, approval and monitoring of country strategies. IMF/IDA, "Review of the Poverty Reduction Strategy Paper (PRSP) Approach: Main Findings", 15 March 2002, available at http://www.imf.org/external/np/prspgen/review/2001/index.htm.

as Petersmann does,[71] the political climate at the time suggests that the founders were driven more by political necessity and lessons learned from the League of Nations than by constitutional considerations.

Given the leading role of the United States and United Kingdom at the Bretton Woods conference, it is also interesting to note that both countries follow a (mixed) dualist system with respect to international law. In such a system, the need for a formal act of the legislator to integrate international law into the national legal order is often seen as a system of checks and balances against abuses of international law and as an instrument to compensate for the—according to this understanding—lack of legitimacy of international law.[72]

If we look at the World Bank and the IMF, we find clear rules of competence, defining a delicate balance between state sovereignty and the decision-making power of the organisations themselves. However, in both organisations, the members of the Board of Executive Directors—the highest level of management—remain representatives of their states or their voting groups. In other words, they are not independent but bound by their states' policies. Each member country is also represented by a governor, who is either the chairperson of the country's central bank or its minister of finance. Overall, the existing rules serve to define clear responsibilities rather than to create a system of checks and balances in the traditional sense.

2.1.3.3. Fundamental Rights

Fundamental rights serve several functions in a constitutional democracy,[73] the instrumental role for economic development being just one of them. While the World Bank and IMF Articles of Agreement do not explicitly refer to human rights,[74] development and social welfare are mentioned several times and can be interpreted according to the practice established within the UN human rights agencies, in particular the Committee on Economic, Social and Cultural Rights. So far, neither the Fund nor the Bank has followed a rights-based approach. As a result, the improvement of labour conditions is seen as a positive side-effect of social policy rather than as an objective in itself. This instrumental approach is fundamentally different from a value—such as human dignity—or rights-based concept. In an instrumental framework, individuals are not the holders of rights but rather the objects of policies.

[71] Petersmann (1996) 431.

[72] Jackson (2003) 793. Several cases pending with the Supreme Court as well as its decision in *Lawrence v Texas* 123 SCR 2472 (2003) and *Atkins v Virginia* 536 USR 304 (2002) sparked scholarly discussions on the relationship between constitutional and international law. See *Agora: The United States Constitution and International Law* (2004) 98 *American Journal of International Law* 42–108 (with contributions by Harold Hongju Koh, Roger Alford, Michael Ramsey, Gerald Neuman and Alexander Aleinikoff).

[73] Petersmann (2001) 18–21.

[74] For a detailed discussion, see Ghazi (2005) 114–15.

Likewise, the compliance of member countries with human rights obligations is not a criterion used by the Bretton Woods Institutions in granting loans.[75] Moreover, there is no judicial protection of individual rights within the BWIs. Similarly, with the exception of the Agreement on Trade-Related Aspects of Intellectual Property Rights (TRIPS)[76] and provisions in the General Agreement on Trade in Services (GATS) on the movement of persons,[77] neither individual nor human rights are mentioned in the WTO agreements. This is not surprising, since the WTO framework is based on the traditional concept of international law with its focus on states.

2.1.3.4. Democratic Participation

Democracy provides legitimacy to a system of governance, thus complementing the rule of law.[78] In addition, economic evidence shows clearly that democratic participation and economic welfare are related.[79]

Democratic participation applies in two ways to the Bretton Woods Institutions: in the establishment of programmes for borrowing countries and within the institutions themselves. As for the World Bank and IMF, the word democracy is not explicitly mentioned in their Articles of Agreement. However, several recently adopted policy papers on "good governance" underline the need for democratic principles such as access to justice.[80]

As far as the decision-making process within the organisations is concerned, there is no institutionalised participation of citizens or NGOs. As Joseph Stiglitz put it, just before he left the World Bank:

> It was finance ministers and central bank governors—and outsiders who often seemed to be representing international financial interests—that had the seats at the table, not labour unions or labour ministers. Indeed, even as debate on reforming the international economic architecture proceeded, these people, who would inevitably face much of the costs of the mistaken policy, were not even invited to sit in on the discussions; and I often felt myself to be the lone voice in these discussions suggesting that basic democratic principles recommended that not only should their voice be heard, but they should actually have a seat at the table.[81]

Similarly, the WTO does not grant any legal position to organisations other than states or individuals. NGOs and citizens neither have standing in dispute

[75] For a discussion of the philosophical aspects of assisting governments that do not protect human rights, see Rawls (2001) 113–20.

[76] Articles 11 and 14–16 TRIPS and the Doha Declaration on the TRIPS Agreement and Public Health, adopted 14 November 2001.

[77] Article I:2(d) GATS.

[78] Stein (2001) at 493–94.

[79] Huber, Rueschemeyer and Stephens (1993) 83; Kirchgässner, Field and Savioz (1999); Sen (2001).

[80] Access to justice is mainly understood in a narrow sense as a tool to protect investment and allow the liberalisation of markets: Alston (1997) 443.

[81] Stiglitz (2000) at 1.

settlement procedures nor are formally included in the WTO's law-making process.

2.1.3.5. Social Justice

Social justice as a constitutional principle acknowledges the fact that political, economic, social and cultural rights are indivisible.[82] Participation in democratic institutions requires the fulfilment of basic needs and fundamental rights inherent to human dignity. Most modern constitutions hold the government responsible for assisting citizens in need.[83] The promotion of social justice, through for instance development aid, is a declared objective of both the World Bank and the IMF and is mentioned in the Articles of Agreement. The Preamble to the Marrakesh Agreement establishing the WTO recognises the relationship between free trade and increased standards of living and sustainable development, thus stating them as goals of the envisaged trade liberalisation.

Historically, as we will see, social justice has played a key role: both the Bretton Woods Institutions as well as what later became the GATT were conceptualised as a means to an end, that is, to foster social justice and peace. Today, this concept seems to have been turned on its head, with economic efficiency becoming the primary objective. Whether this is indeed a valid course of action will be explored further in chapter 4 after the different legal frameworks have been discussed in more detail.

2.2. BRETTON WOODS INSTITUTIONS

2.2.1. The Conceptual Economic Framework of the IMF and World Bank

As mentioned above,[84] the main goal of the Bretton Woods Conference in 1944 was to "win the peace" and avoid repeating the mistakes that had led to the economic instability of the interwar years and the Great Depression in the US.[85] The bitter memories of high unemployment, hyperinflation, recession and fluctuating exchange rates were still fresh, and the world was still at war when the delegates of 45 countries met in Bretton Woods, New Hampshire.[86] Harry Dexter White from the US Treasury Department and the British economist John Maynard Keynes put forward a proposal for a new monetary system and monitoring

[82] Petersmann (2001) 14–15.

[83] Eg the new Swiss Constitution, above note 41, states in Article 12 Right to Aid in Distress: "Persons in distress and incapable of looking after themselves have the right to be helped and assisted, and to receive the means that are indispensable for leading a life in human dignity." The idea of social justice is also reflected in the Preamble: see chapter 1, section 1.1.2.2. above.

[84] Introduction above, note 51 and accompanying text.

[85] These mistakes were analysed by Keynes as early as 1919: Keynes (1919) 2–5, 26–42, 211.

[86] An excellent historical overview can be found in Lastra (2000).

institutions to ensure peace and prosperity. Their proposal[87] finally led to the establishment of the Articles of Agreement for the International Monetary Fund and the International Bank for Reconstruction and Development (IBRD), the World Bank, on 22 July 1944.[88]

What the architects of the IMF and World Bank had in mind were not technocratic organisations but institutions that would contribute to the welfare of humankind and thus put into practice what Winston Churchill and Franklin D Roosevelt had envisioned in the Atlantic Charter in 1941.[89] As John Maynard Keynes stated in his speech on the occasion of the signature of the Articles of Agreement,

> There's never been such a far-reaching proposal on so great a scale to provide employment in the present and increase productivity in the future.[90]

The IMF was expected by its founders to make short-term loans available to countries with balance of payment problems and to advise these countries. Today, the latter encompasses the member countries' economic conditions and policies, which under Article IV of the IMF Agreement are examined annually by the Fund.

The Bank on the other hand, was expected to receive funds from wealthy industrialised countries and redistribute them as loans with the overall goal of post-war reconstruction. Reconstruction has remained an important focus of the Bank's work, given the natural disasters, humanitarian emergencies and post-conflict rehabilitation needs of developing and transition economies. However, the overarching goal of the Bank's work has been refocused on world-wide poverty reduction.

While the IMF and the World Bank did not play significant roles in the years following their establishment,[91] the situation changed dramatically in the 1960s and 1970s.[92] The Bretton Woods system of fixed but adjustable exchange rates came under strain and collapsed in 1973 when free-floating exchange rates replaced the gold/dollar standard and fixed exchange rates.[93] With the new, more flexible system that was negotiated, the Fund sought and found a new role as surveillance authority.

The following decade brought what is often referred to as a "silent revolution".[94] Responding to world-wide fiscal deficits, international debt crises and

87 Newman, Eatwell and Milgate (1987) vol 3, at 38.

88 Lastra (2000) 512–13.

89 See Introduction above, particularly note 51 and accompanying text. Weber (2003) 1344–45.

90 Quoted in Moggridge (1971) 105.

91 Krueger (1998) 1984–88.

92 For an overview see Bordo (1993) 163–83; Krueger (1998) 1988–98; Boughton (2001).

93 According to Article IV(1)(a) of the Articles of Agreement, the value of a currency was defined in terms of gold or in terms of the US dollar as of 1 July 1944. The US dollar had a fixed gold value. This system was called the par value system or Bretton Woods regime.

94 The phrase was introduced by Michel Camdessus, Managing Director of the IMF from 1987 to 2000.

structural rigidities, which led to economic stagnation, the neoclassical theory looked differently at the role of the state: rather than being directly responsible, the state should play an indirect role in ensuring national economic prosperity. The IMF made its loans conditional on the implementation of a package of short- and long-term economic reforms.

At the meeting of the Fund's governors in September 1989, the importance of open trade and the success of liberalising structural reforms was the major topic, and most of the member countries agreed that these policies should become those of the Fund. Named the Washington Consensus, it aimed at raising GDP by improving resource allocation through trade liberalisation, privatisation and stabilisation.[95] Keynes' concept provided the measures to be taken: developing countries confronted with chronic unemployment needed more flexible labour markets. This prescription often meant abolishing minimum wages, decreasing wages, reducing job security and privatising social security—thus lowering labour standards. Latin American countries in particular used IMF loans to service their external debts and avoid default. However, by the end of the 1980s, it had become obvious that the debt burden of some Latin American countries was unsustainable whether or not they complied with IMF conditionalities. To some extent, IMF assistance postponed debt reduction—at the high cost of a longer lasting decline in living standards. Finally, write-downs of Latin American debts were agreed upon at the end of the 1980s under the Brady plan.[96]

In contrast with their original goal of providing short-term lending, a new role has emerged for the IMF and World Bank,[97] namely championing long-term economic development. This new role inherently conflicts with the earlier conceptualisation of them as surveillance authorities for the international monetary system. The ongoing reform discussions within the BWIs concentrate on this point.[98]

2.2.2. Constitutionalism and Core Labour Rights

As we have seen, several steps would have to be undertaken to constitutionalise the BWIs. Supposing that the above-mentioned requirements could be fulfilled, what would this imply for the enhancement of core labour rights?

In a "constitutionalised world", the World Bank and IMF would apply core labour standards as individual rights. Given their binding force and the new rights-based approach, loans would be granted only under the condition that countries comply with labour standards. Sanctions in case of non-compliance

[95] For a detailed discussion see Williamson (1990). For an overview see World Bank (1991). Summary in Fischer (2004b).
[96] Vasquez (1996) 233–44.
[97] Darrow (2003) 10–51.
[98] Krueger (1998) 2015–17; Vines and Gilbert (2004b) 8–35; IMF, Refocusing the IMF, Issues Brief 01/03, April 2001, available at http://www.imf.org.

would be applied. Individuals would be able to have them legally enforced by courts and have access to review procedures within the BWIs. These review procedures would have to be led by an independent body with broader authority than that of the existing Inspection Panel.[99] Finally, the division of labour between the Bretton Woods Institutions and the ILO would have to be resolved.

The next chapter will look at existing policies and examine the extent to which the BWIs adopt any of the three conceptual frameworks—instrumental, mainstreaming and constitutionalism.

2.2.3. Current Policies

2.2.3.1. *The World Bank*

The World Bank has addressed labour rights and standards in the context of both social policies and human rights.

A) Social Policy As set out above, the creation of the modern welfare state is a relatively recent phenomenon.[100] Where does the World Bank fit in? Obviously, its involvement in social protection began relatively late and was influenced by concerns that structural adjustment programmes as they were applied in Africa and Latin America in the 1980s were adversely affecting the welfare of poor people.[101] But these first attempts, in the World Bank's own words, "remained mainly reactive and palliative in nature".[102] Social policy in general gained a higher profile during the 1990s and found its political culmination at the UN 1995 Global Social Summit in Copenhagen.[103] The global financial crisis that first hit East Asia and then Russia and Brazil in 1997–98 finally gave social policy the acknowledgement it deserves as a critical element of sustainable poverty reduction strategy.[104]

In the aftermath of the Asian crisis,[105] both the IMF and the World Bank have started reconsidering their existing social policies. While the IMF is analysing its role in surveillance in the context of regular Article IV reviews, the World Bank—together with UN institutions and the IMF—has prepared a study on *Principles and Good Practice in Social Policy.*[106] The report looks into macroeconomic policy, safety nets, education, housing and labour market policies and the role of correct and timely information. As far as labour is concerned, the

[99] See section 2.2.3.1.D below.
[100] Chapter 1, section 1.1.1.1. above.
[101] See Cornia, Jolly and Stewart (1987).
[102] World Bank (2001b) 2.
[103] See chapter 1 above, note 343.
[104] World Bank (2001b) 3.
[105] For the general economic consequences see Haggard (2000); Horton and Mazumadar (2001) 379–422. For a comparative country study, see Mazumadar and Horton (2000) 451–65.
[106] World Bank (1999).

paper concludes that labour market flexibility is important, but it also recognises the possible implications for wages and social security provisions. Core labour standards are not explicitly mentioned.

In a recent publication on social protection, the 2001 *Social Protection Sector Strategy,* the World Bank formulates the lessons it has learned from earlier experiences, and in particular the East Asian crisis, as follows:

> We have learned from these experiences that social protection projects and programs are needed and in demand by the World Bank's client countries and have, by and large, been effective. However, as the world has evolved, so has the need for the World Bank to modify its approach to social protection. . . . Our experience has shown the need for a new, integrated conceptual framework that builds on previous knowledge but better reflects the world situation at the beginning of the 21st century—a situation where risks and opportunities are on the rise, where it is recognised that neither the state nor the market alone will provide the best solution, and where the plight of more than a billion poor people poses the question of how to manage risk better, not merely providing handouts after a shock has occurred.[107]

Rethinking the concept of social protection resulted in the formulation of a new framework for social risk management.[108] Within this new framework social protection is no longer defined by its different programme components, for example, labour market interventions, but seen as public intervention that assists individuals, households and communities to manage risk better and provide support to the critically poor. Not only does social protection in this new approach provide the necessary safety net and cushion in periods of transition, but it also serves as a *springboard* for poor people. The concept of social risk management relies on the fact that poor people are typically more exposed to risk and have less access to effective risk management instruments than people with greater assets and better education. Thus, while a safety net should exist for all, the programmes should also provide poor people with the capacity to climb out of poverty.[109]

Compared to the first "palliative" social policy measures, the World Bank has indeed come a long way in adopting this new concept of empowerment. It is obvious that this shift in paradigm cannot be prescribed as a medicine for developing countries but requires their active participation. The involvement of the stakeholders in designing and implementing the programmes is therefore crucial. Apart from conveying to participant countries a sense of ownership over social protection programmes,[110] in the context of labour market programmes, this implies consulting with labour market organisations.[111]

[107] World Bank (2001b) 7.

[108] For an extensive discussion of the new concept, see Holzmann and Jorgensen (1999) 1009–20, and Holzmann and Jorgensen (2001) 545–52.

[109] World Bank (2001b) 9.

[110] Especially in the context of the Comprehensive Development Framework (CDF). See note 204 below.

[111] World Bank (2001b) 16.

With regard to labour rights, the World Bank considers equitable access to safe and well-paid employment to be one of the most important aspects of risk reduction. According to this view, "basic" labour standards, including the prohibition of forced labour and discrimination in employment and pay, the freedom of association, and the right to collective bargaining, play an important role in formalising the labour relationship. Nevertheless the World Bank raises two concerns about including these standards in their programmes: first, despite the ILO Declaration on Fundamental Principles and Rights at Work (1998)[112]—which is not mentioned in the strategy paper—not all countries embrace the last two standards because of their political implications. In addition, the empirical evidence about their economic benefits is—according to the Social Protection Strategy—mixed.[113]

In another publication, however, the conclusions are slightly different. The authors of the 2001 *Global Economic Prospects Report* first state that adoption of and compliance with core labour standards is not only desirable on moral grounds but also necessary for promoting broad-based and inclusive economic development. They then differentiate between the impacts of core labour standards—as defined by the ILO—on development on the one hand and economic welfare on the other.

One of the difficulties of assessing the impact of labour standards in general lies in their measurement. In the Social Protection Strategy, development is measured by higher growth rates of GDP per capita. The available data on freedom of association, which was used for the report because it is easier to measure than some of the other standards, is only weakly correlated with both higher levels and higher growth rates of GDP *per capita*.[114] However unfortunate it may seem that the Bank uses the highly debated freedom of association principle for its reasoning, it concludes that on average, more developed countries do indeed have better-than-average compliance with labour standards. In single cases such as that of the newly industrialising countries of East Asia, rising wages have been associated with improved bargaining rights.[115]

Less sceptical conclusions are drawn in an OECD study, where it is stated that countries that strengthen their core labour standards can indeed increase economic efficiency by raising skill levels in the workforce and by creating an

[112] See chapter 1, section 1.2.2.3. above.

[113] World Bank (2001b) 29. With this statement the Bank is still following its approach developed in the World Development Report 1995, 86, where the underlying assumption is that unions need to be restricted to specific policies in order not to impede development:

> Denial of workers' rights is not necessary to achieve growth of incomes. It is possible to identify the conditions and policies under which free trade unions can advance rather than impede development. Unions are likely to have positive effects . . . when they operate in an environment in which product markets are competitive, collective bargaining occurs at the enterprise or the plant level, and labor laws protect the right of individual workers to join the union of their choosing, or none at all.

[114] World Bank (2000a) chapter 3, at 10.

[115] Sceptical Levine (1997) 414–18.

environment that encourages innovation and higher productivity.[116] This statement seems to be heavily influenced by Joseph Stiglitz's challenge of the neoclassical assumption that labour is just another element of production.[117] Stiglitz, having just completed three years' service as chief economist of the World Bank, summarised his view:

> But even more fundamental than the issues of economic efficiency are those concerning economic democracy: the kind of society we are attempting to create. There is more that we can do than just following the dictum of 'do no harm'—though some might argue that that would, by itself, be going a long way. While globalization provides new challenges for sustainable democratic development, it also offers new opportunities to loosen the fetters of the past and to promote the democratic processes essential for long-run success. By becoming advocates of stronger workers' rights and representation, at every level—from the workplace, to the local, regional and national level, to the international level—I believe that we can achieve much more than improvements in efficiency. Labor unions and other genuine forms of popular self-organization are key to democratic economic development. That is why today, the World Bank supports the Labor Standards of the ILO, including the rights to organize and collectively bargain.[118]

Stiglitz's statement relies on a broad notion of development that goes beyond merely increasing the GDP, but includes promoting democratic, equitable, sustainable development. Although highly controversial when it was first presented, the World Bank shares some aspects of this concept when it talks about labour standards and economic welfare. It recognises that adherence to core labour standards can substantially contribute to improving welfare. However, the effects of higher labour standards policies—as demonstrated above in relation to the freedom of association and collective bargaining[119]—depend on the competitive conditions in the affected labour market.[120]

Where do all these economic insights lead us when it comes to including labour standards into social policy programmes? Given the controversy and the different starting levels of affected labour markets, the World Bank opts for a pragmatic and country-by-country approach.[121] With the exception of child labour and gender equality, labour rights are not routinely included in social policy programmes.

[116] OECD (2000) at 14.

[117] Stiglitz (2000) at 4: "Labor is not like other factors. Workers have to be motivated to perform. While under some circumstances, it may be difficult to coach a machine to behave in the way desired (eg, trying to get a computer not to crash), what is entailed in eliciting the desired behavior out of a person and out of a machine are, I would argue, fundamentally different." This view is also reflected in para I(a) of the Declaration Concerning the Aims and Purpose of the ILO, 10 May 1944 (Philadelphia Declaration): "*Labour is not a commodity.*" See chapter 1, section 1.2.2.1. above.

[118] Stiglitz (2000) 22.

[119] See section 2.1.1. above.

[120] World Bank (2000a) chapter 3 at 58.

[121] World Bank (2001b) at 30.

B) Human Rights The World Bank as an international organisation is subject to international law. As such, it could—in theory—accede to international human rights treaties.[122] While no such legal obligations have been entered into, the World Bank has addressed the issue of human rights frequently in recent years.[123]

On the occasion of the 50th anniversary of the Universal Declaration of Human Rights in 1998, the World Bank Group critically reviewed the role of human rights in development. The report, *Development and Human Rights: The Role of the World Bank*, emphasises the fact that the Bank's Articles of Agreement limit its activities,[124] because in all its decisions "only economic considerations shall be relevant".[125] Furthermore, Article III(5)(b) states that the Bank shall make arrangements to ensure that the proceeds of any loan are used only for the purposes for which the loan was granted, with due attention to considerations of economy and efficiency and without regard to political or other non-economic influences or considerations. It is argued by opponents to a World Bank human rights policy that these rules clearly prohibit the Bank from granting or refusing loans based upon a country's human rights record.[126] From this viewpoint, human rights are seen as political issues with which the Bank must refrain from engaging.

Yet, in the Bank's own reading, the same provisions are interpreted less restrictively, prohibiting the promotion of civil and political rights, but allowing for the enhancement of social and economic human rights.[127] The World Bank requires a consensus among its development economists that the social rights included in its programmes will have a positive impact on the economic development of the borrowing countries. Conditionalities with respect to social and economic rights can therefore be imposed on countries receiving financial assistance, to the extent that non-compliance with such obligations would jeopardise the objectives of the assistance programme.[128] The United Nations Committee for Economic, Social and Cultural Rights has called upon the international financial institutions more than once to respect social, economic and cultural rights in their own activities and to tailor their programmes so as to facilitate the promotion of these rights in the respective countries.[129] Most of all,

[122] See the discussion about the adherence of the European Community to the European Convention on Human Rights: the European Court of Justice came to the conclusions that the Treaty of Rome had to be amended before an accession would be possible. Opinion 2/94, [1996] ECR I-1759, reprinted in CMLR Vol 2/1996, 265–91. However, the court's reasoning is influenced far less by legal considerations than by political concerns about the hierarchy between itself and the European Court for Human Rights.

[123] Skogly (2001) 93–110; Ghazi (2005) 59–83.

[124] Ciocari (2000) 336; Darrow (2003) 149–69.

[125] Articles of Agreement of the International Bank for Reconstruction and Development as amended effective 16 February 1989, Article IV(10).

[126] Levinson (1992) 56; Moris (1997) 183.

[127] Schlemmer-Schulte (1999b) 335–36; Shihata (2000b) 448.

[128] Schlemmer-Schulte (1999b) 334–35.

[129] Committee on Economic, Social and Cultural Rights (1998), available on the website of the High Commissioner for Human Rights, http://www.unhchr.ch.

social safety nets should be defined by reference to these rights, giving them a much clearer meaning than that allowed by their existing dependence on political compromise.

The title of Section 10 of Article IV reads "Political activity prohibited" and mainly aims at prohibiting World Bank officials from interfering with domestic policy issues. This principle is known to every international organisation and can in its purest form be found in the UN Charter.[130] However, it does not prevent the Bank from addressing human rights, as these are no longer considered part of the states' *domaine réservé*.[131] In fact, international human rights agreements that have been ratified by the Member States allow international economic institutions to "depoliticise" human rights and to rely on them in formulating and defining development standards.[132]

C) The Special (?) Cases of Child Labour and Gender Equality Because exploitative child labour is one of the most devastating consequences of poverty, the World Bank has started to address this issue in its poverty reduction programmes.[133] Contrary to the assumptions of public opinion, child labour is a complex subject, and well-meaning efforts to stamp it out can easily make matters worse for the children involved.[134] While the Bank had occasionally included child labour issues in its programmes,[135] it started addressing them more systematically when child labour began to receive increased international attention in the late 1990s. In 1998, the Bank established a special child labour initiative, the Global Child Labor Program, based on an extensive study of the effects of child labour and the role of the World Bank.[136] According to this study, the Bank's new approach to child labour should include:[137]

— giving more focus to child labour issues in the policy dialogue with borrowing countries;
— improving partnerships with other relevant international organisations and NGOs;

[130] See Articles 1(2) and 2(1) of the UN Charter. It would go beyond the scope of this paper to discuss the (well-known) argument that the Bank's use of economic aid in order to force compliance with human rights norms violates Article 2(4) of the UN Charter. For an overview, see Moris (1997) 183.

[131] Ciocari (2000) 358–59.

[132] Buergenthal (1999) 100.

[133] Shihata (2000b) 467–69, 473–76.

[134] One of the most serious effects is forcing children into prostitution or causing them to suffer from hunger or starvation by preventing them from working. For an economic overview see Basu (1999) 1091, 1114.

[135] For example, the Bank's credit agreement for the Silk Development Project in Bangladesh, which was approved in late 1997, contains clauses requiring the compliance of contractors who were hired by the Silk Foundation (the agency responsible for the implementation of the project in Bangladesh) with applicable labour laws of Bangladesh, including child labour laws. Quoted in Schlemmer-Schulte (1999b) 337–38.

[136] The study was later published: Fallon and Tzannatos (1998).

[137] *Ibid*, 13–15.

- — raising the awareness and sensitivity of Bank staff regarding child labour issues;
- — giving more emphasis to child labour issues in existing lending activities;
- — requiring compliance with applicable child labour laws and regulations in specific projects where exploitative child labour is otherwise likely to occur; and
- — designing specific projects or components of projects to target the most harmful forms of child labour, possibly starting with a pilot project in a country where child labour is seen as a serious problem.

In launching the Global Child Labor Program in 1998, the World Bank recognised that it does not have the expertise to devise its own definition of exploitative child labour and instead referred to specialised agencies and the existing legal framework established by them. Any work performed by children in conditions inferior to those laid down by UN or ILO conventions is therefore considered economic exploitation. In the words of Zafiris Tzannatos, the leader of the programme,

> We are the new kid on the block. UNICEF and the ILO both have been working directly on child labor issues at the community level and in the labor market for much longer than the Bank. What we can do, together with our partners, is to place child labor in the broader development agenda, to mainstream it, to add further resources in the global fight for the reduction of child labor and the increase in education. The international community has welcomed the Bank's operations on child labor, but this comes with a hefty obligation for us to live up to their expectations.[138]

While official World Bank papers still emphasise that it is an international development finance institution and not a human rights agency, it now regularly imposes conditions regarding child labour standards on its financial assistance, especially when there are good reasons to believe that exploitative child labour may undermine the execution or the developmental objective of its programmes.[139] Moreover, specific programmes to eradicate harmful child labour have been established. However, it is important to note that the eradication of exploitative child labour is not seen by the Bank as an objective in itself but rather as a means to implement its social and development policies; it thus relies on an economic rationale.[140]

Examples of the Bank's efforts to reduce exploitative child labour include a recent programme in Brazil—known under its Portuguese name, *Bolsa Escola*—that provides stipends to poor families in exchange for the commitment that all children aged 7–14 are enrolled in school and have satisfactory attendance and academic performance. The objectives are to reduce the incentives for children to work and to increase school enrolments among poor children.[141] Similar

[138] *Spectrum*, published by the Social Protection Unit of the World Bank, Winter 2001, at 13.
[139] Schlemmer-Schulte (1999b) 335.
[140] Darrow (2003) 164.
[141] World Bank Project ID BRPE65181, Brazil-Program to Eradicate Child Labor, January 2000.

programmes have been set up by the World Bank in Bangladesh, Thailand and Indonesia.[142] Other projects aim to strengthen processes that promote economic development of women and create an environment for social change. One of their components is support for income-earning opportunities for poor women, which allow their children to leave work and attend school.[143]

After having approved a "Policy Statement of Forced and Harmful Child Labor" in March 1998,[144] the International Finance Corporation (IFC), the private investment arm of the World Bank Group, undertook a global study to investigate how IFC clients and the private sector generally were dealing with child labour. As a follow-up, a forthcoming document entitled "Harmful Child Labor Guidance" will address several problems revealed by the study and clarify the terms of the policy statement.

The World Bank's Multinational Investment Guarantee Agency (MIGA) has also included a condition in its general rules for guarantees requiring investors to refrain from using forced child labour.[145] Following up on this initiative, the International Development Association (IDA) recommended that Bank staff pay greater attention to core labour standards in IDA client countries.[146] Specifically, the report requests that each Country Assistance Strategy (CAS)[147] include a diagnostic review of core labour standards. In response to this request, the Bank introduced a *Core Labor Standards Toolkit*[148] to assist its staff in fulfilling these recommendations.

In addition, through its Global Child Labor Program, the Bank also supports research and analyses of these issues. An example is the Inter-agency Research Cooperation Program, which links the ILO, UNICEF and the World Bank by bringing together the different actors with a view to developing a coherent

[142] See also the Andhra Pradesh District Poverty Initiatives project, World Bank Report No 20089-IN, 20 March 2000.

[143] Fallon and Tzannatos (1998) 15, Box 1.

[144] "Harmful Child and Forced Labor", IFC Policy Statement, March 1998, available at http://ifcln1.?ifc.org/ifcext/enviro.nsf/AttachmentsByTitle/pol_ChildLabor/$FILE/ChildForcedLabor.pdf. It states that the IFC will not support projects that use forced labour or harmful child labour. In addition, the IFC will work only on projects that comply with the national laws of the host countries, including those that protect core labour standards and related treaties ratified by the host countries. The IFC focuses on child labour because "harmful child labor is morally unacceptable and in conflict with the World Bank Group's mission to promote socially responsible development".

[145] MIGA, "Environment and Social Review Procedure", para 15, available at http://www.miga.org/ sitelevel2/level2.cfm?id=1184.

[146] IDA, "Additions to IDA Resources: Twelfth Replenishment: A Partnership for Poverty Reduction", 23 December 1998, para 18, 35, 49. Available at http://siteresources.worldbank.org/?IDA/?Resources/?IDA_Retro_Publication.pdf [hereinafter "Twelfth Replenishment"]. In the "Thirteenth Replenishment Report, Supporting Poverty Reduction Strategies", 20 November 2001, core labour standards are mentioned in paras 32, 40 and 65. Yet there is no critical analysis of the steps taken following IDA 12 and there are no further measures foreseen going beyond what is described in IDA 12. See the critical comments AFL-CIO and ICTFU in IDA 13, Comments Received from NGOs on Draft IDA 13 Report, IDA, January 2002, pp 9–10.

[147] See note 211 below and accompanying text.

[148] World Bank, "Core Labor Standards Toolkit", available at http://www.worldbank.org/cls.

framework. One of the goals of the Inter-agency Research Cooperation Program is to define and document the relationship between child labour and sustainable economic development. For this purpose, a basic tool is currently being developed, called the *Child Labor and Child Protection Primer*. It may become an ongoing project that gets periodically updated.[149]

The Bank's approach to gender equality has followed a similar course.[150] Gender issues became part of the Bank's policy against poverty in the 1970s. In 1985 an in-house unit to promote women in development was created, and in 1994 the Bank adopted an official operational policy to "reduce gender disparities and enhance women's participation in the economic development of their countries by integrating gender in its country assistance program".[151] In response to increasing evidence that gender disparities not only are inequitable but also lead to economically inefficient outcomes,[152] the Bank has intensified its efforts to integrate gender into its activities since the Fourth World Conference on Women in Beijing in 1995, recently coming to the conclusion that men and women ought to be addressed differently in its work on poverty reduction.[153] The Bank's mainstreaming approach[154]—institutionalising a gender perspective throughout its lending activities—has led to the virtual doubling of projects that include some consideration of gender issues since 1995, now comprising more than 40% of all Bank projects.[155] Most poverty reduction programmes now explicitly address women and existing gender differences.[156]

The Bank is less reluctant to impose conditionalities on receiving countries when it comes to dealing with harmful forms of child labour or grave violations of women's rights, than when it addresses freedom of association and collective bargaining.[157] In other words, the Bank applies a higher standard of scrutiny in relation to its own actions where the protection of children and women from economic exploitation is involved. Where does this different approach come from? The explanation seems to be twofold: on the one hand, there is, as mentioned above, strong economic evidence suggesting that gender equality and the

[149] *Spectrum*, published by the Social Protection Unit of the World Bank, Winter 2001, at 17.

[150] The World Bank Operational Manual, Operational Policies OP 4.20 "The Gender Dimension of Development", October 1999.

[151] World Bank (2001a) 2.

[152] World Bank (2000b) states that gender inequalities harm well-being and hinder development. Low level of education for example translates into poor quality of care for children leading to higher infant and child mortality and malnutrition. As many NGOs have long been aware, women play a crucial role in development and poverty reduction. See for example the success of Women's World Banking, where the average repayment date for loans in 30 days is 98%. http://www.womensworldbanking.org.

[153] World Bank, *Policy Research Report on Gender and Development* (2000b); World Bank (2001b) at 27–28.

[154] See section 2.1.2. above.

[155] For examples see World Bank (2001a) 10–12. A recent project is the Andhra Pradesh District Poverty Initiatives project, note 142 above.

[156] World Bank (1998) 20–21.

[157] A similar argument is made outside the labour context for the protection of indigenous groups. Cf World Bank (1998) 26.

prevention of exploitative child labour enhance economic progress and welfare and help to create the stable social conditions that are crucial for sustainable development.

Apart from this economic and rather technical argument, which instrumentalises labour rights, there also is what could be called the "humanistic" motivation. As we have seen,[158] the protection of human rights serves many purposes, of which increasing economic welfare is just one; leading a life with human dignity and the "pursuit of happiness" is another.[159] This moral aspect has become apparent in the last few years, as consumer pressure on enterprises in countries with high child labour rates and unequal working conditions for women increases steadily.[160] Boycotts against companies such as Nike and The Gap have made it clear that many consumers will no longer tolerate exploitative working conditions.[161] Consumer boycotts under some circumstances have made the situation for the groups they intended to protect worse.[162] Moreover, in the public opinion and for marketing purposes, protecting helpless children and women is a somewhat "sexy" topic.[163] Who would not be touched by the picture of a skinny six-year-old girl stitching soccer balls in a dusty factory in Pakistan? Union activists taking to the streets to fight for their rights on the other hand seem far less appealing to Western consumers.

In many respects, the World Bank acts like a private corporation. While there are no direct consumers, there are nevertheless stakeholders at all levels of its

[158] See section 2.1.3.3. above.

[159] American Declaration of Independence (1776): "We hold these truth to be self-evident, that all Men are created equal, that they are endowed by their Creator with certain inalienable Rights, that among these are life, liberty, and the Pursuit of Happiness—that to secure these rights, Governments are instituted among men . . ."

[160] An example is the student movement at the University of Michigan, which finally led to the establishment of a Code of Conduct for all University of Michigan Licensees. See also notes 24 and 25 above.

[161] Nike has started to have its factories in Thailand, Vietnam and Indonesia inspected by the Global Alliance for Workers and Communities, a not for profit organisation consisting of corporate (Nike, The Gap) and public members (The World Bank Group) as well as University partners (St Johns University and Penn State University). The last report, "Workers' Voices: An Interim Report on Workers' Needs and Aspirations in Nine Nike Contract Factories in Indonesia", was published on 22 February 2001 and came up with disturbing results on verbal and physical abuse and sexual harassment. The report is available at http://www.theglobalalliance.org/workerssurveys.htm. Comments by Nike as well as updates on the report can be found at http://www.nikebiz.com. Another critical report about Nike was published in May 2001 by The Global Exchange: see Connor (2001). See also the decision by the Supreme Court of California *Kasky v Nike Inc*, No S087859 (California Supreme Court, 2 May 2002), 2002 WL 827173 (CA), holding that Nike's presentation of its labour standards in Asian factories in the course of a public relations campaign are considered commercial speech and can therefore be challenged as being misleading. On 12 September 2003 Nike settled the case by agreeing to pay $1.5 million.

[162] One of the most serious effects is forcing children into prostitution or making them suffer from hunger or starvation by preventing them from working. For an economic overview, see Basu (1999) 1091, 1114. For a detailed discussion see Kristof and WuDunn (1994), who criticise the working conditions in China. See also Kristof and WuDunn (2000) on sweatshops a few years later.

[163] See the examples "Human Rights for Sale" in Schoenberger (2000) 133.

Member States. It is not surprising that the Bank wants to address its stakeholders' legitimate concerns by taking child labour and women's rights into account in its programmes. Not only does this make sense from the viewpoint of political accountability, but also it seems—particularly under the chairmanship of James D Wolfensohn[164]—that there are in fact candid and honest humanistic concerns, that reducing poverty means more than just fulfilling basic needs. The World Bank's actions regarding child labour and women's rights reveal a genuine attempt to empower people and allow them to lead their lives in dignity, free from want, personal exploitation and discrimination.[165] Reducing poverty within the World Bank framework also stands for the protection of the most vulnerable groups in poor communities: women and children. Therefore, the World Bank is very sceptical whenever it encounters child labour or discrimination against women.

Although there is no "official" methodology, if one looks at the various cases, the Bank's approach seems similar to that applied by the US Supreme Court when dealing with the equal protection clause of the Fourteenth Amendment: where children are forced to work and women are treated unequally, the Bank treats these two groups (and outside the labour context, indigenous groups as well)—as "suspect classes",[166] looking very closely at the government's justification and accepting not just any governmental interest but only compelling reasons.[167]

From a legal and humanistic point of view, the Bank's approach in taking a clear position in favour of the most vulnerable groups makes perfect sense. In addition, the Bank's guidelines in this area, although not legally binding, have considerable impact on the behaviour of corporations involved in World Bank projects.[168] However, the question of whether this approach should be extended to the other core labour rights—freedom of association and the right to collective bargaining—remains open. We will consider this issue when assessing the Bank's policy in section 2.2.4. below.

D) Accountability: The Role of the Inspection Panel Unlike the ILO, the World Bank is not a tripartite organisation in which employers, employees and governments are represented. However, participation of non-governmental

164 Ghazi (2005) 95–96.

165 Annan (2000) 19–40.

166 See the famous "Carolene Footnote" in *United States v Carolene Products* 304 USR 144 (1938), footnote 4.

167 This analogy with the Supreme Court applies only to the methodology; the Supreme Court does not treat gender, childhood or poverty as suspect classifications under the equal protection clause and thus declines to investigate discrimination based on these criteria with strict scrutiny. So far, the high standard of strict scrutiny has been applied only to discrimination based on race. Poverty is not a suspect classification: *San Antonio School District v Rodriguez* 411 USR 1 (1973); *Saenz v Roe* 526 USR 489 (1999). In *United States v Virginia* 518 USR 515 (1996), the court applied intermediate scrutiny in a way that came close to strict scrutiny. See also *Plyler v Doe* 457 USR 202, 219–20 (1982).

168 ICHRP (2002) 107.

organisations has been included in the so-called "project cycle" of the World Bank.[169] Over the years, the Bretton Woods Institutions have come under heavy criticism from NGOs, especially in the context of the structural assessment programmes they have imposed on developing countries. In answer to these critics, the Bank set up an Inspection Panel in 1993 to provide an independent forum to groups of private citizens and NGOs who believe that their rights or interests have been or could be directly harmed by a project financed by the World Bank.[170]

The creation of a formal mechanism by which non-state actors can hold the Bank accountable for non-compliance with its own standards, was unprecedented within international organisations and gave the Bank a pioneering role.[171] The panel is a permanent body, consisting of three independent experts.[172] Once the panel considers a request eligible,[173] it recommends the Board to authorise an investigation. If the Boards accepts the recommendation, the panel carries out the investigation by inspecting the relevant Bank records, interviewing Bank staff and other persons and, if needed, making an on-site visit to the project in the territory of the borrowing country. Investigative action in the borrowing country requires that country's prior consent.[174] Since panel operations began in September 1993, 42 formal requests have been received.[175]

The Panel is a review procedure, not an enforcement mechanism. It is not a court. It cannot issue judgments or give remedies in favour of those harmed by the Bank's projects, nor can it monitor projects on its own initiative without first receiving a complaint. Nonetheless, the Panel's non-binding recommendations to the Bank's Board of Executive Directors are often influential, and the publicity surrounding an adverse report can put significant pressure on the Board to change or even end a project.[176] However, the first review of the Resolution Establishing the Panel, which occurred in 1996, resulted in a Board decision to confine the Panel's scope in respect of potential recommendations following investigations to findings on whether the Bank has complied with all relevant Bank policies and procedures.[177] In addition, a proposal to extend the Panel's

[169] Schlemmer-Schulte (2001b) 403–6; Ghazi (2005) 250–51.
[170] Shihata (2000a) 28–33. The Panel was established by Resolution No 93-10 IBRD and Resolution No 93-6 IDA The World Bank Inspection Panel [hereinafter Resolution Establishing the Panel].
[171] Schlemmer-Schulte (2000) 243.
[172] The current members are Edith Brown Weiss from the United States (chairperson), Tongroj Onchan from Thailand and Werner Kiene from Austria.
[173] The requirements for eligibility can be found in the Resolution Establishing the Panel, note 170 above, paras 12–14.
[174] Schlemmer-Schulte (1998) 358.
[175] As of October 2006.
[176] ICHRP (2002) 108–9. In July 2000 for example, the Board decided on significant delays and changes to a controversial poverty reduction resettlement project in western China after a critical panel report, even though Bank staff had recommended that the project should go ahead. See also *The Inspection Panel Annual Report 1998–99* at 24.
[177] "Review of the Resolution Establishing the Inspection Panel—Clarifications of Certain Aspects of the Resolution", 17 October 1996.

function to include the making of recommendations on, for example, possible remedies for harmful effects, or even to discuss the Bank's overall policies and procedures, was rejected.[178]

After an initial, very active period of operation—during which labour issues were not addressed—the Panel was reminded again by the Bank in 1999 that it had to focus on non-compliance with Bank procedures rather than on the harm caused by projects.[179] This means that the violation of labour standards can only be argued before the Inspection Panel if the standards form part of the Bank's policies and impede the implementation of the project.[180] In other words, the violation of freedom of association and collective bargaining by World Bank projects can not be brought before the panel at this stage.

2.2.3.2. The International Monetary Fund

In view of the changing role of the IMF over the years,[181] its goals had to be reviewed.[182] The primary objective, the promotion of international monetary co-operation, can be directly drawn from Article I(i) of the Articles of Agreement. From the beginning, price stability has been one of the major concerns of the IMF, although it was not mentioned in the original Articles of Agreement. The term was introduced into Article IV(1)(i) by the first amendment in 1969. Enhancing price stability is thus the second primary goal. Finally, the next amendment of the Articles of Agreement identified balanced growth—which today is understood as sustainable growth—as the third primary objective. In the Fund's framework, there is no hierarchy among the primary objectives. When conflicts arise, they are resolved in a pragmatic manner.

The economic crises of the 1970s and 1980s initiated further changes in IMF policy. As a result of these crises, developing countries became the primary users of the Fund's financing services. Because their balance of payment problems had a structural dimension that had been absent in the case of industrialised nations, the Fund had to respond with new instruments and new policies. It had become increasingly apparent not only that social, cultural and governance issues had to be addressed by the Fund's programmes, but also that there was a need for policies aimed directly at the poor, allowing them to participate in the growing economies. In addition to its short-term standby arrangements, new facilities[183] for low-income countries, namely the Structural Adjustment Facility (SAF)[184]

[178] Schlemmer-Schulte (1998) 380–81.

[179] Shihata (2000a) 173–203; "Conclusions of the Board's Second Review of the Inspection Panel, 1999 Clarifications", 20 April 1999.

[180] World Bank Inspection Panel on the Chad-Cameroun Project, 17 September 2002, para 212.

[181] See section 2.2.1. above.

[182] This paragraph draws on an internal working paper, "*Konditionalität als Element der Kreditvergabe des Internationalen Währungsfonds*", written by Doris Schiesser-Gachnang, Swiss National Bank, Zürich, 1999 (unpublished manuscript, on file with author).

[183] Lastra (2000) 518.

[184] In November 1993, the Board of Executive Directors agreed that no new commitments would be made under the SAF.

and the Enhanced Structural Adjustment Facility (ESAF), were created.[185] The latter was transformed into the more positively named Poverty Reduction and Growth Facility (PRGF) in November 1999.[186] The PRGF is the result of the IMF's goal of integrating poverty reduction and growth into its operations for the poorest countries and basing these operations on national Poverty Reduction Strategy Papers (PRSP) prepared by the countries involved, with the broad participation of key stakeholders.

Basing a PRGF-supported programme on the country's PRSP should ensure that civil society has been involved in the formulation of the programme, that the country authorities are the clear leaders of the process, and that the programme is properly embedded in the overall strategy for growth and poverty reduction. Thus, Fund staff is required to explain to the Executive Board how these programmes derive from the poverty reduction strategy and how they are complementary to the World Bank's activities and conditionality.[187] As a result, alleviation of poverty was introduced into the IMF's objectives for concessional lending in September 1999. Poverty reduction in the context of a growth-oriented strategy is now considered the Fund's secondary objective.[188] In contrast to the three primary objectives outlined above, this secondary objective does not need to be incorporated into *all* IMF programmes.

Before turning to the analysis of the Fund's core functions and their impact on core labour rights, a few words on the connection between unemployment rates, price stability and labour standards are necessary. There is no explicit legal basis in the Articles of Agreement for supporting human rights. However, high levels of employment and real income are seen as important elements of balanced growth and therefore deserving of the Fund's attention.[189] This raises the question of whether and to what extent monetary policy can contribute to preventing unemployment.

This issue has been highly debated among economists, particularly in the context of the creation of the European Central Bank, which led to heated discussions about the relationship between price stability and unemployment policy. The result was the well-known formulation in the Treaty of Maastricht,[190]

[185] Bradlow (1996) 71.

[186] Currently 78 low-income member countries are eligible for PRGF assistance. Eligibility is defined by the International Development Association (IDA), a member of the World Bank Group. Currently the cut-off point is a per capita gross national income (GNI) level of US$895. See IDA, "Additions to IDA Resources: Fourteenth Replenishment: Working Together to Achieve the Millennium Development Goals", 10 March 2005, available at http://siteresources.worldbank.org/?IDA/?Resources/?14th_Replenishment_Final.pdf, para 14. World Bank (2001c) at 12–15, table 1.1.

[187] IMF, Public Information Notice (PIN) No 02/30, 15 March 2002, "IMF Executive Board Reviews the Poverty Reduction and Growth Facility", available at http://www.imf.org/?external/?np/?sec/?pn/?2002/?pn0230.htm.

[188] IMF, "The IMF's Poverty Reduction and Growth Facility (PRGF)—A Factsheet", 20 September 2005, available at http://www.imf.org/external/np/exr/facts/prgf.htm.

[189] Article I(ii).

[190] Article 105 of the Treaty establishing the European Community.

which affirms that the European Central Bank can support unemployment policies as long as they do not conflict with the overall objective of price stability.[191] Even if this rule were applied to the Fund, there is no economic evidence at this stage for a direct relationship between labour standards and employment policy. For this reason, the following sections will focus on the Fund's aforementioned core functions—ie, surveillance, conditional financial support and technical assistance[192]—and examine if and how labour standards are included.

A) Surveillance According to its statute, the IMF has a mandate to exercise firm surveillance over the exchange rate policies of members in order to oversee the international monetary system and ensure its effective operation.[193] Recently, the prevention of crises has become a major objective in strengthening the effectiveness of surveillance. In fulfilling its mandate, the Fund looks not only at macroeconomic policy, but also at other policies that have a significant impact on macroeconomic performance, such as good political and corporate governance, labour and environmental policies. In its surveys, the IMF often refers to standards established by other international organisations. Could (and should) international labour standards as established by the ILO therefore be included in Article IV consultations?

Economists at the Fund see a major problem in the fact that the Fund does not have the expertise to offer advice to member countries on labour standards. Integrating ILO expertise into well-established and widely accepted IMF surveillance programmes, as well as direct collaboration with the ILO, is therefore currently being considered. Also, although the IMF, like the World Bank, supports core labour rights in *principle*, the Fund argues that these rights are sometimes *applied* in ways that are contrary to Fund policy advice. In fact, the Fund has agreed with the ILO that, from a conceptual point of view, there is nothing inherent in the core labour standards that is contrary to Fund policy advice in support of flexible labour markets.

Core labour rights are very seldom covered in Article IV reports. Like the Bank's approach regarding freedom of association and collective bargaining, core labour rights are only part of IMF programme discussions if they are essential for the success of the programme. Because IMF programmes focus on macroeconomic and monetary issues and not on the micro level of the economy, they

191 Mervyn King, Chief Economist of the Bank of England, compared the Central Bank's role in guaranteeing price stability with that of a football referee:

> . . . a successful central bank is like a good football referee. Inconspicuous for most of the time, thus allowing the game to flow, but not afraid to take centre stage when a difficult decision is necessary. It cannot rouse the players to a fine performance—only supply side reforms can do that—and occasionally it may need to show a red card to cool things down. But, in the end, the central bank is doing its job well when no-one notices that it is there, maintaining stability and allowing the players—economic agents—to display their skills.

Quoted in Hesse (1994) 52.

192 Lastra (2000) 514.

193 Article I of the Articles of Agreement.

are less likely to have a direct effect on the human rights situation of citizens in the Member States. Nevertheless, nothing in the Articles of Agreement prevents the IMF from addressing core labour rights in its Article IV reviews if poor performance negatively affects the macroeconomic situation of the country.[194]

B) Conditional Financial Support The IMF provides financial assistance to countries experiencing balance of payments problems. Such assistance is granted provided the country is implementing an adequate programme of policy adjustments. Conditionality has two objectives: on the one hand, it is intended to give the country confidence that it will continue to receive IMF financing as long as it implements the programme's policies. A country with balance of payments problems is spending more money than it receives. Unless economic reforms take place, this situation will not change. Therefore, conditionality also aims at minimising the credit risk for the Fund by increasing the chances that the country will be able to meet its obligations and pay back the loan.

Conditionality has evolved over the history of the Fund. Until the 1980s, the focus was clearly on macroeconomic variables. This changed with the increasing number of structural adjustment programmes and led to a significant expansion of conditionality. For example, programmes supported by the IMF have incorporated the revision of labour codes and restrictive practices in order to enhance labour mobility and employment. In Côte d'Ivoire, a revision of collective bargaining procedures was included in the programme in order to reverse the steady decline in private sector employment and ensure that labour contracts reflect branch- and firm-specific circumstances.[195] Although these programmes succeeded in making the labour market more flexible, they also resulted in lower labour standards. So far, no programme has included compliance with core labour rights.

The expansion of conditionality has raised concerns among member countries. The Fund responded by streamlining and focusing structural conditionality. In 2001, a relatively broad consensus between the Executive Directors was established, affirming that conditionality should focus on structural reforms that are critical to the achievement of a programme's macroeconomic objectives.[196] For all other programmes, conditionality should be less strict. Nonetheless, some countries have noted that the Fund oversteps its mandate by applying some conditionality outside its areas of responsibility and expertise. Co-operation with the ILO in enhancing labour standards are an example. The

[194] Bradlow (1996) 72–73.

[195] IMF, "Social Dimensions of the IMF's Policy Dialogue", Pamphlet Series No 47, 10 February 1995, available at http://www.imf.org/external/pubs/ft/pam/pam47/pam4703.htm.

[196] IMF, Public Information Notice (PIN) No1/28, 21 March 2001, "IMF Executive Board Discusses Conditionality", available at http://www.imf.org/external/np/sec/pn/2001/pn0128.htm. Background Papers: IMF, "Conditionality in Fund-Supported Programs: Policy Issues", 16 February 2001; IMF, "Structural Conditionality in Fund-Supported Programs", 16 February 2001. Available at http://www.imf.org.

majority of Executive Directors thought that any application of conditionality in these areas should be limited to measures that are critical for a programme's achievement of its macroeconomic objectives. In any case, there was consensus that implementing any measure outside the Fund's core competencies that were included in conditionality, would necessitate ample advice from other agencies like the World Bank and the ILO crucial. As a result, new Guidelines on Conditionality were adopted in September 2002.[197]

The new IMF Guidelines reflect the concerns of borrowing countries by stating that conditions will normally consist of macroeconomic variables and structural measures that are within the Fund's core areas of responsibility. While variables and measures outside the Fund's core areas or responsibility may also be established as conditions, they should be accompanied by detailed explanation of their relevance for the project's success.[198] The Guidelines explicitly exclude cross-conditionality, reasoning that the Fund's resources must not be subjected to the rules or decisions of other organisations. However, the Fund will draw on the advice of other international institutions and aim to tailor its programmes to be consistent with those of other international institutions.[199]

C) Technical Assistance Technical assistance is of crucial importance, particularly for transition economies. The IMF provides training in banking and monetary policy, foreign exchange, fiscal policy and statistics. While core labour rights are not included in these programmes, the issue is sometimes addressed when it comes to institutional questions, such as the establishment of an independent central bank. In this context, the question of freedom of association and collective bargaining has been informally addressed.

2.2.3.3. Responding to the Pressure: Collaboration with other Organisations

The World Bank has led extended discussions on core labour standards not only with the ILO but also with the American Federation of Labor and Congress of Industrial Organizations (AFL-CIO) and the International Conference of Free Trade Unions (ICFTU). While the ILO had previously encouraged the World Bank to use loan-conditionality to enforce core labour standards, the new Director-General of the ILO has moved towards a more promotional role for the World Bank, thus keeping the leadership within the ILO. This attitude is not surprising, given that the ILO is currently looking for an enhanced role to play on the international stage. On the other hand, the IMF has recently shown a tendency to broaden its mandate beyond a purely macroeconomic context. To underline this development, the ILO is now an observer in the IMF's

[197] IMF, "Guidelines on Conditionality", prepared by the Legal and Policy Development and Review Departments, 25 September 2002. Available at http://www.imf.org.

[198] Para 7(b) of the Guidelines.

[199] Para 8 of the Guidelines.

International Monetary and Financial Committee.[200] However, this interpretation of the Fund's role has been strongly criticised by leading politicians and especially by the Meltzer Report.[201]

In the division of labour between the IMF and the World Bank, the IMF focuses on macroeconomic policy, while the World Bank, according to the recent discussions among the member countries, is intended to become an international development agency. As mentioned earlier, the World Bank was asked by the World Bank/IMF Development Committee in 1998 to develop, in consultation with other institutions, "principles of good practice in social policies".[202] The Development Committee considered the resulting paper in 1999. Its members agreed that the further development of these basic social principles was best pursued within the framework of the UN as part of the follow-up on the Copenhagen Declaration of the World Summit for Social Development. Developing countries, especially the Intergovernmental Group of Twenty-Four on International Monetary Affairs (G-24), view these developments critically.[203]

Regardless of ideological differences, the BWIs are co-operating closely with the ILO on a pragmatic basis, setting up new country-led Comprehensive Development Frameworks (CDFs) and Poverty Reduction Strategy Papers (PRSPs). The World Bank proposed the CDF concept in early 1999.[204] It is thought to be a means by which countries can design and implement effective strategies for economic development and poverty reduction. In fact, the CDF was developed as an immediate response to evidence that the pursuit of economic growth in the past has too often been at the expense of social development. The CDF therefore applies a holistic approach to development by including all elements—social, structural and human, and governance, environmental, macroeconomic and financial. Special emphasis is also put on the involvement of the country concerned: CDF is voluntary and emphasises partnership between all stakeholders, ie government, civil society, the private sector and external assistance agencies. The basic principles of CDF can be summarised as a *long-term comprehensive vision* of needs and solutions that are

[200] This committee replaces the former Interim Committee.

[201] Note 70 above; Meltzer (2004) 106–23; Head (2005) 66–67 and 78–81 dismissing such criticism.

[202] See the study with the same name, note 106 above.

[203] Communiqué of the Intergovernmental Group of Twenty-Four on International Monetary Affairs, 23 September 2000, para 11. The reasons for this resistance will be explained in section 2.2.5. below. The G-24 was established in 1971 with the main objective of co-ordinating the position of the developing countries on monetary and development finance issues. It meets twice a year, before the spring and autumn meetings of the Interim and Development Committees of the World Bank and the IMF. Member countries are: Algeria, Argentina, Brazil, Colombia, Côte d'Ivoire, Democratic Republic of Congo, Egypt, Ethiopia, Gabon, Ghana, Guatemala, India, Islamic Republic of Iran, Lebanon, Mexico, Nigeria, Pakistan, Peru, Philippines, Sri Lanka, South Africa, Syrian Arab Republic, Trinidad and Tobago and Venezuela. http://www.g24.org.

[204] For more details see Wolfensohn, "A Proposal for a Comprehensive Development Framework, A Discussion Draft"; The Comprehensive Development Framework (CDF) and Poverty Reduction Strategy Papers—Joint Note by James D Wolfensohn and Stanley Fisher, 5 April 2000.

specific to the country involved and pursued in partnership with internal and external actors with its focus on *development outcomes*. Interestingly, on its web site dealing with frequently asked questions, the World Bank explicitly states:

> Development is therefore about transforming whole societies. Experience shows that unless we look at both sides of a country's balance sheet—macroeconomic and financial aspects on the one side and structural, social and human considerations on the other—we run a grave risk of misjudging a country's performance, as well as inadequately supporting its future development.[205]

Labour issues are of particular importance to the CDF. The World Bank underlines the importance of productive employment for social development, because it creates not only income but also a sense of dignity and self-esteem for the individual. The latter of course depends heavily on the quality of work provided. This is where the ILO comes into play: in the World Bank's view, the ILO's Decent Work concept[206] is an important component of social development. Since minorities and those who are already socially disadvantaged are more likely to be the subject of adverse effects of structural adjustment policies, labour standards for women and children are a particular concern for the Bank.

Supplementing a CDF, a PRSP has to be prepared by the country involved. The PRSPs are expected to be country-driven and more clearly focused on growth and poverty reduction. They are at the heart of the new poverty reduction approach. All programmes supported by the PRGF are being framed around a comprehensive, nationally owned PRSP. At the September 1999 Annual Meetings, the IMF and the World Bank Group agreed that country-owned poverty reduction strategies should provide the basis for all World Bank and IMF concessional lending as well as debt relief under the Heavily Indebted Poor Countries (HPIC) Initiative. In March 2002, the Executive Boards of the IMF and the World Bank reviewed the PRSP approach.[207]

Within the ILO, the Working Party on the Social Dimension of Globalization is strongly affected by this process. Furthermore, the Committee on Employment and Social Policy (ESP) examined to what extent the ILO's decent work agenda can contribute to PRSPs in Cambodia, Honduras, Mali, Nepal and the United Republic of Tanzania.[208] As in all CDFs and PRSPs, the involvement of the ILO must be invited and developed in the context of a nationally owned

205 Frequently Asked Questions about CDF, para A.4, available at http://worldbank.org/cdf.

206 Somavia (1999).

207 IMF, Public Information Notice (PIN) No 02/31, 15 March 2002, "IMF Executive Board Reviews the Poverty Reduction Strategy Paper (PRSP) Approach", available at http://www.imf.org/?external/?np/?sec/?pn/ 2002/pn0231.htm; IMF/IDA, "Review of the Poverty Reduction Strategy Paper (PRSP) Approach: Main Findings", 15 March 2002, available at http://www.imf.org/?external/?np/?prspgen/?review/?2001/?index.htm.

208 ILO, Governing Body, Committee on Employment and Social Policy, "Poverty Reduction Strategy Papers (PRSPs): an Assessment of the ILO's experience", GB 283/ESP/3, 283rd Session, Geneva, March 2002.

process.[209] In addition, the ILO established a high-level World Commission on the Social Dimension of Globalization in February 2002.[210]

Finally, in close co-operation with the ILO, the World Bank has developed a toolkit on labour standards for use by Bank staff members who are working with governments in the development of Country Assistance Strategies (CASs).[211] As requested by the IDA, core labour standards are now reviewed in CASs.[212] The country assistance strategy is a development framework for the World Bank's assistance in a client country. Its objective is to identify the areas in which Bank assistance can have the largest impact on poverty reduction. It is the central instrument in the Board's review of assistance programmes and is prepared with the participation of the government and other stakeholders.[213] In accordance with IDA recommendations, labour standards have been included in several CASs so far. One recent example is the country assistance strategy for Bangladesh:

> Bangladesh has ratified six of the eight International Labor Organization conventions on core labor standards, but not the two pertaining to child labor. Despite the formal ratification, the Government still restricts freedom of association in export processing zones to attract foreign investment. Discrimination against women and religious minorities in the labor market and extensive trafficking in both women and children primarily for forced prostitution continue, notwithstanding efforts by the Government to address these social problems. The issue of child labor is particularly worrisome because 6.3 million children below 14 years of age, constituting 12% of Bangladesh's labor force, are working and out-of-school. Improvement is, however, expected in the future as a result of the growing support of the Government, civil society and international organizations for efforts to abolish child labor and provide working children with alternatives that would allow them to resume schooling.[214]

2.2.4. Assessing Current Policies

In assessing existing policies, it is important to keep in mind what the mandate of the BWIs is really all about. In the words of Juan Somavia, the Director-General of the ILO:

> In any of the things we do, the final question is: Are we helping to better the life of individual men, women, and children? And that's the bottom line. The rest are

[209] ILO, Governing Body, Committee on Employment and Social Policy, "ILO Relations with the Bretton Woods Institutions", GB.279./ESP/1, 279th Session, Geneva, November 2000, at paras 10–12.

[210] See chapter 1, section 1.2.2.4., note 401 and accompanying text.

[211] World Bank, "Core Labor Standards Toolkit", available at http://www.worldbank.org/cls. See also text accompanying note 148 above.

[212] Section 2.2.3.1. above.

[213] "The World Bank Operational Manual, Bank Procedures 2.11: Country Assesment Strategies", January 2005.

[214] Quoted in step 3 of the "Core Labor Standards Toolkit", note 211 above.

> bureaucratic stories within institutions that, as I say seen from outside of the institutions, look pretty ridiculous.[215]

The following sections will look first at the legal framework governing the BWIs: the general principles of international law that are applicable to the BWIs and their statutes. After outlining the broader framework, the analysis will then turn to the Bank's and Fund's Articles of Agreement and whether they allow the promotion of labour rights according to the principles established by the International Court of Justice (ICJ).

Similar to the WTO, but unlike in the ILO framework, the BWI's argue that the ICJ cannot authoritatively interpret the World Bank's or the IMF's Articles of Agreement because of special procedures that were established to resolve disputes between members or between the institution and members over questions of interpretation. The World Bank maintains that according to these mechanisms, the authoritative decision on interpretation lies with the Executive Board and finally the Board of Governors. As a result, there is no judicial control, either directly or indirectly through advisory opinions of the ICJ.[216] Although the IMF established a Committee on Interpretation,[217] in practice formal interpretations are usually issued by the Executive Board and Board of Governors.[218] Nevertheless, decisions of the ICJ on the general sources of international law are of relevance for the BWIs. In addition, in a procedure similar to that of the ILO,[219] where questions arise, they are usually solved by "informal" interpretation; the institutional mechanisms have hardly played any role in the past, and this is unlikely to change in the future.[220] In light of this legal framework, sections 2.2.4.2. and 2.2.4.3. will then critically examine specific rationales and currently applied policies.[221]

2.2.4.1. *The Legal Context of Bretton Woods Institutions*

A) General Principles of International Law As international organisations, both the IMF and the World Bank are subjects of international law[222] and as such "bound by any obligations incumbent upon them under general rules of international law."[223] While this principle does not itself determine which rights

215 Somavia (2000).
216 Fawcett (1960) 328.
217 For the history of the committee see Schermers and Blokker (1995) 843, note 68.
218 For the World Bank Institutions: Article IX of the IBRD Articles of Agreement, Article X of the IDA Articles of Agreement, Article VIII of the IFC Articles of Agreement, Article 56 of the Convention Establishing the Multilateral Investment Guarantee Agency. For the IMF: Article XXIX of the IMF Articles of Agreement.
219 See chapter 1, section 1.2.3.2. above.
220 Gold (1996) 16, 30–41.
221 For discussion of current policies, see section 2.2.3. above.
222 For an extensive discussion, see Ghazi (2005) 103–6.
223 "Interpretation of the Agreement of 25 March 1951 between the World Health Organization and Egypt", ICJ Reports 1980, 73, at 89–90 (Advisory Opinion of 20 December 1980).

and obligations international organisations have, the ICJ has stated[224] that their scope has to be defined in relationship with the constituent treaty of the organisation concerned.[225] Legal obligations of international organisations can thus be found in their constituent treaty or other recognised sources of international law: international agreements and conventions that the international organisations have ratified, customary international law, general principles of law common to the major legal systems of the world and the judicial decisions and teachings of distinguished scholars.[226]

Neither the World Bank nor the International Monetary Fund is party to the ILO Conventions and UN Covenants relevant to core labour rights. Nor have they adopted the ILO Declaration on Fundamental Principles and Rights at Work.[227] Also, the Conventions and Covenants mainly address obligations of states rather than those of international institutions. Finally, Article 24 ICESCR is often put forward to underline the argument that specialised agencies are subject to their own charters.[228] This position can be challenged by two facts: first, core labour rights as defined by the ILO Declaration have reached the status of at least emerging general principles of law according to Article 38 of the ICJ statute. Second, and even more striking, most Member States of the BWIs are also members of the ILO and thus bound by the Declaration and the conventions mentioned therein.

It is important to note that the obligations of states to protect labour rights also extend to their participation in international organisations, where they act collectively.[229] The obligation to protect labour rights does not stop at the domestic level but requires states to apply the same standards when they participate in international organisations. This approach is reflected in Article 5 of the International Law Commission's draft on state responsibility[230] and has also been emphasised by the Committee on Economic, Social and Cultural Rights on several occasions.[231] It translates into an obligation for international economic institutions not to require measures that would hinder a member's ability to comply with core labour rights.[232]

224 "Reparation for Injuries Suffered in the Service of the United Nations", ICJ Reports 1949, 174 [hereinafter "Reparations for Injuries"], at 179 (Advisory Opinion of 11 April 1949).

225 Handl (1998) 654–55.

226 Article 38, Statute of the International Court of Justice.

227 On the ILO Declaration, see chapter 1, section 1.2.2.3. above.

228 Gianviti (2002) para 12.

229 "Maastricht Guidelines on Violations of Economic, Social and Cultural Rights", Maastricht, January 22–26, 1997, para 19, available at http://heiwww.unige.ch/humanrts/instree/-Maastrichtguidelines_.html [hereinafter Maastricht Guidelines].

230 Note 34 above.

231 Examples are the concluding observations on Belgium, UN Doc E/C.12/1/Add 54, 1 December 2000, para 31; the concluding observations on Italy, UN Doc E./C.12/1/Add.43, 23 May 2000, para 20; and the concluding observations on Morocco, UN Doc E/C.12/1/Add.55, 1 December 2000, para 38.

232 For human rights in general, see Bradlow (1996) 72–73. For a very critical view, see Gianviti (2002) paras 28, 34–36, who states that the IMF has neither the mandate nor the capacity to consider all of a member's international commitments.

B) Articles of Agreement

a) **World Bank** A very strong argument for supporting labour standards can be found in Article I of the Bank's Articles of Agreement, where it is stated: Article I Purposes

> The purposes of the Bank are: . . .
>
> (iii) To promote the long-range balanced growth of international trade and the maintenance of equilibrium in balances of payments by encouraging international investment for the development of the productive resources of members, thereby assisting in raising productivity, the standard of living and conditions of labour in their territories.
>
> . . .
>
> The Bank shall be guided in all its decisions by the purposes set forth above.

According to this provision, raising the standard of labour conditions is an explicit goal. On the other hand, as we have seen in section 2.2.3.1.B above, Articles III(5)(b) and IV(10) are often referred to as confining the Bank's mandate to purely economic considerations and prohibiting it from taking into account political or other non-economic influences. These concerns have led to the adoption of a very cautious approach by the Bank in applying labour rights. Is this approach consistent with the Bank's practice in other human rights areas? However reluctant the World Bank feels about some core labour standards, it does not apply the same caution when addressing the delicate question of access to justice. Indeed, it defines a strong, accessible and independent judiciary as a primary condition for guaranteeing human rights. The Bank sees any country's system of justice as an important factor of good governance and as "the ultimate guarantor of equality under the law between the rich and poor, the powerful and the weak, the state and the citizen".[233] In its absence, corruption and theft will undermine not only the integrity of the economy but also the stability of society.[234] In addition, the Bank considers judicial reform as crucial to the success of the projects it supports and therefore includes judicial reform in its programmes. To put it bluntly, access to justice is about participation and democracy. By its practice, the Bank thus actively promotes the establishment of democratic legal structures and thereby abandons the principle of neutrality towards political systems.

As astonishing as this may seem at first glance, a broad debate about a right to democratic governance has been going on among international legal scholars since the late 1980s.[235] The collapse of communism in Eastern Europe, together with the idea put forward by Francis Fukuyama that there is an emerging worldwide consensus in favour of liberalism as the basis for economic and political

233 World Bank (1998) 15.

234 This statement reflects precisely the reasoning that is behind the rule-of-law-principle as it is applied in theories of constitutionalism. See section 2.1.3. above.

235 For an excellent analysis, see Marks (2000) 33–50.

life,[236] has inspired international legal scholars to reconsider the relationship between international law and domestic constitutions. In a groundbreaking article, Thomas Franck concluded that a norm of democratic governance has begun to emerge as a result of a post-Cold War consensus that governments must be the result of periodic and genuine elections.[237] The Commission on Human Rights confirmed this notion of democracy in 1999 in a Resolution on the Promotion of the Right to Democracy.[238] A similar conclusion was reached by Anne-Marie Slaughter with different reasoning:[239] her emphasis lies on empirical evidence that suggests that prospects for peace would be best if all states embraced not just market economics but also liberal democracy.[240] Moreover, numerous UN Resolutions, starting with the Vienna Declaration and Programme of Action in 1993, have confirmed the correlation between democracy, development and human rights and the need to promote them.[241]

Process-oriented core labour rights aim at levelling the playing field in the labour market. Freedom of association and collective bargaining in particular relate directly to the political rights of democratic participation and access to justice. They are the equivalent to civil and political rights in the world of work.

It thus becomes clear that interpreting the Bank's statute as precluding it from actively promoting labour rights, and in particular freedom of association and collective bargaining, is flawed in two respects. First, such an interpretation neglects important developments in international law that recognise a right to participate fully in a democratic society and to have access to justice and legal protection.[242] Second, the Bank's reluctance to include core labour rights in its programmes is inconsistent with its policy regarding access to justice. These programmes prove that substantial progress can be made without undermining the sovereignty of Member States and without overstepping the Bank's mandate.

b) The International Monetary Fund The only legal basis for promoting human rights in the IMF's Articles of Agreement can be found in Article I(ii):

Article I Purposes

The purposes of the International Monetary Fund are: . . .

(ii) To facilitate the expansion and balanced growth of international trade, and to contribute thereby to the promotion and maintenance of high levels of employment and real income and to the development of the productive resources of all members as primary objectives of economic policy.

236 Fukuyama (1992) chapter 4.
237 Franck (1992) 63–77.
238 Commission on Human Rights Resolution 1999/57, E/CN.4/RES/1999/57, 28 April 1999. The resolution was adopted by 51 votes to nil (China and Cuba abstaining).
239 Slaughter (1995) 503.
240 Slaughter (1992) 403; Slaughter (1993) 236–37. See also the critique of Slaughter's concept by Alvarez (2001) 183–246.
241 United Nations, World Conference on Human Rights, Vienna Declaration and Programme of Action, A/CONF.157/23, 12 July 1993, para II.66.
242 Resolution on the Promotion of a Right to Democracy, above note 238, para 2(c) and (e).

This provision reflects the general objective pursued by the framers of the BWIs to generate welfare by creating stable economic conditions worldwide.[243] The Fund's policy is seen as an economic means to reach this goal. Consequently, labour rights are not found in IMF programmes unless there is a strong economic correlation between the rights and the programme's objective.

The Fund was invited to participate in the negotiations of the ICESCR but declined because the limits set on the IMF's activities at the time did not appear to cover this field. The Fund saw itself as an agency that relies on technical and economic considerations rather than the political or economic rights of individuals.[244]

Much like the World Bank, however, the Fund is subject to the general principles of international law as outlined above. Also like the World Bank, the Fund has now begun considering the issue of good governance in many of its activities, emphasising in particular the prevention of corruption.[245] Therefore, the legal situation for the Fund is no different from that for the World Bank: general principles of international law as well as the need for consistent policy require the inclusion of labour rights into the Fund's programmes.[246]

In summary, the legal framework for the BWIs as comprised in their statutes and derived from general principles of international law not only allows them to integrate labour rights into their programmes but creates an obligation to do so.

2.2.4.2. *Shortcomings of the Purely Economic Approach to Labour Rights*

It is often argued that the rights-based approach described in section 2.1.3.3. above does not add any value to ongoing discussion about improving working conditions. Why not focus on the long-term goal of increased welfare and improvement of economic conditions? In adhering to a narrow interpretation of their mandates, both the IMF and the World Bank put economic criteria first. Labour rights are to be pursued only if they contribute to objectives defined in

243 See section 2.2.1. above.

244 ECOSOC, "Co-operation between the Commission on Human Rights and the Specialized Agencies and other Organs of the United Nations in the Consideration of Economic, Social and Cultural Rights", UN Doc E/CN.4/534, 28 March 1951, Annex, pp 4–5. The World Bank also declined the invitation. *Ibid*, p 4; Gianviti (2002) para 4.

245 Communiqué of the International Monetary and Financial Committee (IMFC) of the Board of Governors of the IMF, Third meeting, Washington DC, 29 April 2001. Reprinted in IMF Survey Vol 30, No 9, 7 May 2001 at 136–40, available at: http://www.imf.org/imfsurvey.

246 One of the most recent programmes for Vietnam does not mention labour rights, although severe measures are taken to liberalise the labour market: IMF Country Report No 01/59, "Vietnam—Request for a Three-year Arrangement under the Poverty Reduction and Growth Facility", International Monetary Fund, Washington DC, April 2001, available at http://www.imf.org. It is interesting to note that the US Commission on International Religious Freedom in a letter to Treasury Secretary Paul O'Neill on 29 March 2001 called on the US government to withhold backing for World Bank and IMF fund lending to Vietnam in protest at "grievous violations" of religious freedom. World Bank, Press Review, 11 April 2001, available at http://worldbank.org/?developmentnews.

economic terms. This means–end instrumentalist or welfare-maximising approach sharply contrasts with the language of human rights advocates[247] and furthermore excludes labour rights with controversial economic effects—such as freedom of association and collective bargaining.

In traditional economic terms, labour standards can be perceived as aiming mainly at the correction of market failures, such as asymmetric information etc. However, this concept neglects the fact that labour standards also express human values as they are reflected in the ILO Declaration on Fundamental Principles.

The two main arguments against the traditional economic approach are as follows. First, the Washington consensus is too narrow in focusing on the GDP and also in choosing the instruments of development. Second, development cannot be limited to raising the GDP but must involve a transformation of society and a change in mindsets.[248]

The dividing line between the economic and legal approaches used to be very clear, but recent legal scholarship tends either to acknowledge complementarity[249] between the two approaches or to apply economic analysis to international law.[250] While the former is a valuable attempt to merge the language of economics with legal terminology and pursue goals that many development economists and human rights advocates have in common,[251] the latter is more problematic. It overlooks the fact that economic theories can neither define the values that are to be protected nor provide a concept that is universally accepted—unlike international law (according to some scholars).[252]

For this reason, the proposals of Ernst-Ulrich Petersmann to "constitutionalise" the WTO[253] have been heavily criticised by human rights lawyers, notably Philip Alston.[254] Petersmann claims that what he calls "market freedoms"[255] are inevitable consequences and complements of the protection of human rights; these "market freedoms" must therefore be taken into account and protected by the WTO. Alston rejects his ideas as a "merger and acquisition of human rights by trade law", fearing that Petersmann's approach would sever human rights from their foundations in human dignity and instead treat them primarily as instrumental means for the achievement of economic policy objectives.[256] Alston would be correct if Petersmann had really put forward such an

[247] Steiner (1998) 25.
[248] Stiglitz (2000) 2; similarly Weber (2003) 1340–42.
[249] Kennedy (1999) 39–48, 61; Steiner (1998) 40.
[250] Dunoff and Trachtman (1999)1–56; Goldsmith and Posner (1999) 1113?77.
[251] Illustrated by two decisions of the South African Supreme Court: *Soobramoney v Minister of Health (Kwazulu-Natal)* 1997 (12) BCLR 1696 (CC) para 31, concurring opinion by J Sachs, paras 54–59; and *The Government of South Africa v Grootboom* 2001 (1) SA 46 (CC) 4 October 2000, para 24. See also Stiglitz (2000) 1.
[252] Mutua (1996) 589.
[253] Petersmann (2002a) and Petersmann (2002b).
[254] Alston (2002).
[255] Including rights to property, contract and freedom of trade.
[256] Alston (2002) 843.

argument. Yet he has not; what Petersmann provides is not an immediately applicable concept for which all the details have been thought through, but a *vision* of a regime that reconciles human rights and principles of free trade. In contrast, Alston focuses on the consequences of implementing this vision in real life, which inevitably reveals shortcomings in Petersmann's concept. As a result, the debate has led not to concrete results but to a list of questions that need to be studied further.

2.2.4.3. *Difficulties with Mainstreaming*

If mainstreaming is understood as a legal concept[257] in contrast to a simple management tool,[258] it is about including the core labour rights as defined by the ILO into the activities of the BWIs. Political statements, as found in numerous World Bank and IMF documents and the speeches of their respective chairpersons, are important but not sufficient. If mainstreaming is to have a real impact on the rights of the people concerned, the details are crucial. As mentioned earlier, the World Bank is currently attempting to mainstream gender equality and child labour into its programmes,[259] yet their recently published study "Engendering Development"[260] does not address the specific role of the BWIs, concentrating instead on states' obligations. Declaring that gender equality is to be considered in all lending activities simply does not go far enough. The same is true for programmes on child labour: the Bank refers to the domestic regulations of the country concerned, not to international standards. In other words, defining the standard is left to the states.

In addition to the lack of a clear legal framework, the mainstreaming concept as applied by the Bank does not clarify responsibilities. For credibility reasons, transparency of the process (accountability) is essential. What happens if a country does not comply with core labour rights?

The BWIs could in fact learn a lot from the Northern Ireland experience:[261] above all, in order to establish democratic legitimacy, a clear *legal* commitment by the organisations is necessary. This could be achieved by an explicit formal acceptance of the ILO Declaration on Fundamental Principles and Rights at Work (1998) by the Fund and the Bank. This formal commitment at the Board level, where Member States are represented, is preferable to a single-minded concentration on consultation and participation, because the latter could undermine the position of the Member States and give too much influence to NGOs. In addition, like other international organisations, the BWIs are under considerable pressure to cut costs and provide their services as efficiently as possible.

[257] See Vienna Declaration and Programme of Action, above note 241, para II(1–3).
[258] Schlemmer-Schulte (1999a) 240–41.
[259] See World Bank, "Integrating Gender into the World Bank's Work: A Strategy for Action", January 2002, Washington DC.
[260] World Bank (2000b).
[261] McCrudden (1999a) 1720–21.

The additional bureaucratic burden and extra costs involved are therefore often used as arguments against dealing with labour rights. However, this concern could easily be addressed by co-operation with other agencies such as the ILO.

Finally, in the national context, the inclusion of protected groups has often created concern.[262] Given the legal mandate of both the Fund and the Bank, inclusion is necessary and therefore strongly supports the concept of mainstreaming. The idea has already been partially implemented by the ownership concept in the CDF and PRSP framework.[263]

2.2.5. Member State Sovereignty and BWI Enforcement of Labour Rights

Is it legitimate for the World Bank and the IMF to include labour standards in their policies? Should these organisations be "constitutionalised" in order to enhance labour standards? Unlike the WTO agreement and the GATT, the Articles of Agreement for the World Bank and the IMF contain no explicit dispute settlement procedures, let alone the possibility of taking sanctions. However, according to the conditionality approach, loans depend on complying with economic standards set up by the Fund and the Bank.

While the authority of the Bank and the Fund in establishing economic standards is rarely debated by its member countries, this is not true for "soft" issues such as human rights. The debate about the inclusion of labour standards into the WTO/GATT Agreements that took place in Singapore and resulted in paragraph 4 of the 1996 Singapore Declaration,[264] demonstrated the sensitive nature of asking developing countries to accept external guidance in this regard.[265]

As mentioned earlier, developing countries have urged the World Bank and IMF to "resist non-economic considerations in their decision-making" about labour standards.[266] This scepticism is not limited to the BWIs but applies to international labour regulations in general; it is feared that developed nations will use exaggerated labour standards to limit economic liberalisation and thus deprive developing countries of their competitive advantage.[267]

According to developing countries, the World Bank's approach to human rights gives the market too important a role and shifts the burden of political and legal reform to the developing countries.[268] The World Bank's approach seems to imply that the long-discussed tension between civil and political rights on the one hand, and economic and social rights on the other, has been resolved;

[262] For Northern Ireland, see McCrudden (1999a) 1735.

[263] See note 204 above and accompanying text.

[264] For discussion of the Singapore Declaration, see chapter 1 above, notes 348–49 and accompanying text.

[265] Kennedy (1999) 43–45.

[266] Communiqué of the Intergovernmental Group of Twenty-Four on International Monetary Affairs, 23 September 2000, para 11.

[267] For an extended discussion, see Howse and Langille (2000).

[268] Anghie (2000) 254–55.

the market provides the answer by calling for good governance, which protects all human rights and is thus essential for a country's economic and social progress. In the eyes of the developing world, this policy presents them with a double challenge: not only do they feel themselves compelled to make significant financial concessions in order to attract foreign capital and fulfil the requirements of structural adjustment programmes but they are also expected to minimise the social impact of globalisation by providing complementary social policy programmes.[269]

Human rights advocates are familiar with the postulate that enforcing or monitoring compliance with human rights obligations violates the principle of state sovereignty. In the context of World Bank policies—the argument goes—linking economic aid with mandatory human rights policies infringes the sovereignty of recipient countries and thus results in an unlawful interference with their domestic affairs.[270] As previously discussed, this discussion reflects the major change in global governance we are currently experiencing and its impact on the old Westphalian system of sovereign nation states.[271]

The Fund and the Bank are aware of the fragile balance between donor and recipient countries within the institutional structure. The concerns of developing countries about being paternalised are addressed in the ongoing discussion on institutional reform.

At the heart of the discussion are structural adjustment programmes, which, as a rule, will affect the labour market. While the reform programmes might be perfectly sensible from an economic point of view, they can lead to internal political difficulties in several respects. For example, a country might have a law about collective bargaining. In the process of privatising public enterprises collective bargaining is often suspended, thus leaving the country in a situation where it does not comply with its own rules. As a result, the question of consistency arises.

2.2.6. Conclusions: The Need for a Legal Framework

The IMF and World Bank have adapted their policies following the Asian crisis, having learned that it is impossible to implement quick remedies in crises like the one experienced by East Asia and that long periods of economic growth are not necessarily backed by sustainable social protection policies. The lesson is that social policies must be established *before* crises occur. These insights are reflected in recent IMF and World Bank policy statements, as discussed above. In addition, the language of human rights has increasingly found its way into their documents.[272]

[269] Rodrik (1997) 26.
[270] Moris (1997) 184 with further references.
[271] See chapter 1, section 1.1.1.3. above.
[272] Steiner (1998) 38.

As yet, neither the World Bank nor the IMF has adopted a comprehensive legal framework for addressing labour rights. If labour rights are discussed at all, the debate is driven by economic considerations. The promotion of human rights is often seen as a positive side-effect of development policy. It also seems that public relations play a role when highly emotive issues such as child labour are addressed. What is the problem with this approach? One could argue that there is no added value in applying a rights-based approach as long as core labour rights are *de facto* protected. But this means overlooking the fact that despite the cultural diversity of BWI member countries, universal standards are necessary in order to guarantee equal treatment of all borrowing countries. The importance of equal treatment of aid-receiving countries is underlined by the fact that several developing nations challenged the preferential trade systems set up by the European Union in the WTO, protesting what they viewed as unequal treatment, ie violations of the Most Favoured Nation principle.[273]

There is no need to reinvent the wheel, however; legal standards for core labour rights already exist, and most countries adhere to them. Introducing a new concept would in fact mean weakening the existing one: the social policy standards adopted by the BWIs are not legally binding and thus likely to dilute the legal obligations imposed on states by international law. A second danger lies in the tendency of international institutions to focus on minimum standards or basic needs when it comes to the implementation of human rights and especially economic, social and cultural rights. If the already reduced set of core labour rights is further limited by economic considerations, there will not be much left. While focusing on minimum standards may be legitimate as a temporary solution in circumstances where resources are limited or political obstacles impede full implementation, notwithstanding its good intentions, it can undermine the content of the right in question. An illustration is the concentration on *extreme* poverty in recent UN declarations.[274] Poverty has already been defined as a condition impairing the full enjoyment of fundamental human rights; lowering that standard makes it hard to imagine how Kofi Annan's vision for the twenty-first century—of all people living free from want[275]—will ever become reality.[276] Indeed, the combination of the core concept with the economisation of labour rights would lead to a significant lowering of applicable standards.

Instead of introducing new concepts to deal with labour rights and thereby reinventing the wheel, several arguments can be made for BWIs to formulate and establish an appropriate legal framework:

[273] See note 294 below and accompanying text.

[274] Eg ECOSOC, Human Rights and Extreme Poverty, Commission on Human Rights Resolution 2001/31, UN Doc E./CN.4/RES/2001/31, 20 April 2001. The UN international development goals that have been adopted by the World Bank and the IMF aim at halving the proportion of people who live in extreme poverty between 1990 and 2015. World Bank (2001c) at 3–5.

[275] Annan (2000) 19–40.

[276] Chinkin (2001) 565–66 notes a general weakening of language and objectives, for example from social security to social safety nets, from development to eradication of poverty, from poverty to extreme poverty.

1. Almost all BWI member countries are also members of the ILO and thus bound by the ILO Declaration on Fundamental Principles and Rights at Work (1998).[277] This legal obligation does not end at the door to the IMF and World Bank boardroom. The obligation to protect core labour rights includes the obligation of states to ensure that international institutions of which they are members do not violate these rights. States have to fulfil their obligations whether they act in an international or domestic context. Thus in the interest of consistency, they must ensure that collective decisions within the BWIs are made in accordance with their obligation to comply with the ILO Declaration.[278] Before programmes and policies are implemented, assessments of their effects on core labour rights are therefore necessary.[279]
2. A rights-based approach entitles workers to the guarantees enshrined in the ILO Declaration, whereas the basic needs theory treats them as passive recipients of social benefits. If respect for human dignity is taken seriously, empowerment of people is crucial. Moreover, the "mother" of all human rights, the Universal Declaration of Human Rights, talks about rights and responsibilities, not about development and needs.
3. Whereas complying with social policies is voluntary for states, a rights-based approach imposes clear legal obligations on them, thus holding them legally accountable for the implementation of core labour rights.
4. Given their broad acceptance, core labour rights have reached the status of emerging general principles of international law, according to Article 38 of the ICJ statute. Hence, these rights also bind international organisations such as the IMF and the World Bank. They oblige the BWIs not only to follow a "do no harm policy" but also actively to promote core labour standards within their respective mandates. This reflects a general shift in international law away from bilateralism towards a system that functions as a large community whose members are comprised of not just states but also individuals and international organisations.[280] In fact, holding the entire international community responsible for protecting human rights was exactly the intention of early documents such as the Universal Declaration of Human Rights.
5. By adopting a legal framework for addressing core labour rights, the debate about their economic advantages becomes less important.

How should the Bank and the Fund proceed in establishing a legal framework for labour rights? The first step would be an official commitment to the ILO Declaration by the respective Governors and Boards of Executive Directors,

[277] For discussion of the ILO Declaration, see chapter 1 above, particularly section 1.2.2.3.

[278] Dankwa, Flinterman and Leckie (1998) 724–25; "Maastricht Guidelines on Violations of Economic, Social and Cultural Rights", Maastricht, 22–26 January, 1997, para 19, available at http://heiwww.?unige.ch/?humanrts/instree/Maastrichtguidelines.html.

[279] Darrow (2003) 221–94.

[280] Simma (1994) 234.

explicitly accepting the rights and obligations enshrined therein.[281] Because the ILO has established a very elaborate set of standards to measure compliance with core labour rights, both the Bank in its loan agreements and the Fund in its Article IV consultations could refer to these standards and thereby overcome concerns that core labour rights would be unenforceable.

In a second step, BWI activities would have to be coordinated. Given that labour rights are not the only human rights to be dealt with, a central human rights unit would be advisable. The Bank has already set up thematic networks in several fields, which would facilitate the establishment of a human rights network.[282]

In the implementation of core labour rights, many of the current activities could be continued. Existing programmes such as those for child labour and gender equality would in fact have a greater impact and become more focused if they were embedded in a consistent legal framework.

From a state's perspective, the suggestions outlined above have several consequences: the state would be obliged to adhere to the core labour standards when acting as a member of the BWIs. This requirement stems first from the state's own legally-binding obligation to adhere to the respective covenants and the ILO Declaration. It is also a result of the BWIs' obligation to comply with core labour standards, which indirectly applies to individual states when acting as organs of the BWIs. A state therefore cannot refer to state sovereignty in order to oppose the inclusion of core labour standards into World Bank or IMF programmes. Yet, for reasons outlined earlier, the core labour rights need to be defined by concrete criteria in order to be applicable to real problems. Here, of course, the collaboration of the state is necessary.

2.3. GATT/WTO

2.3.1. Formation of the GATT

In addition to the controversy over the role that BWIs play with regard to labour rights, conflicting obligations may also occur in the relationship between core labour rights and international trade law as it has been codified in the GATT/WTO framework. With the end of the Second World War in sight, the UK and US agreed on a framework for the creation of three key international institutions that would be the basis of a new co-operative international

[281] The former Managing Director of the Fund, Horst Köhler, was obviously in favour of enforcing labour standards. In a public statement made at the annual meeting in Prague in September 2000, he emphasised the importance of core labour standards. However, this statement does not reflect the official position of the Fund.

[282] The four Bank networks are Human Development (HD); Environmentally and Socially Sustainable Development (ESSD); Finance, Private Sector, and Infrastructure (FPSI); and Poverty Reduction and Economic Management (PREM). The networks bring together all World Bank staff working in a particular functional area, wherever they are in the World Bank, to increase the capacity to capture the experience of others.

economic environment. The Bretton Woods agreement called for the establishment of the International Monetary Fund, the World Bank and the International Trade Organisation (ITO). However, the ITO never came into existence, mainly because of opposition in the US Congress, which was concerned about restrictions on domestic sovereignty. As a result, a provisional agreement, the General Agreement on Tariffs and Trade (GATT), was negotiated between 23 major trading countries and finally adopted in 1947.

Although considered a temporary solution until the ITO and the Havana Charter were adopted, the GATT became the permanent institutional basis for the multilateral world trading regime.[283] Unlike the Havana Charter, however, which contained a stipulation that members were to take measures against "unfair labor conditions", neither the GATT nor the WTO agreement contains a similar provision on labour rights, apart from Article XX(e) of the GATT, which preserves the members' right to take measures—that would otherwise be inconsistent with the GATT—against "products of prison labour".

Following the Uruguay round of negotiations, the original GATT of 1947 became the GATT of 1994. The WTO Agreement of 1994 is an umbrella agreement that not only establishes the structure of the WTO structure and but also includes GATT 1947 and many other agreements to which all Member States must, with few exceptions, subscribe.[284]

2.3.2. The Main Principles of the WTO/GATT

There are two major approaches to defining the goals of the WTO/GATT.[285] The first emphasises the principle of non-discrimination, which is often seen as the cornerstone of the GATT. It is referred to in the preamble and in Article I, adopting the Most Favoured Nation principle (MFN), and in Article III, adopting the principle of National Treatment. According to this model, regulation is only a problem if it leads to discrimination. It is however disputed whether Article III is about market access or protectionism.[286] From the second point of view, free trade as trade free of burdens—a "laissez-faire" principle—is the key objective of the GATT/WTO. Following this approach, liberalisation and deregulation are essential.

While the earlier GATT panels showed a tendency to adopt a laissez-faire attitude, the Appellate Body now applies a mixed approach, interpreting the text of the WTO/GATT as a product of compromise.[287]

[283] For the Havana Charter, see chapter 1 above, note 345 and accompanying text.

[284] Marceau (1995) 153–63; Trebilcock and Howse (2005) 23–25.

[285] Driesen (2001) 287–91; Sykes (1999) 24–33; Heiskanen (2004) 2–4.

[286] Howse and Regan (2000) 276.

[287] *United States—Restrictions on Imports of Tuna*, Report of the Panel, 16 August 1991 (unadopted), reprinted in ILM, vol 3, 1594–623, para 5.27 [hereinafter *US—Tuna/Dolphin I*]; *United States—Restrictions on Imports of Tuna*, Report of the Panel, 16 June 1994 (unadopted), GATT Doc DS29/R, paras 5.25–5.27, 5.38–5.39 [hereinafter *US—Tuna/Dolphin II*]; *United*

2.3.2.1. *The Most Favoured Nation (MFN) Principle*

Article I of GATT states that a member cannot provide more favourable treatment[288] to some WTO members than to others with respect to "like products". All benefits must be conferred unconditionally, which means on a non-reciprocal basis.[289] Thus, all members can benefit from MFN treatment regardless of whether they provide it themselves. If a member is denied MFN treatment, the appropriate recourse is a dispute settlement complaint and not retaliation.[290] In summary, Article I prohibits discrimination between different *foreign* "like products". If a product from country A is considered the same as a product from country B, Article I requires that they to be treated the same.

With regard to the discussion on labour rights, the following exceptions are important:[291] Part IV of the GATT and the so-called "Enabling Clause"[292] allow for a General System of Preferences (GSP) in favour of developing countries, which otherwise violates the MFN principle. As we shall see in chapter three, the EU and US make ample use of GSP measures in the context of labour rights.[293] The European Union's GSP regime was challenged by India.[294] The argument was that the selective choice of countries that receive preferential treatment is contrary to, *inter alia*, the MFN principle. In its decision, the Appellate Body clarified two important conceptual issues that had previously been controversial: it first held that the Enabling Clause is an "exception" to the MFN principle;[295] second, it made clear that the conditions mentioned in footnote 3[296] of the Enabling Clause are binding.[297]

States—Import Prohibition of Certain Shrimp and Shrimp Products, Report of the Appellate Body, WT/DS58/AB/R, adopted 6 November 1998, paras 172–76 [hereinafter *US—Shrimp/Turtles*]. The *Tuna/Dolphin* decisions both criticise the use of national trade restrictions to force foreign countries to protect dolphins. Similarly, in *US—Shrimp/Turtles* the Appellate Body held that the United States may not seek to force other countries to adopt regulatory regimes identical to its own through trade restrictions. These decisions thus define free trade as including a principle of non-coercion, at least through trade measures. Driesen (2001) 307.

288 With respect to tariffs, privileges, immunities, charges and other measures.

289 *Canada—Certain Measures Affecting the Automotive Industry*, Report of the Appellate Body, WT/DS139/AB/R, WT/DS142/AB/R, 31 May 2000 [hereinafter *Canada—Automotive*], para 84; Senti (2000) Rz 379.

290 Jackson (1997) 125.

291 For a complete list, see Trebilcock and Howse (2005) 54–55.

292 "Differential and More Favourable Treatment, Reciprocity and Fuller Participation of Developing Countries", Decision of 28 November 1979 (L/4903, GATT BISD 26S/203). The Appellate Body confirmed that the Enabling Clause is an exception to Article I:1 GATT: *European Communities—Conditions for the Granting of Tariff Preferences to Developing Countries*, Report of the Appellate Body, WT/DS246/AB/R, 7 April 2004, para 99 [hereinafter *EC—Tariff Preferences*].

293 For the US, see section 3.2.2.1. and for the EU, see section 3.2.2.4.

294 Request for the Establishment of a Panel by India, *European Communities—Conditions for the Granting of Tariff Preferences to Developing Countries*, 9 December 2002, WT/DS246/4.

295 *EC—Tariff Preferences*, note 292 above, para 99.

296 Footnote 3 to paragraph 2(a) stipulates that, in addition to being "non-discriminatory", tariff preferences granted under GSP schemes must be "generalized".

297 *EC—Tariff Preferences*, note 292 above, para 174. See also Bartels (2003) 518–21; Howse (2003a) 395; Charnovitz, Bartels, Howse, Bradley, Pauwelyn and Regan (2004).

2.3.2.2. *The National Treatment Principle*

A) Principle and Scope Article III of GATT allows the government of an importing country to apply the same regulatory standards for domestic products as imported products, as long as these products are not treated less favourably than similar domestic products. For our discussion, it is important to note the conceptual differences between sections 1, 2 and 4 of Article III. Article III:1 states that domestic taxation should not be applied so as to afford protection to domestic production. According to the first sentence of Article III:2, imports must be taxed identically to "like" domestic products. In the interpretation of the Appellate Body, this means that if two products are "like" and the imported product is taxed in excess of the domestic product, then the measure is inconsistent with Article III:2.[298]

If the two products are not alike but are directly competitive or substitutable,[299] the imported product must not be taxed dissimilarly from the domestic product so as to "afford protection to domestic production". In contrast to the first sentence of Article III:2, the first sentence of Article III:2 explicitly refers to Article III:1. Therefore in the view of the Appellate Body, a three-pronged test is required for determining whether an internal tax measure is consistent with the second sentence of Article III:2.

The three issues are:[300]

1. whether the imported products and the domestic products are "directly competitive or substitutable products" that are in competition with each other;
2. whether the directly competitive or substitutable imported and domestic products are "not similarly taxed"; and
3. whether the dissimilar taxation of the directly competitive or substitutable imported domestic products is "applied . . . so as to afford protection to domestic production".

The third prong obviously requires some kind of objective analysis of the measures taken. To what extent regulatory purpose plays a role will be examined in the next section.

Article III:4 finally brings other internal regulations (not taxes) within the scope of the non-discrimination principle. The crucial question here is: when are products considered like products? What are the criteria?

[298] *Japan—Taxes on Alcoholic Beverages*, Report of the Appellate Body, 4 October 1996, WT/DS8/AB/R, WT/DS10/AB/R, WT/DS11/AB/R [hereinafter *Japan—Alcoholic Beverages*] at 19.

[299] "Like products are a subset of directly competitive or substitutable products: All like products are by definition, directly competitive or substitutable products, whereas not all directly competitive or substitutable products are like." *Korea—Taxes on Alcoholic Beverages*, Report of the Appellate Body, 19 January 1999, WT/DS75/AB/R [hereinafter *Korea—Alcoholic Beverages*] para 118.

[300] *Japan—Alcoholic Beverages*, note 298 above at 26.

B) Product versus Process and Production Methods (PPMs) At first glance, one might think that Article III provides ample room for considering labour rights. A country could, for example, decide that no products, whether imported or domestic, are to be sold if they are not produced in compliance with ILO core labour standards. Unfortunately, it is not that simple. In two strongly criticised panel decisions[301] a distinction between regulatory measures that aim at products on the one hand and measures that relate to the manner in which the products are produced on the other hand—for example Process and Production Methods (PPMs)[302]—was introduced. According to these decisions, Article III deals only with products and not with the process of manufacturing them. In the *Tuna/Dolphin* cases, the US banned tuna that was produced in a manner that resulted in high rates of dolphin mortality, and was found to have treated physically identical products differently. Because the production method has no effect on the physical constitution of the product, the regulation relating to this method is not a regulation of products but an import restriction. Thus, Article III:4 does not cover process and production-related measures; these must instead be examined under Article XI.[303] As a result, although the measures were non-discriminatory as import restrictions, they were considered prima facie violations of Article XI. Only if they fulfil the requirements of Article XX of the GATT—which the panels denied in the *Tuna/Dolphin* cases—can they be justified.

In a recent decision, however, the Appellate Body left the door open for future consideration of process and production methods.[304] In the *Asbestos* case it decided that physical characteristics are not the only criterion for treating products differently. In fact, a product is not considered a like product if, for example, consumers treat it differently because of potential health risks. Therefore, the crucial criterion is the "competitive relationship" between the two products. Article III is not about market entry but about avoiding protectionism for domestic products. In the words of the Appellate Body,

> The broad and fundamental purpose of Article III is to avoid protectionism in the application of internal tax and regulatory measures. More specifically, the purpose of

[301] *US—Tuna Dolphin I*, note 287 above, at para 5.15; *US—Tuna/Dolphin II*, note 287 above, at para 5.9. Neither of the decisions was adopted by the United States. For a critique of the product/process distinction see Howse and Regan (2000) and the reply by Jackson (2000). While Howse and Regan argue that there is no textual basis in the WTO agreement for the product/process distinction, Jackson raises institutional and textual concerns about drawing the line between PPMs that should be considered and those that should not. The first decision on PPMs related to Article I GATT and found that non-products-related PPMs were incompatible with Article I: *Belgian Familiy Allowance*, 7 November 1952 (G/32-1S/59) GATT, B.I.S.D. (1st Supp) 59–63.

[302] For a conceptual framework of PPMs see OECD (1996b) 11–18. Charnovitz (2002b) 64–74.

[303] *US—Tuna Dolphin I*, note 287 above at para 5.15; *US—Tuna/Dolphin II*, note 287 above at para 5.9. Hudec (1998) 624; Howse and Regan (2000) 254.

[304] *European Communities—Measures Affecting Asbestos and Asbestos-Containing Products*, AB 2000-11, Report of the Appellate Body, 12 March 2001, WT/DS135/AB/R [hereinafter *EC—Asbestos*] especially para 100. For a review of this decision see Breining-Kaufmann (2001).

> Article III 'is to ensure that internal measures not be applied to imported and domestic products so as to afford protection to domestic production'. Toward this end, Article III obliges Members of the WTO to provide equality of competitive conditions for imported products in relation to domestic products . . . Article III protects expectations not of any particular trade volume but rather of the equal competitive relationship between imported and domestic products.[305]

In determining whether such a competitive relationship exists, the Appellate Body in *Asbestos* nevertheless relied to a great extent on the physical characteristics of the products, namely their carcinogenicity. While it stated that the physical characteristics were just one of four applicable criteria, the decision could also be interpreted as imposing a high burden of proof on a Member State that wants to contradict physical evidence.[306] In other words, WTO jurisprudence has not yet answered the question of whether PPMs can result in the "unlikeness" of two products under Article III.

C) Country-based and Origin-neutral Measures Article III prohibits discrimination on the basis of the origin of a product, because the national origin is not relevant from an economic point of view if the products are otherwise "like". Therefore, measures that prohibit sales of products from a country because of, for example, its systematic and consistent violation of core labour rights, seem prima facie illegal under Article III and can be upheld only if they can be justified under Article XX. The reason for this strict approach is that such measures also exclude products from the particular country that, for whatever reason, *are* produced in compliance with core labour rights. In other words, the ban is overinclusive by affecting all products regardless of concrete circumstances.[307]

An example of such a regulation that is likely to violate Article III—assuming that it aims at a general trade embargo—is the *Burmese Freedom and Democracy Act* adopted by the US Congress in 2003.[308] The bill introduces an import ban on all products manufactured or grown in Burma/Myanmar. It refers to the ILO declarations in respect of Burma/Myanmar[309] and explicitly quotes the gross violations of core labour rights as one of the reasons for the ban. However, because the ban is imposed according to the national origin of the products and not according to whether the products are produced in violation of core labour rights, it could be seen as a violation of Article III. In defending the bill, one would have to argue that consumers perceive products from Burma/Myanmar differently from physically identical products from other countries. If it were possible to demonstrate that consumer preferences lead to a different treatment of products made in Burma/Myanmar in the market, they

[305] *EC—Asbestos, ibid*, para 97.
[306] Marceau (2002) 808.
[307] Howse and Regan (2000) 252, 269–70.
[308] HR 2330, 108th Congress (2003) Pub Law No 108-61. A similar proposal had been introduced before, the Harkin-Helms Bill, Senate 926, 107th Cong (2001) HR 2211, 107th Cong (2001).
[309] See chapter 1, section 1.2.2.2.B. above.

could be treated differently under Article III because they would not be considered "like" products. However, unlike in the environmental context,[310] there is as yet no evidence of such consumer behaviour. On the other hand, Senator Tom Harkin, when introducing an earlier similar bill in the Senate, rightly pointed out that in a WTO dispute settlement procedure, Burma/Myanmar would have to claim that the bill discriminates against it by allowing the importation of other products that are also manufactured using forced and child labour.[311] Given its experience with the ILO, Burma/Myanmar seems highly unlikely to take such a step.

D) Protectionism and Regulatory Purpose Suggesting that the WTO dispute settlement mechanisms should eliminate protectionism makes a definition of this concept necessary. Not all regulations are as clear as the apparently discriminatory US bill about Burma/Myanmar. When there is no such apparent discrimination, the question remains as to whether the measures are nonetheless protectionist. Unfortunately, although much has been written, no legal definition of protectionism has yet been agreed upon.[312]

In an effort to bring the "like product" concept of Article III GATT in line with the general non-protectionism policy, the so-called "aim and effects" test was developed by the panel in *US—Malt Beverages*.[313] Canada had *inter alia* challenged several US state regulations that imposed sale restrictions on beer with alcohol levels exceeding 3.2 per cent, arguing that all beer was a "like product". The panel looked at Article III:1 and interpreted the phrase "so as to afford protection to domestic production" as depending on the aim and the effects of the regulation. It concluded that the regulation needs to have a bona fide regulatory purpose[314] and its effect on conditions of competition must not be protective.[315] With regard to Canada's allegation about the treatment of beer, the panel identified several reasons of social welfare and revenue-collection for the distinction between beer products. In addition, it found that the product distinction did not create adverse conditions of competition for Canadian brewers and thus did not violate Article III.[316]

310 With respect to genetically modified food, an industry-sponsored poll in the United States in 1997 showed that 93 per cent of consumers wanted such food to be labelled, thus indicating that they considered the genetically modified products unlike. Stilwell and Van Dyke (1999) note 8 and accompanying text.

311 Cong Rec S5455–56 (daily edition, 22 May 2001).

312 See for example the different definitions by Alan Sykes (Sykes (1999) 3–5) and Donald Regan (Regan (1986) 1094–98; Regan (2001) 1879–89). For a detailed discussion of the different concepts, see Driesen (2001) 353–60.

313 United States—Measures Affecting Alcohol and Malt Beverages, 19 June 1992, DS23/R- 39S/206 [hereinafter *US—Malt Beverages*].

314 The most comprehensive analysis of regulatory purpose in the context of like products has just been provided by Regan (2002).

315 *US—Malt Beverages*, note 313 above, paras 5.74–5.76.

316 *Ibid.*

The problem with this new approach was that it was difficult to reconcile with the wording of Article III:2.[317] Since only the second sentence of Article III:2 explicitly refers to the general policy in Article III:1, it seemed difficult to read the same notion into the first sentence. In addition, it was argued that allowing a consideration of the regulatory purpose in the context of Article III would make the exceptions in Article XX virtually redundant because all possible justifications enumerated in Article XX would already have been taken into account when determining a violation of Article III.

Not surprisingly, in the first case to raise these issues under WTO law, the *Japanese—Alcoholic Beverages* case, the Appellate Body put the idea of relying on the regulatory purpose in determining the likeness of products in perspective:

> No one approach to exercising judgment will be appropriate for all cases . . . The concept of "likeness" is a relative one that evokes the image of an accordion. The accordion of "likeness" stretches and squeezes in different places as different provisions of the WTO Agreement are applied. The width of the accordion in any one of those places must be determined by the particular provision in which the term "like" is encountered as well as by the context and the circumstances that prevail in any given case to which that provision may apply.[318]

That case involved a three-country complaint by Canada, the European Community and the US, arguing that certain alcoholic beverage taxes in Japan violated Article III:2 in two respects: first, they imposed taxes on certain foreign beverages which were higher than the taxes upon like domestic products in violation of the first sentence of Article III:2; second, they imposed higher taxes upon a broader group of foreign beverages "so as to afford protection" to directly competitive domestic products and therefore violated the second sentence of Article III:2.[319]

After its introductory statement, the Appellate Body then moved on to clarify that the first sentence of Article III:2 leaves no room for an aim and effects test but instead requires a strict interpretation of "like products". The Appellate Body argued that the explicit instruction contained in the second sentence made it likely that the drafters would have included a similar reference in the first sentence if they had wanted to apply the general policy stated in Article III:1. With regard to the second sentence, the Appellate Body stated that it rejected the aim and effects approach and instead investigated the "protective application" of the measure:

> As in that case, we believe that an examination in any case of whether dissimilar taxation has been applied so as to afford protection requires a comprehensive and objective analysis of the structure and application of the measure in question on

[317] The aim and effects test was applied in a second GATT panel decision in 1994: United States—Taxes on Automobiles, 11 October 1994, para 5.10. The European Union blocked the adoption of the panel report and made it clear that it would challenge the aim and effects approach at the earliest possible occasion. See Hudec (1998a) 629.

[318] *Japan—Alcoholic Beverages*, note 298 above, at 23.

[319] Hudec (1998a) 630.

domestic as compared to imported products. We believe it is possible to examine objectively the underlying criteria used in a particular tax measure, its structure, and its overall application to ascertain whether it is applied in a way that affords protection to domestic products.

Although it is true that the aim of a measure may not be easily ascertained, nevertheless its protective application can most often be discerned from the design, the architecture, and the revealing structure of a measure. The very magnitude of the dissimilar taxation in a particular case may be evidence of such a protective application, as the panel rightly concluded in this case. Most often, there will be other factors to be considered as well. In conducting this inquiry, panels should give full consideration to all the relevant facts and all the relevant circumstances in any given case.[320]

In the view of the Appellate Body, emphasis must be put on the objective analysis of purpose and not on the intent of legislators or regulators. Although the Appellate Body wanted to indicate a clear departure from the aim and effect approach, it left many questions unanswered, in particular the impact of the new ruling on the interpretation of Article III:4 in which the text leaves more room for interpretation than does Article III:2. As Howse notes, in many taxation contexts, the avoidance of protectionism may call for the application of objective criteria such as consumer preferences.[321] In other areas, when the measures are clearly aimed at regulating or influencing behaviour for legitimate, non-commercial policy purposes—such as labour rights—regulatory purpose may play a much larger role.

A year after *Japan—Alcoholic Beverages*, the Appellate Body decided on *Bananas III*.[322] A panel had suggested interpreting Article III:4 so as to include the protective application analysis the Appellate Body had called for in applying the second sentence of Article III:2. This interpretation was sharply rejected by the Appellate Body, who held that because there was no explicit reference in Article III:4 to the general principles of Article III:1, it was inappropriate for a panel to make any further inquiry about "protective application" when applying the like product test of Article III:4.[323]

Although the WTO organs have not yet had the opportunity to decide a case involving labour rights, decisions related to the protection of the environment are relevant, especially with regard to the exception clauses in Article XX.

2.3.2.3. Non-tariff Border Restrictions

Article XI prohibits quantitative restrictions in a broad sense, ie the use of quotas or import or export licenses, on the importation or exportation of goods into or out of a member country. The provision reflects the idea of the framers that

[320] *Japan—Alcoholic Beverages*, above note 298, at 31.
[321] Howse (1999) 141.
[322] *European Communities—Regime for the Importation, Sale and Distribution of Bananas*, Report of the Appellate Body, 9 September 1997, WT DS27/AB [hereinafter *Bananas III*].
[323] *Ibid*, at para 216.

protection and border restrictions with respect to trade should take the form of tariffs.[324] While tariffs are subject to reduction over time, quantitative restrictions are to be eliminated: Article XI assumes that such restrictions always protect domestic producers.

What is the relationship between Articles III and XI? At first glance it seems fairly straightforward: Article III applies to internal measures applied after a product has crossed the border while Article XI deals with restrictions at the border. A pure import ban would therefore be examined under Article XI whereas sales restrictions would fall under Article III. However, in practice, measures are often of a hybrid nature and cover both areas: an import ban may be combined with a ban on sales such as in *EC—Asbestos*. In this case, the panel applied Article III, relying on the Note to Article III and emphasising that the measure applied to *both* domestic and imported products.[325] This approach was upheld by the Appellate Body. However, the question of whether Article XI might apply as well remained unaddressed. In *India—Autos* the panel clarified that Article III is applicable where competitive opportunities in the domestic market are affected, while Article XI addresses competitive opportunities for importation itself, ie *entering* the market.[326] Moreover, it noted that there may be measures with a range of effects that cover both provisions.[327]

Why is it important which of the two provisions applies? A violation of Article XI is much easier to prove, and the only defence is to claim an exception under Article XX. If Article III is applicable in addition to the general exception of Article XX, an argument can be made by the defendant that the products are not "like". In addition, as mentioned in section 2.3.2.2.B above, in the two unadopted *Tuna—Dolphin* decisions, panels argued that Article III deals only with products and not with process production methods.[328] As a result, even if measures are being applied to sales of domestic and imported products, Article XI would be applicable. Scholars have strongly criticised this view,[329] and since the decisions are unadopted, they have little precedential value; the Appellate Body has not yet clarified the issue.

2.3.2.4. Exceptions in Article XX

In order for Article XX to be applicable, the measures taken by a Member State in violation of the GATT must fit under one of the specific exception headings in Article XX. For measures related to labour rights, the exceptions of public

[324] Senti (2000) Rz 531.

[325] *European Communities—Measures Affecting Asbestos and Asbestos-Containing Products*, Report of the Panel, 18 September 2000, WT/DS135/R [hereinafter *EC—Asbestos, Report of the Panel*] paras 8.91–8.95.

[326] *India—Measures Affecting the Automotive Sector*, Report of the Panel, 21 December 2001, WT/DS146,175/R [hereinafter *India—Autos*] paras 7.218, 7.223–7.224.

[327] *Ibid*, para 7.296.

[328] See note 287 above.

[329] Howse (1999) 139.

morals (Article XX(a)) or human life and health (Article XX(b)) can be invoked. In addition, Article XX(e) preserves the right to take measures against prison labour. If measures fall under one of these provisions, they still have to be necessary and proportional.[330] The scheme in question must also be applied so as not to create arbitrary or unjustified discrimination; it thus has to comply with the Chapeau of Article XX.[331]

Finally, a word is needed here about the extraterritorial effects of measures under Article XX(a) and (b). It is not clear whether a Member State can invoke these provisions in order, for example, to protect the health of the workers in another country or to fight child labour abroad. In *US—Tuna/Dolphin I* the panel held that measures taken under Article XX(b) must not jeopardise the rights of other contracting parties to determine their life and health protection policies, thus rejecting extra-jurisdictional application.[332] In *US-Tuna/Dolphin II* the panel concluded that the GATT does not proscribe in an absolute manner measures that relate to things or actions outside the territorial jurisdiction of the party taking the measures.[333] Thus,

> the policy to conserve dolphins in the eastern tropical Pacific Ocean, which the US pursued within its jurisdiction over its nationals and vessels, fell within the range of policies covered by Article XX(g).[334]

Four years later, the Appellate Body in *US—Turtles* avoided discussing the sensitive issue by merely stating that there was a "sufficient nexus" between endangered migratory turtles and the US to justify measures under Article XX(g).[335] According to the holdings in *US—Gasoline*[336] and *EC—Asbestos,*[337] it seems that the nexus required will vary based on the particular policies and the legal provisions at issue.[338]

While it has become clear that pursuing a multilateral approach is much more likely to be successful in relying on an Article XX argument, the impact of this approach on the issue of extraterritorial application is not yet clear.[339] It is possible that the Appellate Body would accept measures taken under Article XX to protect core labour rights as defined by the ILO, so long as the countries involved are ILO members and therefore required to comply with core labour rights.

330 The necessity test applies to all measures under Article XX(a)–(d).

331 For a compilation of the WTO practice to Article XX, see WTO, Committee on Trade and Environment, "GATT/WTO Dispute Settlement Practice Relating to GATT Article XX, Paragraphs (b), (d) and (g)", WT/CTE/W/203, 8 March 2002 [hereinafter "WTO, Practice Article XX"].

332 See note 301 above, paras 5.24–5.27.

333 *Ibid.*

334 *Ibid*, para 5.17.

335 *US—Shrimp/Turtles*, note 287 above, para 133.

336 *United States—Standards for Reformulated and Conventional Gasoline*, Report of the Appellate Body, 29 April 1996 WT/DS2/AB/R, [hereinafter *US—Gasoline*] p 16.

337 See note 304 above, para 103.

338 Marceau (2002) 810.

339 For a more detailed discussion, see Bartels (2002) 358–65.

A) Public Morals: Article XX(a) So far, there is no jurisprudence on the interpretation of Article XX(a). Given the explicit reference to labour in Article XX(e) and the fact that the Havana Charter never came into force,[340] the exception of public morals does not seem to encompass labour rights. However, this perspective relies on a static interpretation of the term "public morals", freezing it at the meaning it had in 1948 and excluding recent developments in international law.

Such an interpretation is contrary to Article 31 of the Vienna Convention on the Law of Treaties (VCLT), which declares the subsequent practice and subsequent relevant agreements between the parties as well as any relevant rules of international law to be sources of treaty interpretation. The idea of the GATT being a "self-contained" system[341] was brought to an end by the very first report of the Appellate Body,[342] wherein it stated that the WTO system cannot be construed in "clinical isolation" from the widespread sources of public international law.[343]

Two years later, the Appellate Body held for the first time that the Vienna Convention is the key to finding additional sources for the interpretation of the GATT. In *US—Shrimp/Turtles* it held that the exception in Article XX(g) ("conservation of exhaustible natural resources") had evolved since the drafting of the GATT and, given the developments in international law and policy, would now encompass the protection of living species.[344] To develop this approach a step further, a panel recently employed rules and principles of customary international law to fill unintended gaps in the WTO agreements.[345] To sum up, the WTO regime cannot be seen as a special regime, but as part of the international legal system as a whole.[346]

All of this leads to the conclusion that public morals cannot be interpreted in isolation from developments in international law. Nevertheless, the danger of protectionist abuse is real: virtually anything can be characterised as a moral issue.[347] At least since the Second World War, human rights have been considered a core element of public morality. In the context of labour rights, the ILO Declaration on Fundamental Principles and Rights at Work now represents a universal consensus on core human labour rights.[348] This development forces

[340] See chapter 1, section 1.2.3.3. above, note 344 and accompanying text.
[341] For the notion of self-contained regimes, see Simma (1985).
[342] *US—Gasoline* above note 336, p 16.
[343] This is supported widely by the doctrine: Jackson (1997) 25; McRae (2000) 36–38; Pauwelyn (2001) 538.
[344] *US—Shrimp/Turtles*, note 287, paras 128–29.
[345] *Korea—Measures Affecting Government Procurement*, Report of the Panel, 1 May 2000 WT/DS163/R, [hereinafter *Korea—Government Procurement*] para 7.101.
[346] Hilf (2001) 121–24; Feddersen (2002) 70–73.
[347] Charnovitz (1998) 731.
[348] For discussion of the ILO Declaration, see chapter 1, section 1.2.2.3. above. For a summary, see Feddersen (2002) 212–18.

WTO authorities to interpret Article XX in light of the duty of Members States to comply with rules of general international law.[349]

Feddersen and others have argued that the provisions of Article XX encompass only measures with respect to physical characteristics and not PPMs.[350] The fact that Article XX(e) is the only provision to address production methods (prison labour)—the argument goes—indicates that the other sections of Article XX do not include measures based on production methods.[351] As Howse[352] correctly points out—along with Feddersen, who gave up his earlier view[353]—such an interpretation is flawed for several reasons. First, there is no evidence whatsoever that the drafters of the GATT intended to exclude PPMs from the scope of Article XX. Second, such an analysis would restrict the scope of Article XX(a) to an extent that would make it almost irrelevant in practice. For example, any product manufactured in the context of organised crime would have to be given the full protection of the GATT, unless it were independently harmful. Not surprisingly, the language of the Appellate Body in *US—Shrimp/Turtles* could hardly have been clearer when making this point.[354]

B) Human Life and Health: Article XX(b) The exception in Article XX(b) also leaves room for the inclusion of labour rights as far as they are related to the protection of human life and health.[355] The decision in *EC—Asbestos* made it clear that the exception in Article XX(b) and the notion of risk are subject to dynamic interpretation,[356] which can take into account developments in other international organisations such as the World Health Organization (WHO) and the ILO. In fact, the decision in *EC—Asbestos* was the first case in which WTO dispute settlement organs referred to ILO conventions, the main issue being the protection of workers against the harmful effects of asbestos.

349 Diller and Levy (1997) 694.

350 Feddersen (1998) 109.

351 Notably, the inclusion of Article XX(e) in the GATT of 1947 was motivated by concerns of social dumping, not by ethical considerations.

352 Howse (1999) 143–44.

353 Feddersen (2002) 189, note 151. See also pp 188–206 where Feddersen provides an excellent analysis of both scholarly work and jurisprudence leading to the conclusion that PPMs are not excluded from the scope of Article XX.

354 Note 344 above, para 121:

> It is not necessary to assume that requiring from exporting countries compliance with, or adoption of, certain policies (although covered in principle by one or another of the exceptions) prescribed by the importing country, renders a measure a priori incapable of justification under Article XX. Such an interpretation renders most, if not all, of the specific exceptions of Article XX inutile, a result abhorrent to the principles of interpretation we are bound to apply.

355 According to *Thailand—Restrictions on Importation of and Internal Taxes on Cigarettes*, Report of the Panel, DS10/R - 37S/200 [hereinafter *Thailand—Cigarettes*], para 73, the use of the word "protection" implies the existence of a risk, and a panel therefore must begin any analysis by identifying a risk for public health.

356 *EC—Asbestos*, note 304 above, para 162.

Given that almost all countries ratified the United Nations Convention on the Rights of the Child,[357] intolerable forms of exploitative child labour that put children's health at risk fit within the exception of Article XX(b). Measures aiming at banning importation of products made using exploitative child labour would not involve a change in the official policy of other contracting parties.[358] Therefore, the argument of extraterritorial jurisdiction is invalid in such cases.[359]

Could other labour rights be considered under the exception of human health? The ILO has launched the Safe Work Programme, which aims, *inter alia*, at establishing preventive policies and programmes to protect workers in hazardous occupations and sectors and at extending effective protection to vulnerable groups of workers who fall outside the scope of traditional protective measures. In its report on the Decent Work Deficit, the ILO emphasises the importance of reducing health risks at work by implementing the ILO Declaration on Fundamental Principles and Rights at Work.[360] In addition, the WHO refers to equity, solidarity and social justice in its "Health for All" strategy.[361] Health risks are obviously involved in the context of forced labour. Experiences from Mexican *maquiladoras* also show that hazardous practices can be involved in measures that discriminate against women.[362] With regard to freedom of association and collective bargaining, the 2005 Review of Annual Reports under the Follow-up to the ILO Declaration contains several examples of links to health and safety standards.[363] As a result, Article XX(b) gives Member States some room for manoeuvre in protecting labour standards.

Nevertheless, in order to comply with the exception of Article XX, all measures taken must be necessary and comply with the Chapeau of this provision. The country invoking Article XX(b) bears the burden of proving that the contested measure meets the requirements contained in that provision. In *US—Gasoline* the panel determined that this demonstration includes the following steps:

> (1) [T]hat the policy in respect of the measures for which the provision was invoked fell within the range of policies designed to protect human, animal or plant life or health;

[357] See discussion in chapter 1, section 1.2.1.5. above. For Arts 32 and 35 of the Convention on the Rights of the Child, see Appendix A.5.

[358] Diller and Levy (1997) 683.

[359] See section 2.3.2.4. above.

[360] ILO (2001b). For the ILO Declaration, see chapter 1, section 1.2.2.3. above.

[361] Available at http://www.who.int/.

[362] For a description of the practices in the context of the North American Agreement on Labor Cooperation (NAALC), the NAFTA Labor Side Agreement, see United States National Administrative Office, "Public Report of Review of NAO Submission No 9701", 12 January 1998, available at the Department of Labor's website, http://www.dol.gov/ilab/media/reports/nao.

[363] ILO, Review 2005, Part II, p 29 quotes the new Chinese Work Safety Law of 2003, which gives workers a right to stop work and leave the workplace when they encounter a situation that directly endangers personal safety.

(2) that the inconsistent measures for which the exception was being invoked were necessary to fulfil the policy objective; and
(3) that the measures were applied in conformity with the requirements of the introductory clause of Article XX.[364]

C) The Necessity/Proportionality Test None of the Appellate Body and panel reports have questioned the environmental or health policy choices made by governments. Instead, Article XX is seen as designed to permit the consideration of important state interests. Member States therefore have a significant degree of autonomy in determining their own policies.[365] In order to assess their compatibility with WTO law, the Appellate Body developed a bifurcated necessity test that applies to the measure, not to the policy:[366] while under some circumstances a Member State may claim that the measure taken was the only one available to achieve its chosen level of protection, there are other situations in which a not indispensable measure is nevertheless necessary. In other words, if a measure is not indispensable, it must be proportional. If there is no alternative "reasonably available", the measure is consistent with Article XX(b).[367]

The values and interests at stake will in addition determine the level of scrutiny a panel has to apply in defining the necessity of the measures.[368] The protection of human life and health is considered "both vital and important in the highest degree" by the Appellate Body.[369]

D) Compliance with the Chapeau of Article XX The introductory clause or Chapeau of Article XX refers to the application of the measures taken by a Member State. It is seen as an expression of the principle of good faith.[370] It states that in order to be justified under any paragraph of this Article, the application of measures must not constitute "a means of arbitrary or unjustifiable discrimination between countries where the same conditions prevail, or a disguised restriction of international trade". The Appellate Body has stated that the word "discrimination" covers both discrimination between products from different supplier countries and discrimination between domestic and imported products.[371] In the context of labour rights, this means that a country cannot impose an import ban on, for example, products from Burma/Myanmar, while allowing the importation of similar products manufactured under similar

364 *United States—Standards for Reformulated and Conventional Gasoline*, Report of the Panel WT/DS2/R, 29 January 1996, para 6.20.
365 *US—Gasoline,* Report of the Appellate Body, note 336 above, at p 28.
366 *Korea—Measures Affecting Imports of Fresh, Chilled and Frozen Beef*, Report of the Appellate Body, 11 December 2000, WT/DS161/AB/R, WT/DS169/AB/R [hereinafter *Korea—Beef*] para 164.
367 This test was first developed in the *US—Section 337 of the Tariff Act of 1930*, Report of the Panel, 36S/345, adopted on 7 November 1989 [hereinafter *US—Section 337*], on Article XX(d) and then applied to Article XX(b) by the panel in *Thailand—Cigarettes*, note 355 above, para 75.
368 *EC—Asbestos*, note 304 above, para 172; *Korea—Beef*, note 366 above, paras 166 and 163.
369 *EC—Asbestos*, note 304 above, para 172.
370 *US—Shrimp/Turtles*, note 287 above, paras 158–59.
371 *US—Gasoline*, note 336 above, p 22.

conditions from China. Such a policy is unjustified discrimination under Article XX. Also, the same standards regarding labour rights must be applied to both domestic and imported products.

If the measures are not based on clear, transparent rules and do not comply with due process, it constitutes arbitrary discrimination.[372]

Finally, when is a measure a "disguised restriction of international trade"? In *Japan – Alcoholic Beverages* the Appellate Body suggested that the protective application of a measure can most often be discerned from its design, architecture and revealing structure.[373] The panel in *EC—Asbestos* conducted a particularly thorough analysis. As a result, three criteria have been established by the WTO dispute settlement organs to determine whether a measure is a disguised restriction on international trade: (1) the publicity test; (2) consideration of whether the application of a measure also amounts to arbitrary or unjustifiable discrimination; and (3) examination of "the design, architecture and revealing structure" of the measure.[374] In recent cases, emphasis has been put on the last of these three criteria.[375]

2.4. THE OECD

2.4.1. The General Purpose of the OECD

The history of the OECD begins with the Marshall Plan, which was set up for the reconstruction of Europe after the Second World War. The predecessor of the OECD, the Organisation for European Economic Cooperation (OEEC), was charged with the administration of the Marshall Plan. The goals of the organisation were the promotion of co-operation and commerce among Europe's reconstructed economies, development of a European customs union and ultimately, a free trade area. After the abrupt end of Marshall Plan aid in 1952, the OEEC remained active, focusing on free trade and European economic development, which later laid the ground for the creation of the European Economic Community (EEC) and the European Free Trade Area (EFTA).

The establishment of the EEC and the Cold War changed the role of the OEEC. Its role became more political in the ideological battle over centrally-controlled economies versus market economies. This was the reason why in 1960 the member countries decided to create a new organisation in its place, the

372 *US—Shrimp/Turtles*, note 287 above, paras 177, 180, 183.

373 *Japan—Alcoholic Beverages*, note 298 above, p 32. This analysis was undertaken in the context of Article III:4 but is applicable to Article XX too: *EC—Asbestos, Report of the Panel*, note 325 above, para 8.236.

374 WTO, Practice Article XX, note 331 above, para 79.

375 *United States—Import Prohibition of Certain Shrimp and Shrimp Products, Recourse to Article 21.5 of the DSU by Malaysia*, WT/DS58/AB/RW, 22 October 2001 [hereinafter *US—Shrimp (Article 21.5)*] paras 135–44.

Organisation for Economic Co-operation and Development (OECD). The founding treaty requires the organisation to promote policies designed:

(a) to achieve the highest sustainable economic growth and employment and a rising standard of living in Member countries, while maintaining financial stability, and thus to contribute to the development of the world economy;
(b) to contribute to sound economic expansion in Member as well as non-Member countries in the process of economic development; and
(c) to contribute to the expansion of world trade on a multilateral, non-discriminatory basis in accordance with international obligations.[376]

Today, the OECD has 30 members.[377] The only legal requirement for membership apart from unanimous approval of existing members is that an applicant has a market-based economy.[378] In contrast to other international organisations such as the Bretton Woods Institutions or the UN, the OECD is a very homogenous organisation of wealthy nations that produce two-thirds of the world's good and services.[379] In fact, it operates in a club-like atmosphere.

2.4.2. Labour Rights within the OECD

2.4.2.1. Consideration of Labour Rights

The OEEC's mission was more than simply disbursing funds and rebuilding a Europe based on free markets. Its core mission was equally to prevent support for communism and the re-emergence of fascism. This explains its longstanding consideration of labour issues. As a result of the emphasis that communist regimes put on workers, policy-makers in the West saw the need to give workers a voice in reconstruction, hoping to pre-empt their support of socialist communist parties.[380] Also, it must be borne in mind that attempts to democratise the regimes in East Germany (1953), Hungary (1956) and Czechoslovakia (1968) were violently suppressed by Soviet armed forces. As a result, the OECD created two non-governmental bodies in the field of labour: the Trade Union Advisory Committee (TUAC) and the Business Industry Advisory Committee (BIAC). TUAC consults regularly with OECD committees and provides feedback from the international labour community.

[376] Convention on the Organisation for Economic Co-operation and Development, 14 December 1960; SR 0.970.4.

[377] The member countries include the 21 original members (Western European countries, United States, Canada and the key NATO allies Turkey and Iceland) and 9 countries that joined later. The full list follows: Australia, Austria, Belgium, Canada, the Czech Republic, Denmark, Finland, France, Germany, Greece, Hungary, Iceland, Ireland, Italy, Japan, Korea, Luxemburg, Mexico, the Netherlands, New Zealand, Norway, Poland, Portugal, Spain, Sweden, Switzerland, Slovak Republic, Turkey, the United Kingdom, the United States.

[378] Articles 2 and 16 of the OECD Convention.

[379] http://www.oecd.org/about.

[380] Salzman (2000) 785–86.

The OECD has never established labour standards, and labour rights played no role in the OECD accession process until the 1990s when the Republic of Korea (South Korea) applied for membership. Human rights and labour rights are mentioned nowhere in the OECD Convention (and neither is democracy). As mentioned above, the only formal requirement is a commitment to a market-based economy. Since every new membership requires the consensus of the Council of Ministers, accession decisions are not legal in nature but largely determined by political considerations. TUAC and the International Confederation of Free Trade Unions (ICFTU) had long been concerned about Korean labour rights and seized the opportunity when Korea announced its wish to join the OECD. As a result, the Korean government promised to improve compliance with international labour standards in exchange for OECD membership. Although the relevant standards were never clearly defined, it was understood that the emphasis should lie on freedom of association and collective bargaining, in other words, the content of ILO Conventions Nos 87 and 98.[381]

Because several OECD member countries—including the US—have not ratified Conventions Nos 87 and 98, Korea was never asked formally to ratify them but rather to comply with their important requirements—as the US does. However, a few months after acceding to the OECD, Korea introduced new national laws that weakened labour rights and violated this understanding. The OECD Council then saw itself as being forced to react in order not to lose its credibility. For the first time, it set up a Special Monitoring Process, and the Secretariat is now in charge of monitoring labour developments in Korea.

The taken by the Council did not go as far as those of the ILO in the case of Burma/Myanmar, yet it has been widely acknowledged that the labour situation in South Korea improved in the following years. In light of this progress, Korea asked for the Monitoring Process to be suspended in June 2000. While Japan and other member countries supported Korea, the TUAC lobbied successfully to defeat the motion in the Council. Monitoring activities remain in place as of today.[382] Nevertheless there have been numerous incidents of police attacks on peacefully protesting union workers.

2.4.2.2. Reports on Labour Standards 1996 and 2000

The Directorate for Education, Employment, Labor and Social Affairs (ELSA) is the OECD's think tank. It focuses on analytical research, leaving political issues to the tripartite ILO. As a result, ELSA does not intend to develop labour standards but sticks to its core competence, economic analysis.

The first ELSA study, *Trade, Employment and Labour Standards: A Study of Core Worker's Rights and Labour Standards*, was published in 1996. A principal finding was the lack of evidence that countries with low core labour

[381] For relevant articles to Convention Nos 87 and 98, see Appendix A.9 and A.10.

[382] Salzman (2000), 801–4.

standards enjoy a better global export performance than countries with high standards. Moreover, there was no evidence that labour standards worsened in countries that liberalised trade or that labour rights impeded liberalisation. In summary, the study concluded that respect for core labour rights and economic development were mutually reinforcing.[383] In identifying core labour standards, ELSA worked closely with the ILO, thus paving the way for the later ILO Declaration on Fundamental Principles and Rights at Work.[384]

Because the publication of OECD studies and reports requires a complicated process of consultation among the Member States and ultimately their consensus,[385] there was considerable debate on the statement in the report about the respective roles of the WTO and ILO. The result was a vague statement that

> while some countries continue to call for a discussion of the issue [of core labour standards] in the WTO and others are opposed, this remains an issue for international consideration. The debate on this issue and on the associated conceptual and practical difficulties will continue.[386]

The study was conducted at a time of public discussion regarding possible linkages between trade and labour rights, and many had hoped for a clear statement from the experts at the OECD; unsurprisingly, they were disappointed.[387]

Although labour standards are not a traditional topic for the OECD, the 1996 study proved very influential because it was framed in terms of economic analysis—translating rights into economic impacts—and thereby brought labour rights into the ambit of the OECD.[388]

In 2000, a second OECD study, *International Trade and Core Labour Standards*, was published. It included important recent developments, in particular the first WTO Ministerial Meeting in Singapore in December 1996, the ILO Declaration on the Fundamental Principles and Rights at Work of 1998 and a review of the economic literature published since then. The study largely confirmed the results of the 1996 report and, in relation to freedom of association, clarified a somewhat controversial aspect of the 1996 study by stating that there is a positive association between the level of economic development and the respect for freedom of association.[389]

2.4.2.3. Multinational Agreement on Investment (MAI)

In 1995 the OECD Council decided, on the basis of research carried out by the Committee on Capital Movements and Invisible Transactions (CMIT), to negotiate a Multinational Agreement on Investment (MAI) in order to harmonise the

[383] For relevant articles to Convention Nos 87 and 98, see Appendix A.9 and A.10, 796–97.
[384] See chapter 1, section 1.2.2.3. above.
[385] This process is known as "derestriction". See Salzman (2000) 778.
[386] OECD (1996a) at 17.
[387] For a detailed critique, see Charnovitz (1997) 131–52.
[388] Salzman (2000) 800.
[389] OECD (2000) at 27 Box 3.

many existing investment treaties. The goal was to create by the end of 1997 the first comprehensive international investment treaty with uniform rules for foreign direct investment (FDI) protection, liberalisation and dispute settlement. The treaty would be open for non-member countries, and these countries would be granted observer status during the negotiations. The whole undertaking was thus seen as a mainly technical issue, fitting perfectly within the OECD's acknowledged role as the leading organisation for the protection of FDI.

The first phase of the negotiations passed without much public notice. However, the situation suddenly changed when the first draft was finished.[390] The draft was based on the principles of national treatment, most-favoured nation treatment and transparency. It required governments to treat foreign and local investment equally, thus giving new rights to multinational enterprises. For several countries and for many NGOs, a balance between these rights and corresponding obligations was missing. The main concern was that the proposed MAI would lead to a "race to the bottom", with governments lowering labour standards in the competition to attract foreign investment.

TUAC had raised the "race to the bottom" concern at an early stage of the negotiations by requesting *inter alia* that a binding obligation be included, such that parties would undertake not to attract foreign investment by suppressing domestic labour standards or violating internationally recognised workers' rights. Although the negotiators rejected this proposal, TUAC never publicly opposed the MAI. Instead, other NGOs stepped in. The spark was ignited in February 1997 when Ralph Nader's public citizens' group got hold of the Chairman's draft and published it on its website. Within months, a global campaign against the MAI was launched. The OECD, taken completely by surprise, was quick to include TUAC's demands, but it was too late. The NGO campaign had developed a life of its own and was used by several political leaders to address issues of domestic policy. As a case in point, when President Clinton made an attempt to revive the Fast Track procedure in Congress in early 1998, he sought support from NGOs by stating that the MAI was fatally flawed. In France, Prime Minister Jospin declared that the MAI jeopardised the sovereignty of the country and that as a result France would pull out of the negotiations. These actions doomed the MAI to failure, and the OECD announced on 3 December 1998 that there would be no more negotiations on the MAI.[391]

With this outcome, it seems likely that investment issues and their possible link to labour rights will be discussed at the WTO. In fact, investment is on the agenda for the negotiations on a new trade round under the Doha agreement.[392]

[390] The OECD has just released the documents on the negotiations. Of particular importance for labour rights issues are OECD, Negotiating Group on the Multilateral Agreement on Investment (MAI), "MAI and Environment and Labour Standards (Note by the Chairman)", DAFFE/MAI(97)30, 21 October 1997; and OECD, Negotiating Group on the Multilateral Agreement on Investment (MAI), "The MAI and Labour Standards (Note by the Chairman)", DAFFE/MAI(96)32, 3 December 1996.

[391] Salzman (2000) 814–28.

[392] Doha Declaration, para 20. See chapter 1 above, note 352 and accompanying text.

Whether a social clause will be included is unclear, given the Doha Declaration's reaffirmation of the Singapore Declaration.[393] However, the question remains: what have we learnt from the MAI experience, and how has the framework changed since?

2.5. CONCLUSIONS

The analysis of international economic organisations' approach to core labour rights shows that the current practice may result in conflicting obligations for member states and consequently inconsistencies in the international legal system.

However, international economic organisations can affect core labour rights in several respects. They can first *respect* them by adopting a "do no harm policy" and complying with core labour rights in their own activities. In addition, international organisations can actively *protect* core labour rights by incorporating them into their own programmes such as the World Bank does with child labour and gender equality. As we have seen, this mainstreaming approach carries the risk that institutions outside the ILO will interpret the content of the core labour standards for themselves. Since the BWIs tend to be economically focused, the already minimised core content of labour rights will be further limited by means of "economisation".

Furthermore, the analysis of the different organisations shows that, with the exception of the WTO, core labour rights—if addressed at all—are not framed as legally binding instruments but rather as soft law or expert advice. Whereas trade-related measures rely on detailed legal rules in the WTO framework, financial institutions are governed by soft law subject to the considerable influence of expert advice.

As a result, the nation-state is faced with the challenge of accommodating the different interests of different international organisations and of reconciling what seem to be inconsistent legal obligations. In addition, the key role of expert advice and soft law in financial institutions weakens the influence of the Member States and instead focuses on market participants. This shift away from the nation-state will be further explored in chapter 3 below, where the impact of cross-border activities and multinational enterprises in particular will be examined. Chapter 3 will look at the linkages between trade and core labour rights and at the different solutions available to address the tensions between the different fields and the different actors.

[393] See chapter 1 above, note 352 and accompanying text.

3

Cross-border Economic Activities: Multinational Enterprises and the Linkage Debate

Globalization, like golf, requires a handicapping system that allows the new players to catch up.

Patricia A Sto Tomas, President of the International Labour Conference 2001[1]

THE PREVIOUS TWO chapters have established the potential for conflicting obligations for states under international economic law and core labour standards. This chapter will now add another dimension to the relationship between states, international economic organisations and core labour standards by looking at non-state actors: multinational enterprises (MNEs).

Increasing cross-border economic activities have started to blur the boundaries not only between domestic and foreign companies but also between (international) trade law and (often domestically regulated) rights. This situation leaves states the dual problem of determining the extent of their regulatory authority and avoiding clashes between different legal regimes. Two examples illustrate this challenge: the role being played by the multinational enterprises and the relationship between labour rights and trade regulations. Chapter 3 will therefore first look at how the international community is addressing the problem of multinational enterprises. The relationship between trade and labour rights will then be explored. Should there be a link? What conflicts occur?

3.1. MULTINATIONAL ENTERPRISES (MNES)

3.1.1. MNEs under General International Law

Traditionally, international law has applied to sovereign states; acknowledging individuals as subjects of international law is a relatively recent phenomenon. While some human rights treaties such as the European Convention on Human

[1] In her presidential address to the International Labour Conference, 89th session, 2001.

Rights are interpreted in such a way as to grant specific rights to multinational enterprises,[2] their obligations under international law are less clear.[3] After the Second World War, private enterprises were *indirectly* held responsible for crimes against humanity if they had acted on behalf of the state[4] or if individuals in leading positions had been involved in the crime of genocide.[5] So far, no general *direct* legal responsibility of private enterprises has been established in international law. The Statute of the International Criminal Court (ICC) does not impose obligations on enterprises; they can be held accountable only if their actions can be attributed to individuals or states. Some scholars extend the concept of second liability as it is contained in Article 25(3)(c) and (d) of the ICC Statute, to include enterprises.[6] However, so far neither state practice nor the jurisprudence of international courts has confirmed this approach. Similarly, the new provisions on state responsibility suggested by the International Law Commission do not touch on corporate responsibility.[7]

The fact that MNEs do not fit into traditional legal systems has led to a need for specific regulations. Because they can organise production transnationally, MNEs have enormous corporate power and are often perceived as harmful to labour. The ease with which technology can be transferred abroad means that skilled jobs are often lost to low-wage countries.[8] In the 1970s, the number of reports about unethical and illegal activities undertaken by multinational corporations increased significantly,[9] leading to intensive discussions within international organisations, especially the United Nations, the Organisation for Economic Co-operation and Development (OECD) and the International Labour Organization (ILO). As a result, codes of conduct have been established to provide a stable and predictable framework in which MNEs conduct their business, with the intention of preventing abuse of workers and the environment on the one hand, and governments from trying to control MNEs on the other hand.[10]

Although the initiatives undertaken by several international bodies overlap widely, there are differences in motivation and results (Figure 3.1.).

[2] For a critical view, see Müller, JP (2005) 560–62, 571–72. The granted rights are rights to free speech in Article 10, to a fair trial in Article 6 and the right to privacy in Article 8. In addition, Article 1, Protocol 1 grants the right to property. Muchlinski (2001) 32.

[3] For a more detailed discussion see Breining-Kaufmann (2005) 119–35.

[4] International Military Tribunal (Nuremberg), Judgments and Decisions, 1 October 1946, reprinted in (1947) 41 *American Journal of International Law* 172–333, 241–43. See also *Barcelona Traction, Light and Power Co (Belgium v Spain)*, ICJ Reports 1970, 3, 42 at para 70.

[5] International Military Tribunal (Nuremberg), Judgments and Decisions, note 4 above, at 220.

[6] Clapham and Jerbi (2001) 342–49. For a detailed discussion see Clapham (2006) 237–51.

[7] Article 5 of the ILC Draft on State Responsibility holds states accountable for the conduct of entities that act with governmental authority. See International Law Commission, "State Responsibility, Draft Articles adopted by the International Law Commission at its fifty-third session", UN Doc A/CN.4/L.602 Rev.1 [Hereinafter ILC, Draft State Responsibility]. See also chapter 1 above, note 272.

[8] Held, McGrew, Goldblatt and Perraton (1999) 278.

[9] High-profile examples include the involvement of ITT and other US companies in the 1973 Chilean coup that overthrew President Allende and the series of bribes Lockheed paid to Japanese politicians for military contracts.

[10] According to the most comprehensive study available by Aaronson and Reeves (2002).

Figure 3.1. *Different Approaches to Dealing with Multinational Enterprises*

Year	Organisation	Motivation	Results
1976	**OECD** *Guidelines for Multinational Enterprises* as part of the Declaration and Decision on International Investment and Multinational Enterprises.	Response to MNEs as new players on the market and concerns of governments and international trade unions. Guidelines were drafted with input not only from governments, but also from social partners (BIAC and TUAC). Guidelines remained mainly untouched by revisions of the Declaration in 1979, 1984 and 1991. Substantial revision in June 2000 (see below).	Guidelines had some influence on conflict over labour rights in Europe in the early days of their adoption but eventually became less important.
1977	**United Nations** Commission on Transnational Corporations (established by ECOSOC) started work on a *Code of Conduct on Transnational Corporations* (TNCs). A draft code was published in 1983.[11] The draft code has 2 parts: one addresses the participating countries, the other, transnational corporations. For the definition of TNCs the draft refers to the relevant ILO documents.	The issue of a new International Economic Order was raised in general discussion. The main goal was to control the activities of TNCs in order to prevent abuses of TNC power and to bring them in line with the development goals of their host countries, especially developing countries. Focus was on partnership between developing and developed countries, less on human rights. Para 13: "Transnational corporations should/shall respect human rights and fundamental freedoms in the countries in which they operate."	The discussions did not come to a conclusion. In particular, no consensus was reached on provisions on the treatment of foreign investment.

[11] The draft can be found in UN Document E/1983/17/Rev. 1, Annex II, the report of the Secretary General on outstanding issues in UN Document E/C.10/1984/S/5, 29 May 1984.

Figure 3.1. *cont.*

Year	Organisation	Motivation	Results
1977	**ILO** *Tripartite Declaration of Principles concerning Multinational Enterprises and Social Policy*	Largely inspired by the OECD *Guidelines* (above). Concentrates on employment, training, working conditions and industrial relations. Addresses not only governments but employers, workers and MNEs. They do not go further than the OECD guidelines but are more detailed. The Declaration was revised in 2001 to include the Declaration on Fundamental Principles and Rights at Work	Widely accepted by governments but has little effect in practice.
1992	**World Bank** Report to the Development Committee and *Guidelines on the Treatment of Foreign Direct Investment*	Guidelines rely on the work of the UN Commission on TNCs and on the OECD Declaration on Multinational Enterprises and the work done by the ILO. They are meant to be a "checklist for national legislators" and attempt to reflect generally acceptable international standards. The Guidelines incorporate the OECD Declaration into the World Bank Group legal framework.	Substantial effect on several programmes within the World Bank and IMF Group.
1999	**UN** *Global Compact*	Aims to encourage global corporate citizenship with an instrument that does not rely on state regulations but holds companies	Many prominent companies have responded. Views of corporations are mixed.

		responsible on moral grounds. It is aimed directly at companies and covers labour rights, human rights and the environment. There is no formal accountability mechanism, but the Compact can be linked to SA 8000.	
2000	**OECD** *Guidelines for Multinational Enterprises* as part of the Declaration and Decision on International Investment and Multinational Enterprises	Substantial revision of the 1976 *Guidelines*, focusing on chapter entitled "Employment and Industrial Relations" in order to cover the new challenges by globalisation and to take into account recent legal developments within the ILO, EU and NAFTA. Corporations are now asked to try to hold their suppliers and subcontractors accountable.	Currently the most comprehensive guidelines, covering human rights, labour standards, environmental protection, corruption and information disclosure. 39 nations, including the non-members Argentina, Brazil, Chile, Estonia, Israel, Latvia, Lithuania, Romania and Slovenia, have signed the Guidelines.
2003	**UN Economic and Social Council** *Norms on the responsibilities of transnational corporations and other business enterprises with regard to human rights*	Emphasise the need to clarify business responsibilities. The *Norms* propose an implementation and monitoring process while leaving the primary responsibility to comply with human rights obligations with the respective Member States.	Welcomed by NGOs, although governments and enterprises have reacted cautiously.

3.1.2. Standards as Solutions?

Susan Aaronson, who has done extensive research on corporate responsibility, differentiates between four categories of strategies that address corporate conduct.[12] Codes of conduct are *aspirational*: they describe how companies and their employees should behave. Such codes include the UN Global Compact, the Caux Principles and the Global Sullivan Principles. They are non-binding, and most of them do not include enforcement or follow-up mechanisms. Because of the drawbacks of these strategies, a different approach was sought by encouraging executives to report and monitor their own social and environmental performance. *Reporting standards* are tools to facilitate reporting of what and how companies are doing. They include the Global Reporting Initiative (GRI) and Social Accountability 8000 (SA 8000). These standards are widely used; an estimated 64 per cent of the world's largest companies disclose social and environmental activities and progress on their websites.[13] However, there are no uniform or universally accepted reporting standards. As a result, *general standards* were developed as a framework with which stakeholders can assess corporate codes of conduct. These include the Principles for Global Corporate Responsibility-Benchmarks. Finally, scholars have called on governments to pass national legislation that requires businesses to adhere to high standards regardless of where they operate. International institutions have responded to these calls, and *Government-sponsored codes* now include the OECD Guidelines and the ILO Principles. The most recent example, the UN Draft Norms on Corporate Responsibilities belongs in this category.[14]

Of the four types of strategies for dealing with corporate conduct, the following sections will focus on international responses.

3.1.2.1. The UN Global Compact

In 1999, after several failed attempts to insert a social clause into WTO law and thereby formally link trade and labour rights, and under the pressure of increasing frustration among NGOs and civil society, the UN Secretary-General Kofi Annan proposed a different strategy and a different forum at the World Economic Forum in Davos. He challenged business leaders to enact the *Global Compact*—ten core principles on labour standards, human rights and environmental protection (Figure 3.2.).[15]

[12] Aaronson and Reeves (2002). For an excellent overview on existing standards, see Aaronson (2001), Chart 1 at 42–45. See also Hepple (2005) 72–76.

[13] Aaronson and Reeves (2002) note 5 and accompanying text.

[14] UN Sub-Commission on the Promotion and Protection of Human Rights, "Norms on the Responsibilities of Transnational Corporations and Other Business Enterprises with Regard to Human Rights", 13 August 2003, UN Doc E/CN.4/Sub.2/2003/12/Rev.2.

[15] The Global Compact is available at http://www.globalcompact.org.

What is the global compact?

"A global compact of shared values and principles, which will give a human face to the global market" (Kofi Annan)

Human Rights

The Secretary-General asked world business to:

Principle 1: support and respect the protection of international human rights within their spheres of influence; and

Principle 2: make sure their own corporations are not complicit in human rights abuses.

Labour

The Secretary-General asked world business to uphold:

Principle 3: freedom of association and the effective recognition of the right to collective bargaining;

Principle 4: the elimination of all forms of forced and compulsory labour;

Principle 5: the effective abolition of child labour; and

Principle 6: the elimination of discrimination in respect of employment and occupation.

Environment

The Secretary-General asked world business to:

Principle 7: support a precautionary approach to environmental challenges;

Principle 8: undertake initiatives to promote greater environmental responsibility; and

Principle 9: encourage the development and diffusion of environmentally friendly technologies.

Anti-Corruption

Principle 10: Businesses should work against all forms of corruption, including extortion and bribery.

Figure 3.2. *The Global Compact*

The Secretary-General hoped that the compact would improve global corporate governance without the need for national or international regulation, ie "hard law". If the ten principles become an integral part of economic activities, economic rules and social principles might be more balanced. As a merely aspirational tool, however, the compact includes no enforcement or accountability mechanisms, and companies can only demonstrate their adherence to it by taking (corporate) action. Company reports on the measures taken are published on the UN Global Compact website. Most recently, the Compact has established an Advisory Council to disseminate the idea more effectively. Governments do not play an active role in the global compact.

3.1.2.2. The UN Norms on Corporate Responsibilities

In August 2003, the UN Sub-Commission on the Promotion and Protection of Human Rights unanimously adopted the Norms on the Responsibilities of Transnational Corporations and Other Business Enterprises with Regard to Human Rights.[16] The Norms do not define new responsibilities but restate existing international legal principles that are applicable to businesses. Paragraph 1 of the Norms emphasise that states have primary responsibility for compliance with human rights. This responsibility includes ensuring that transnational corporations and other business enterprises respect human rights. The Norms cover a broad range of human rights, including labour rights in paragraphs 5–9. In its commentary, the sub-commission refers to the respective ILO Conventions and applies their main principles to corporations and businesses.[17] The principle of non-discrimination is not contained in the section on workers' rights but in paragraph 2 of the Norms where a general right to equal opportunity and non-discriminatory treatment is affirmed.

The Norms are the result of a long drafting process that involved various stakeholders, including other international organisations such as the ILO and several NGOs.[18] What makes the Norms so important is that they are the first non-voluntary initiative to be accepted at the international level.[19] Ideally, from the drafters' point of view, the Commission on Human Rights will eventually adopt the Norms.

Reactions to the Norms at the 60th session of the Commission on Human Rights in spring 2004 were mixed: while NGOs welcomed them as a step towards more clarity regarding obligatory business responsibilities, several governments, including the United States, United Kingdom, Saudi Arabia, Egypt and India, argued that the Norms are a duplication of work of other bodies of the UN system and should therefore be taken off the agenda of the Commission on Human Rights. Very few states, such as Switzerland, declared their support for the Norms.

In addition to government resistance, the norms were opposed by business groups, chiefly the International Chamber of Commerce and others. Their key argument was that the proposed Norms, by introducing new obligations to respect what were only vaguely-defined human rights, would discourage investment and therefore be counterproductive. In addition, it was argued that existing voluntary standards were sufficient to protect human rights and were more flexible in their application. Finally, it was pointed out that private companies

[16] Note 14 above.

[17] UN Sub-Commission on the Promotion and Protection of Human Rights, "Commentary on the Norms on the Responsibilities of Transnational Corporations and Other Business Enterprises with Regard to Human Rights", 26 August 2003, UN Doc E/CN.4/Sub.2/2003/Rev.2.

[18] Weissbrodt and Kruger (2003) 903–7; Lucke (2005) 148–50.

[19] Weissbrodt and Kruger (2003) 903.

are not subjects of international law and are therefore bound only by domestic rules.[20]

Given the complexity of the legal issues surrounding the Norms, the UN Secretary General in 2005 appointed a Special Representative for human rights, transnational corporations and other business enterprises, John Ruggie.[21]

3.1.2.3. The OECD Guidelines

In 1976, the OECD Council of Ministers adopted a recommendation entitled the Declaration and Decision on International Investment and Multinational Enterprises. As its name suggests, the main purpose of the Declaration was to promote transnational investment. One of the seven chapters of the Declaration outlined a set of voluntary rules of conduct for MNEs that are referred to as Guidelines. It was hoped that the Guidelines would ensure that the operations of MNEs would live up to the expectations of host countries by establishing a baseline of labour rights. Both the Trade Union Advisory Council (TUAC) and the Business and Industry Advisory Council (BIAC) supported the Guidelines.

The Guidelines have been amended four times: in 1979, 1984, 1991 and 2000. In 1991, a new chapter on the environment was added. Since the most recent revision, approved in June 2000, the preamble to the Guidelines explicitly refers to the ILO Declaration on Fundamental Principles and Rights at Work; and in Chapter IV, the most significant additions focus on human rights.[22] As a result of the MAI experience,[23] the revision process was more inclusive than ever before. For the first time, the responsible Committee on International Investment and Multinational Enterprises (CIME) actively sought input from outside the OECD, asking for public comments and the opinion of the ILO.[24]

A) The legal nature of the Guidelines The Guidelines are recommendations addressed by governments to multinational enterprises that operate in or from countries that adhere to the Guidelines. Although they are not substitutes for national laws, to which MNEs are fully subject, they can be used as a means of clarification when interpreting national laws. A good example are the OECD rules on money laundering, which while not legally binding, are applied by most Member States when interpreting and reviewing domestic regulations. Some states have even incorporated them into national legislation.

[20] United States Council for International Business, "Talking Points on the Draft Norms on the Responsibilities of Transnational Corporations and Other Business Enterprises with Regard to Human Rights", 2003.

[21] UN DocE/CN.4/Res.2005/69 establishing the mandate and the first interim report, E/CN.4/2006/97, 22 February 2006.

[22] OECD, Working Party on the OECD Guidelines for Multinational Enterprises, "The OECD Guidelines for Multinational Enterprises: Text, Commentary and Clarifications", DAFFE/IME/WPG (2000)15/FINAL, 31 October 2001.

[23] See chapter 2, section 2.4.2.3. above.

[24] Salzman (2000) 795.

There are several ways in which the Guidelines appear to function as soft law. First of all, they rely on a broad consensus of not only governments but also the BIAC and the TUAC. In addition, the Guidelines are based on the most recent research and are thus "state of the art". Because of the OECD's reputation as a premier economic research institution, its standards and guidelines are widely respected and applied by those in the industry, including rating agencies and investment firms. This creates a fact-based, economic pressure and incentive for countries to comply with OECD standards, which then have some legal effect.

With regard to labour and human rights issues, the Guidelines aim to deal with the effects of globalisation and especially of new developments in international business such as structural change, large-scale international mergers and the blurring boundaries between enterprises. It is the Guidelines' explicit goal to balance the positive contributions that multinational enterprises can make to economic and social progress against the difficulties to which their activities may give rise.

Because the Guidelines are seen as principles and standards of good practice and not as legally binding, there is no need for a precise definition of what constitutes a multinational enterprise. This open approach reflects the fact that there is no "typical" multinational enterprise in the business world today.

Given the non-binding character of the Guidelines, their successful implementation is heavily dependent on their being known by the businesses concerned. Participating national governments have therefore established National Contact Points as forums for discussion on all issues related to the Guidelines. The role that these contact points play in practice varies widely from country to country. Generally, they play a much more active role in Europe than in the US.[25]

B) General Policies The Guidelines very carefully position themselves in relation to other relevant international agreements and regulations such as those of the WTO. The Guidelines recognise that national laws concerning human rights differ between the member countries and that these differences can lead to conflicts in practice. When dealing with this issue earlier, the OECD came to the conclusion that such conflicting requirements on multinational enterprises could indeed create difficulties, which ought to be brought to then attention of the Committee on International Investment and Multinational Enterprises (CIME).[26] Not surprisingly, it is now clearly stated that multinational enterprises are required in the first place to comply with the rules of their host country.[27]

In addition, the Guidelines also deal with new developments in the markets they are aiming at. In particular, given that many multinational enterprises have

[25] Aaronson and Reeves (2002); OECD, "OECD Guidelines for Multinational Enterprises: 2005 Annual Meeting of the National Contact Points", Report by the Chair, Paris, 2005.

[26] "Conflicting requirements imposed on multinational enterprises: General considerations and practical approaches", Decision of the OECD Council (June 1991).

[27] Section II(2).

established internal codes of conduct and that supervisory authorities in different areas of business have abandoned their former authoritative approach in favour of self-regulation procedures, the Guidelines encourage the application and the further development of self-regulatory practices.[28]

The Guidelines assume that enterprises should be seen by governments as partners and vice versa. On the one hand, this provision aims at providing multinational enterprises with the stability and predictability that are required by governmental policy. On the other hand, it also reflects the fact that governments depend heavily on the information made available by multinational enterprises. As recent international mergers have shown, governments are quite often not informed early enough of important developments and as a consequence are not able to handle efficiently the repercussions of, for example, large lay-offs.

C) Disclosure The provisions on disclosure in section III of the OECD Guidelines reflect the fact that multinational enterprises as such are not subject to the implementation procedures set up by the OECD. The only possible way to keep track of their activities and their internationally diversified organisational structures is to encourage them to provide transparent, high-quality information. This requirement, as stated by the Guidelines, has to be seen together with current accounting and auditing standards, as set up by the relevant international accounting organisations.

These requirements on disclosure provide a relatively firm basis for the human rights discussed in the next paragraph.

D) Employment and industrial relations As far as substantive human rights are concerned, section IV(1) of the Guidelines refers to the core principles and core human rights as defined by the ILO. In addition to the general information that is needed to exercise the rights, section IV(2) and (3) require more detailed information for employees as well as the provision of facilities to allow them to exercise their rights. As simple as these provisions seem at first sight, they have played a significant role in some of the major labour conflicts in Europe over the last few years. In many European countries the managements of industries are no longer willing to negotiate wages with the trade unions of an entire sector, dealing instead only with the employees' representatives within the corporation, and only for each individual business unit. Information and transparency have therefore become major issues.

Although geographical boundaries are becoming less important for multinational enterprises, the Guidelines nevertheless state that, as a minimum requirement, standards of employment and industrial relations must reach a level that is comparable to others in the host country. However, this leaves open the possibility of applying lower standards in a less developed country than in

[28] Section II(7).

an industrialised one. This provision must therefore be seen as a way to protect multinational enterprises from conflicting requirements.

Lastly, in an attempt to address the concerns of developing countries, the Guidelines encourage multinational companies to employ and train local personnel.

E) Implementation In setting up a formal procedure to handle disputes related to the Guidelines, the OECD Council decided on a package for implementation.[29] The implementation of the Guidelines relies on two bodies: the National Contact Points and the Committee on Investment and Multinational Enterprises (CIME).

In principle, National Contact Points are set up by the adhering countries for undertaking promotional activities and handling inquiries and discussion. The National Contact Points in the different countries should co-operate and exchange views. For this purpose, they should meet annually and report to the CIME. In practice so far, the effect of these National Contact Points, which are often government offices, varies greatly from country to country.

Within the OECD, the CIME is the body responsible for overseeing the functioning of the Guidelines, but because the Guidelines are non-binding, the CIME cannot act as a judicial body. Its main tasks consist in organising exchanges of view, issuing clarifications and in reporting to the OECD Council. It is important that—because of the non-binding character of the Guidelines—clarifications are not judgments in individual cases but rather more general interpretations of the Guidelines.[30]

Business and labour representatives are not formally bound to the implementing structure. However, they can request consultations with the National Contact Point on issues related to the OECD Guidelines.

3.1.2.4. The ILO Tripartite Declaration

The ILO Tripartite Declaration on Principles Concerning Multinational Enterprises and Social Policy grew out of a consensus reached in 1977 by the ILO's Governing Body. Unlike the Declaration on Fundamental Principles and Rights at Work, it was not adopted by the Annual Conference but by the Governing Body with a limited membership of governments, workers' organisations and employers' organisations. It therefore has less formal standing than the Declaration on Fundamental Principles and Rights at Work.

A) The Legal Nature of the ILO Tripartite Declaration Paragraph 7 of the Declaration states that the principles should be observed on a voluntary basis.

[29] "The OECD Guidelines for Multinational Enterprises", Decision of the Council and Procedural Guidance, June 2000, available at http://www.oecd.org/.

[30] OECD, Working Party on the OECD Guidelines for Multinational Enterprises, "The OECD Guidelines for Multinational Enterprises: Text, Commentary and Clarifications", DAFFE/IME/WPG (2000)?15/FINAL, 31 October 2001, pp 45, 48.

The use of the terms "encourage", "commended" and "recommended" throughout the Declaration underlines its non-binding character. The fact that the principles were adopted in a non-binding manner and by the Governing Body only, is due to political obstacles at the time. In addition, legal reasons played a role: it was difficult to define precisely what constitutes an MNE, so the term was deliberately left vague; moreover the attempt to encompass non-state actors that are not subjects of international law (eg, workers' and employers' organisations) created conceptual difficulties.

B) The Contents of the Tripartite Declaration The Declaration on Principles addresses the responsibilities of both public and private sectors. It seeks to integrate corporate activities in international investment with public pursuit of sustainable development and core labour rights in general and the ILO decent work agenda specifically.[31] It is thought of as a guideline for governments, employers' and workers' organisations as well as the MNEs themselves in adopting social policies. It thus attempts to balance responsibilities among the players.

The Declaration recommends a set of minimum benchmarks for good investment policy and practice by private and public actors and contains four main principles. Above all it aims at the realisation of the fundamental principles and rights at work according to the corresponding ILO Declaration. Along the lines of the general ILO mandate, it then attempts to promote employment and income, to enhance social protection and social security and finally to strengthen dialogue among the key players—government, business and labour. The benchmarks are based on ILO conventions and recommendations. They cover employment issues such as training, non-discrimination, security of employment, wages, benefits and working conditions, health and safety, freedom of association and the right to organise.

Article 8 refers to the Universal Declaration of Human Rights and the corresponding international covenants on civil and political rights and on economic, social and cultural rights, stating that governments, employers and trade unions should respect them. Significantly, it also emphasises the importance of freedom of expression and freedom of association for workers' rights.[32]

C) Implementation The Tripartite Declaration establishes a follow-up procedure based on three pillars: reporting through global surveys; an interpretation procedure; and an office-coordinated programme of applied research, promotional activities and advisory and liaison services.

A key element of the survey process is the three-way input by governments, business and labour. A questionnaire is first agreed on by business, labour and governments and then sent to governments, workers' and employers' organisations in all ILO member countries. The procedure results in a lengthy report that provides extensive details on the activities of MNEs but does not disclose their

[31] Diller (2001) at I.
[32] ICHRP (2002) 69.

names.[33] The reports would be more useful if specific MNEs were named and if they were given an opportunity to reply to allegations of non-compliance with the Tripartite Declaration. In addition, the conclusions that are drawn from the extensive compilation of data are restricted to fairly minor procedural improvements.

When the meaning of the Tripartite Declaration is disputed, governments can ask a sub-committee of the Governing Body to provide interpretation. Workers' and employers' organisations can also ask for interpretation, but only if their governments take no action. According to the ILO tradition, the sub-committee is a tripartite organ. When a request is admitted, the chairpersons and the International Labour Office draft a response that must be adopted by the sub-committee and the Governing Body.

Since the procedure began in 1986, a number of requests for assistance have been made, but only four of these have resulted in interpretations.[34] Similar to the case of the OECD, an interpretation does not judge the conduct of a specific company or even suggest remedies for victims. However, because the ILO is now recognised as the leading authority on labour rights,[35] NGOs see the interpretation mechanism as a potential tool for clarifying ambiguities about the standards that companies should follow.[36]

These implementation procedures are complemented by the third pillar of the ILO follow-up, which is comprised of studies and research as well as promotional and advisory activities.

The as yet limited effect of the Tripartite Declaration can be traced to the fact that it is institutionalised within a sub-committee of the Governing Body, a relatively low level for ILO standards. Virginia Leary brings the situation into focus when she states:

> The timidity of the ILO twenty-two years ago when the Declaration was adopted was perhaps understandable, but is less so today when the subject of labor rights and multinational enterprises is so clearly on the international agenda. At a minimum, the ILO might reconsider the manner in which the Report is written to make it more readable, more understandable and more focused on issues.[37]

3.1.3. Conclusions

Although the concept of core labour rights provides a sufficient basis for extending obligations to multinational enterprises, the existing codes and guidelines show a strong preference for voluntary approaches. As already noted with

[33] ILO, Seventh Survey, GB 280/MNE/1 and GB 280/MNE/2, March 2001.
[34] Five cases have so far been brought before the Committee on Multinational Enterprises for interpretation: http://www.ilo.org/public/english/employment/multi/case.htm.
[35] Singapore and Doha Declaration, see chapter 1 above, note 352 and accompanying text.
[36] ICHRP (2002) 103.
[37] Leary (2003) 196.

respect to the ILO Declaration on Fundamental Principles and Rights at work, the main problem with these approaches is the lack of efficient monitoring procedures.[38] They are, in Bob Hepple's words, "rich in Principles but weak in enforcement".[39]

Core labour rights impose an obligation on states to prevent abuses of these rights by businesses, thus holding businesses indirectly accountable. Given the political difficulties of reaching a consensus for an international legally binding agreement, the legal gap left open by the voluntary instruments could be best filled by the state. By incorporating voluntary standards such as the OECD Guidelines and the ILO Tripartite Declaration into domestic law, states could play an important role in the building of an international law of business responsibility.[40]

3.2. LINKS BETWEEN FREE TRADE AND LABOUR RIGHTS

While the first section of this chapter has dealt with the emergence of MNEs as new actors, this section will address the question of a potential link between core labour rights and (international) trade law. The focus will therefore be on substantial law.

3.2.1. The Current Debate

Philip Alston's early grasp of the problem notwithstanding,[41] the debate about a possible link between free trade and labour rights seems fairly new.[42] Its inception can be traced to the time of the establishment of the WTO in 1994. The relationship between trade liberalisation and human rights generally has been on the international agenda, primarily at the behest of NGOs. In the context of core labour rights specifically, developing countries argue that they risk losing their competitive advantage if they are compelled to adhere to higher labour standards. In contrast, NGOs and some developed countries contend that trade liberalisation must not be governed solely by economic considerations but should also take into account fundamental human rights such as core labour rights; these rights are as important as, if not *more* important than trade regulations.

Widespread dispute over the relationship between trade and labour rights has meant that there are many and varied approaches to the issue of regulation (see Figure 3.3.),[43] and the transnational labour regulations adopted by states differ

[38] ICHRP (2002) 159–63.
[39] Hepple (2005) 83.
[40] Breining-Kaufmann (2005) 120–30.
[41] Alston (1980) 126–58; Alston (1982) 155–83.
[42] Cottier (2002); Alston (2005b) 1–24.
[43] The most comprehensive analysis on which this section draws is that by Van Wezel Stone (1996) 470.

from country to country. A first distinction within the large body of transnational labour regulations can be made with regard to participants: regulation can be unilateral or multilateral. A second criterion refers to the level and scope of legislation: is it transnational or domestic?

Transnational rules that have an *integrative* effect can be established by preemptive rules or harmonisation. *Preemptive* rules set an international standard that is binding for all the contracting parties and directly applicable. *Harmonisation* on the other hand sets the framework for domestic legislation.

Figure 3.3. *Models of Labour Regulation*

		Multilateral Implementation	**Unilateral Implementation**
Transnational Regulations	*Integrative* approaches	*Pre-emptive legislation* — EC Treaty: Arts 39–42 — EC Regulations	*Harmonisation* — EC Directive on Equal Treatment[44] — EC Directives on Public Procurement[45] — EC Directive on the Posting of Workers[46] — ILO Convention
	Interpenetrative approaches	*Cross-border monitoring and enforcement* — NAFTA Labor Side Agreement (NAALC)[47] — US–Jordan Free Trade Agreement[48]	*Extraterritorial jurisdiction* — *Aramco* case[49] — Generalized System of Preferences (GSP)[50]
National Regulations	*Integrative* approaches		*Universal jurisdiction* — *Pinochet* case
			Extraterritorial jurisdiction — Alien Tort Claims Act (ATCA)
			Domestic regulations

[44] Directive 76/207/EEC on the Implementation of the Principle of Equal Treatment for Men and Women, OJ 1976 L 39, p 40; Decision of the ECJ in *Tanja Kreil v Bundesrepublik Deutschland* [2000] ECR I-00069, 11 January 2000.

[45] Section 3.2.2.4. below.

[46] Note 293 below and accompanying text.

[47] Section 3.2.2.2. below.

[48] Section 3.2.2.3. below.

[49] *EEOC v Arabian American Oil Co* 499 USR 246.

[50] Section 3.2.2.1. below for the USA and section 3.2.2.4. below for the EU.

In other words, such rules are not directly applicable but need to be implemented unilaterally by national law. Yet even pure domestic legislation can become internationally relevant or *interpenetrative*—using the word of Katherine Van Wezel Stone—either by allowing for extraterritorial jurisdiction or establishing cross-border monitoring and enforcement. In addition, unilateral provisions and measures can refer to international legal standards and thus be simultaneously unilateral and integrative. Examples are the US Alien Tort Claims Act,[51] which refers to international human rights and provides for extraterritorial jurisdiction, and the decisions in the *Pinochet* case,[52] which have been viewed as a step towards universal jurisdiction for severe violations of fundamental human rights—a highly controversial issue.[53]

The main approaches will be discussed in the next chapters, followed by a discussion on how labour rights actually enter WTO law and what legal problems occur. Some remarks on regulatory competition and the feared race to the bottom will conclude the topic.

3.2.2. Unilateral and Regional Approaches to Labour Rights

3.2.2.1. The United States

Attempts to link trade and labour rights started in early 1890 when the importation of slaves was prohibited and foreign goods manufactured by convicted labour were banned. In 1930, the Hawley-Smoot Tariff Act was enacted to forbid imports made by forced labour or indentured labour under penal sanctions.[54] The law is still in effect but only sporadically enforced.

The American Federation of Labor (AFL), established in 1881 as the Federation of Organized Trades and Labor Unions, urged Congress to protect American industry against imports from low-wage countries. The principle was incorporated in the Tariff Acts of 1922 and 1930 and became known as "cost equalization". The President was empowered to adjust tariffs in order to equalise the differences in the costs of production between a domestic article and a similar foreign article from the principal competing country.[55] With the National Industrial Recovery Act of 1933, Congress gave the President the authority to impose codes of "fair competition" on domestic industries.

[51] 28 USC § 1350 (1994).

[52] Decision by the House of Lords, 24 March 1999, *Regina v Bow Street Stipendiary Magistrate, ex parte Pinochet Ugarte (No 3)* [2000] 1 AC 147.

[53] The decision of the ICJ in the *Case Concerning the Arrest Warrant of 11 April 2000 (Democratic Republic of the Congo v Belgium)*, 14 February 2002, ICJ Reports 2002, 3, and in particular the separate opinion of President Guillaume cast some doubt as to the future position of the ICJ towards universal jurisdiction. See also the joint separate opinion of judges Higgins, Kooijmans and Buergenthal.

[54] Tariff Act of 1930, chapter 497, 46 Stat 689 (1930); current version at 19 USC § 1307.

[55] Charnovitz (1987) 568.

More recent initiatives include the Generalized System of Preferences (GSP) under the 1974 Trade Act,[56] the Caribbean Basin Initiative (CBI) of 1983,[57] the Overseas Private Investment Corporation (OPIC),[58] the Omnibus Trade and Competitiveness Act of 1988,[59] which amended the 1974 Trade Act with regard to labour rights, and finally Executive Order 13126 on Child Labor.[60] In addition, selective purchasing laws have been adopted by several states. The following chapter will focus on the most relevant policies: the measures adopted under the Trade Act, the Executive Order on Child Labor, the selective purchasing laws and finally the Alien Tort Claims Act.

A) The Trade Act (1974)

a) **Sections 301–106[61]** The predecessor of Section 301, the Trade and Expansion Act of 1962, had been adopted to address the fear that European integration would shut out the US from the European market. Its Section 252 gave the President the authority to retaliate against foreign practices that discriminated against US exports. Section 301 of the Trade Act of 1974 was a response to the fact that many markets seemed too closed in comparison to the relatively open US market. It enabled the President to take an even wider range of retaliatory actions against any country that has "unjustifiable" or "unreasonable" import restrictions or any export subsidies that reduce the sales of US goods abroad. Thus, it broadened both the definition of unfair trade and the scope of retaliatory measures.[62] Although a powerful tool, Section 301 was seldom used and rarely successfully. Frustrated by presidential unwillingness to promote it more actively, Congress amended Section 301 with the Omnibus Trade and Competitiveness Act of 1988, which included, *inter alia*, the compliance with labour rights as a condition for most-favoured nation status. This amendment is often referred to as "Super 301".[63]

Section 301 contains two branches. First, the United States Trade Representative (USTR) can take action if a foreign country violates legal provisions. Section 301(c) provides a broad spectrum of measures, including bringing the case to the WTO dispute settlement organs. As such, Section 301 could serve as a vehicle for unions to bring a claim to the WTO. Section 304 gives the USTR discretion in unilaterally determining whether US rights are being denied before any procedure is started under the Dispute Settlement Understanding (DSU) of the

[56] 19 USC § 2462(c)(7) (2000).

[57] *Ibid*, § 2702(c)(8) (1994) with amendment in 19 USC § 2703(b)(5)(B)(iii) (2000). Caribbean Basin Economic Recovery Act, PL 98-67 (1983), Section 212(c)(8).

[58] 22 USC §§ 2191a (a)(1) (1994) and 2199(i) (1982 and Supp III 1985).

[59] 19 USC § 2901, PubL No 100-418, § 2423(a), 102 Stat 1107 (1988).

[60] Executive Order 13126 of 12 June 1999: Prohibition of Acquisition of Products produced by Forced or Indentured Child Labor.

[61] 19 USC § 2411–20.

[62] Milner (1990) 165.

[63] *Ibid*, 163; Hudec (1999) 13.

WTO.[64] This could be seen as a violation of Article 23 DSU, which requires member countries to follow the multilateral rules and procedures of the DSU in the case of a dispute. In fact, precisely this claim was brought before the WTO by the European Communities.[65] However, the US Statement of Administrative Action (SAA),[66] which accompanied the US legislation that implemented the results of the Uruguay Round, clarifies that the administration intends to use its discretion *in compliance* with the DSU. The panel considered this statement to be sufficient to guarantee the application of Section 304 in accordance with the rules of the DSU.[67]

The second branch of Section 301 addresses situations in which no legal rights are breached but allows measures to be taken against acts, policies or practices of a foreign country that are unreasonable or unjustifiable and burden or restrict US commerce. The provision is very controversial, especially when it comes to defining what "unreasonable" means. The amendment of 1988 clarified this point with regard to labour rights: Section 301(d) 3B now states that the denial of specifically enumerated worker rights constitutes an unreasonable trade practice.[68] A country engaging in such a practice may be subjected to a wide variety of sanctions imposed by the executive branch without further reference to Congress and without the right to appeal.[69]

As noted in chapter 1,[70] the US has made several attempts to include labour rights in the GATT/WTO agreement. These initiatives can be traced back to Section 121(a)(4) of the 1974 Trade Act, where it was recognised that the best way of linking trade and labour rights is within a multilateral framework.

Developing countries in particular argued that Section 301 expresses US cultural values and attempts to impose them on every country. From a domestic point of view, Helen Milner referred to these as "US revenge fantasy".[71] She pointed out that "Super 301" makes the US into a judge assessing foreign countries—an infringement on their sovereignty that will provoke resistance. In addition, the US would be judging its own case. On the other hand, there is a civil disobedience aspect to the concept: trade will become freer because countries have to eliminate barriers. The US does not need to apply Section 301 to reach its goal; all it takes is the threat.[72]

[64] Understanding on Rules and Procedures Governing the Settlement of Disputes, Annex 2 to the Marrakesh Agreement Establishing the World Trade Organization.

[65] *United States—Sections 301–10 of the Trade Act of 1974*, Report of the Panel, WT/DS152/R, 22 December 1999 [hereinafter *US—Sections 301*].

[66] Submitted by the President to Congress: 1994 House Report No 103-826, 1994 US Code Cong and Admin News, p 3773.

[67] *US—Sections 301*, note 65 above, paras 7.125–7.126.

[68] The rights include the right of association and the right to organise and bargain collectively, the abolition of forced or compulsory labour, the provision of a minimum age for the employment of children and the provision of standards for minimum wages, hours of work and occupational safety and health for workers. Non-discrimination is not included in the list.

[69] Alston (1993) 4.

[70] Chapter 1 above, note 346 above and accompanying text.

[71] Milner (1990) 168–74.

[72] *Ibid*, 176; Sykes (1992) 250–51.

Notably, Section 301 and especially "Super 301" have rarely been applied.

Before engaging in a more detailed discussion on unilateral and regional measures, it must be borne in mind that unilateral sanctions do not violate customary international law but might be incompatible with treaty obligations.[73]

b) Most-Favoured Nation Status The granting of most-favoured nation (MFN) status to communist countries is conditioned on the state's overall protection of fundamental human rights.[74] Under this policy, MFN status was withdrawn from Poland in 1982, following the suppression of the solidarity labour union movement by the martial law government.[75]

Another constant source of controversy has been China's MFN status. While President Clinton made MFN treatment conditional on compliance with various human rights after the Tiananmen massacre in 1989, business support for trade relations with China and the need to win China's co-operation with non-nuclear proliferation policies aimed at North Korea led him to renew China's MFN status and unlink trade from human rights in 1994. Finally, trade relations with China were normalised in 2000 despite the deteriorating human rights situation.[76]

c) Sections 501–5[77] Sections 501–5 make the status of a privileged trading partner conditional on, *inter alia*,

> taking steps to afford internationally recognised worker rights to workers in the country (including any designated zone in that country).[78]

The reference to worker rights was included in 1984 under the Generalized System of Preferences (GSP) Renewal Act.[79] Unlike Section 301, the GSP provisions apply to only countries designated by the President, in other words, developing countries. The scope of the protected worker rights is the same as under Section 301. Again, non-discrimination is excluded.

The GSP system has been the primary trade provision utilised to promote labour rights. Both labour unions and NGOs frequently request review of GSP

[73] See the decision of the ICJ in the Nicaragua case: *Military and Paramilitary Activities in and against Nicaragua, Nicaragua v United States of America*, Jurisdiction and Admissibility, ICJ Reports 1984, 319, at 447.

[74] Section 402 of the Trade Act of 1974, introduced by the Jackson-Vanik Amendment of the Trade Act of 1974, 19 USC § 2432 (1994).

[75] Suspension of the Application of Column 1 Rates of Duty of the Tariff Schedules of the United States to the Products of Poland, 47 Fed Reg 49,005 (1982). Poland's MFN status was restored in 1987: Restoration of the Application of Column 1 Rates of Duty of the Tariff Schedules of the United States to the products of Poland, 52, Fed Reg 5425 (1987).

[76] People's Republic of China—Trade Relations, 114 Stat 880, Pub L No 106–286, § 101. The only provision remaining that deals with human rights is Sec 513 stating that financial aid may not be provided if there is credible evidence that the recipient authorities or institutions are materially responsible for the commission of human rights violations. Cleveland (2001) 43–44.

[77] 19 USC § 2461–65.

[78] Trade Act of 1974, *ibid*, Section 502(b)(7).

[79] Enacted as Title V of the Trade and Tariff Act of 1984, PubL No 98-573, § 502, 98 Stat 3020, codified at 19 USC § 2462.

status.[80] Recalling the discussion about China, the decision to impose sanctions depends much more on political considerations than on human rights implications. In practice, few countries are denied GSP benefits because of labour rights violations. The closer its trade relations with the US, the less likely a country is to face sanctions in the case of labour rights violations. Indonesia is a typical example.[81] The question therefore remains whether the mere threat of sanctions and the institutionalised review of human rights situations are enough to encourage compliance with labour rights by GSP recipients.

d) Critical Assessment Since the Trade Act speaks of internationally recognised worker rights, one would expect reference to the relevant ILO Conventions. However, this is not the case. Most noticeably, one key labour right, the principle of non-discrimination, is mentioned neither in the context of Section 301 nor in the GSP provisions of Sections 501 and 502. The US, with the exceptions of the Child Labour (No 182) and the Forced Labour (No 105) Conventions, has not ratified any of the ILO Fundamental Conventions; this means that the competent US authorities can opt to set whatever standards they choose in any given situation.[82]

The US approach has been heavily criticised because it applies to any state regardless of whether it has ratified the relevant international conventions.[83] However, as we saw earlier in chapter 1,[84] the 1998 ILO Declaration on Fundamental Principles and Rights at Work expresses a universal consensus on core labour rights; and to the extent that the US refers to these core labour rights, the US is engaging with an internationally accepted concept and is not imposing its own standards on other countries.[85]

B) Child Labour In 1999, another attempt was made in Congress to pass legislation that would prohibit import products manufactured with child labour, with the threat of civil and criminal penalties for those who intentionally violate the law.[86] The bill promotes international co-operation to supplement

[80] For an overview of recent cases, see Cleveland (2001) 44–45.

[81] Cleveland (2001) 46 with further references.

[82] Alston (1993) 8.

[83] *Ibid*, 12–16.

[84] Section 1.2.2.3. above.

[85] In this sense, the rights listed as customary international law in the Restatement would have to be amended: Restatement (Third) of the Foreign Relations Law of the United States § 702, American Law Institute (1987), vol 2, 161. In 1994, the International Law Association Committee suggested a number of possible additions to the Restatement, *inter alia*, the right to form and join trade unions, the right to free choice of employment and the prohibition against sex discrimination in employment. Commentary on the Enforcement of Human Rights Law, International Law Association, Final Report on the Status of the Universal Declaration of Human Rights in National and International Law, in: International Law Association, Report of the Sixty-Sixth Conference 525, 544–49 (1994).

[86] Child Labor Deterrence Act, Senate 1551 106th Cong (1999); United States Department of Labor, Bureau of International Labor Affairs, The Apparel Industry and Codes of Conduct: A Solution to the International Child Labor Problem, 1996/1998.

international trading rules with a view to renouncing the use of underage children in the production of goods for export as a means of competitive advantage[87] and urges the President to seek an agreement with each US trading partner for the purpose of securing an international ban on trade in products of child labour.[88] This is very much in line with the numerous initiatives taken by the US to include a social clause into the WTO/GATT Agreement.

Unlike other unilateral regulations, the Bill refers to the ILO Minimum Age Convention (No 138) and the Worst Forms of Child Labour Convention (No 182). Although this so-called Child Labour Deterrence Act was not passed, parts of it were given legal effect when President Clinton issued an Executive Order on Child Labor in 1999.[89] The Order essentially prohibits procurement by the US government of goods produced by "forced or indentured child labor." A child is defined as a person less than 18 years of age. Yet unlike Section 307 of the Tariff Act,[90] which employs *verbatim* the definition of the ILO Forced Labour Convention (No 29), the Executive Order on child labour applies a much narrower definition than the respective ILO Convention (No 182) on the Worst Forms of Child Labour.[91] The Executive Order does not apply if the foreign country is a WTO or North American Free Trade Agreement (NAFTA) member and the contract in question meets the WTO Agreement or NAFTA threshold.[92] As a result, the Order mainly applies to developing countries.

Section 307 of the Tariff Act was invoked several times to ban the import of products from Mexico[93] and China[94] that were produced with prison or convict labour. While child labour was not mentioned in the original provision, in 1997 an amendment was made to prohibit the use of customs service funds for imports of goods produced by indentured child labour.[95] As a result, a petition

87 Child Labor Deterrence Act, Senate 1551 106th Cong § 2 (1999).

88 *Ibid.*

89 Executive Order 13126 of 12 June 1999, Prohibition of Acquisition of Products Produced by Forced or Indentured Child Labor, 64 Fed Reg 32, 383.

90 19 USCA § 1307.

91 Section 6(c) defines forced or indentured child labor as "all work or service (1) exacted from any person under the age of 18 under the menace of any penalty for its nonperformance and for which the worker does not offer himself voluntarily; or (2) performed by any person under the age of 18 pursuant to a contract the enforcement of which can be accomplished by process or penalties." For relevant articles of ILO Conventions Nos 29 and 182, see Appendix A.7. and A.14.

92 Section 5(b) of the Executive Order, note 89 above.

93 Merchandise Produced by Convict, Forced or Indentured Labor, 19 CFR § 12.42 (h) (2000).

94 Determination that Merchandise Imported from the People's Republic of China is being Produced with Convict, Forced or Indentured Labor by the Qinghai Hide and Garment Factory, 58 Fed Reg 32,746 (1993); Determination that Merchandise Imported from the People's Republic of China is being Produced Using Convict, Forced, or Indentured Labor by the Tianjin Malleable Iron Factory, 61 Fed Reg 17,956 (1996).

95 Treasury, Postal Service and General Government Appropriations Act of 1998. Pub L No 105-61, § 634, 111 Stat 1272 (1997), barring the use of customs service funds "to allow the importation into the United States of any good, ware, article or merchandise minded, produced or manufactured by forced or indentured child labor, as determined pursuant to section 307 of the Tariff Act of 1930".

to ban the importation of rugs from South Asia that are knotted by hand using child labour was filed.[96] In 1999, a bill introduced by Senator Harkin to include forced or indentured child labour in Section 307 was passed.[97]

C) Selective Purchasing Laws Selective purchasing laws have a longstanding tradition in the US. States targeted by national and state or local selective purchasing laws are Burma/Myanmar, Nigeria, China, Cuba and Indonesia. As already mentioned, in 1999 President Clinton barred federal agencies from purchasing products made using child labour. Outside the labour context, the most controversial statute is the Helms-Burton Act regarding Cuba.[98] Helms-Burton was adopted in March 1996 in response to Cuba's attack on two airplanes operated by a Miami-based Cuban liberation group. The extraterritorial provisions of Helms-Burton and the related Iran and Libyan Sanctions Act[99] spurred formal protests from the international community, which considered them to be a violation of both customary international law and the GATT.[100]

At the local level, North Olmsted, Ohio, in 1998 was one of the first cities to bar the local government from doing business with countries where "sweatshop" labour—defined as child labour, forced labour, sub-living wages or a work week that is longer than 48 hours—is employed.[101]

The most prominent recent example is the sanctions imposed by the Commonwealth of Massachusetts on Burma/Myanmar. In 1989, the US had indefinitely suspended Burma/Myanmar's preferred trading status due to the country's labour rights violations.[102] In 1996, Massachusetts enacted legislation restricting its agencies from purchasing goods and services from companies in or doing business with Burma/Myanmar.[103] The legislation was based directly on previous legislation regulating state contracts with companies that had South African links. The statute generally bars state entities from buying goods or services from any person (defined to include a business organisation) identified on a "restricted purchase list" of those doing business with Burma/Myanmar.

[96] International Labor Rights Fund, Labor Rights and Trade, at n 35 (1998) at www.laborrights.org. Cleveland (2001) 47.

[97] Senate 281, 106th Cong (1999).

[98] The Cuban Liberty and Democratic Solidarity (LIBERTAD) Act of 1996, 1996, Pub L No 104–114; 110 Stat 785.

[99] Iran and Libyan Sanctions Act of 1996, 1996 Pub L No 104–172, 110 Stat 1541. The Act imposed extraterritorial sanctions on domestic and foreign entities investing in the Iranian and Libyan petroleum industries.

[100] Canada, Mexico and the European Union adopted legislation prohibiting, *inter alia*, their companies from complying with Helms-Burton. Canada and Mexico pursued dispute resolution mechanisms under NAFTA and the European Community formally initiated dispute resolution proceedings in the WTO. Cleveland (2001) 60 with references. See also note 73 above and accompanying text.

[101] City of North Olmsted Resolution 97-9 (1998).

[102] Proclamation No 6245, 3CFR 7, 7–9 (1992), reprinted in 105 Stat 2484, 2484–86 (1991); Proclamation No 5955, 3CFR 29, 29–31 (1990), reprinted in 103 Stat 3010, 3011–13 (1989).

[103] An Act Regulating Contracts with Companies Doing Business with or in Burma/Myanmar, 25 June 1996, Massachusetts General Laws §§ 7:22G–7:22M.

Doing business with Burma/Myanmar is defined broadly.[104] Although the statute has no general provision for waiver or termination of its ban, it does exempt from boycott any entities present in Burma/Myanmar solely to report the news or to provide international telecommunication goods and services or medical supplies.

Three months after the Massachusetts law was enacted, Congress passed a statute imposing a set of mandatory conditional sanctions on Burma/Myanmar.[105] The Act has five basic parts:

(1) It imposes sanctions directly on Burma/Myanmar, banning all aid to the Burmese Government except for humanitarian assistance, counter-narcotics efforts and promotion of human rights and democracy.
(2) It authorises the President to impose further sanctions subject to certain conditions, for example he may prohibit "United States persons" from initiating new investment in Burma/Myanmar.
(3) It directs the President to work to develop "a comprehensive, multilateral strategy to bring democracy to and improve human rights practices and the quality of life in Myanmar/Burma".
(4) It requires the President to report periodically to Congress on the progress in Burma/Myanmar towards democratisation and better living conditions as well as on the development of the required strategy.
(5) It gives the President the power to waive "temporarily or permanently any sanction [under this Act], if he determines and certifies to Congress that the application of such sanction would be contrary to the national security interests of the United States".

The Massachusetts law created concern at home and abroad. In 1998, following the federal legislation, the National Foreign Trade Council, a non-profit corporation representing companies engaged in foreign commerce, brought a claim challenging the Massachusetts law. It argued that the state law is contrary to the Constitution and the Federal Act. Japan and the European Community formally complained to the US and the WTO that the Massachusetts law is contrary to the Agreement on Government Procurement (GPA) as it was adopted in 1994.[106]

[104] See § 7:22G, *ibid*. Most state entities may only procure goods or services from persons on the restricted purchase list if the procurement is essential and if elimination of the person would result in inadequate competition among bidders. Even then, it would seem that where any procurement includes bidders who are on the restricted purchase list, the state authority may award the contract to a person on the list only if there is no "comparable low bid or offer" by a person not on the list. A bid by a person not on the list can be up to 10 per cent greater than a bid submitted by a person on the restricted list and still remain comparably low. McCrudden (1999b) 6.

[105] Foreign Operations, Export Financing, and Related Programs Appropriations Act, 1997, Pub L No 104–208, § 570, 110 Stat 3009-166–3009-167 (enacted by the Omnibus Consolidated Appropriations Act, 1997 § 9002(c), 110 Stat 3009-121–3009-172).

[106] Request by Japan in GPA/W/39, reply by the United States in GPA/W/52. Request by the European Union for consultations WT/DS88/1 and GPA/D2/1, in which Japan joined (WT/DS88/2) and the request for the establishment of a panel WT/DS88/3. In a separate

After a Boston District Court ruled that the Massachusetts law was unconstitutional,[107] the EC und Japan requested the suspension of the panel proceedings at the WTO.[108] On appeal, the US Supreme Court upheld the claim by the National Foreign Trade Council and declared the Massachusetts law unconstitutional because it conflicts with the power to impose sanctions, which Congress delegates to the President:

> Therefore, the state law is an obstacle to the accomplishment of Congress's full objectives under the Federal Act. We find that the state law undermines the intended purpose and "natural effect" of at least three provisions of the Federal Act, that is its delegation of effective discretion to the President to control economic sanctions against Burma, its limitation of sanctions solely to United States persons and new investment, and its directive to the President to proceed diplomatically in developing a comprehensive multilateral strategy towards Burma.[109]

However, the Supreme Court neither addressed the possible violations of the relevant WTO/GATT rules nor referred to the dormant commerce clause.[110]

D) The Alien Tort Claims Act (ATCA)

a) The Origins and Scope of the ATCA Currently the most controversial statute is the Alien Tort Claims Act (ATCA).[111] It was adopted by the first Congress of the United States in Section 9 of the Judiciary Act of 1789.[112] It reads:

> The district court shall have original jurisdiction of a civil action by an alien for a tort only, committed in violation of the law of nations or a treaty of the United States.[113]

While hardly any claims were brought under the ATCA for a long time, the situation changed dramatically in 1980 with the groundbreaking decision in *Filartiga v Pena-Irala*.[114] In this case, the relatives of a Paraguayan citizen who had been murdered by a police official in Paraguay successfully sued the official for torture before a US court. The court held that

> . . . deliberate torture perpetrated under color of official authority violates universally accepted norms of the international law of human rights, regardless of the nationality of the parties. Thus whenever an alleged torturer is found and served with process within Untied States borders, the ATCA provides jurisdiction.[115]

procedure, Japan, joined by the European Union requested the establishment of a panel WT/DS95/3. We will return to this issue in section 3.2.3. below when discussing labour rights and the existing law of the WTO.

[107] *National Foreign Trade Council v Baker* 26 F Supp 2d 287, 291 (Mass 1998).

[108] Letter sent to the Chairman of the Panel on 9 February 1999 in accordance with Article 12.12 of the DSU, note 64 above.

[109] *Crosby v National Foreign Trade Council* 530 USR 366, 373 (2000).

[110] Halberstam (2001b). On the dormant commerce clause, see chapter 1 above, note 71.

[111] For a more extensive discussion see Breining-Kaufmann (2005) 122–30.

[112] Act of 24 September 1789, chapter 20, s 9(b) 1. Statute 73, 77 (1789).

[113] 28 USC § 1350 (1994).

[114] *Filartiga v Pena-Irala* 630 F.2d 876 (2d Cir 1980).

[115] *Ibid*, at 878.

After a more restrictive decision in *Tel-Oren v Libyan Arab Republic*,[116] Congress breathed new life into the ATCA by passing the Torture Victim Protection Act of 1991 and explicitly adopting the interpretation offered in *Filartiga*.[117] Subsequent decisions have consistently found that Congress intended the ATCA to provide subject matter jurisdiction and a cause of action for violations of the law of nations.[118]

Today, the statute thus provides both a federal cause of action and a federal forum for claims (1) brought by an alien; (2) alleging a tort; (3) committed in violation of a US treaty or the law of nations.[119] To be actionable, the suit must state a claim for a tortious violation of contemporary international law (whether customary law or a treaty), and the plaintiff must establish personal jurisdiction over the defendant. An alleged violation must be of an international norm that is "specific, universal and obligatory".[120] Such obligations certainly include norms of *ius cogens*.[121] In recent decisions, the Ninth Circuit Court of Appeals has made clear that while a violation of *ius cogens* is *sufficient* to warrant an actionable claim under the ATCA, it is not *necessary*. In so doing, the court overruled an interpretation of the law of nations as encompassing only norms of *ius cogens*, an interpretation that would be contrary to the text of the ATCA.

Similarly, the Second Circuit Court of Appeals defines the "law of nations" as "clear and unambiguous rules of customary international law".[122] In *Filartiga*, the court left open the question of whether the ATCA applies *only* to state actors or also to non-state actors.[123] Four years later, in *Tel-Oren*, Judge Edwards commented that individual liability was available under the ATCA for

116 *Tel-Oren v Libyan Arab Republic* 726 F.2d 774, 817 (DC Cir 1984). Judge Bork held that "international law typically does not authorize individuals to vindicate rights by bringing actions in either international or municipal tribunals". According to this view, individuals are not considered subjects of international law.

117 Torture Victim Protection Act of 1991, 12 March 1992, Pub L 102–256, 106 Stat 73, 28 USCA § 1350 note.

118 *Kadic v Karadzic* 74 F.3d 377, 378 (2d Cir1996), citing HR Rep No 367, 102d Cong, 2d Sess, at 4 (1991), reprinted in 1992 USCCAN 84, 86.

119 *Alvarez-Machain v Sosa* 331 F.3d 604, at 612; *Hilao v Estate of Marcos [Marcos II]* 25 F3d 1467 (9th Cir 1994) at 1475; Cleveland (1998) 1562; Clapham (2006) 252–62.

120 *Filartiga v Pena-Irala* 630 F.2d 876 (2d Cir 1980) at 881. In *re World War II Era Japanese Forced Labor Litigation* 164 F Supp 2d 1160 (ND Cal 2001) at 1177. Several courts stated that the list of claims actionable under the ATCA should at least include the rights recognised by the Restatement (Third) of the Foreign Relations Law of the United States as peremptory norms of customary international law. These include (a) genocide; (b) slavery or slave trade; (c) murder or causing the disappearance of individuals; (d) torture or other cruel, inhuman or degrading treatment or punishment; prolonged arbitrary detention, systematic racial discrimination and a consistent pattern of gross violations of internationally recognised human rights. *Kadic v Karadzic* 70 F.3d 232 (2d Cir 1995) at 240–41. *Alvarez-Machain v Sosa* 331 F.3d 604 (9th Cir 2003) at 612.

121 *Alvarez-Machain v Sosa* 331 F.3d 604 (9th Cir 2003) at 612; *Hilao v Estate of Marcos [Marcos II]* 25 F3d 1467 (9th Cir 1994) at 1475; *Filartiga v Pena-Irala* 630 F.2d 876, at 885–87.

122 *Flores v Southern Peru Copper Corp* 343 F.3d 140 (2d Cir 2003) at 160.

123 *Filartiga v Pena-Irala* 630 F.2d 876 (2d Cir 1980) at 878.

a handful of acts including piracy and slave trading. However, Judge Edwards limited the application of the ATCA to private defendants by declining

> . . . to read section 1350 to cover torture by non-state actors, absent guidance from the Supreme Court on the statute's use of the term "law of nations".[124]

As a result, although the ATCA does not require that the defendant has acted under colour of law, most courts have held that customary international law itself imposes a state action requirement for claims of torture, summary execution and disappearance, cruel, inhuman or degrading treatment, arbitrary detention, and systematic race discrimination. Nevertheless, in *Kadic v Karadzic* the court held that

> . . . certain forms of conduct violate the law of nations whether undertaken by those acting under the auspices of a state or only as private individuals.[125]

On the basis of this statement, it might therefore be possible to bring a claim under the ATCA against private actors.

b) Labour Rights Cases The prohibition of forced labour is considered a norm of *ius cogens* by the courts and can therefore be the object of an ATCA suit.[126] In fact, in recent years several cases concerning forced labour have been filed under the ATCA. A first group dealt with claims brought by Burmese villagers against the American oil company Unocal. Unocal was involved in a joint venture to build a pipeline for natural gas off the coast of Burma/Myanmar, extending to the Thai border. The villagers claimed that Unocal was liable for international human rights violations and in particular for the use of forced labour perpetrated by the Burmese military for the benefit of the pipeline. While one class action was dismissed on procedural grounds by the Ninth Circuit Court of Appeals,[127] another was decided on the merits, the District Court finding that Unocal did not actively participate in the forced labour practices and therefore was not liable under international law:

> The evidence does suggest that Unocal knew that forced labor was being utilized and that the Joint Venturers benefited from the practice. However, because such a showing is insufficient to establish liability under international law Plaintiffs' claim against Unocal for forced labor under the Alien Tort Claims Act fails as a matter of law.[128]

The court referred to the industrialist cases brought against German companies and their owners after the Second World War.[129] Because Unocal did not

[124] *Tel-Oren v Libyan Arab Republic* 726 F.2d.774 (DC Cir 1984) at 795.

[125] *Kadic v Karadzic* 70 F.3d 232 (2d Cir 1995) at 239.

[126] *John Doe I v Unocal Corp* Nos 00-56603, 00-57197, DC No CV-96-06959-RSWL, 2002 WL 31063976 (CA 9th Cir Cal, 18 Sept 2002) at *8, 9.

[127] *Doe v Unocal Corp* 248 F.3d 915 (9th Cir 2001).

[128] *Doe v Unocal* 110 F Supp 2d 1294, 1310 (CD Cal 2000).

[129] *United States of America v Friedrich Flick [The Flick Case]*, 6 Trials of War Criminals Before the Nuremberg Military Tribunals Under Control Council Law No 10 (1952), *United States of America v Carl Krauch [The Farben Case]*, 8 Trials of War Criminals Before the Nuremberg

directly employ or seek to employ forced labour, the court denied the application of the principles developed in *Iwanowa v Ford Motor Company*.[130] On appeal,[131] the Ninth Circuit Court rejected this argument, stating that the District Court had erred in relying on the "active participation" standard, which had been applied by the Nuremberg Military Tribunals only in cases to overcome the defendants "necessity defense".[132] The Ninth Circuit Court held instead that the standard developed by the International Criminal Tribunal for the former Yugoslavia in the *Furundzija*[133] case was applicable. Under this standard, aiding and abetting liability under international criminal law means knowing and practical assistance, encouragement, or moral support that has a substantial effect on the perpetration of the crime.

In assessing the facts, the court concluded that Unocal knew or should reasonably have known that its conduct—including hiring the Burma/Myanmar Military to provide security and build infrastructure along the pipeline route in exchange for money or food—would assist or encourage the Burma/Myanmar Military to subject the plaintiffs to forced labour, a "modern form of slavery", and thus violate international *ius cogens*. As a result, the court reversed the District Court's grant of Unocal's motion for summary judgment on forced labour claims under the ATCA.

Judge Reinhardt filed a concurring opinion in which he agreed with the result of the decision but sharply criticised the application of international law instead of federal common law in determining Unocal's third-party tort liability.[134] In his view, recourse to *ius cogens* was unnecessary because Unocal could be held liable as a third party by virtue of Burma/Myanmar's violation of customary international law against forced labour. He concluded that federal common law better meets the policy interest as it is set out in the Restatement (Second) of Conflict of Laws.[135]

Following this judgment of the Ninth Circuit, the *Unocal* case would normally have gone back to the District Court. However, in February 2003 a motion for

Military Tribunals Under Control Council Law No 10 (1953); *United States of America v Alfred Felix Alwyn Krupp von Bohlen und Halbach [The Krupp Case]*, 9 Trials of War Criminals Before the Nuremberg Military Tribunals Under Control Council Law No 10 (1950). See also *Flick v Johnson* 174 F.2d 983, 984 (DC Cir 1949).

130 *Iwanowa v Ford Motor Co* 67 F Supp 2d 424, 440 (DNMJ 1999). The court held that Ford's "use of unpaid, forced labor during World War II violated clearly established norms of customary international law". The plaintiff Iwanowa had been literally purchased by Ford together with 38 other children from Rostock.

131 *John Doe I v Unocal Corp* Nos 00-56603, 00-57197, DC No CV-96-06959-RSWL, 2002 WL 31063976 (CA 9th Cir, Cal, 18 Sept 2002) at *13.

132 These were cases where the defendants argued that the act they were charged with was necessary to avoid an evil both serious and irreparable; that there was no other adequate means of escape; and that the remedy was not disproportionate to the evil. *United States v Krupp*, note 129 above, at 1436.

133 *Prosecutor v Furundzija* IT-95-17/1-T, 10 December 1998, reprinted in (1999) 38 ILM 317.

134 *John Doe I v Unocal Corp* Nos 00-56603, 00-57197, DC No CV-96-06959-RSWL, 2002 WL 31063976 (CA 9th Cir Cal, 18 Sept 2002) at *24–30.

135 Restatement (Second) of Conflicts of Laws, § 6 cmt d and f (1971).

rehearing the case *en banc* was granted, and it was ordered that the panel decision could not be cited as precedent with the Circuit.[136] On 17 June 2003, the Ninth Circuit Court of Appeals, *en banc*, heard the case. Before the hearing, the US Department of Justice submitted an unsolicited *amicus curiae brief* claiming that the panel in the Ninth Circuit had made several analytical errors:

> The court has construed a statute that on its face merely confers subject matter jurisdiction as also affording an implied private right of action. Recent Supreme Court precedent, however, prohibits finding an implied private right of action in this jurisdictional grant. Moreover, it is clearly error to infer a right of action to enforce unratified or non-self-executing treaties, and non-binding UN General Assembly resolutions. Finally, contrary to the long-established presumption against extraterritorial application of a statute, this court has extended the causes oaf action recognized under the [Alien Tort Claims Act] to conduct occurring wholly within the boundaries of other nations, involving only foreign sovereign or nationals, and causing no direct or substantial impact in the United States.
>
> Under this new view of the [ATCA], it has become the role of the federal courts to discern, and enforce through money damage actions, norms of international law from unratified or non-self-executing treaties, non-binding Untied Nations General Assembly resolutions, and purely political statements. Although often asserted against rogues and terrorists, these claims are without bounds, and can easily be asserted against allies of our Nation. [. . .] This court's approach to the [ATCA] bears serious implications for our current war against terrorism, and permits [ATCA] claims to be easily asserted against our allies in that war. [. . .]
>
> Wide-ranging claims the courts have entertained regarding the acts of aliens in foreign countries necessarily call upon our courts to render judgments over matters that implicate our Nation's foreign affairs. In the view of the United States, the assumption of this role by the courts under the [ATCA] not only has no historical basis, but more important, raises significant potential for serious interference with the important foreign policy interests of the United States, and is contrary to our constitutional framework and democratic principles.
>
> While the United States unequivocally deplores and strongly condemns the anti-democratic policies an blatant human rights abuses of the Burmese (Myanmar) military government, it is the function of the political Branches, not the courts, to respond (as the US Government actively is) to bring about change in such situations. Although it may be tempting to open our courts to right every wrong all over the world, that function has not been assigned to the federal courts. When Congress wants the courts to play such a role, it enacts specific and carefully crafted rules, such as in the Torture Victim Protection Act of 1991 (TVPA), 28 USC § 1350 note. The [ATCA], which is a simple grant of jurisdiction, cannot properly be construed as a broad grant of authority for the courts to decipher and enforce their own concepts of international law. Thus, respectfully, the Government asks the court to reconsider its approach to the [ATCA].[137]

[136] *Doe v Unocal Corp* Nos 00-56603, 0056628, Doc Nos CV-96-06959-RSWL, CV-96-06112-RSWL, 2003 WL 359787 (CA 9th Cir Cal, 14 Feb 2003).

[137] Brief for the United States of America, as Amicus Curiae, filed 8 May 2003, at 2–4. Available at http://www.lchr.org/?Issues/ATCA/atca_02.pdf .

Two weeks earlier, the same court had held that a foreigner had a right to bring suit in the US over alleged human rights abuses abroad.[138] Therefore, in the hearing, the judges focused on the question of which standards should be applied to Unocal's actions: should standards be drawn from federal case law or from international law, and if from international law, from civil law or criminal law, including jurisprudence of the Nuremberg, Yugoslavia and Rwanda tribunals?[139] In March 2005, Unocal and the plaintiffs agreed on an out-of-court settlement, the details of which were not disclosed.

A second group of cases relates to forced labour during the Second World War. In the most recent cases, Korean and Chinese plaintiffs sought damages and other remedies from Japanese corporations.[140] The court held that the forced labour practices during the Second World War undoubtedly violated international law and that therefore the ATCA was applicable. However, because the conduct took place more than 50 years ago, the court concluded that the claims must be dismissed because they were time-barred.[141] Since the ATCA does not contain a statute of limitations, the court, following instructions by the Supreme Court,[142] had to "borrow" the most suitable limitations period from some other source, traditionally the law of the forum state. The court concluded that the Torture Victim Protection Act (TVPA), which was enacted by Congress in 1991[143] as a statutory note to the ATCA, serves as the closest federal statute to the ATCA.[144] The TVPA provides a ten-year limitations period. Because the Korean and Chinese plaintiffs gave no reasons why their claims could not have been brought under the ATCA within ten years of the war's end, the court finally concluded that the ten-year limitations period on the international law claims under the ATCA had expired.[145] While it is certainly remarkable how the courts are applying international labour rights, it does not seem convincing to refer to national law with regard to time limitations.

[138] *Alvarez-Machain v US* 331 F.3d 604 (9th Cir 2003).

[139] Lisa Girion, "Unocal Case Focuses on Liability Standards", *Los Angeles Times*, 18 June 2003.

[140] Other cases, which involved United States and Allied veterans, were dismissed because the 1951 Treaty of peace with Japan waived all such claims: *In re World War II Era Japanese Forced Labor Litigation* 114 F Supp 2d 939, 942 (ND Cal 2000). In 2001, a similar claim by Filipino plaintiffs who were not members of the armed forces of the United States or its allies was dismissed, because the Philippines is specifically named in Article 23 of the Peace Treaty, and the country both signed and ratified the treaty; it is therefore an Allied power for the purpose of the Treaty. As a result, the Treaty of Peace with Japan precludes the claims of the Filipino plaintiffs regardless of the authority under which these claims are brought: *In re World War II Era Japanese Forced Labor Litigation* 164 F Supp 2d 1153, at 1157, 1159 (ND Cal 2001). Both decisions were affirmed by *Deutsch v Turner Corp* 324 F.3d 692 (9th Cir 2003).

[141] *In re World War II Era Japanese Forced Labor Litigation* 164 F Supp2d 1160 (ND Cal 2001) at 1179, 1180. Affirmed by *Deutsch v Turner Corp* 324 F.3d 692 (9th Cir 2003).

[142] *DelCostello v International Brotherhood of Teamsters* 462 USR 151, 158 (1983).

[143] Note 117 above and accompanying text.

[144] In *re World War II Era Japanese Forced Labor Litigation* 164 F Supp2d 1160 (ND Cal, 2001) at 1180. Affirmed by *Deutsch v Turner Corp* 324 F.3d 692 (9th Cir 2003).

[145] *Ibid*, at 1181.

Finally, a case relating to Chinese prison labour was brought before a Washington DC District Court.[146] Four Chinese citizens who were current or former inmates of a "Shanghai Reeducation Through Coerced Labour" prison camp claimed that they had been the victims of various human rights abuses perpetrated by the Chinese government, *inter alia*, to engage in prison labour, which included the sewing of soccer balls. The defendants were the Politburo of the Central Communist Party of China in Beijing and its chairman Li Peng, the Bank of China, a commercial Chinese bank owned by the Chinese government, and Adidas America. The court dismissed the claim for lack of subject matter jurisdiction. While there was no doubt that the plaintiffs were aliens and the claim was for a tort, the third requirement to establish jurisdiction under the ATCA was less clear. The court took the view that under the ATCA, private entities such as Adidas can only be found to have violated the law of nations if acting either as an officer of the state or under colour of state law or if extreme forms of egregious misconduct had occurred.[147]

The court stated first that the only factual allegation tying Adidas to the soccer ball project was the presence of its logos on the soccer balls that Chinese inmates were forced to assemble. Therefore, a formal agreement between Adidas and the Chinese Government and a direct role of the company in the plaintiffs' incarceration and their treatment could not be established. As a result, the court considered the case different from *Iwanowa v Ford Motor Co*[148] and *Doe I v Unocal*.[149]

The court then moved on to examine whether jurisdiction could be established under the private actor doctrine, finding that

> . . . forced prison labor under dire conditions may be condemnable in its own right, it is not the equivalent of the acts of genocide at issue in Kadic, or the slave labor practices at issue in *Unocal* or *Iwanowa*. Moreover, forced prison labor is not a state practice proscribed by international law [. . .] It therefore cannot be within the "handful of crimes" to which the law of nations attributes individual responsibility.[150]

While the court referred to § 702 of the Restatement (Third),[151] it clearly erred in excluding the prohibition of forced prison labour from international law. The prisoners in this case had not been convicted in a court of law—they were political prisoners. Article 8(3)(b) ICCPR contains an exception for prison labour but only for prisoners who have been convicted in court. This is an important point that the court missed in this case.

[146] *Bao Ge v Li Peng* 201 F Supp 2d 14 (DDC 2000).
[147] *Ibid*, at 20.
[148] *Iwanowa v Ford Motor Co* 67 F Supp 2d 424 (DNMJ 1999) at 445–46.
[149] *John Doe I v Unocal Corp* 963 F Supp 880 (CD Cal 1997) at 891–92.
[150] *Bao Ge v Li Peng* 201 F Supp 2d 14 (DDC 2000) at 22.
[151] Note 85 above.

With respect to the government, the court applied the Foreign Sovereign Immunities Act of 1976 (FSIA)[152] and concluded that although products of Chinese forced prison labour are being imported into the US, the operation of the Chinese judicial and penal systems is still not a commercial activity and therefore does not constitute an exception to foreign state immunity under the FSIA.[153] It quoted the Supreme Court, which in 1993 had ruled that

> . . . however monstrous such abuse undoubtedly may be, a foreign state's exercise of the power of its police has long been understood [. . .] as peculiarly sovereign in nature. [. . .] Exercise of the powers of police and penal officers is not the sort of action by which private parties can engage in commerce.[154]

With similar arguments, the claim against the Bank of China was dismissed.[155]

c) **Current Issues and Conclusions** In a long awaited landmark decision, the Supreme Court decided in June 2004 on some of the controversial issues with respect to the applicability of the ATCA.[156] The court held that the ATCA gave federal courts jurisdiction to hear "claims in a very limited category defined by the law of nations and recognised as common law".[157] It thus unanimously defined the ATCA as a jurisdictional statute creating no new causes of action. However, its history makes clear that the ATCA was enacted on the understanding that common law would provide a cause of action for the modest number of violations of international law that have a potential for personal liability.[158] Historically, only three offences were recognised as violations of the law of nations: piracy, infringement of the rights of ambassadors and violations of safe conducts.

[152] 28 USC §§ 1330, 1391(f) and 1602–11. The FSIA permits jurisdiction and thus an exception to foreign state immunity, if the foreign sovereign's acts are commercial and have a direct effect in the United States.

[153] *Bao Ge v Li Peng* 201 F Supp 2d 14 (DDC 2000) at 24–25. Similarly in *Hwang Geum v Japan* 172 F Supp 2d 52 (DDC 2001) at 63:

> The described conduct is unquestionably barbaric, but certainly is not commercial in nature. Japan's use of its war-time military to impose "a premeditated master plan" of sexual slavery upon the women of occupied Asian countries might be characterized properly as a war crime or a crime against humanity. This conduct, however, was not in connection with a commercial activity. [. . .] As plaintiffs correctly recognize, this system "required" the resources at the government's disposal. Such conduct is not typically engaged in by private players in the market.

In 1996, an exception was added to the FSIA, permitting suits against countries designated as state sponsors of terrorism. 28 USC § 1605(a)(7). See *Cicippio v Islamic Republic of Iran* 18 F Supp 2d 62 (DDC 1998).

[154] *Saudi Arabia v Nelson* 507 USR 349, 361–62 (1993).

[155] The decision was also criticised because there were arguable issues in this case that should have gone to trial. It seemed inappropriate that the court dismissed the case so early on.

[156] *Sosa v Alvarez-Machain* 124 SCR 2739 (2004). For a comment, see Vàzquez (2005) 137–47.

[157] *Sosa v Alvarez-Machain*, *ibid*, at 2754.

[158] *Ibid*, at 2761.

The court then moved on to a discussion of what the law of nations encompasses today. In a split decision,[159] it held that federal courts could still receive claims under the ATCA provided that they were based on

> the present-day law of nations to rest on a norm of international character accepted by the civilized world and defined with a specificity comparable to the features of the 18th-century paradigms we have recognised.[160]

In other words, the court refers to customary international law. Given the difficulties in defining the contents of customary international law and the discretion of judges in doing so, the court establishes a set of specific requirements for the creation of causes of action under the ATCA. As a rule, federal courts should look for legislative guidance before exercising what the Supreme Court calls "innovative authority over substantive law". Overall, the creation of a private right of action is a decision that should be left to legislative judgment. In addition, the possible collateral consequences and implications for the foreign relations of the US of making international rules privately actionable argue for judicial caution:

> It is one thing for American courts to enforce constitutional limits on our own State and Federal Governments' power, but quite another to consider suits under rules that would go so far as to claim a limit on the power of foreign governments over their own citizens, and to hold that a foreign government or its agent has transgressed those limits.[161]

Balancing these interests, the majority of the court concluded that a narrow class of international norms is still actionable and that "the door is still ajar subject to vigilant doorkeeping".[162] As a result, in order to establish a cause of action, the norm needs to be recognised as a norm of customary international law and needs to be sufficiently definite. In the view of the Supreme Court, the latter criterion implies an assessment of the practical consequences of making such a cause available to litigants in federal court. Foreign policy considerations as they have been raised by the administration in its submission can play a role here.[163]

In sum, there is a strong argument that the ATCA provides a cause of action for at least one core labour right: the abolition of forced labour.[164] The Supreme Court did not decide on the question of whether private corporations can be held accountable under the ATCA. Therefore, the respective decisions by the Court of Appeals are still good law. Overall, as noted above, litigation under the

[159] Chief Justice Scalia and Justice Thomas limit the scope of the ATCA to the three violations of international law recognised at the time of the ATCA's passage.

[160] *Sosa v Alvarez-Machain*, note 156 above, at 2761–62.

[161] *Ibid*, at 2763.

[162] *Ibid*, at 2764.

[163] Reply Brief for the United States as Respondent Supporting Petitioner, *Sosa v Alvarez-Machain*, Nos 03-339, 03-485, 29 June 2004, 2004 WL 577654.

[164] See also the concurring opinion of Justice Breyer, *Sosa v Alvarez-Machain*, note 156 above, at 2782–83.

ATCA faces a number of procedural hurdles, the most difficult being to establish a forum somewhere in the United States.

According to the *forum non conveniens* rule[165] a defendant has to prove that a better alternative forum exists[166] and that private and public interests warrant a trial abroad.[167] It is more difficult for foreign plaintiffs to make a sufficiently strong showing of convenience for their choice of a forum in the United States. If multinational enterprises are involved, a headquarters or incorporated branch in the US is usually required by the courts.[168] However, in the case against Union Carbide following the gas disaster in Bhopal, the courts held that although Union Carbide had its headquarters in the US, the *forum non conveniens* rule would apply because all the witnesses and evidence were in India.[169] In addition, violations of human rights, no matter how severe, cannot be brought before an American court under the ATCA if personal jurisdiction cannot be established. Foreign companies that lack sufficient US contacts to support personal jurisdiction are therefore effectively immune from liability.[170] For all other companies, the threat of ATCA liability may indeed influence their decisions on foreign direct investment and thus indirectly affect host countries' possible labour rights policies. Similar to the question of compliance with OECD guidelines, a country may have an interest in complying with core labour standards in order to attract investment by foreign companies.

3.2.2.2. *The NAFTA Labor Side Agreement (NAALC)*

A) Objectives and Principles of NAALC When the North American Free Trade Agreement (NAFTA) was adopted in 1993 by the US, Canada and

[165] 28 USC § 1404 (a): "[F]or the convenience of parties and witnesses, in the interest of justice, a district court may transfer any civil action to any other district or division where it might have been brought." See also Anderes (2001) 173–75.

[166] *Piper Aircraft v Reyno* 454 USR 235, 257 (1981).

[167] *In re Union Carbide Corp Gas Plant Disaster at Bhopal, India in December 1984* 809 F.2d 195 (2d Cir 1987), cert denied, 484 USR 871 (1987); *In re Air Crash Disaster near New Orleans, LA, on July 1982* 821 F.2d 1164 (5th Cir 1987); *Gulf Oil Corp v Gilbert* 330 USR 508 (1947).

[168] *Jota v Texaco* 157 F.3d 153 (2d Cir 1998): the defendant had its headquarters in the US and all evidence was in the US; *Lony v EI Du Pont de Nemours & C* 935 F.2d 604 (3d Cir 1991) at 608.

[169] *In re Union Carbide Corp Gas Plant Disaster at Bhopal, India in December 1984* 809 F.2d 195 (2d Cir 1987) at 199–203.

[170] *In Doe v Unocal Corp* 27 F Supp 2d 1174, 1190 (CD Cal 1998) the district court dismissed a suit against the French oil company Total S.A. because Total's contacts with California were insufficient to give rise to either specific or general jurisdiction. The court rejected the plaintiffs' argument that the California contracts of Total's subsidiaries could be attributed to Total itself. By contrast, in *Wiwa v Royal Dutch Petroleum Co* 226 F.3d 88 (2d Cir 2000) at 93–99, the US Court of Appeals for the Second Circuit upheld the trial's court ruling that personal jurisdiction over the defendants both of whom were foreign corporations, was proper. The court held that the activities of the defendants' investor relations office in New York City were sufficient to establish general personal jurisdiction. Cert denied in 532 USR 941 (2001). "Developments in the Law: International Criminal Law: Corporate Liability for Violations of International Human Rights Law" (2001) 114 *Harvard Law Review* 2025, 2039. See also Sacharoff (1998) 927. Confirmed in *Wiwa v Royal Dutch Petroleum Co* No 96 CIV. 8386(KMW), US Dist 2002 WL 319887 (SDNY, 28 Feb 2002) at *12.

Mexico, it led to strong criticism particularly in the US that it did "nothing to reaffirm our right to insist that the Mexicans follow their own labour standards, now frequently violated".[171] It was argued that unfair competitive advantages might result from lower labour standards in Mexico, thus leading to a "race to the bottom". Indeed, NAFTA includes no provisions for labour rights. However, before NAFTA was submitted to the US Congress for approval in August 1993,[172] President Clinton negotiated a Side Accord on Labor Cooperation,[173] known as the NAFTA Labor Side Agreement (NAALC).

The NAALC is an example of cross-border monitoring and enforcement of labour regulation. It does not harmonise labour standards between different countries. Unlike some of the unilateral mechanisms discussed above, the NAALC does not affirm extraterritorial jurisdiction, ie it does not apply the labour laws of one country to actions and parties in another country.[174] Instead, a NAFTA country can challenge another NAFTA member's application of the second country's national labour laws.[175]

The NAALC establishes objectives, obligations and principles for the parties. The objectives and obligations are enumerated in Articles 1–7. Article 1 sets out the main objectives of the Agreement, namely, to improve working conditions and living standards in each party's territory and to encourage an exchange of information related to labour laws and institutions in the Member States. Although some of the obligations are broad, such as the requirement to have high labour standards, they go beyond a mere statement of intent. The member parties are, *inter alia*, required to ensure access to justice[176] and due process.[177] Of crucial importance is the parties' obligation to enforce their own labour laws.[178] Yet, if a party can demonstrate that its failure to enforce a law stemmed from the legitimate pursuit of higher priorities, it will not be held in violation of the Agreement.[179]

Substantial labour rights are referred to as "principles". There are eleven labour principles in Annex 1 of the NAALC. On closer inspection, they resemble the principles in the European Social Charter. However, it is important to note that they are not understood as common minimum standards but as

[171] Then-candidate Bill Clinton during his 1992 presidential campaign.

[172] In 1991, President Bush had assured the United States Congress that Mexico's labour standards were compatible to those in the United States and what was lacking was not commitment but budgetary resources. The Bush administration needed a renewal of fast-track negotiating authority to move forward with the NAFTA trade negotiations. In return, the administration assured Congress that it would include "new initiatives to expand US-Mexico labor cooperation", including labour standards. Human Rights Watch (2001) notes 35–38 and accompanying text.

[173] North American Agreement on Labor Cooperation (NAALC).

[174] Van Wezel Stone (1996) 447.

[175] Articles 2 and 22 NAALC.

[176] Article 4(1) NAALC.

[177] Article 5(1) NAALC.

[178] Article 6 NAALC.

[179] Article 49 NAALC.

guiding principles for each country's domestic legislation, thus prioritising sovereignty in internal labour affairs.[180]

Article 42 clearly excludes extraterritorial jurisdiction by stating that

> Nothing in this Agreement shall be construed to empower a Party's authorities to undertake labor law enforcement activities in the territory of another Party.

Not surprisingly, this cautious approach is reflected in the enforcement mechanism: the Agreement embodies a three-tiered hierarchy of labour rights, with each level subject to additional action by the state parties to address a violation (Figure 3.4.). The most basic level, which allows for the least intervention, includes freedom of association, the right to bargain collectively and the right to strike. Collective labour rights are therefore only subject to review and consultation. In case of a violation, there is no effective remedy.

Figure 3.4. *NAALC: Levels of Supervision*

Measure	Scope	Initiative	Possible outcome
Consultation between NAOs	*All* principles in Annex 1	Anybody	Evaluation and recommendations
Ministerial consultations	*All* principles in Annex 1	NAOs, Governments	Evaluation, non-binding recommendations
Evaluation by Committee of Experts (ECE)	• Enforcement of *technical standards*: principles 4–11 • Issue must be *trade-related* and covered by mutually recognised labour laws	Governments	Analysis and non-binding recommendation
Arbitration	Consistent pattern of failure to enforce national rules on principles Nos 5, 6, 9.	Council with 2/3 majority upon Government request	Binding decisions, penalties, sanctions

At the second level are the so-called technical labour standards, which are comprised of the prohibition on forced labour, elimination of employment discrimination, equal pay for men and women, compensation in cases of occupational injuries and illnesses and the protection of migrant workers. In case of a violation, a Committee of Experts may evaluate these standards.[181] Finally, only

[180] Compa (1995) 354.

[181] Articles 23(2) and 49 NAALC.

labour principles regarding minimum wage, child labour and occupational safety and health laws may be examined by a multilateral Arbitration panel.[182] National Administration Offices (NAOs) serve as contact points in each of the member countries. Although the Agreement provides a forum for government-to-government talks in case of enforcement problems, further non-consensual steps can be taken only if the rights involved are of the second or highest tier.

B) The NAALC in Practice: Unfulfilled Promises? As of October 2005, 32 submissions have been filed under the NAALC. Seventeen have alleged violations of labour rights in Mexico; eleven have alleged violations in the US; and four have concerned Canada.[183] Six of the submissions were not accepted for review, and four were subsequently withdrawn. The three National Administration Offices have issued 19 case reports, recommending ministerial consultations in all but three cases. As a result of such consultations, the Member States have adopted Agreements on Implementation or Joint Declarations. In one case regarding an alleged lack of enforcement by the US of minimum wage and overtime protection legislation in workplaces employing foreign nationals, files were closed. The closure was the result of a new Memorandum of Understanding between the US Department of Labor and the Immigration and Naturalization Service and the signature of an Action Plan between the US and Mexican Secretaries of Labor.[184]

As we have seen, the NAALC does not attempt to set substantive minimum labour standards for the parties. One of the most debated cases was Submission 9701, which was filed by Human Rights Watch, the International Labor Rights Fund and the Mexican National Association of Democratic Lawyers in 1997. The organisations alleged that employers in Mexico's export processing sector, the *maquiladora* industry, regularly required female job applicants to verify that they were not pregnant as a condition of employment and furthermore denied employment to pregnant women. Additionally, the organisations alleged that some *maquiladora* employers discharged pregnant employees or deliberately mistreated them in order to provoke them to resign. After holding a public hearing, the US NAO published its report in 1998.[185]

While Mexican law contains no explicit prohibition of pre-employment discrimination, Mexico had ratified *inter alia* ILO Convention No 111, which prohibits sex discrimination. The NAO found that while the legality of pre-employment screening was questionable under both international and domestic law, the illegality of dismissal because of pregnancy was clearly established under Mexican law. The NAO thus recommended ministerial consultations

[182] Principles Nos 5, 6 and 9. Article 29(1) NAALC.
[183] http://www.dol.gov/ILAB/programs/nao/naalc.htm.
[184] Case No CAN 98–2 and MEX 9804.
[185] US NAO, Public Report of Review of NAO Submission No 9701, 12 January 1998. The Report is available at http://www.dol.gov/ilab/media/reports/nao/public-reports-of-review.htm.

> for the purpose of ascertaining the extent of the protections against pregnancy-based gender discrimination afforded by Mexico's law and their effective enforcement by the appropriate institutions.[186]

As a result, several conferences were held in Mexico and the US in 1999 and 2000 to address issues related to women's rights at work.

This and other examples show that the (deliberate) inherent weakness of the Agreement is increased by several other factors:[187] the parties use the Agreement only hesitantly, although the NAOs have ample authority to bring forward important labour issues and initiate reviews and consultations. In addition, the interpretation of several obligations in the Agreement has so far remained unclear. In order to make the Agreement more effective, an institutionalised process of interpretation should be established.

Given the limited scope of the Agreement, the problems with its application are hardly surprising. For the NAALC to become more efficient, it would have to be amended.[188] The issues that receive the most criticism are not application problems but lie in the very structure of the Agreement.[189]

3.2.2.3. Free Trade Agreements of the United States

A) The US–Jordan Agreement An attempt to overcome the structural difficulties of the NAALC can be found in the Free Trade Agreement between the US and Jordan, which entered into force on 17 December 2001.[190] This Agreement is different from the NAALC in several respects.[191] First, it explicitly refers to the ILO Declaration on Fundamental Principles and Rights at Work[192] and defines labour laws as rules relating to core *international* labour standards.[193] However, in contrast to the NAALC, this agreement rather noticeably leaves out non-discrimination in employment.

In balancing international obligations and national sovereignty, the Agreement states that

> A Party shall not fail to effectively enforce its labor law, through a sustained or recurring course of action or inaction, in a manner affecting trade between the Parties, after the date of entry into force of this Agreement.[194]

[186] US NAO, Public Report of Review of NAO Submission No 9701, 12 January 1998. The Report is available at http://www.dol.gov/ilab/media/reports/nao/public-reports-of-review.htm.

[187] Human Rights Watch (2001) at II and VI.

[188] Compa (1995) 362.

[189] See, eg, criticism from Summers (1999) 173–87; and Alston (2004) 479.

[190] Agreement between the United States of America and the Hashemite Kingdom of Jordan on the Establishment of a Free Trade Area [hereinafter US–Jordan], available at http://www.ustr.gov/Trade_Agreements/Bilateral/Jordan/Section_Index.html.

[191] See Human Rights Watch (2001) at III.

[192] Article 6(1) US–Jordan. For the ILO Declaration, see chapter 1 above, section 1.2.2.3.

[193] Article 6(6) US–Jordan.

[194] Article 6(4)(a).

Although the Agreement treats labour rights and trade obligations equally and, unlike the NAALC, does not establish different levels of protection, this provision limits the scope of the Agreement to persistent violations of labour rights that affect trade. Furthermore, an important limitation can be found in Article 6(4)(b), which excludes violations of labour rights that result from the exercise "of investigatory, prosecutorial or regulatory discretion" or from a "bona fide decision regarding the allocation of resources".

In case of an alleged violation, a Joint Committee shall resolve the dispute, taking recourse to a panel if necessary.[195] If the Committee does not succeed in settling the dispute, the affected Party is "entitled to take any appropriate and commensurate measure".[196] Non-compliance with labour rights might therefore ultimately result in a withdrawal of trade benefits under the Agreement.

Finally, Article 18 makes it clear that the US–Jordan Agreement does not establish extraterritorial jurisdiction—the ATCA notwithstanding. Claims by individuals that Jordan violates the Agreement can therefore not be brought before US Courts and vice versa.

The US–Jordan Agreement is the first trade agreement in the history of the US to address labour issues within the text of the agreement itself. In order to avoid possible conflicts with the WTO, Article 1 reaffirms the parties' commitments under WTO law. In addition, it explicitly states that the parties are not authorised to apply measures, namely sanctions, that are inconsistent with WTO law.[197] An additional Joint Statement on WTO Issues clarifies the relationship further.[198] Because the US–Jordan Agreement goes much further in protecting labour rights than WTO law, it could be seen as a means of circumventing the WTO's focus on trade and slipping in a social clause through the back door. In fact, however, increasing regionalism and bilateralism were seen as major impediments to international trade and the major reasons for the revision of the GATT. For this reason, only one day after the signature of the US–Jordan Agreement, the US Chamber of Commerce vowed to seek the removal of provisions dealing with workers' rights when Congress discussed the implementation of the Agreement.[199]

B) The US–Morocco Agreement The recent Free Trade Agreement with Morocco, signed in June 2004, follows the approach of the US–Jordan Agreement[200] yet further develops the standard with respect to labour rights. It reaffirms the obligations of both parties as members of the ILO[201] and

[195] Article 17(1) US–Jordan.
[196] Article 17(2)(b) US–Jordan.
[197] Article 1(4) US–Jordan.
[198] http://www.jordanembassyus.org/new/commercial/fta/joint_wto.pdf.
[199] "The Chamber has consistently maintained that the best means to achieve improvements in labor and environmental conditions is to pursue these improvements in separate, albeit parallel efforts." 17 BNA's International Trade Reporter, Africa/Middle East, 2 November 2000.
[200] Article 1.2 of the Agreement.
[201] Article 16.1.

condemns the weakening or lowering of domestic labour standards in order to attract trade or investment.[202]

An interesting provision can be found in Article 16.2.1, which requires the parties to effectively enforce its labour laws but respects their discretion. In exercising this discretion, the parties have to ensure that a systematic failure to enforce labour laws does not affect the trade between the parties. A letter attached to the Agreement clarifies that this provision applies to situations "in which there is a sustained or recurring failure to effectively enforce domestic law *and* the failure affects trade between the United States and Morocco."[203]

With respect to co-operation, the Agreement includes a mechanism to promote respect for the ILO Declaration on Fundamental Principles and Rights at Work and Convention No 182 on the Worst Forms of Child Labour.[204] All core obligations, including the labour provisions, are subject to the Agreement's special dispute settlement procedures. These procedures provide for open public hearings, the public release of legal submissions by governments and the opportunity for interested third parties to submit views.

The Free Trade Agreement led to substantial labour rights reforms in Morocco with a new labour law entering into force on 8 June 2004. As of October 2006, Morocco has ratified the ILO fundamental conventions except for Convention No 87 on Freedom of Association.

C) The US–Australia Agreement On 15 July 2004, a Free Trade Agreement with Australia was approved by the US Senate. Its labour rights provisions follow the Moroccan example, with the exception that it defines in a separate provision what it considers to be internationally recognised labour principles and rights.[205] This provision was introduced mainly because Australia provides labour protection for children primarily not through labour laws but through regulations about compulsory education.

3.2.2.4. *The European Union*

A) Social Policy in General The protection of labour rights has a long tradition in Europe. Respect for core labour rights is a requirement for membership in the Council of Europe.[206] The European Convention on Human Rights was complemented by the Council of Europe Social Charter in 1961, which was revised

[202] Article 16.2.

[203] Letter of 15 June 2004 by Catherine A Novelli, Assistant USTR for Europe and the Mediterranean to Taib Fassi Fihri, Minister Delegate for Foreign Affairs and Cooperation, Kingdom of Morocco. http://www.ustr.gov/Trade_Agreements/Bilateral/Morocco_FTA/Section_Index.html

[204] Article 16.5 and Annex 16-A of the Agreement. For the text of the ILO Declaration and relevant articles of Convention No 182, see Appendix A.15. and A.14. respectively.

[205] Chapter 18 of the Agreement.

[206] Article 3 of the Constitution for the Council of Europe requires new members to guarantee their citizens fundamental and human rights. More recently, new members have been required to adhere to the European Convention on Human Rights.

in 1996. It includes the obligation to work towards the protection of the four core labour rights as defined by the ILO.

As a result of the significant differences between the different European Countries with respect to the standard of living and working conditions after the Second World War, social dumping was a constant concern during the creation of the European Single Market.[207] In the 1970s the European Community organs started paying more attention to human rights. However, efforts to include the legally non-binding Community Charter of the Fundamental Social Rights of Workers (1989)[208] in the Maastricht Treaty failed due to strong opposition from the United Kingdom. Instead, a protocol was annexed to the Treaty indicating the goal of closer harmonisation among EC members.[209] The Maastricht Treaty did however contain important labour-related rights, such as a very strong provision against employment discrimination.

In 1997, the Treaty of Amsterdam brought the so-called "opt-out" by the United Kingdom to an end and incorporated the Community Social Charter into EU law, thus restoring unity to social policy.[210] Although Article 137 of the EC Treaty still provides that Member States remain primarily responsible for social policy,[211] the competence of the Community has been expanded by the Amsterdam Treaty, because social policy is now based on human rights and allows room for a dynamic interpretation of Article 3(j) of the EC Treaty.

It is now established within the European Union that sustainable economic growth and social cohesion—which requires respect for core labour standards—go hand in hand.[212] At the European Council meeting held in Nice in December 2000, a new European Social Policy Agenda was adopted. It explicitly stated the mutual reinforcement of economic and social policy.[213] The Charter of Fundamental Rights of the European Union, which was also adopted at the Nice Summit, commits EU members to observing fundamental labour rights.[214] The respective provisions are now included in the draft Treaty establishing a Constitution for Europe of June 2004.[215]

[207] Fredman, McCrudden and Freedland (2000) 178; Morici and Schultz (2001) 67–68.

[208] COM 89(248) final.

[209] Treaty on European Union—Agreement on Social Policy, European Social Policy, OJ 1992 C 191/91. Because amending the EEC Treaty requires unanimity, the Agreement did not amend the Treaty and it is not binding on the United Kingdom. See Van Wezel Stone (1999) 109.

[210] Articles 136–45 of the Treaty on Establishing the European Community as amended by the Treaty of Amsterdam.

[211] This has been criticised, *inter alia*, by Blanpain (1999) 498, who characterises the Treaty of Amsterdam as "High Goals, meager means".

[212] EC Commission (2001), 3.

[213] Social Policy Agenda, COM (2000)379 final, 28 June 2000.

[214] Charter of Fundamental Rights of the European Union, Articles 5 (Prohibition of slavery and forced labour), 27 (Workers' right to information and consultation within the undertaking), 28 (Right of collective bargaining and action), 31 (Fair and just working conditions), 32 (Prohibition of child labour and protection of young people at work). OJ 2000 C 364/1.

[215] Conference of the Representatives of the Governments of the Member States, Provisional consolidated version of the draft Treaty establishing a Constitution for Europe, 25 June 2004, CIG 86/04, Articles II-5, II-27, II-28, II-31 and II-32.

B) The Cotonou Agreement Since 1992 all agreements concluded between the European Community and third countries have been required to incorporate a clause defining human rights as a basic element.[216] This clause also encompasses core labour rights as set out in the eight fundamental ILO Conventions.[217] Furthermore, since the Copenhagen World Summit for Social Development in 1995, all agreements between the European Communities and third countries incorporate a reference to the final declaration of this summit, on the same footing as the reference to human rights.

The 2000 Cotonou Agreement[218] between the European Communities and 77 African, Caribbean and Pacific (ACP) states goes a step further by including a specific provision on trade and labour standards, which confirms the parties' commitment to core labour standards:[219]

> Article 50 Trade and labour standards
>
> 1. The Parties reaffirm their commitment to the internationally recognised core labour standards, as defined by the relevant ILO Conventions, and in particular the freedom of association and the right to collective bargaining, the abolition of forced labour, the elimination of worst forms of child labour and non-discrimination in respect of employment.
> 2. . . .
> 3. The Parties agree that labour standards should not be used for protectionist trade purposes.

In addition, the Cotonou Agreement names the promotion of core labour standards as part of the overall development strategy of the Agreement, which provides that

> co-operation shall support ACP States' efforts at developing general sectoral policies and reforms which improve the coverage, quality of and access to basic social infrastructure and services . . .[220]

It also provides that co-operation shall aim, *inter alia*, at "encouraging the promotion of participatory methods of social dialogue as well as respect of basic social rights".

The Cotonou Agreement is seen as a potential role model for future trade and co-operation agreements. From the point of view of the European Community, the commitment to core labour rights in co-operation agreements will make these autonomous instruments complementary to efforts in the multilateral

[216] This development started with Article 5 of the Lomé IV Convention of 1989. The legal basis for the extension on other agreements is Article 310 EC Treaty. Nogueras and Martínez (2001) 318; Brandtner and Rosas (1999) 701–2.

[217] On the ILO Conventions, see chapter 1 above, section 1.2.2.2.

[218] Partnership agreement between the members of the African, Caribbean and Pacific Group of States of the one part, and the European Community and its Member States, of the other part, signed in Cotonou on 23 June 2000, OJ 2000 L 317/3.

[219] EC Commission (2001), 12.

[220] Article 25 of the Cotonou Agreement, "Social Sector Development", note 218 above.

framework to promote such rights. In its long-term strategy, the Commission considers development assistance as an excellent opportunity to discuss the implementation of core labour rights with ACP countries.[221] It therefore aims to better integrate core labour rights in the EC's development policy, especially the poverty reduction programmes. Although still very much a "work in progress", this approach goes a lot further than the current policy of the Bretton Woods Institutions.

C) The General System of Preferences (GSP) The Community General System of Preferences (GSP) scheme provides market access on a preferential basis to developing countries.[222] The modalities are set out in Council Regulations.[223] Social incentives under the GSP are an important tool for the promotion of core labour rights. Until December 2001, compliance with core labour standards qualified for additional trade preferences.[224] However, a withdrawal of preferences, in whole or in part, was possible when beneficiary countries practised any form of slavery or forced labour.

In 2002, a new GSP scheme entered into force.[225] Since the special incentive arrangements were not as successful as had been hoped at the time of their original adoption in 1994,[226] the new scheme aimed to make them more attractive.[227] Under the new regulation, *additional* preferences would double the general preferences.[228] As it turned out, the double conditionality established by the earlier social incentive arrangements did not work in practice. Under the old rules, a country had first to qualify for the status of a beneficiary country under the arrangements; second, exports from that country had to be certified as being manufactured in accordance with the labour standards concerned. This included all inputs, even imported ones. Because countries were not in a position to control compliance in that respect, the Commission decided to drop this requirement.[229] With regard to the definition of core labour rights, the new regulation referred to the Fundamental ILO Conventions mentioned in the ILO Declaration on Fundamental Principles and Rights at Work of 1998.[230]

[221] EC Commission (2001), 18–19.

[222] For a detailed discussion, see Brandtner and Rosas (1999) 713–21.

[223] Council Regulation (EC) No 980/2005 of 27 June 2005, applying a scheme of generalised tariff preferences for the period 1 January 2006 to 31 December 2008.

[224] Under the special incentives, additional trade preferences may be granted to countries that effectively apply the standards laid down in ILO Conventions Nos 87 and 98 on freedom of association and the right to collective bargaining and those of Convention No 138 on Child labour.

[225] Council Regulation (EC) No 2501/2001 of 10 December 2001, applying a scheme of generalised tariff preferences for the period 1 January 2002 to 31 December 2005.

[226] COM (2001) 688 final, paras 28–29. Council Regulation (EC) No 3281/94 of 19 December 1994.

[227] In the view of one commentator, the Community has moved from a "carrot and stick" approach to a "more carrots" approach. Brandtner and Rosas (1999) 714.

[228] COM (2001) 688 final, paras 28–29.

[229] *Ibid*, para 31.

[230] Article 14.

Following the Appellate Body in *EC—Tariff Preferences*[231] the scheme had to be amended again.[232] The Fundamental Conventions are now explicitly referred to Article 9 (1) and Annex III, part A of the Regulation.

These special arrangements for the protection of core labour rights are available on request. In making a request, an applying country must specify the laws and regulations that in substance incorporate the eight fundamental ILO Conventions as well as the measures adopted to implement them. Ratification of the conventions is not required. The Commission will then publish the request in the Official Journal and invite interested parties to submit relevant comments and information. The examination takes into account information by competent organisations such as the ILO. After consultation with the GSP committee the Commission will decide on whether to grant the special incentive arrangements.

With the adoption of the new definition in 2001, the scope of labour rights addressed by the special incentives programme has significantly increased. By explicitly referring to the ILO Conventions mentioned in the ILO Declaration on Fundamental Principles and Rights at Work, the European Community confirms the universal character of the core labour standards. In addition, under the new regulation, general GSP benefits can be fully or partially withdrawn if a country is found to violate seriously and systematically the freedom of association, the right to collective bargaining or the principle of non-discrimination or use of child labour.[233] While the limitation to serious and systematic violations might restrict the already basic core labour rights even further, one has to bear in mind that the Commission's proposal is based on a long-term strategy: it intends to refine the link to the ILO fundamental conventions in the context of future reviews of the GSP regulation.[234]

As before, the export of goods made by prison labour is reason enough to withdraw benefits.[235] Accordingly, following an investigation into allegations by European trade union organisations of forced labour in Burma/Myanmar, the country's access to the GSP was removed in 1997.[236]

Although the GSP system has generally been viewed as compatible with WTO law, and in particular with Part IV of the GATT and the Enabling Clause,

[231] *European Communities—Conditions for the Granting of Tariff Preferences to Developing Countries*, Report of the Appellate Body, WT/DS246/AB/R, 7 April 2004, para 99 [hereinafter *EC—Tariff Preferences*].

[232] Note 223 above.

[233] Article 26.1(b) of the Council Regulation 2001, note 225 above; Article 16.1(a) of the Council Regulation 2005, note 223 above.

[234] EC Commission (2001), 17. Communication from the commission on developing countries international trade and sustainable development: the function of the community's generalized system of preferences (6SP) for the ten year period from 2006 to 2015, COM (2004) 461, paras 63 and 65.

[235] Article 26.1.(c) of the Council Regulation 2001, note 225 above; Article 16.1(b) of the Council Regulation 2005, note 223 above.

[236] Council Regulation 552/97 (EC) of 24 March 1997, temporarily withdrawing access to generalised tariff preferences from the Union of Myanmar, OJ L 85/8, 27.3.1997.

India challenged the system in the WTO.[237] In general, GSP is an exception to the MFN principle in Article I of the GATT. In 1979, the Enabling Clause was introduced to allow positive discrimination in favour of developing countries. A Resolution 21(II) adopted by UNCTAD in New Delhi in 1968 characterised GSP as a "non-reciprocal and non-discriminatory generalized system of preferences in favor of developing countries". This definition implied that differences of treatment between developing countries cannot be established and that the system should benefit them all and be based on objective criteria. However, in reality, concessions under GSP are unilateral and voluntary. The country that applies a GSP system has great freedom in its design and, as we have seen, establishes differences according to different criteria, such as the competitive relationship of the products or the relative development level of the beneficiaries.[238]

In its original request for a panel, India had claimed that the labour conditionality violated the MFN obligation in Article I:1 GATT. It then conceded that the Enabling Clause affected the application of Article I GATT to GSP schemes. However, India argued that the EC scheme violated several parts of the Enabling Clause. Although India finally withdrew its complaint with respect to labour rights, the case is still being discussed among scholars. The first question is whether the EC special preference agreement is covered by the Enabling Clause. If so, it will be necessary to examine whether the requirements of the Enabling Clause are being met. Article XX GATT would apply if the Enabling Clause were violated. A strong argument can be made, with different reasoning, that the Appellate Body might be likely to uphold the EC programme.[239]

D) Public Procurement The European Communities' public procurement policy is contained in several directives[240] that have recently been revised with the objective of clarifying and simplifying procedures.[241] Social considerations such as compliance with core labour rights can be taken into account at different

[237] Request for the Establishment of a Panel by India, *European Communities—Conditions for the Granting of Tariff Preferences to Developing Countries*, 9 December 2002, WT/DS246/4. Oppermann (1999) Rz 1828. See also chapter 2 above, note 294 and accompanying text.

[238] Nogueras and Martínez (2001) 331.

[239] Bartels (2003) 525–26; Howse (2003b) 1378–81; Charnovitz et al (2004) 244–46.

[240] Council Directive 92/50/EEC of 18 June 1992 relating to the coordination of procedures for the award of public service contracts; Council Directive 93/36/EEC of 14 June 1993 coordinating procedures for the award of public supply contracts; and Council Directive 93/37/EEC of 14 June 1993 concerning the coordination of procedures for the award of public works contracts, as amended by European Parliament and Council Directive 97/52/EC of 13 October 1997; Council Directive 93/38/EEC of 14 June 1993 coordinating the procurement procedures of entities operating in the water, energy, transport and telecommunications sectors, as amended by Directive 98/4/EC of the European Parliament and of the Council of 16 February 1998.

[241] Directive 2004/18/EC of the European Parliament and of the Council of 31 March 2004 on the coordination of procedures for the award of public works contracts, public supply contracts and public service contracts; Directive 2004/17/EC of the European Parliament and of the Council of 31 March 2004 coordinating the procurement procedures of entities operating in the water, energy, transport and postal services sectors. Both directives entered into force on 30 April 2004.

stages of the procurement process.[242] The first step is of course the choice by the public authority as to which goods or services it wants to purchase, thus the definition of the subject matter. At this stage, community law permits member countries to set technical standards and, for instance, to require compliance with specific production processes as long as they characterise the product in relation to other competing products and in such a way as to meet the needs of the contracting authority. Therefore, requirements that bear no relation to the product or the service itself are not technical specifications within the meaning of the public procurement directives.

In the *Beentjes*[243] case, the European Court of Justice (ECJ) held that a condition regarding the employment of long-term unemployed persons was not related to a tenderer's economic, financial or technical capacity and suitability under the relevant procurement directive. However, the contracting authorities can include conditions relating to the employment of long-term unemployed people but only when setting conditions relating to the execution of a contract. Such conditions must of course comply with Community law and not discriminate directly or indirectly against non-national tenderers. They should not be disguised as technical specifications. Contract performance conditions are compatible with the Directives provided that they are not directly or indirectly discriminatory and are indicated in the notice used to make the call for competition or in the specifications. Mention may be made of:

> requirements [. . .] to comply in substance with the provisions of the basic International Labour Organization (ILO) conventions, assuming that such provisions have not been implemented in national law.[244]

The same is true for measures designed to promote equality between men and women. Although the ECJ has not yet had the opportunity to decide a case, it seems that contractual clauses relating to the manner in which supply contracts are executed would be more problematic because requiring changes to the organisation, structure or policy of an undertaking established on the territory of another Member State might be considered discriminatory or to constitute an unjustified restriction of trade.[245]

Although the public procurement directives do not contain specific provisions on core labour rights, it is undisputed that the core labour rights laid down in the ILO Declaration on Fundamental Principles and Rights at Work apply without exception to all Member States. The issue becomes more difficult, however, when the stipulated working conditions go beyond the ILO minimum standard.

242 For a detailed analysis see EC, Interpretative Communication of the Commission on the Community law applicable to public procurement and the possibilities for integrating social considerations into public procurement, COM (2001) 566 final, 15 October 2001.

243 Case 31/87 *Gebroeders Beentjes BV v The Netherlands* [1988] ECR 4635. The *Beentjes* decision leaves room for different interpretations. See McCrudden (1998) 231–33.

244 Directive 2004/17/EC, note 241 above, at para 44 of the preamble; and Directive 2004/18/EC, note 241 above, at para 33 of the preamble.

245 Note 242 above, at 1.6, p 17.

The ECJ has recognised that ensuring social protection of workers is an imperative requirement of general interest and may justify national measures restricting the exercise of one of the fundamental freedoms of Community law.[246] Notwithstanding this, purely administrative considerations would not justify such a derogation from Community law by a Member State.[247]

To sum up, the public procurement directives offer various possibilities to consider core labour rights. While the cases in which the personal situation of a tenderer may lead to its exclusion from a procurement procedure are interpreted strictly, the member countries have relatively broad room for manoeuvre once the contract has been awarded.

3.2.2.5. *Switzerland*

Switzerland is a small and open economy and, as such, is necessarily outward oriented. Its exports rank twentieth, its imports seventeenth among the international community.[248] Nevertheless, the effect of unilateral measures would be very limited. After a period of "splendid isolation" based on neutrality concerns, Switzerland has now adopted a course of "selective integration", ie participation in those international organisations that are compatible with the country's neutrality and its specific needs and objectives.

A) The Framework: Neutrality and Foreign Policy While the concept of neutrality held Switzerland back from regional and international integration in the past, it was more a deliberate political decision rather than legal reasoning that kept Switzerland from becoming a member of the United Nations until September 2002. The fact that the system of collective security as it was established by the UN requires the *whole* international community to discriminate against aggressors, coupled with the end of the cold war, led to a review of Switzerland's neutrality concept[249] and eventually to a radical change in Swiss foreign policy.[250] In 1990, Switzerland for the first time participated in UN sanctions.[251] The reasoning behind the federal government's decision left no doubt: when the inter-

[246] Case 279/80 *Webb* [1981] ECR 3305; Joined Cases 62/81 and 63/81 *Seco and Desquenne & Giral* [1982] ECR 223; Case C-113/89 *Rush Portuguesa* [1990] ECR I-1417; Case C-272/94 *Guiot* [1996] ECR I-1905; Joined Cases C-369/96 and C-376/96 *Arblade* [1999] ECR I-8453.

[247] Case C-18/95 *Terhoeve* [1999] ECR I-345, paras 43–47.

[248] Source: WTO, World Trade in 2002, available at http://www.wto.org/english/res_e/statis_e/its2003_e/ its03_overview_e.htm. In comparison, the country ranks 110th with respect to its size: Bericht zur Aussenwirtschaftspolitik 2000, BBl 2000 I 824-958, 834 [hereinafter Aussenwirtschaftspolitik 2000].

[249] Malinverni (1998) 112–14; Bericht zur Neutralität, Anhang zum Bericht über die Aussenpolitik der Schweiz in den 90er Jahren vom 29. November 1993 [hereinafter Neutralitätsbericht 1993], BBl 1994 I 206 (White Paper on Neutrality, Annex to the Report on Swiss Foreign Policy for the Nineties of 29 November 1993, English translation available at http://www.eda.admin.ch).

[250] Schindler (1992) 106; Thürer (1992) 63–85.

[251] Sanctions against Iraq: Verordnung vom 7. August 1992 über Wirtschaftsmassnahmen gegenüber der Republik Irak und dem Staat Kuwait, AS 1990 1316; See UN Doc S/RES/661 (1991).

national community takes steps against flagrant violations of international law, there is no room for neutrality. Not joining the international community in its attempts would come nothing short of supporting the offender.[252]

After the change in policy had been initiated with the sanctions against Iraq, the Federal Council gradually expanded Switzerland's engagement in collective actions taken by the UN. In parallel with the resolutions of the UN Security Council, Switzerland imposed trade and financial sanctions on Libya,[253] Yugoslavia (Serbia and Montenegro),[254] Haiti,[255] Sierra Leone,[256] the National Union for the Total Independence of Angola (UNITA),[257] the Taliban (Afghanistan)[258] and Liberia.[259]

In a dispute about the application of the sanctions against Libya, the Federal Council expressed the view that Switzerland's participation was an act of solidarity with the international community's effort to combat terrorism and in compliance with the country's neutrality.[260] With regard to the sanctions against UNITA, Sierra Leone and Liberia, the aim of the UN Security Council was to restrict trade with conflict diamonds in order to cut down the resources available for financing the civil wars in these countries. Since Switzerland is one of the main trading areas for diamonds, it has an interest in avoiding conflict diamonds. It therefore actively supported international efforts to create a special certificate/label for raw diamonds in the framework of the Kimberley Process.[261]

To sum up, it is now recognised—at least by legal scholars—that the law of neutrality is applicable only in traditional interstate wars where the UN Security Council has not yet made a decision to act. It does not apply to enforcement measures decided by the Security Council, even if such measures involve military actions. Switzerland therefore now allows forces under the Security

[252] Neutralitätsbericht 1993, para 412; Villiger (1995) 178.

[253] Verordnungen über Massnahmen gegenüber Libyen vom 15. April 1992 und 12. Januar 1994, SR 946.208, AS 1992 598, AS 1994 108. UN Doc S/RES/748 (1992). The measures were suspended in 1999 after the suspects for the attacks on the PAN-AM and UTA airplanes were extradited to the Netherlands for trial: AS 1999 1544. UN Doc S/RES/1192 (1998).

[254] Verordnung über Massnahmen gegenüber Jugoslawien (Serbien und Montenegro) vom 3. Juni 1992, AS 1992 1203. See UN Doc S/RES/757 (1992).

[255] Verordnungen vom 30. Juni 1993 und vom 22. Juni 1994 über Massnahmen gegenüber der Republik Haiti, AS 1993 2053 and AS 1994 1453; UN Doc S/RES/917 (1994) and S/RES/944 (1994).

[256] Verordnung vom 8. Dezember 1997 über Massnahmen gegenüber Sierra Leone, AS 1997 3010; UN Doc S/RES/1132 (1997).

[257] Verordnung über Massnahmen gegenüber der UNITA, AS 1999 151, amended by AS 2001 3583.

[258] Verordnung über Massnahmen gegenüber den Taliban (Afghanistan), AS 2000 2642. UN Doc S/RES/1267 (1999). The sanctions were imposed after the Taliban refused to extradite Osama bin Laden after the attacks on the US embassies in Kenya and Tanzania. The sanctions were intensified several times, especially after 11 September 2001: AS 2001 1353, AS 2002 155; UN Doc S/RES/1373 (2001).

[259] Verordnung über Massnahmen gegenüber Liberia vom 27. Juni 2001, AS 2001 1686; UN Doc S/RES/1343 (2001).

[260] VPB 1996-60/III 60.88.

[261] Verordnung vom 29. November 2002 über den Handel mit Rohdiamanten, SR 946.231.11. Pauwelyn (2003b) 1177; Nadakavukaren Schefer (2005) 391–450.

Council's authorisation to fly over its territory but for political reasons does not itself participate in military operations.[262]

In 1993, the Federal Council made an effort to bring the conceptual framework in line with practice and defined five major goals to be pursued by foreign policy (Figure 3.5.). These goals were later reformulated by the new Constitution[263] and include: the preservation of Switzerland's independence and social welfare; the alleviation of need and poverty in the world; the promotion of human rights and democracy; the peaceful coexistence of nations; and the preservation of natural resources.[264]

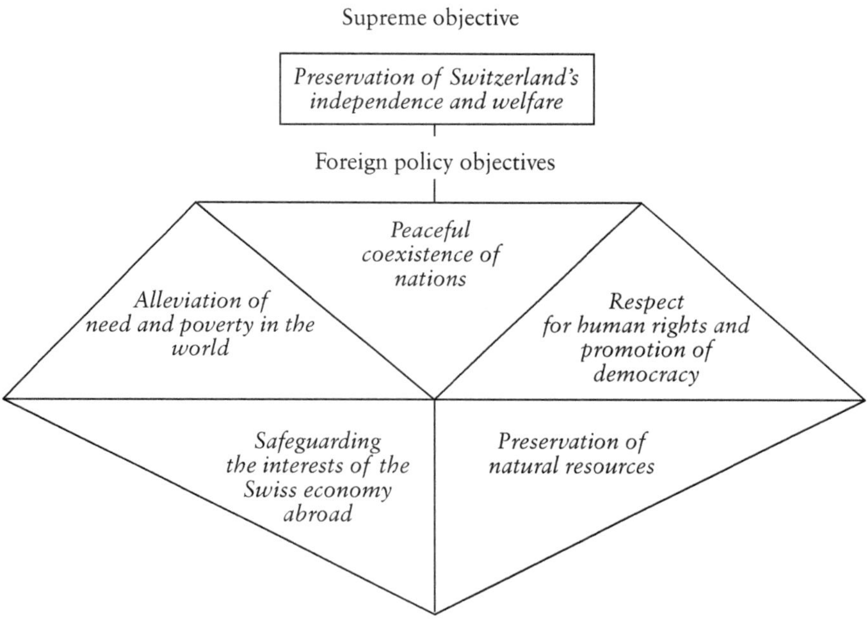

Source: Aussenpolitik 2000.

Figure 3.5. *The Five Major Goals of Swiss Foreign Policy*

262 Schindler (1998a) 162; Schindler (1991) 20–21; Botschaft über die Volksinitiative Für den Beitritt der Schweiz zur Organisation der Vereinten Nationen BBl 2001 1212–15; Neutralitätspraxis der Schweiz—aktuelle Aspekte, Bericht der interdepartementalen Arbeitsgruppe vom 30. August 2000. On 3 March 2002, the States and the population agreed to Switzerland's membership to the United Nations.

263 Bericht über die Aussenpolitik der Schweiz in den 90er Jahren vom 29. November 1993, BBl 1994 I 153 [hereinafter Aussenpolitik 1993].

264 Article 54(2) of the Constitution; Präsenz und Kooperation: Interessenwahrung in einer zusammenwachsenden Welt, Aussenpolitischer Bericht 2000, BBl 2001 I 261, 299–312 [hereinafter Aussenpolitik 2000]. Unofficial English translation: Presence and Cooperation: Safeguarding Switzerland's Interests in an Integrating World, Foreign Policy Report 2000, at 3.1.2.2. p 23, available at http://www.eda.admin.ch.

This set of goals for foreign policy is a clear departure from the earlier concept where neutrality, solidarity and universality played key roles.[265] The new goals of promoting human rights and democracy were further elaborated by a comprehensive report in 2000.[266]

B) Principles of Foreign Trade Policy For foreign trade policy, free access to markets is crucial. This goal can however be at odds with other important economic goals such as full employment. Therefore, a broad consensus has been reached in Switzerland: trade liberalisation is an essential but not exclusive objective of trade policy.[267] Other goals include fairness in economic relations and solidarity with developing countries as well as public health and security.

The Federal Council has made it clear that the goals of economic development and respect for human rights are complementary: in the long term, one cannot be reached without the other.[268] However, formulating a coherent policy that prioritises both foreign trade and human rights has proven difficult in practice. In order to facilitate this process, the decision to apply "political conditionality" to specific countries has lain with the Federal Council alone since 1999. When the label "political conditionality" is applied to a country, co-operation can be partially or completely suspended in the event of serious human rights violations.

The constitutional basis for foreign trade measures in Switzerland is Article 101. Section 2 allows the Confederation to depart from the principle of economic freedom if necessary. While such measures can be based on a variety of motives—such as the protection of public health and security, the policy of neutrality or even retaliation of measures taken by other countries[269]—with regard to the protection of core labour rights, compliance with international law is one of the major motivating factors.

Since Switzerland's trade measures on their own can seldom have a significant impact on a targeted country without the support of the international community, the Federal Council has maintained that unilateral trade sanctions are usually not an option; instead the emphasis lies on measures that are "positive in nature". Commonly applied trade measures hence range from discussion of human rights issues during bilateral economic negotiations to promotion of fair trade and investment to increase economic development and welfare, incentives to co-operate with countries that actively engage in the promotion of human rights, refusal to grant export and investment guarantees, and participation in economic sanctions imposed by the international community.[270]

265 Aussenpolitik 1993, note 263 above, at 159. Rhinow, Schmid and Biaggini (1998) § 32 Rz 15.
266 Bericht über die Menschenrechtspolitik der Schweiz vom 16. Februar 2000, BBl 2000 2586 [hereinafter Menschenrechtspolitik 2000].
267 Biaggini, Müller, Richli and Zimmerli (2005) 84–85 with further references; Rhinow, Schmid and Biaggini (1998) § 32 Rz 14.
268 Menschenrechtspolitik 2000, note 266 above, at 2594.
269 Biaggini, Müller, Richli and Zimmerli (2005) 90–92.
270 Menschenrechtspolitik 2000, note 266 above, at 2595.

The concept of "positive" trade measures might be seen as a first step towards mainstreaming human rights into government activities. However, the Federal Council assesses every situation on a case-by-case basis, taking into account the particular circumstances and the policies applied by other countries.[271] In other words, so far, there is no direct institutional link between core labour rights and international trade in Swiss law. The Federal Law on Foreign Trade Measures[272] provides guidance only for what have been called "pathological" cases by commentators.[273] According to the law, the government can restrict the import, export and transit of goods if measures taken by other countries or extraordinary circumstances abroad have a devastating impact on major Swiss economic interests. In other words, labour rights violations cannot justify measures under this law unless they seriously affect major national economic interests. This has never been the case so far and is unlikely to be so in the future. In a similar fashion, gross and systematic violations of human rights can also be considered under the Federal Law on Export Risk Guarantee[274] and the Law on Investment Protection.[275, 276]

After the 1996 WTO Ministerial Conference in Singapore, the Swiss government was asked by a member of Parliament about its position on the relationship between trade and core labour rights. The government's reply made it clear that it would support the ILO's activities in this field and that it was in favour of an "adequate" reference to core labour standards in the WTO framework.[277] At the Geneva 2000 Forum, a follow-up event to the 1995 Global Social Summit in Copenhagen, Switzerland proposed an initiative to analyse and discuss the impacts of globalisation, including the relationship between trade and core labour standards, under the leadership of the ILO; the initiative was supported by the US, the EU and some developing countries but emphatically rejected by other developing nations.[278]

C) Bilateral Agreements with the European Communities The number of regional and bilateral trade agreements has increased recently. There are several reasons that account for this phenomenon: first, bilateral agreements became increasingly popular when the Uruguay Round of the GATT seemed about to fail. The threat of that failure prompted several countries to ensure free trade by incorporating some of the basic trading rules that were negotiated during the Uruguay Round into bilateral or regional agreements. In addition, the fall of the

[271] *Ibid*, at 2598–99.
[272] Artikel 1 Bundesgesetz über aussenwirtschaftliche Massnahmen vom 25. Juni 1982, SR 946.201.
[273] Biaggini, Múller, Richli and Zimmerli (2005) 92.
[274] Bundesgesetz über die Exportrisikogarantie vom 26. September 1958, SR 946.11.
[275] Bundesgesetz über die Investitionsrisikogarantie vom 20. März 1970, SR 977.0.
[276] Menschenrechtspolitik 2000, note 266 above, at 2595.
[277] Question (einfache Anfrage) submitted by Rep Rennwald of 30 April 1997 (NR 97.1059); accepted by the Federal Council on 9 June 1997.
[278] Aussenwirtschaftspolitik 2000, note 248 above, at 878. This initiative also called on the BWIs, but it seems that it was never mentioned by the Swiss representatives in the relevant bodies.

iron curtain and the collapse of the Council for Mutual Economic Assistance (COMECON) led to a number of new trade arrangements. The success of the EC's common market stimulated efforts in the rest of Europe and other regions of the world. Finally, the expansion of increasingly effective free trade agreements outside Europe, including most notably NAFTA and Mercosur,[279] caused the EU to seek similar arrangements in order to avoid discrimination in these crucial markets.[280]

It is in this context that the Swiss government decided to expand its existing network of bilateral and regional trade agreements.[281] After the rejection of the proposal to join the European Economic Area in a 1992 referendum, Switzerland found itself institutionally isolated and faced with the threat of losing its competitiveness with regard to other European countries. From the 15 topics that the Federal Council considered desirable subjects of a trade agreement with the EC, ten were of mutual interest for the European Council and consequently grouped into seven mandates for negotiations: free movement of persons, civil aviation, overland transport, agriculture, technical barriers to trade, public procurement and research.[282] After long and difficult negotiations, seven agreements covering the ten identified issues were finally signed on 21 June 1999 and entered into force on 1 June 2002.[283]

The Agreement between Switzerland and the European Communities on the free movement of persons[284] establishes a gradual opening of the labour market and a right of entry, residence and access to work for all nationals of the contracting parties.[285] A mixed committee is in charge of implementation of the agreement.[286] With increasing immigration in the 1970s and 1980s, Switzerland became concerned not only about the number of immigrants but also about social dumping and the mistreatment of immigrant workers. For this reason, ample control mechanisms to ensure compliance with existing standards for working conditions and minimum wages were established.[287] Under existing law, work permits are granted to non-indigenous workers only if the local

[279] Argentina, Brazil, Paraguay and Uruguay.

[280] Cottier (1996) 152–53.

[281] Aussenwirtschaftspolitik 2000, note 248 above, at 846.

[282] Botschaft des Bundesrates zur Genehmigung der sektoriellen Abkommen zwischen der Schweiz und der EG vom 23. Juni 1999, BBl 1999 6128 [hereinafter Botschaft Sektorielle Abkommen], Separatum pp 11–13.

[283] Although the agreements are commonly referred to as the "Bilateral Agreements", technically the agreement on the free movement of persons is not bilateral because it had to be ratified not only by the European Community but also by the Member States. The agreement is considered a mixed treaty according to Articles 300, 310 of the Treaty establishing the European Community. Thürer and Hillemanns (2002) 18; Oppermann (1999) Rz 1711–13.

[284] Botschaft Sektorielle Abkommen, above note 282, at p 6489; Bericht zur Aussenwirtschaftspolitik 2003, BBl 2004 1 [hereinafter Aussenwirtschaftspolitik 2003] at 10–21.

[285] Article 1(a). For an overview, see Kälin (2002) 12–16.

[286] For a detailed description of the mixed committees established by the bilateral agreements, see Jaag, Institutionen, 48–60.

[287] Verordnung vom 6. Oktober 1986 über die Begrenzung der Zahl der Ausländer (BVO), SR 823.2. For an overview, see Thürer and Kaufmann (1990) 47–48 and 51–53.

standards for working conditions and wages are met.[288] The agreement with the EC allows contracting parties to maintain preferential treatment such as special discriminatory controls for a maximum period of two years.[289] Given the high costs of living and the related relatively high wages in Switzerland, this provision raised concerns not only within the government but also within labour unions.[290]

In order to prevent the feared social dumping, the Swiss Parliament adopted a set of *flanking* or companion measures. The Federal Law on Minimum Wages and Working Conditions for Posted Workers and Flanking Measures, which entered into force together with the Agreement, provides for a set of minimum labour standards that must be applied to *all* workers in Switzerland regardless of nationality or residence.[291] Since working contracts that are established in Switzerland are already subject to Swiss law and its labour standards and regulations, the new provisions focus on workers sent to Switzerland by their foreign employers for a limited time, so-called "posted workers" *(entsandte Arbeitnehmer)*. These workers are still bound by their working contract and therefore – depending on country of origin – subject to lower labour standards than are required in Switzerland.

The risk of social dumping is not unique to Switzerland. In 1990, the European Communities started to look into this issue and after lengthy discussions and negotiations adopted a directive in 1996.[292] The new Swiss law follows this approach to a large extent and also takes into account the experiences of Germany and France in relation to the domestic regulations that they established to bridge the gap until the Directive finally entered into force. The law covers the following minimum labour standards: minimum wages, maximum work periods and minimum rest periods, minimum paid annual holidays, safety and health at work, protection of pregnant women and women who have recently given birth and protection of children and young people; it also provides for non-discrimination and equality of treatment between men and women.[293] In these fields, the workers have a right to *at least* the labour standards as they are defined in federal laws, federal ordinances, collective agreements that have been extended by the government to cover third parties *(allgemein verbindlich erklärte Gesamtarbeitsverträge)* and minimum wages set according to the new Article 360a of the Code of Obligations.[294]

[288] Article 9 BVO (SR 823.21).
[289] Article 10(2) of the Agreement.[290] Portmann (2002) 269.
[291] Bundesgesetz über die minimalen Arbeits- und Lohnbedingungen für in die Schweiz entsandte Arbeitnehmerinnen und Arbeitnehmer und flankierende Massnahmen vom 8. Oktober 1999, BBl 1999 8744 [hereinafter Law on Flanking Measures] Botschaft des Bundesrates above note 284.
[292] Directive 96/71/EC of the European Parliament and of the Council of 16 December 1996 concerning the posting of workers in the framework of the provision of services, OJ No L 18/1, 21.1.1997.
[293] Article 2 of the Law on Flanking Measures, note 292 above. Portmann (2002) 278–84.
[294] SR 220.

Notably, the new law and flanking measures apply not only to workers from countries within the European Union but also to those from other countries. For the latter, Article 9 of the Federal Ordinance limiting the number of foreigners (BVO) remains applicable.[295]

D) Sanctions In addition to international collaboration, Switzerland employs two other major tools in the attempt to link trade with core labour rights: sanctions and development assistance. It has been argued that the recent Swiss sanctions imposed against Iraq, former Yugoslavia and other countries were motivated by neutrality policy.[296] While this argument was true in the case of what was then South Rhodesia in 1965,[297] where the importation of goods was frozen to the *courant normal* in order not to undermine the sanctions imposed by the UN or other countries, the situation as we have seen changed drastically in the 1990s when Switzerland took a stand and actively participated in economic sanctions that involved prohibiting trade, payments and loans.[298]

Sanctions are an important tool not only within the UN but also at the regional level. Of particular importance for Switzerland is the EU, which because of its mandate for a Common Foreign and Security Policy,[299] can also decree sanctions.[300] The principles for the Common Foreign and Security Policy refer explicitly, *inter alia*, to the UN Charter and allow for sanctions against a state breaking the peace or violating international law. Such measures can therefore have the function of restoring order and thus serving the peace. In this context, according to the Swiss Federal Council, the same considerations of neutrality apply as in the case of UN sanctions. Therefore, in 1993 the Swiss government came to the conclusions that it was, in principle, willing to join in non-UN economic sanctions.[301] After carefully assessing the situation, it will decide on a case-by-case basis whether abstention or participation is in Switzerland's interest and which course will most effectively serve to re-establish a situation that complies with international law.

The first sanctions taken by Switzerland outside the UN were against the Federal Republic of Yugoslavia (Serbia and Montenegro). The European Union reacted to the violent actions by Serbian forces in Kosovo by imposing selected trade sanctions on the Federal Republic of Yugoslavia. Since Switzerland felt

[295] SR 823.21.

[296] Biaggini, Múller, Richli and Zimmerli (2005) 90 now correctly state that this was only the case until the 1990s.

[297] This was the only time Switzerland participated in sanctions taken by the United Nations before the change in concept in the 1990s.

[298] For an overview of sanctions taken by Switzerland since 1990, see Botschaft zu einem Bundesgesetz über die Durchsetzung von internationalen Sanktionen, BBl 2000 1433 [hereinafter Botschaft EmbG], at 1437–46.

[299] Common Foreign and Security Policy is the so-called Second Pillar of the European Union: Article 11 of the Treaty Establishing the European Union.

[300] Article 301 of the Treaty Establishing the European Community.

[301] Neutralitätsbericht 1993, note 249 above, para 42.

equally affected by the events in Kosovo, similar measures were taken by the Swiss government.[302]

Later, Switzerland followed the lead of the European Union[303] in imposing financial sanctions on Burma/Myanmar.[304] Although the government identified the serious violations of core labour rights in its report to the ILO as the main reason for the sanctions,[305] in actuality, the autonomous implementation of the respective EU regulation played a much more important role.[306] It is interesting to note that the EU strongly opposes a sanctions-based approach to enforcing core labour standards.[307]

E) Development Assistance The second major tool outside of international collaboration that Switzerland employs in the attempt to link trade with labour rights is development assistance. Development assistance aims, *inter alia*, at the promotion of human rights including labour rights.[308] The responsible government body, the Swiss Agency for Development and Cooperation (*Direktion für Entwicklung und Zusammenarbeit* (DEZA)), therefore actively supports programmes within the ILO while also aiming to avoid any negative impacts of development programmes on human rights.

3.2.3. Labour Rights and the Existing Law of the WTO

As we have seen with the case of Switzerland in particular, compliance with core labour rights can be an element of national trade policy and thus raise the

[302] Verordnungen über Massnahmen gegenüber der Bundesrepublik Jugoslawien vom 1. Juli bzw. 1. Oktober 1998 und 23. Juni 1999, AS 1998 1845, AS 1998, 2696, AS 1999 2224, amended by AS 2000 2589, AS 2001 110 and last 19 on December 2001, AS 2002 238.

[303] The EU took a common position in 1996 that confirmed already existing sanctions (an arms embargo imposed in 1990, the suspension of defence co-operation since 1991 and the suspension of all bilateral aid other than strictly humanitarian aid) and introduced a visa ban on the members of the military regime, the members of the government and other senior officials including their families as well as the suspension of high-level governmental visits to Burma/Myanmar. The common position was strengthened in October 1998 by extending the sanctions to transit visas and covering the tourism administration in Burma/Myanmar. In April 2000 it was further strengthened by adding the following measures: a ban on the export from the EU of any equipment that might be used for internal repression or terrorism, the publication of the list of persons affected by the visa ban and a freeze on the funds held abroad by the persons named in the list. Following a visit of the EU Troika to Burma/Myanmar in March 2002, the Common position was again renewed and extended for another six months: Council Common position of 22 April 2002 extending Common Position 96/635/CFSP on Burma/Myanmar (2002/310/CFSP), OJL 107/1, 24.4.2002. In addition, GSP preferences were suspended in 1997; see note 236 above and accompanying text.

[304] Verordnung über Massnahmen gegenüber Myanmar vom 2. Oktober 2000, AS 2000 2648. See chapter 1 above, section 1.2.2.B.

[305] ILO, GB 280/6, para 17.

[306] See chapter 1 above, note 291 and accompanying text.

[307] EC Commission (2001), 11.

[308] Menschenrechtspolitik 2000, note 266 above, at 2596; Leitlinien Nord-Süd des Bundesrates vom 7. März 1994 (Report by the Federal Council on Switzerland's North-South Relations in the 1980's).

question of linkages and consistency. This chapter will now shift the focus from states to the international level, namely the WTO.

There are several possibilities regarding the method by which core labour rights can become an issue in the WTO.[309] We have already looked at import restrictions when discussing the problem of like products under Article III GATT.[310] Also, the most recent challenge to the GSP schemes has already been mentioned above. The following sections will focus on the remaining major current debates: social labelling and government procurement.

Although core labour rights might become an issue in the context of services,[311] once the agenda for negotiations under the Doha framework has been agreed upon, there is not enough substantial evidence upon which to base a discussion that would go beyond theoretical and to some extent speculative arguments. For this reason, the General Agreement on Trade in Services (GATS) is not discussed in this chapter.

3.2.3.1. The Agreement on Technical Barriers to Trade (TBT)[312] and Social Labelling Programmes

A) The Nature of Social Labelling Programmes Labelling programmes have become common in the environmental context[313] and are now increasingly discussed in the field of labour.[314] Because proposals for social labelling schemes related to labour have so far mostly been voluntary programmes, the following section will concentrate on voluntary government-sponsored labelling schemes, so-called *social labels*.[315] Under such schemes, governments define certain labour-related criteria to promote, for example the abolition of child labour, and then award "seals of approval" labels to products that embody the criteria.[316] The idea is that consumers will prefer these labelled products to competing products that do not meet the standards. The Belgian label on socially responsible production is an example (Figure 3.6.).

309 For an excellent overview and analysis of the current discussion, see McCrudden and Davies (2000).

310 See chapter 2 above, section 2.3.2.2.

311 One of the open questions is whether Member States can take measures against child prostitution by limiting tourist services. In addition, there is currently a proposal on the table to include prostitution in the list of liberalised services, which if accepted would raise new questions on, eg, measures against trafficking.

312 SR 0.632.20 Anhang I A.6.

313 Appleton (2000) 196–97; Bartenhagen (1997) 54–59; Tietje (1995) 126–30.

314 For an overview see Lopez-Hurtado (2002) 720–24; Urminsky (2002) 38–46.

315 Social labelling is understood as a means of communicating information through a physical label about the social conditions surrounding the production of a product or rendering of a service. Social labels may be affixed to products or their packaging or displayed on shelving or shop windows at the retail site. Some labels are assigned to enterprises, usually producers or manufacturers. They are aimed at consumers and/or potential business partners. Social labelling programms are considered to be voluntary responses to market incentives rather than to public law or regulation. ILO (2000b) para 68.

316 Bartenhagen (1997) 56.

Figure 3.6. *Selected Labelling Programmes*

Monitoring	Programme	Product	Labour Rights Addressed: Child Labour	Forced Labour	Discri-mination	FoA/ CB*	Countries affected (producers (P) and buyers (B))	Reference to ILO standards
Third-party monitoring by NGOs or professional auditor	**Fair trade Labelling Org International**	Agricultural products	x	x	x	x	P: About 20 in Africa, Asia and Latin America B: Western Europe, US, Canada, Japan	no
	Forest Stewardship Council (FSC)	Forestry products, incl. timber					P: About 33 countries worldwide B: Australia, Japan, Western Europe, North America	yes
	RUGMARK	Hand-knotted carpets	x				P: India, Nepal, Pakistan B: Western Europe, US, Canada	no
	STEP	Hand-knotted carpets	x	x		x	P: India, Nepal, Pakistan, Morocco, Egypt B: Switzerland	yes
	Reebok	Soccer balls	x				P: Pakistan B: US, Europe, Latin America	no
Monitoring by governmental agency	**Kateen**	Hand-knotted carpets	x				P: India B: Germany, Nordic countries	no
	Belgian label on socially responsible production	Any product on the Belgian market	x	x	x	x	P: all B: Belgium	yes
Self-monitoring	**Baden**	Balls for sports	x	x			P: China B: Primarily N. America and Western Europe, some Latin American countries, Pacific Rim	no

*FoA: Freedom of Association; CB: Right to Collective Bargaining
Sources: Diller (1999); Urminsky (2002).

In addition to government-sponsored programmes, there are *private* labelling schemes, such as Fair Trade, FSC and others mentioned in Figure 3.6., which involve assessment of appropriate labour standards by organisations that are independent of the producers or manufacturers of a product. Finally, several companies apply *self-declaration* labelling programmes, stating for example that their products are not made by child labour. These programmes usually refer to the individual companies' or groups' code of conduct regarding labour rights (Figure 3.6.).

B) Social Labelling Programmes in Practice In the US, several attempts have been made to introduce social labelling programmes in federal legislation. Although so far only one of the bills has been enacted, their history reflects developments in international law and the repercussions of these developments on national regulations and state sovereignty.

In 1999, the Child Labor Free Consumer Information Act of 1999, a proposal for a social labelling programme, was put forward by Senator Tom Harkin.[317] The bill aimed to establish a labelling scheme for clothing and sporting goods. It provided that the Secretary of Labor, in consultation with a new Child Labor Free Commission, would

> . . . issue regulations to ensure that a label using the terms "Not Made with Child Labor", "Child Labor Free" or any other term or symbol referring to child labor does not make a false statement or suggestion that an article or section of wearing apparel or sporting good was not made with child labor. The regulations developed under this section shall encourage the use of an easily identifiable symbol or term indicating that the article or section of wearing apparel or sporting good was not made with child labor.[318]

While the labelling standards are voluntary, permission of the Secretary of Labor would be required for the use of the label. In case of an alleged violation of the labelling standards, the Child Labor Free Commission would review the petitions and forward them to the Secretary of Labor together with a report on the merits of the case. The Secretary of Labor in collaboration with the Federal Trade Commission would then decide on the case. If a violation was determined, the label could be withdrawn and a civil penalty according to the Federal Trade Commission Act imposed.[319]

The social labelling programme proposed by the Child Labor Free Consumer Information Act was very much in line with existing schemes in the environmental sector. The defeated bill did not refer to ILO standards but defined a child as a person under the age of 15 years, leaving the Secretary of Labor to determine what constitutes abusive or exploitative practice.[320] The bill was

[317] The Child Labor Free Consumer Information Act of 1999, Senate 1549, 106th Cong (1999). An earlier attempt was made in 1997: The Child Labor Free Consumer Information Act of 1997, Senate 554, 105th Congress, 1st Session (1997).

[318] The Child Labor Free Consumer Information Act of 1999, Senate 1549, 106th Cong § 101(a)(1) (1999).

[319] Federal Trade Commission Act, 15 USC § 45(m)(1).

[320] The Child Labor Free Consumer Information Act of 1999, Senate 1549, 106th Cong § 401 (1999).

inspired by motives similar to those of the Child Labor Deterrence Act of 1999.[321]

In 2001, two less ambitious bills were introduced. The first, the Socially Responsible Consumers' Choice and Anti-Child Labor Bill[322] intended to eliminate the consumptive demand exception in Section 307 of the Tariff Act,[323] thus prohibiting the import of *all* products manufactured with forced labour and indentured child labour regardless of whether they are manufactured in sufficient quantities within the US to meet consumer demand.[324]

The second bill, the United States–Commonwealth of the Northern Marianas Human Dignity Bill[325] would amend existing federal law to prohibit the affixation of the "Made in the USA" label to products from the Northern Mariana Islands unless:

(1) each worker producing such product is paid a minimum wage equal or greater than the wage set by the Fair Labor Standards Act of 1938;[326]
(2) the product is manufactured in compliance with all federal laws relating to labour rights and working conditions; and
(3) the factory or other business producing the product does not employ individuals under conditions of indentured servitude.

In 1999, temporary contract workers from foreign countries held more than 85 per cent of all private sector jobs in the Northern Mariana Islands. In fact,

> [t]he Commonwealth of the Northern Mariana Islands has used its immigration policy to recruit a large, low-cost foreign workforce of desperately poor individuals with virtually no voice to demand safe living and working conditions or better wage and benefit options. The Human Dignity Bill[327] addresses these issues by applying the minimum wage provisions of the Fair Labor Standards Act and the Immigration and Nationality Act to the Northern Mariana Islands. It prohibits any product of the Northern Mariana Islands from entering the customs territory of the US duty-free or not subject to quota as a product of an insular possession, unless specified requirements relating to fair labour practices and country of origin are met. In addition, a study on human and labour rights violations in the Northern Mariana Islands is required.

[321] See note 87 above and accompanying text.
[322] Senate 1353, 107th Cong (2001), introduced by Senator Tom Harkin.
[323] The consumptive demand exception allows importation of prohibited goods if sufficient quantities of similar goods are not produced in the US to meet US consumer demand. For the Tariff Act, see note 90 above and accompanying text.
[324] See notes 93–97 above and accompanying text.
[325] HR 2661, 107th Cong (2001), introduced by Congressman George Miller. The Northern Mariana Islands were a United States territory as part of the United Nations Trust Territory of the Pacific Islands. In 1976, the United States agreed to form the Commonwealth of the Northern Mariana Islands. This agreement came into effect in November 1986, making the people US citizens. The government of the Commonwealth controls its internal affairs, but the US remains responsible for foreign affairs and defence.
[326] 29 USC §§ 201 et seq.
[327] HR 2661, 107th Cong § 2(5) (2001).

The bill addresses two concerns: first, it aims to protect consumers who trust that garments carrying "Made in USA" labels are produced by workers who are paid a living wage and working in safe environments. Second, the bill is intended to prevent the Northern Mariana Islands from violating labour rights in order to obtain a competitive advantage over products made on the US mainland.

Finally, in 2001, an amendment to the fiscal year 2002 Agriculture Appropriations Bill, which provides the Food and Drug Administration with funding to create a "no-child slavery label" for chocolate products, was passed by the House of Representatives overwhelmingly with 291:115 votes.[328] However, it was abandoned at the final conference on establishing the budget, for reasons that seemed to be essentially lack of funds. Encouraged by the success in the House, an Agreement with the global chocolate industry, the so-called Harkin-Engel Protocol, was established.[329] It aims to eliminate the worst forms of child labour on cocoa farms in West Africa and explicitly refers to ILO Convention No 182.[330] A detailed Action Plan lays out the steps to be taken and is summarised in Figure 3.7. A short progress report was released on 1 July 2005.[331]

In Belgium, a law to promote socially responsible production entered into force on 1 September 2002.[332] The law created a label that enterprises may use to promote products that fulfil certain standards and criteria, which are stipulated in the law. In contrast to the US—Northern Marianas Human Dignity Act, the Belgian law explicitly refers to international labour standards as defined by the ILO's fundamental conventions: forced labour (Nos 29 and 105), freedom of association and collective bargaining (Nos 87 and 98), discrimination and equal remuneration (Nos 100 and 111) and minimum age/child labour (No 138).[333] The label is awarded by the Minister of Economic Affairs and can be withdrawn if the stipulated conditions are no longer met. Labels established by other countries or organisations can be recognised if they require the same level of protection for labour standards and if they are imposed by official bodies in the respective countries.[334]

328 HR 2330, 107th Cong (2001), amended by H amdt 142, 147 Cong Rec H3781–83, 3786–87 (daily edition, 28 June 2001); Became Public Law No 107-76.

329 Protocol for the Growing and Processing of Cocoa Beans and their Derivative products in a Manner that Complies with ILO Convention 182 Concerning the Prohibition and Immediate Action for the Elimination of the Worst Forms of Child Labor, available at http://www.NCA-CMA.org.

330 For ILO Convention No 182 banning the worst forms of child labour, see chapter 1 above, section 1.2.3.2. and Figure 1.2.

331 Joint Statement from US Senator Tom Harkin, Representative Eliot Engel and the Chocolate/Cacoa Industry on Efforts to Address the Worst Forms of Child Labor in Coca Growing. Protocol Work Continues, Washington DC 1 July 2005.

332 Loi visant à promouvoir la production socialement responsable du 27 février 2002, published in Moniteur belge, 26 mars 2002, 2 edn, p 12428–32.

333 Article 3 §2 of the law, *ibid*. For text of the relevant articles of the ILO Conventions, see the Appendix of this volume.

334 Article 3 §7 of the law, *ibid*.

The Protocol contains a Key Action Plan with six steps to eliminate the worst forms of child labor:

(1) *Public Statement of Need for and Terms of Action Plan*

The Chocolate Industry as well as West African nations have acknowledged the problem of forced child labor in West Africa.

(2) *Formation of Multi-Sectoral Advisory Groups*

By October 1, 2001 multi-sectoral advisory groups comprising industry, government, cocoa growers, organized labor, NGO, and consumer representatives will begin the task of investigating labor practices in West Africa. By December 1, 2001 a broad consultative group will be constituted to advise in the formulation of appropriate remedies for the elimination of the worst forms of child labor in the growing and processing of cocoa beans and their derivative products.

(3) *Signed Joint Statement on Child Labor to Be Witnessed at the ILO*

By December 1, 2001 a joint statement made by the major stakeholders will recognize, as a matter of urgency, the need to end the worst forms of child labor in connection with the growing and processing of West African cocoa beans and their derivative products and the need to identify positive developmental alternatives for the children affected.

(4) *Memorandum of Cooperation*

By May 1, 2002 there will be a binding memorandum of cooperation among the major stakeholders that establishes a joint action program of research, information exchange, and action to enforce the internationally-recognized and mutually-agreed upon standards to eliminate the worst forms of child labor and to establish independent means of monitoring and public reporting on compliance with those standards.

(5) *Establishment of a Joint Foundation*

By July 1, 2002, a joint international foundation will be established to oversee and sustain efforts to eliminate abusive child labor in the growing and processing of cocoa worldwide. This private, non-profit foundation will be governed by a board comprised of representatives of industry and the other major partners. The Industry will be the primary source of the financial support needed by the foundation to carry out its work.

(6) *Building toward Credible Standards*

In conjunction with governmental agencies and other parties, the industry is currently conducting baseline-investigative surveys of child labor practices in West Africa to be completed by December 31, 2001. Taking into account those surveys, by July 1, 2005 the industry in partnership with other major stakeholders will develop and implement credible, mutually-acceptable, voluntary, industry-wide standards of public certification, consistent with applicable federal law, that cocoa beans and their derivative products have been grown and/or processed without any of the worst forms of child labor.

Figure 3.7. *The Harkin-Engel Protocol: Action Plan*

Before we move on to the applicable WTO rules, the ILO's own efforts regarding social labelling must be noted. In his 1997 report "The ILO, Standard Setting and Globalization", the Director-General of the ILO gave a detailed analysis of the strengths and weaknesses of social labelling programmes.[335] The proposed labelling programme sought to label countries rather than products or companies. Countries whose legislation and practices complied with fundamental ILO standards would receive the label. For this purpose, the Director-General suggested a new ILO convention on labelling and monitoring to thereby provide the opportunity, on a strictly voluntary basis, for Member States to claim the right to use a global social label.[336] Because of strong opposition by developing countries, the proposal did not even survive infancy and was put on the sidelines almost immediately.[337]

C) Applicability of the TBT Within the WTO, social labels have been discussed in the context of Article III GATT and the Agreement on Technical Barriers to Trade. We will first examine how the TBT applies to labelling schemes and then look into the relationship between TBT and GATT.

a) Labelling Schemes as Standards or Regulations under the TBT The TBT Agreement applies to all products, including industrial and agricultural products, but not to services or intellectual property.[338] With regard to measures, the TBT Agreement covers technical regulations and standards. Regulations are defined as

> documents which lay down product characteristics or their related processes and production methods, including the applicable administrative provisions, with which compliance is *mandatory*.[339]

In *EC—Asbestos*, the Appellate Body held that the core of the definition of "technical regulation" is the laying down of one or more product characteristics, in either positive or negative form, that is, as a requirement or as a prohibition.[340]

Standards on the other hand are:

> documents approved by a recognised body, that provide, for common and repeated use, rules, guidelines or characteristics for products or related processes and production methods, with which compliance is *not mandatory*.[341]

[335] ILO (1997) at I.B.2.
[336] Langille (1999) 252. See also Trebilcock and Howse (1998) 29.
[337] Langille (1999) 253.
[338] Article 1.3. TBT. Services fall under the GATS, and intellectual property is covered by the TRIPS.
[339] TBT Annex 1.1 (emphasis added).
[340] *European Communities—Measures Affecting Asbestos and Asbestos-Containing Products*, AB 2000-11, Report of the Appellate Body, 12 March 2001, WT/DS135/AB/R [hereinafter *EC—Asbestos*], paras 72–75.
[341] TBT Annex 1.2 (emphasis added).

Both regulations and standards may also include "labelling requirements as they apply to a product, process or production method".[342] Since the applicable rules for regulations and standards are different, it is important to determine whether a social labelling scheme is considered a regulation or a standard.

Most current initiatives for labels related to core labour rights, such as the abovementioned Belgian law on socially responsible production, are of a voluntary nature; the label is not required by government.[343] However, as we have seen, governments can be involved indirectly, for example, by setting the criteria that must be fulfilled to obtain the label. By such means, governments can create an economic necessity for companies to comply with these criteria in order to survive on the market. As a result, such labels, while voluntary in theory, become mandatory for companies wishing to remain competitive.

Moreover, by establishing legally binding criteria for a label, a government can regulate the process of obtaining the label, regardless of whether or not the label itself is mandatory. Although the WTO dispute settlement organs have not yet had the opportunity to decide on this interpretation of the TBT, a panel report issued under the GATT 1947 in *Canada—FIRA* touched on this question.[344] The Canadian Foreign Investment Review Act and the Foreign Investment Review Regulations (FIRA) provided the *possibility* to foreign investors of submitting written undertakings to purchase goods of Canadian origin[345] or to purchase goods from Canadian sources. Although these undertakings were not required by the FIRA, once they had been accepted they became part of the conditions under which the investment proposals were approved, and compliance could be legally enforced. The panel argued that because of this practice the submission of undertakings to purchase Canadian goods had to be qualified as a requirement in the meaning of Article III:4 GATT.[346]

In the context of the TBT, this argument gains weight because Annex 1.1 explicitly includes the applicable administrative provisions. Therefore, to return to the Belgian example, once a company decides to apply for the label, compliance with the criteria established by the government is mandatory in order to obtain that label. Moreover, if the criteria are no being longer met, the government can withdraw the label; this demonstrates clearly that we are in fact dealing with technical regulations under the TBT.

With regard to standards, the concern is more of an antitrust type: standards, although voluntary by definition, might be set up in a cartel-like manner and

[342] TBT Annex 1.1 and 1.2.

[343] The representative of the European Communities in the Committee on Technical Barriers to Trade clarified that the Belgian proposal was of a voluntary nature and had only been notified to inform other member states. G/TBT/M/23 paras 17–18.

[344] *Canada—Administration of the Foreign Investment Review Act*, Report of the Panel adopted on 7 February 1984 (L/5504—30S/140) [hereinafter *Canada—FIRA*].

[345] In preference to imported goods or in specified amounts or proportions.

[346] *Canada—FIRA*, note 344 above, para 5.4.

impede access to the market for anyone who is not a member of the standard-setting organisations. The provisions on standards apply only if the rules are not legally enforceable and therefore not considered governmental and mandatory. As described above, government involvement in establishing such rules will, in many cases, lead to their qualification as regulations.

Article 4 requires all central government standardising bodies to comply with the TBT Agreement's Code of Good Practice. Whether or not a local, regional or non-governmental standardising body accepts the Code of Good Practice, WTO Members are required under Article 4 to take such reasonable measures as may be available to them to ensure that they comply with the provisions of the Code. In addition, members must not take measures that have the effect, directly or indirectly, of requiring or encouraging the standardising body to act in a manner inconsistent with the Code of Good Practice.[347] The Code offers guidelines on how standards can be developed and implemented in ways that prevent unjustifiable non-tariff barriers. As a result, the term "standards" seems to include, at least potentially, private labour rights initiatives such as the social labelling schemes described in Figure 3.6. above.

The question about how strictly Article 4.1 should be interpreted still remains. Especially for federal states, this issue is of crucial importance. Under the GATT 1947, a panel had to decide on the meaning of an identical provision in Article XXIV:12.[348] The issue was whether the Canadian government had taken all reasonably available measures to ensure that its provinces complied with the relevant provisions of the GATT when enacting legislation on the supply and distribution of alcoholic beverages. Challenged by the European Communities, the Canadian government argued that the "federal clause" included in Article XXIV:12 should be given a restrictive interpretation in order to avoid "imbalances" in the rights and obligations created by the treaty.[349] In particular, Canada pleaded that ultimately only the Supreme Court of Canada could decide whether the Canadian Federal Authority had the legislative authority to control the provincial measures relating to the treatment of imported alcohol and the measures under consideration.[350] The European Communities replied *inter alia* that Canada could at least have initiated a constitutional challenge against the provinces.[351] Similar arguments were made by the intervening US.[352] As a result, the panel declined to adopt the Canadian view and held that Canada had not taken all measures reasonably available to it,[353] thus applying a strict approach in interpreting Article XXIV:12 GATT.

[347] WTO (1995) para 3(b).
[348] *Panel on Import, Distribution and Sale of Alcoholic Drinks by Canadian Provincial Marketing Agencies*, Report of the Panel, adopted on 22 March 1988 (L/6304—35S/37) [hereinafter *Canada—Alcoholic Drinks*].
[349] *Ibid*, para 3.53.
[350] *Ibid*, para 3.65.
[351] *Ibid*, para 3.72.
[352] *Ibid*, para 3.95.
[353] *Ibid*, para 4.35.

b) Labelling Programmes and PPMs The TBT Agreement applies only to standards and regulations that relate to "characteristics for products or related process and production methods".[354] Thus, the TBT Agreement covers process and production methods (PPMs) that have an effect on product characteristics such as quality or performance, so-called *incorporated* PPMs.[355] However, there is controversy as to whether measures based on non-product-related PPMs such as labour standards are covered by the TBT:

> The negotiating history of the TBT suggests that many participants were of the view that standards based *inter alia* on PPMs unrelated to a product's characteristics should not be considered eligible for being treated as being in conformity with the TBT Agreement.[356]

Some scholars therefore argue that this was a deliberate choice by the Members and reflects a long history in WTO and GATT practice of defining like products based on the physical characteristics of the product at issue, and not permitting discrimination between physically identical products because of non-product-related PPMs or other reasons.[357] Nevertheless, several WTO members have insisted on an interpretation of the definitions in Annex 1 to the TBT as including unincorporated PPMs by arguing that the phrase, "Standard: [. . .] may also include [. . .] labelling requirements as they apply to a product, process or production method" must be understood as an addition to the first sentence and thus includes all labels that refer to PPMs whether product-related or not.[358] Furthermore, one can argue that the phrase reflects the drafters' intention to exclude services and intellectual property, as self-standing PPMs, from the scope of the TBT.

In June 2001, Switzerland submitted a request for clarification of the scope of the TBT with regard to labelling schemes and pointed out that the vague definitions lead to considerable difficulties in the application of the agreement.[359]

One way of looking at this issue is to view labels as part of the product, similar to its packaging or content. In this view, all social labels become "product-related", even if they pursue a goal that is process-related, such as the abolition of child labour.[360] On the other hand, the first sentence of Annexes 1.1 and 1.2 to the TBT could be interpreted as stating the general principle that applies also to the second sentence, thus including only labels that refer to product-related PPMs. In the same vein as the discussions about like products under Article III

[354] TBT, Annex 1.1 and 1.2.
[355] Tietje (1995) 134.
[356] WTO, History TBT, para 3(c).
[357] Ambrose (2000) 867. WTO, Secretariat (1995), paras 103–51.
[358] For example, see the position of the United States in the Committee on TBT, G/TBT/M/4, para 93, 1 March 1996. See also Charnovitz (2002b) 75–102.
[359] Marking and Labelling Requirements, Submission from Switzerland, WT/CTE/W/192, G/TBT/W/162, 19 June 2001.
[360] For an overview on social labelling programmes see Diller (1999) 105, 114; Morici and Schulz (2001) 70–73.

GATT,[361] one could argue that the fact that a soccer ball is produced with child labour has no impact on its quality or performance. According to this reasoning, a government-sponsored labelling programme for soccer balls (eg, the one set up by Reebok in 1996[362]) would not fall under the TBT Agreement. However, if labels are considered part of the product, the soccer ball carrying a label would be different from the one without, and the label would therefore be covered by the TBT Agreement.

The key question of whether labour-related labelling programmes refer to "products or related processes and production methods" in light of the definition in Annexes 1.1 and 1.2 of the TBT Agreement has not yet been answered by the WTO dispute settlement organs. But we can refer to the recent *EC—Asbestos* decision, where the Appellate Body interpreted exactly the same phrase in the context of health-related measures.[363] It provided the following interpretation of product characteristics:

> Thus, the "characteristics" of a product include, in our view, any objectively definable "features", "qualities", "attributes", or other "distinguishing mark" of a product. Such "characteristics" might relate, *inter alia*, to a product's composition, size, shape, colour, texture, hardness, tensile strength, flammability, conductivity, density, or viscosity. In the definition of a "technical regulation" in Annex 1.1, the *TBT Agreement* itself gives certain examples of "product characteristics"—"terminology, symbols, packaging, marking or labelling requirements". These examples indicate that "product characteristics" include, not only features and qualities intrinsic to the product itself, but also related "characteristics", such as the means of identification, the presentation and the appearance of a product.

According to the Appellate Body and the wording of Annexes 1.1 and 1.2, any label related to the product is, as such, a product characteristic. This definition includes all PPMs except those that have nothing to do with the product. An example of the latter would be a label that refers to the compliance of distributors with core labour standards vis-à-vis their employees. Such a regulation would not be related to a specific product and thus not fall within the scope of the TBT Agreement.[364]

Even if one disagrees with the concept of viewing PPM-related labels as product characteristics, there is still a strong argument for the coverage of such labelling programmes by the TBT Agreement. If we turn to the analysis of like products under Article III GATT and the criterion of competitive relationship,[365] it could be envisioned that the Appellate Body would interpret Annex

361 See chapter 2 above, section 2.3.2.2.

362 Details of the programme are available at http://www.reebok.com/Static/global/initiatives/rights/?home.html.

363 *EC—Asbestos*, note 340 above, para 67.

364 A different way of looking at this problem would be to interpret the process and production methods narrowly, thus excluding all procedures that are not specifically applicable to the product in question but of a general nature.

365 See chapter 2 above, section 2.3.2.2.

1.1 and 1.2 similarly, ie in such a way as to include PPMs if they have an impact on the product's market appearance and performance. What would this mean in practice? If, for example, a product carrying a label that refers to child labour was treated differently by consumers from a like product without a label, the TBT Agreement would cover the labelling programme.

With these considerations in mind, we can move on to the issue of whether voluntary labour rights-related labelling programmes that are established by private organisations are covered by the TBT Agreement.

c) **Private Organisations** So far, exept for the Belgian law on socially responsible production all labour-related labels have been established by private organisations.[366] As such, non-governmental organisations and private businesses are not subject to the TBT Agreement. However, Articles 3.1 and 4 do refer to non-governmental bodies and non-governmental standardising bodies. What organisations are meant to be included by these terms? Annex 1.8 defines non-governmental bodies as organisations that have legal power to enforce a technical regulation. Therefore with regard to *regulations*, only in situations where the government delegates the authority to enforce technical regulations to local governments or institutions outside the government, are these entities subject to the TBT Agreement. Whether a non-governmental body is vested with the power of legal enforcement depends on the law of the Member State. If such a delegation is to comply with the Swiss constitutional order of legislative authority, it needs a legal basis and its mandate should be limited to issues of minor importance.[367]

While it has become rather common to delegate legislative power to private organisations in the context of the self-regulation of financial markets, there have as yet been no similar developments with regard to labour rights. So far, labelling programmes are conducted solely either by private enterprises and NGOs without any official function,[368] or remain with the government.[369]

With respect to *standards*, Article 4.1 refers to non-governmental and regional standardising bodies. Bearing in mind that standards were included in the TBT Agreement out of a concern about possible cartel-like behaviour of standardising organisations, Article 4.1 holds governments responsible for taking reasonable measures to prevent such behaviour. This means that governments should ensure that such organisations accept and comply with the Code of Good Practice in Annex 3 of the TBT Agreement. All the initiatives outlined in Figure 3.6. above are undertaken by private organisations. By establishing a labelling programme, these organisations set standards in the sense of Annex 1.2 TBT. The code requires these organisations to grant MFN treatment to all

[366] See figure 3.6. above.
[367] Häfelin and Haller (2005) Rz 1890.
[368] See list at note __.
[369] For example the proposals for 'child labour free' labels in th US. See note 317 above and accompanying text.

products regardless of their national origin. In addition, standards must not be adopted or applied when they would create an unnecessary obstacle to international trade.

D) The Relationship between the TBT Agreement and the GATT Does the coverage of social labelling programmes by the TBT Agreement mean that the GATT, Article III:4 in particular, does not apply?

There are different ways to look at the relationship between TBT and GATT.[370] The first view is that TBT can be understood as a *lex specialis* to the general obligations in Articles III and XX of the GATT. This would mean that if a measure falls within the definition of a regulation or standard in the TBT Agreement, its legality would be considered only under that Agreement.[371] The second view is that a complainant may choose to bring a claim under either the GATT or the TBT but not both. A third and final view is that the obligations and rights in GATT and TBT operate concurrently, and both may apply to a single dispute, provided of course that the measure falls within the ambit of some provision in both agreements.

This third view is consistent with the way in which, to date, panels and the Appellate Body have understood the relationship between GATT and other WTO treaties.[372] As a result, the provisions in the TBT Agreement cannot be interpreted in isolation from the GATT. In particular, the application of the TBT must not undermine the general principles as stated in the GATT.

With respect to voluntary labelling schemes, the TBT Agreement is of particular importance in cases where there is no facial discrimination but a *discriminatory impact* can nevertheless be established. Regulations and standards that discriminate *de iure* between domestic and non-domestic products would first be considered under Article III:4 GATT, thus shifting the burden of proof for justification under Article XX to the defendant. In the case of a non-origin-based labelling scheme, a panel would first apply the TBT Agreement, thus requiring the complainant to prove that the programme is an unnecessary obstacle to trade, ie it cannot be justified by the legitimate objectives mentioned in Article 2.2. TBT.[373]

E) Government Responsibility? Assuming that the TBT Agreement does apply to labour rights-related labelling programmes, what requirements need to be fulfilled in order to comply with the Agreement? To what extent is the sovereignty of the Member States in regulation limited?

The TBT Agreement is somewhat of a hybrid model in adapting voluntary private-sector guidelines to a legally binding conventional system of multilateral

[370] For a detailed analysis, see Howse and Tuerk (2001) 308–13.

[371] This view is supported by Tietje (1995) 137.

[372] *EC—Asbestos*, note 340 above, para 80.

[373] For standards see Annex 3.E. The meaning of "unnecessary obstacle to trade" must be interpreted in line with Article 2.2. TBT. For a detailed discussion see Howse and Tuerk (2001) 312–13.

public regulation. States assume certain obligations with regard to private sector standardising activities while acknowledging the voluntary and non-state character of the underlying private initiatives.[374]

The TBT Agreement differs from the GATT/WTO agreement in two respects. First, its obligations apply to all technical regulations whether or not they are discriminatory. Second, the focus of the TBT Agreement is on due process, ensuring transparency, coherence and consistency in the regulatory process.[375] In particular, the TBT Agreement requires Member States to refer to existing international standards where they exist and does not attempt to establish its own regime.[376]

Once the TBT Agreement becomes applicable it imposes several obligations on states. The main principles are compliance with national treatment and MFN obligation and the prohibition of the creation of unnecessary obstacles to international trade. With regard to technical regulations, Article 3 holds governments responsible for the acts of local and non-governmental bodies.

Article 4 requires Member States to ensure that all organisations involved in standardisation and its enforcement accept and comply with the Code of Good Practice in Annex 3 of the TBT Agreement. Annex 3.D. provides a national treatment and most-favoured nation obligation with respect to standards. Annex 3.E. addresses the concern of developing countries that they might not be able to meet standards without losing their competitive advantage, by determining that

> the standardizing body shall ensure that standards are not prepared, adopted or applied with a view to, or with the effect of, creating unnecessary obstacles to international trade.

In contrast to Article XX GATT,[377] under the TBT Agreement the challenging state has to prove that the regulating state has failed to ensure that its measure is an unnecessary obstacle to international trade.[378] The meaning of this notion can be drawn from Article 2.2, which, *inter alia*, names national security requirements, the prevention of deceptive practices, protection of human health or safety, animal or plant life or health or the environment as legitimate objectives.

In the context of labour rights-related labels, the protection of human health or safety is of particular relevance. The list in Article 2.2, however, is not exhaustive. Although public morals is not explicitly mentioned it could be argued that it is a legitimate objective not only in the context of Article XX GATT but also for the TBT Agreement. It is important to keep in mind that the

[374] Diller (1999) 125.
[375] See for example Article 2.7.
[376] Article 2.4.
[377] Under Article XX GATT, the defending state has to prove the requirements of the necessity test, because a violation of the GATT has already been established and the burden of proof for its justification then shifts to the defendant.
[378] Unlike for technical regulations, the requirement that the measures are "no more trade-restrictive than necessary" is not repeated in Article 4.

focus of the TBT Agreement is on the regulatory process. Therefore, the obligation to ensure the least trade-restrictive regulations/standards is relative to the kinds of risks that would arise in the absence of the regulations or standards.[379] With regard to labour-related social labelling programmes, the question arises of whether not meeting certain labour standards would actually create a risk for human health. Assuming that labelling is a valid means of reducing the use of child labour,[380] it is hard to imagine any less restrictive alternatives.

Furthermore, the Code states that international standards should be used where they exist. Thus, ILO labour standards are relevant for the interpretation of the TBT Agreement and its annexes.[381]

Government responsibility according to Article 4 is an obligation *to ensure.* As we have seen in the context of the ICESCR, states enjoy a margin of discretion in the fulfilment of their obligations.[382] This margin becomes even larger because under Article 4 only *reasonable* measures that are *available* must be taken. However, looking at the practice of the dispute settlement organs under the GATT 1947,[383] it seems likely that a panel would interpret the government's obligation strictly.

To summarise, the state has a positive obligation to ensure that local and non-governmental bodies comply with Article 2 when setting or enforcing regulations. With respect to standards, the state has to create rules or incentives for private standard-setting organisations to comply with the Code of Good Practice. However, the impact of this obligation is softened by several factors: first, it does not contain any substantial rights but deals with the *process* of standard setting; second, the Code of Good Practice does not establish a new set of rules but mainly refers to obligations already formulated elsewhere, for example, the GATT or international standards that already exist.[384] Overall, this concept corresponds to the voluntary nature of the labelling programmes discussed above and the general attitude of the TBT Agreement, which is to concentrate on the regulatory process and to leave the authority for substantial standard-setting with states.

F) Conclusions What does the fact that labels can be considered product characteristics mean for the new Belgian law on socially responsible production[385]

379 Article 2.2. TBT; Howse and Tuerk (2001) 314–15.

380 This assumption is the most debated point in the whole argument.

381 ILO (2000b) para 81.

382 See chapter 1 above, section 1.2.1.2.; Maastricht Guidelines on Violations of Economic, Social and Cultural Rights, Maastricht, 22–26 January 1997, available at http://heiwww.unige.ch/?humanrts/?instree/?Maastrichtguidelines.html [hereinafter Maastricht Guidelines], paras 6–8. For Arts 6–10 ICESCR, see Appendix A.2.

383 *Canada—Alcoholic Drinks*, note 348 above.

384 With Annex I, Article 4 ILO standards are recognised as relevant for the interpretation of the TBT. In addition, the ISO/IEC Directory of International Standardizing Bodies, 7th edn, (1995) lists the ILO and the specified standards.

385 Note 332 above and accompanying text.

and for the US Human Dignity Bill?[386] Following the approach outlined in Figure 3.8., a panel would first examine whether the proposed regulations provide a different treatment based on the origin of the product and thus possibly violate Article III GATT. Neither the Belgian law nor the Human Dignity Bill discriminates *de iure* between domestic and foreign products. While the Belgian law explicitly applies to all enterprises that sell goods on the Belgian market,[387] the Human Dignity Bill imposes US labour laws on the Northern Mariana Islands and therefore treats them equally with domestic producers.[388] As a result, a panel would move on to examine the labelling schemes under the TBT. The question here is whether the schemes, although facially neutral, have a discriminatory impact and could create an *unnecessary obstacle to trade*. In addition, voluntary labelling schemes have to comply with the Code of Good Practice in Annex 3 of the TBT and respect the MFN rules.

The new Belgian law led to intensive discussions by the Committee on TBT.[389] Three major arguments were put forward. First, Malaysia on behalf of the ASEAN countries stated that the law would bring labour issues back into the

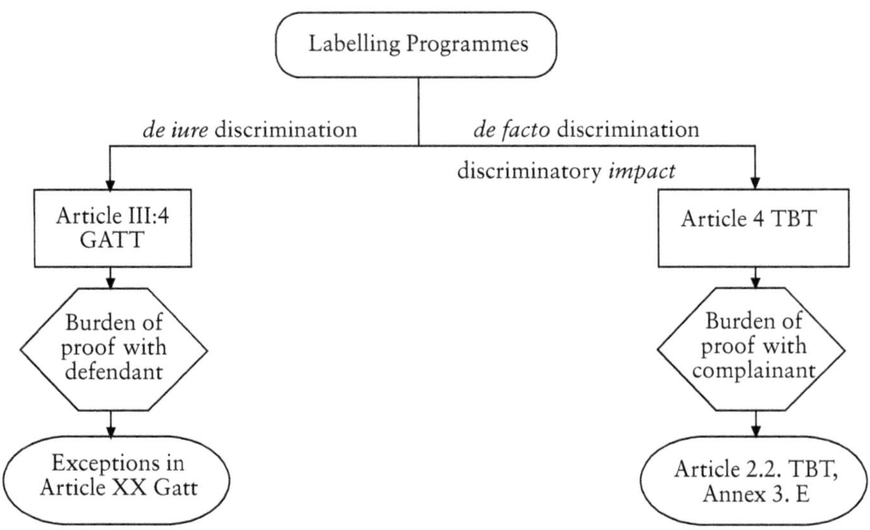

Figure 3.8. *Labelling Programmes under GATT/TBT*

[386] Note 327 above and accompanying text.

[387] Article 2(3).

[388] However, because other countries are not affected by the measure, it might be seen as a violation of MFN. Also it would be necessary to examine whether the requirements could be seen as quantitative measures under Article XI. It is likely that a panel would first examine these additional aspects before moving on to the TBT.

[389] Committee on Technical Barriers to Trade. Minutes of the discussions in G/TBT/M/23, 8 May 2001 and G/TBT/M/24, 14 August 2001.

WTO, which was contrary to the Singapore Declaration.[390] In addition, some delegations considered the law discriminatory and to be creating unnecessary obstacles to trade.[391] While it is still disputed whether the TBT also covers non-product-related PPMs,[392] the issue comes down to the question of alternative, less trade-restrictive means for Belgium to achieve the objective, ie the promotion of core labour rights. Because the proposed label is voluntary, this seems a very difficult point for the complainant to prove. Assuming that the TBT covers all PPMs, the Belgian law is unlikely to be in violation of the agreement.

3.2.3.2. The Agreement on Government Procurement (GPA 1994)

In this section, the legality of selective purchasing laws under the WTO Procurement Agreement of 1994 is considered. The issue here is whether the goals set by the GPA conflict with international labour rights and in particular with social and human rights policies.

As we have seen, the use of sanctions and selective purchasing laws has increased significantly over the last few years,[393] one of the most prominent recent examples being the legislation of Massachusetts regarding Burma/Myanmar.[394]

It should be noted in this context that the ILO established a *Labour Clauses (Public Contracts) Convention (No 94)* as early as 1949.[395] The Convention applies to contracts in which at least one of the parties is a public authority. It requires the inclusion of labour clauses to ensure standards that "are not less favourable than those established for work of the same character in the trade or industry concerned in the district where the works is carried on".[396]

A) The History of the GPA 1994 During the International Trade Organisation (ITO) negotiations in 1947, the US proposed subjecting government procurement to the national treatment and MFN principles.[397] Instead, the GATT dealt with the issue in Article III.

Article III:8 GATT exempts purchases by "governmental agencies of products purchased for governmental purposes". Because the MFN obligation in Article 1 GATT makes reference to the obligations of Article III:2 and III:4, it is argued that government procurement is also an exception to MFN rules. Practice under GATT confirms this argument.[398]

390 G/TBT/M/23, para 15. The whole statement of ASEAN can be found in: ASEAN concerns regarding the proposed Belgian law for the promotion of socially responsible production, Committee on Technical Barriers to Trade, G/TBT/W/159, 28 May 2001.
391 G/TBT/M/23, paras 9, 10, 15.
392 This argument was made by Hong Kong in the context of the Belgian law: *ibid*, para 10. See also Charnovitz (2002b) 65–66.
393 McCrudden (1999b) 4–7. See section 3.2.2. above.
394 Section 3.2.2.1. above, especially note 103.
395 The Convention was ratified by 59 Member States.
396 Article 2(1) Labour Clauses (Public Contracts) Convention (No 94) 1949.
397 For a detailed analysis of the History of the GPA, see Blank and Marceau (1997).
398 Jackson (1997) 225.

This exception had become troublesome by the 1970s for two reasons: first, the government sector increased and in some countries reached 40% of the GDP; and second, it was very difficult to define what "governmental agencies" and "governmental purposes" meant in practice. There was no universal consensus on what activities a government should undertake. For example, in some but not all countries such activities include owning and running railways, telecommunication companies, all electricity generation, airlines etc.[399]

Although the situation was ameliorated by the growing trend to privatise such activities, government procurement still accounted for a substantial part of trade volume. Therefore, at the time of the Tokyo and Uruguay round, the negotiators felt a need for an Agreement on Government Procurement (GPA). Inspired by the work that had already been undertaken within the European Communities and the OECD,[400] a solution was finally found in a voluntary agreement that was intended to serve as a code of conduct for governments. The key principles were non-discrimination and MFN. The first GPA was adopted in 1979 and entered into force in 1981. Only 13 industrialised countries ratified it, and developing nations were reluctant to open up their markets for procurement.

During the Uruguay round, two topics were of particular interest: while the inclusion of services was agreed upon without any major resistance, the coverage of purchases by regional and communal governmental agencies was highly controversial, especially between the EU and the US. After lengthy debates and several interruptions of the negotiating process,[401] the EU and the US agreed in December 1993 to limit the MFN principle to the extent that it should be granted only on a reciprocal basis. As a result, the amended GPA was finally adopted in 1994 and replaced the Tokyo GPA on 1 January 1996. The GPA is a voluntary plurilateral agreement and is thus binding only for those states that ratify it.[402] As of October 2006, 36 states have become parties to the agreement, this number being considerably smaller than the membership of the WTO (149 states).[403]

B) Key Provisions Although the GPA seems to be far-reaching, its scope is limited by Article I, which states that the Agreement applies only to sub-national entities that are specified in Appendix I. In addition, access to procurement by sub-central governments, public utilities, and for services is contingent on other

[399] *Ibid.*

[400] Blank and Marceau (1997) 37–41.

[401] *Ibid*, 47–48.

[402] Multilateral agreements such as GATT, GATS and TRIPS bind all WTO member states. Senti (2000) Rz 1419.

[403] States that have ratified: Canada, the 25 Member States of the European Communities (Austria, Belgium, Cyprus, Czech Republic, Denmark, Estonia, Finland, France, Germany, Greece, Hungary, Ireland, Italy, Latvia, Lithuania, Luxemburg, Malta, Netherlands, Poland, Portugal, Slovak Republic, Slovenia, Spain, Sweden, United Kingdom), Hong Kong China, Iceland, Israel, Japan, Korea, Liechtenstein, Netherlands with respect to Aruba, Norway, Singapore, Switzerland, United States. Negotiating accession are Albania, Bulgaria, Georgia, Jordan, Kyrgyz Republic, Moldova, Oman, Panama, Chinese Taipei.

parties making acceptable reciprocal offers.[404] Furthermore, the coverage of the Agreement depends on whether the value of the procurement is above a specified threshold (Article I:4).

Article III contains the basic principles of the GPA, namely, non-discrimination and MFN.[405] Because of the plurilateral character of the GPA, non-discrimination does not apply to every GATT member but only to those parties that have ratified the agreement.[406] The MFN principle does not go that far: The parties to the agreement have the right to denounce MFN to other parties if they consider the reciprocal benefits unsatisfactory. Such reservations are published in Annex I under "General notes and derogations from the provisions of Article III". This exception is known as "basic reciprocity" or the "system of variable geometry".[407]

C) Exceptions: Article XXIII Does the GPA prevent states from adopting social policy measures? Article XXIII, *inter alia*, names measures relating to public morals, order and safety or to the products and services of prison labour as legitimate.

Debates over social policy had already taken place under the GPA 1979. The US, for example, succeeded in renegotiating the draft Agreement to include an exemption related to its labour surplus and the small business and minority set-aside programmes.[408] Years later, several countries sought exemptions from the coverage of the GPA 1994 for particular social policies. Although the GPA 1994 answers many questions, there are many national provisions attaching social policy requirements to public procurement that may appear to be in breach of the GPA.[409] In particular it has been argued that the GPA prevents governments from protecting their countries against the adverse effects of globalisation.[410]

Although Article XXIII GPA has not yet been the subject of a dispute settlement proceeding, some guidance can be obtained from its relationship to Article XX (a) GATT[411] and Article XIV(a) GATS. In contrast to article XX(a) GATT, Article XXIII GPA and Article XIV(a) GATS contain both the exception of public morals *and* public order.This seems to indicate that the scope for exceptions is broader in the GPA than under Article XX (a) of the GATT. Given that the GPA attempts to respect state sovereignty in procurement and focuses on trade restrictions, such an interpretation seems plausible. In US-Gambling[411] the

404 McCrudden (1999b) 14.

405 Hoekman and Mavroidis (1997) 16–17.

406 This approach if further underlined by Article V:12, which allows the parties to grant special treatment to developing countries that have not ratified the Agreement.

407 Senti (2000) Rz 1449.

408 The exemption was granted "in return" for the inclusion of NASA on the entity list. McCrudden (1999b) 17–18.

409 McCrudden (1999b) 21.

410 Shuman (1994) 529.

411 United States–Measures Affecting the Cross-Border Supply of Gambling and Betting Services, Report of the Appellate Body, 7 April 2005, WT/DS285/AB/R [hereinafter US–Gambling], para 296–299. For analysis see Breining-kaufmann and Weber (2007).

Appellate Body confirmed the panel's findings with regard to Article XIV (a) GATS that

> the term 'public morals' denotes standards of right and wrong conduct maintained by or on behalf of a community or nation [and] the definition of the term 'order,' read in conjunction with footnote 5 of the GATS, suggests that 'public order' refers to the preservation of the fundamental interests of society, as relected in publc policy and law.

Moreover, the concept of public order or *ordre public* in the French text is well established in many civil law jurisdictions, in the European Community law and in many international treaties. In the domestic civil law context, the concept of public order is a tool for resolving conflicts between fundamental societal values or principles and personal liberties. An example is the Swiss Federal Law on Private International Law, which states that foreign law is to be applied by Swiss courts only if it is not in conflict with the Swiss *ordre public*. Similarly, decisions by foreign courts or authorities are not acknowledged if contrary to the *ordre public*.[412] As such, the Swiss law goes much further than classic police measures, which protect public health, security or morals. The Swiss Supreme Court held that fundamental human rights are binding for everyone performing state functions and thus part of the *ordre public*.[413]

In the international context, the focus is somewhat different. Because international (trade) agreements are usually based on compromises between the different levels of domestic legislation among the Member States, invoking the exception of public order could easily undermine the purpose of the agreement.[414] As a result, the European Court of Justice has interpreted the concept of public policy—which corresponds to the notion of public order—in the Treaty of Rome in a narrow fashion.[415] Stating that public policy exceptions cover only "a genuine and sufficiently serious threat to one of the fundamental interests of society", the ECJ requires that measures be *necessary* for the maintenance of public order.[416] Similar concerns have been raised in the WTO, especially the risk of a "de-legalization of international trade relations".[417] In the context of the GPA, the question comes down to whether the exceptions of public order or public morals can be interpreted without encouraging protectionist measures.

412 Articles 17 and 27 Bundesgesetz über das Internationale Privatrecht vom 18. Dezember 1987, SR 291. Kokott (1998) 93–96.

413 BGE 126 II 324, 327–28; similarly BGE 123 II 595, which differentiates between Swiss *ordre public* and international human rights obligations but treats them at the same level. For a definition of the international *ordre public* that includes human rights which are considered customary international law or obligations *erga omnes*, see Kälin (1994b) 39 f, 154; Kokott (1998) 87–89, who in contrast to Kälin elaborates on the distinction between customary international law, *ius cogens* and obligations *erga omnes*.

414 In the context of the WTO, there is a risk of undermining the rule-based approach to the conduct of international trade that is the basis for the new system: Jackson (1997) 28. See also McCrudden (1999b) 41.

415 Articles 30, 39, 46, 58 and 186 of the Treaty establishing the European Community.

416 ECJ case 30/77 *Régina v Bouchereau* [1977] ECR 1999, para 35 at p 2015.

417 Roessler (1998) 514. See also note 414 above.

As discussed previously, the Appellate Body has made clear that the GATT cannot be read "in clinical isolation from public international law".[418] Naturally, the same is true for the GPA. Because of the relatively consistent international practice on the content of *ordre public*, referring to international human rights appears to be accepted. Indeed, linking the exception of public order to existing international human rights law seems to prevent the pursuit of domestic interests for protectionist purposes. Under the GPA a state could therefore justify unilateral measures in the interest of public order if the measures are based on international human rights law such as the ILO Conventions or the ILO Declaration on Fundamental Principles and Rights at Work. In addition, following the Appellate Body's approach in *US–Gambling*, the concept of public order could also be understood as including the state's authority to ensure regulatory consistency within its territory in dealing with domestic and imported products.[419] If a state is a party to international human rights treaties, importing goods that are produced in violation of these treaties would undermine the domestic legal order and ridicule the democratic *Rechtsstaat*.

However, in order for these measures to be compatible with the GPA, a second requirement needs to be fulfilled: the necessity test. Here, the difficulties that we have already encountered in the context of Article XX GATT emerge again. Under Article XX GATT and Article XIV GATS, panels and the Appellate Body have given a narrow meaning to the exceptions,[420] an approach that could easily be applied in the context of the GPA. Concerns about the legitimacy of allowing the WTO dispute settlement organs to decide on the necessity of a measure are even more serious under the GPA given its general emphasis on state sovereignty in procurement. Certainly, the Appellate Body's approach in considering a measure necessary if an alternative means that is consistent with the GATT or GATS is not reasonably available[421] could serve as a basis for claims under the GPA too. Moreover, the concept of *proportionality*,[422] as it has been developed by many European countries and the ECJ,[423] could be helpful.[424]

418 *United States—Standards for Reformulated and Conventional Gasoline*, Report of the Appellate Body, 29 April 1996 WT/DS2/AB/R [hereinafter *US—Gasoline*]; see also chapter 2 above, notes 336 and 342 and accompanying text.

419 *US–Gambling*, note 411 above; Kokott (1998) 76.

420 For Article XX GATT see chapter 2 above, section 2.3.2.4. For Article XIV GATS see *US–Gambling*, note 411 above.

421 *US—Section 337 of the Tariff Act of 1930*, Report of the Panel, 36S/345, adopted on 7 November 1989 [hereinafter *US—Section 337*], para 5.26; *US–Gambling*, note 411 above, paras 309–311.

422 For a similar concept, see McCrudden (1999b) 48.

423 Article 5(3) of the Treaty establishing the European Community. ECJ Case 11/70 *Internationale Handelsgesellschaft v Einfuhr- und Vorratsstelle für Getreide und Futtermittel* [1970] ECR 1125, 1135 f; ECJ Case C-331/88 *The Queen v Fedesa* [1990] ECR I-4023, para 13; ECJ Case C- 272/94 *Guiot* [1996] ECR I-1905, paras 13–16.

424 However, it must be kept in mind that the WTO and the EU legal system are different in that the EU system creates a regional constitutional order with the goal of integrating a group of fairly homogenous societies. The WTO on the other hand has a much more limited agenda.

The concept of proportionality dictates that a measure has to be capable of achieving a legitimate public interest or policy objective. Furthermore, the measure must be the least restrictive means available and must not go beyond what is necessary in order to achieve that objective. Finally, the public and private interests at stake have to be assessed. In other words, a qualified public interest is required in order to outweigh legitimate private interests.[425]

With a different approach, the US Supreme Court has reached the same conclusions: it applies different levels of scrutiny to cases involving the fourteenth amendment. While in general governmental measures must have a "legitimate purpose" under the rational basis review in order to justify unequal treatment without violating the fourteenth amendment, a "compelling governmental interest" is necessary to justify unequal treatment based on race, such as in affirmative action programs. The rational basis test reflects an almost complete deference to government and as a result, almost every purpose will pass the Supreme Court's examination under this test.[426] Obviously, in an international organisation such as the WTO, the perspective is different; in order to avoid the creation of impediments to international trade, governmental discretion has to be limited. The US Supreme Court's approach follows a similar line of thought by applying strict scrutiny to discrimination based on race and national origin. Because historically the primary purpose of the fourteenth amendment was to protect African Americans,[427] the government must show an extremely important reason for its actions and must demonstrate that the goal cannot be achieved through any less discriminatory alternatives.[428]

What are the consequences of applying the concept of proportionality to Article XXIII GPA? Although it would imply a strict scrutiny of the policy interests raised by the government, it would still allow for a relatively broad margin of discretion in the pursuit of legitimate social and human rights policies, as long

[425] *US–Gambling*, note 411 above, para 307, requiring 'weighing and balancing' of the values and interests at stake. The approach of the Swiss Supreme Court can be applied as a general methodology: BGE 109 Ia 33, 36; 118 Ia 175, 181–83. See also Weber-Dürler (2000) 139. Moor (2001) § 16, Rz 40–57. For a comprehensive study of the concept of public interest, see Wyss (2001).

[426] *McGowan v Maryland* 366 USR 420 (1961) where the court upheld a law using public morals as a sufficient basis. One of the few examples where a governmental purpose did not pass as legitimate is *Romer v Evans* 517 USR 620 (1996) in which the court held that an amendment to the Colorado Constitution, which repealed all laws protecting gays, lesbians, and bisexuals from discrimination and prohibited all future government action to protect these individuals from discrimination, violated the Fourteenth Amendment: "We must conclude that Amendment 2 classifies homosexuals not to further a proper legislative end but to make them unequal to everyone else. This Colorado cannot do" (at 635). A minority of the court led by Justice Scalia argued that the provision was a permissible moral judgment by the voters of Colorado "to preserve traditional sexual mores against efforts of a politically powerful minority to revise those mores through use of the laws" (at 636, Scalia J dissenting).

[427] "A core purpose of the Fourteenth Amendment was to do away with all governmentally imposed discrimination based on race. Classifying persons according to their race is more likely to reflect racial prejudice than legitimate public concerns." Chief Justice Warren Burger in *Palmore v Sidoti* 466 USR 429, 432 (1984).

[428] *Wygant v Jackson Board of Education* 476 USR 267, 274 (1986); *Grutter v Bollinger* 539 USR 306, 326, 333 (2003); Chemerinsky (1997) 550; Spann (2000) 21–24.

as the measures taken were not protectionist in nature.[429] Governments would be required to adduce evidence "sufficient to suggest that the choice [of instruments] is not patently unreasonable or a grossly disproportionate adaptation of means to ends".[430] Such an approach would not only reflect the basic philosophy of the GPA to concentrate on governmental procurement policies that threaten international trade, but also acknowledge the authority of national governments to determine the level of social and human rights policies for their countries in compliance with international law.

3.2.4. Regulatory Competition and the Race to the Bottom

Having addressed the linkage debate at the domestic and international level, we will now address several conceptual questions.

A key reason for the establishment of global core labour standards is the fear that low labour standards might reduce the cost of labour and subsequently lead to what some scholars call a "race to the bottom". According to this view, companies prefer to operate in legal environments that offer the least protection for labour. If necessary, they shift production abroad to capture lower labour costs. The prospect of races to the bottom places unions in a classical prisoner's dilemma:[431] unions want to improve domestic labour protection legislation but at the same time are acutely vulnerable to the capital flight that increased labour standards can trigger.[432] Universal labour standards are therefore often the perceived solution.

3.2.4.1. The Concept of Regulatory Competition

At the state level, globalisation encourages regulatory competition: nations compete for business by setting labour standards that are advantageous vis-à-vis the economies of other states.[433] Regulatory competition is a familiar phenomenon not only at the international level but also within federal states. The regulatory experiences of a federal state such as the US are therefore helpful for analysis of the international level.

A) Different Types of Jurisdictional Competition With regard to labour standards, there are several types of jurisdictional competition.[434] One type occurs

429 For a European example see Case 31/87 *Gebroeders Beentjes BV v The Netherlands* [1988] ECR 4635 and comments in McCrudden (1998) 229–33.

430 Trebilcock and Howse (1998) 32; McCrudden (1999b) 45.

431 Because there is no evidence that regulatory decisions have led to a situation that could be described as being at "the bottom", many commentators have suggested avoiding the use of this term, calling it a misnomer. See for example Oates (1997) 1321.

432 Van Wezel Stone (1999) 95–96.

433 Charny (2000) 282–83.

434 This section draws on the work by Kyle Bagwell and Robert W Staiger and David Charny. Of particular relevance are Bagwell and Staiger (2001b), Bagwell and Staiger (2000) and Charny (2000), Regulatory Competition. A comprehensive summary of the argument can be found in Bagwell and Staiger (2001a).

when jurisdictions set rules to affect terms of trade. In a country that imports goods that are also produced domestically, the levels of tariffs and non-tariff barriers are determined by a trade agreement, but the jurisdiction is free to set labour standards for the industry. Higher labour standards will increase the cost of labour. If the country is economically large enough to influence world markets and affect world prices, it might opt for higher labour standards that affect terms of trade. As a result, some of the costs of higher labour standards are externalised because they are passed on either to foreign producers who now sell less of their goods at the higher price or to foreign purchasers of the goods. This effect will in turn encourage an import-competing country to promote higher labour standards. However, the situation changes when trade is liberalised and the opportunity to externalise the cost of the labour standard is limited: higher labour standards become more costly than before liberalisation. Thus, an import-competing country might be inclined to lower its labour standards compared to the pre-liberalisation level in order to reduce costs.

This model of regulatory competition/race to the bottom is based on the assumption that lowering labour standards facilitates market access and thus increases competitive advantage. Under WTO law, a government has no option to raise tariffs unilaterally in order to grant import relief to its producers. In this situation, it might be tempted to choose an indirect way of doing so by lowering labour standards for domestic producers and thus eliminate some of their production costs. Without an efficient non-violation right available, such a measure would be difficult to challenge under WTO law because according to the jurisprudence of the WTO dispute settlement organs, the requirements for a complaint under Article XXIII:1(b) GATT would not be fulfilled.[435]

As Kyle Bagwell and Robert Staiger have shown, this possibility of international cost-shifting makes weakening domestic labour standards an especially attractive method for governments that have bound their tariffs with WTO commitments, because the reciprocal nature of their available tariff options would prevent them from shifting costs.[436] In principle, the costs of higher labour standards could be offset by the government with adjustments in other policies such as import tariffs or domestic producer subsidies, with the effect of preserving the balance of market access commitments. Therefore, race to the bottom or regulatory chill problems will only occur when WTO law prevents such compensatory measures.

A second type of regulatory distortion might arise from incentives that are established to influence investment. However, studies by the OECD show that no further gains can be aggregated by manipulating labour standards.[437]

[435] Article XXIII:1(b) GATT on nullification and impairment protects legitimate expectations without requiring a violation of the GATT. One of the requirements for a successful complaint is the nullification of a benefit based on tariff concessions or on legitimate expectations for better market access. *Japan—Measures Affecting Consumer Photographic Film and Paper*, Report of the Panel, 22 April 1998, WT/SD44/R, paras 10–41.

[436] Bagwell and Staiger (2001b) 20–25.

[437] OECD (2000) 34; Charny (2000) 285.

Finally, there are labour regulations that refer to imperfections in the market. Here, the main question is why governments would not apply direct measures like subsidies to influence, for example, unemployment instead of relaxing labour standards. Often, governments will lack the information to determine the ideal level of direct intervention, like for instance tax reductions.

B) The Impact of Regulatory Decisions on Labour Rights Regulatory decisions have different effects on the different types of labour rights. While many labour standards are not affected by jurisdictional competition because the jurisdiction gains no competitive advantage by relaxing them, core labour rights that have strong distributive effects such as the freedom of association are indeed threatened.[438] Enterprises facing the costs of being required to bargain collectively with unions may choose to produce in a country where no such obligation exists.

If labour standards are established not primarily as tools for economic efficiency but as individual human rights, workers are entitled to a regime of labour standards that enforces these rights regardless of the effects on trade.[439] Consider the example of an import-competing country whose trading partner permits sweatshop conditions—ie, hazardous work at extremely low wages—and suppresses unions. The workers in the import-competing country suffer an economic disadvantage because of the exporting jurisdiction's low labour standards. They face lower wages and a deterioration of labour protection. The argument goes that there is a general right to be free of the adverse consequences of another's wrongful act. In order to violate a core labour right, the deterioration has to go far, though. While the ILO Declaration on Fundamental Principles and Rights at Work reflects a consensus on core labour rights, the concrete details of what exactly they encompass still need to be worked out. As elaborated earlier, cultural diversities cannot justify the violation of core labour rights.[440]

3.2.4.2. A Design for Enforcing Core Labour Rights Internationally

The basic normative question asked by the theory of regulatory competition in the context of international labour rights is not new: when is international regulation superior to regulation at the national level?[441] While superiority is commonly defined as maximisation of aggregate welfare, measured by maximisation of monetary wealth, other objectives may play a role in the context of core labour rights. As described earlier, core labour rights also aim at redistributing decision-making power and, to some extent, income.[442] In designing inter-

[438] Charny (2000) 291–92, 294.
[439] Howse and Trebilcock (1996) 77.
[440] Chapter 1 above, section 1.2.3. For a different opinion see Charny (2000) 296–97.
[441] This paragraph draws on Barenberg (2000).
[442] At the national level, the same objectives play a crucial role in US labor law. Barenberg (2000) 307.

national regulation, the question is whether regulatory competition and co-ordination will encourage upward or downward regulatory races and whether the regulatory process will promote or diminish democratic participation.

The decentralisation of bargaining units—from federal to state level and from sectors to individual enterprises—that we find at the national level is paralleled by similar developments at the global level in low-wage sovereign states.[443] Since capital may lawfully move across the boundaries of nation states, export processing zones and multinational enterprises, national and sub-national entities compete in attracting foreign investment. If capital moves to countries with low labour standards and possibly non-democratic, repressive regimes, the political weight of these countries in international forums increases, thus further weakening movements that attempt to strengthen labour standards.

Whether at the national or international level, legal rules aimed at redistribution will unavoidably disrupt the political and economic balance. As a result, interest groups threatened by these rules will strongly oppose their enforcement. In a federal state or an international organisation, regulatory co-ordination therefore becomes crucial in overcoming competition at the national or subnational level. The establishment and enforcement of international labour rights can avoid such competition. However, low-wage countries doubt the equal application and enforcement of such standards because they fear that high-wage countries dominate international bodies such as the ILO and the WTO. How can international law address these concerns?

Above all, it is important to notice that there are two different issues involved in answering the question about the possible necessity of international labour standards. On the one hand, there is the humanitarian aspect, for example the concern about the welfare of children throughout the world. In terms of economics, this is a public goods issue,[444] which as such has nothing to do with market access. Regulatory competition and the threat of a race to the bottom on the other hand are connected to market access as we have seen above. Therefore, to the extent that international labour standards aim at redistribution, they operate in the public goods context. This distinction will be important in determining which institutions should deal with which problems.

The fact that international labour standards touch on both political and economic issues means that legitimacy in their design becomes all the more important. Legitimacy is crucial not only in the establishment of the standards

[443] For the United States, see Barenberg (2000) 311–14.

[444] Wouters and De Meester (2003) 4; chapter 1 above, section 1.1.1.2.

[445] An illustrative example is the New Deal coalition in the United States. A broad New Deal coalition led by president Franklin D Roosevelt during the American Great Depression declined to enforce legislation and court rulings that would have allowed the removal of striking workers from the property of General Motors in Detroit. However, the same coalition also proved to be incapable of sustaining this "upward race" towards higher labour standards by letting the Southern racialist wing of the Democratic Party have its way. Roosevelt's failure to purge the Party in the 1938 election led in fact to a *downward* spiral for the United States labour movement.

but also in their enforcement.[445] To achieve the goal of legitimacy, procedural and substantive labour rights must go hand in hand. International labour standards are only as legitimate as the representatives who set them up. From that point of view, the ILO's tripartite structure adds to the legitimacy of its core labour rights.[446]

Because globalisation can induce a democratic deficit by shifting power from the national to the international level, international organisations must provide some compensation in the form of co-ordinating mechanisms that ensure the participation of national actors in interpreting, monitoring and enforcing compliance with core labour rights.[447] The emergence of the European social dialogue in the mid-1980s following the United Kingdom's opposition to the adoption of community legislation on labour policy illustrates this point: the dialogue between the social partners at the European level was recognised by the Protocol and Agreement on Social Policy annexed to the Treaty of Maastricht in 1992.[448] It explicitly provided for the implementation of community labour law through collective bargaining within member states,[449] thus "constitutionalising" the social dialogue. The Treaty of Amsterdam then went a step further and formally enshrined the role of the social dialogue in EC labour law-making in the EC Treaty,[450] therefore also binding the United Kingdom. The court of First Instance confirmed the constitutional nature of the integration of social dialogue into the EC Treaty.[451]

3.2.4.3. *The Normative Debate about Distributive Justice*

While the above arguments show that regulatory competition does not necessarily lead to a race to the bottom but can indeed encourage tighter labour standards, the question remains: are there distributive goals that justify the establishment of

The 1936/37 strike of General Motors workers in Michigan was the most important strike in the United States in the 20th century. Because the strike took place in form of sit-down on factory premises, it was illegal under Michigan state property law. A Michigan court thus awarded General Motors injunction. Yet, Michigan Governor Frank Murphy and President Roosevelt declined to use state coercion against the workers. Barenberg (2000) 316–17, 320 note 44; See the detailed study by Fine (1969).

446 To what extent unions successfully represent worker communities would of course need to be analysed further.

447 As Barenberg has pointed out, four challenges need to be addressed. First, the central organisation must implement rules that assess the representativity of the public and private entities that participate in co-ordinating mechanisms at the international level. Second, the international regime must implement norms that determine which decentralised interests and social groups shall be so represented. Third, the regime must implement norms that determine how these decentralised actors participate in interpreting, monitoring, and enforcing compliance with core labour rights. Finally, with regard to all these basic norms, the regime must choose a combination of procedural and substantive rights. Barenberg (2000) 323.

448 See section 3.2.2.4.1. above.

449 Bercusson (2001) 246–49.

450 Articles 136–45 Treaty establishing the European Community.

451 Court of First Instance, Case T-135/36 *Union Européenne de l'Artisanat et des Petites et Moyennes Entreprises (UEAPME) v Council of Europe* [1998] ECR II-2335.

international core labour standards? There are three main arguments in favour of centralised—federal or international—core labour rights.

The first is an argument for democracy. Generally, federal rules will carry greater constitutional legitimacy than regional standards. However, this argument is not as such applicable to international organisations. As pointed out above, international organisations can only meet the demand for democratic legitimacy if their design allows for representation of various interest groups. A good example is the ILO Declaration on Fundamental Principles and Rights at Work. As for the inherent conflict between sovereignty and democracy—and this is the second argument for international core labour standards—it seems that democracy should override sovereignty because it is the democratic process that restricts sovereignty by adhering to international standards. This leads us to the third argument: as elaborated earlier, states with low labour standards can have a spill-over effect by limiting the policy options of another state that prefers higher labour standards. The sovereignty approach as it is defended by many developing countries in essence prioritises the sovereignty to suppress labour rights over the sovereignty to enforce these rights. Even if the decision to accept lower labour standards is based on considerations of comparative advantage, it still stands for a particular distributive outcome that must be justified by a substantive concept of distributive justice, and is thus a normative decision.[452] As a result, it is impossible to avoid the debate about the weight of national sovereignty as a value when discussing international core labour rights.

Related to this question is the issue of power allocation between domestic and international law and between different international organisations.[453] It is in this broader context that the debate on cross-border justice and extraterritorial jurisdiction, such as the question of whether European citizens are in a legitimate position to protect core labour rights in Asia must be placed.

3.2.4.4. Conclusions

Regulatory competition lies at the core of the debate about linking trade and core labour rights. As such it can lead to a race to the bottom or to a regulatory chill if there are no universally agreed and enforced core labour standards and/or if countries lose their comparative advantage when tightening labour standards. As shown, there are two issues involved here: public goods and market access.

A solution could lie in the consensual agreement by states not only to adhere to international core labour rights but also to enforce them effectively in practice. For developed nations, this would mean not only implementing core labour rights within their own jurisdiction but also not increasing their demands for develop-

[452] Barenberg (2000) 325.

[453] Jackson (2003) 790–94, observing that in current debates "sovereignty" mostly refers to questions about the allocation of power.

ing countries to enforce labour rights at a level that cannot be realistically met. A step in this direction is the guarantee of developing countries' competitive advantage with regard to labour standards in the WTO's Singapore Declaration as it was confirmed at the Doha summit in December 2001.[454] Since this aspect of the problem deals with the nature of labour standards as global commons it is not, as such, covered by the mandate of the WTO. Therefore, the establishment, interpretation and enforcement of core labour standards is the responsibility of the ILO. This by no means suggests that the WTO is not required to apply core labour standards according to its obligation to comply with international law.

In addition, with respect to the problem of market access, the feared race to the bottom can be avoided if the comparative advantage of the countries concerned are maintained. Under exiting WTO law, this can be achieved by effective use of the non-violation complaints together with a broader interpretation of WTO renegotiating provisions. As a result, a country that opts for stricter labour standards could renegotiate its tariffs more easily and thus have a better chance at being compensated for the higher standards. Its trading partners on the other hand would obtain an efficient tool for challenging the lowering of labour standards as a means of indirectly impairing their market access. In this respect, the race to the bottom is in fact a result of an imperfect protection of market access rights, ie one of the main factors of the WTO's trade liberalisation model. It can be corrected by applying measures that are already contained in existing WTO law.

3.3. ARE TRADE SANCTIONS A SOLUTION?

It is beyond the scope of this book to examine in detail the concept of sanctions in international law. However, some general conclusions can be drawn from what has been said so far.

Before proceeding, a clarification of the terminology is necessary. The term "sanctions" here refers to measures taken against a state that violates an international obligation in order to influence governmental behaviour. Sanctions therefore go beyond simple punishment. They form part of the general notion of countermeasures applied by the International Law Commission in its draft on state responsibility.[455] Following the elimination of military force as a valid tool for enforcing international law, trade measures have become very important.[456] The use of sanctions has significantly increased over the last few years: prior to 1990, the UN Security Council had imposed sanctions in only two cases.[457]

[454] WTO, Doha Ministerial Declaration, adopted on 14 November 2001, WT/MIN(01)/DEC/W/1, para 8; see also chapter 1 above, note 352 and accompanying text.

[455] International Law Commission, "State Responsibility, Draft Articles adopted by the International Law Commission at its fifty-third session", UN Doc A/CN.4/L.602 Rev.1 [Hereinafter ILC, Draft State Responsibility]; see also chapter 1 above, note 272.

[456] For a detailed analysis, see Vázquez (2003) 799–800.

[457] Sanctions aganist Southern Rhodesia, S/RES/217 (1965) and against South Africa, S/RES/418 (1977).

With the increasing number of sanctions, their focus has shifted from complete trade and financial embargoes to more targeted measures, with an emphasis on financial sanctions. Such "smart sanctions"[458] not only are more effective[459] but are also aimed directly at the political, military or economic elite who have the power to change the policy or behaviour that provoked an international response and spare those who have not.

While it has been said that such sanctions are a policy-maker's dream because they are not only right but also more effective,[460] the relationship between sanctions and the validity or credibility of a norm is also a key factor of the new approach. In fact, what we are experiencing right now is a revival of a concept that was developed in the early twentieth century by Hans Morgenthau.[461] In Morgenthau's view, sanctions bridged the *Sein* (reality) and *Sollen* (ought) in Hans Kelsen's theory by turning the "pure ought" into a "legal ought" that can be observed in reality. If the expectation of sanctions is missing, a norm lacks reality. The effectiveness of sanctions therefore becomes a key element of credibility.[462] This insight is one of the reasons why some groups try to bring non-trade-related issues onto the agenda of the WTO, which, because of its binding dispute settlement process, is seen as one of the most effective international organisations.[463]

Behind the new concept of smart sanctions is the experience that broad economic sanctions often negatively affect the poor and the middle classes who are unable to influence the policies targeted by the sanctions and who have few or no resources to cushion the effects of sanctions.[464] While the sanctions imposed on Iraq are the most prominent example of this phenomenon, there is also evidence for the devastating effects of trade sanctions imposed in the form of boycotts as a reaction to the use of child labour. Recent measures have therefore focused on financial sanctions and include blocking private accounts held by the government officials of a targeted country. Whether this new concept is effective in practice or just the result of an "internationalist fantasy" has been discussed intensively among scholars following the first smart sanctions.[465]

In addition to this humanitarian argument, the logic of the WTO system suggests that in most cases trade sanctions are not an appropriate means to enforce compliance with labour standards. In fact, trade sanctions are contrary to the

[458] See the Interlaken Seminars on Targeting United Nations Financial Sanctions, organised by the Swiss Federal Office for Foreign Economic Affairs in co-operation with United Nations Secretariat in 1998 and 1999.

[459] Elliott (1999) 192–93. For a critical view, see Craven (2002) 43–61, who suggests that there is little evidence that the initial attempts at targeting have made sanctions more humane in practice.

[460] Craven (2002) 47.

[461] Morgenthau (1935) 478–83.

[462] Koskenniemi (2002a) 455–59.

[463] With regard to sanctions, the WTO/GATT has not yet played an important role. The few sanctions imposed have not succeed in inducing compliance. Charnovitz (2001) 808–9.

[464] Serious negative impacts of the sanctions against Iraq on the civilian population were the reason why the Security Council established the oil-for-food programme in Iraq: UN, Sanctions, 150–52; Craven (2002) 45; Doxey (1999) 208 with further references; Breining-Kaufmann (1991) 242–47 for food sanctions; Elliott (1999) 199–203.

[465] Howse (2002a) 89.

WTO system as such. Although international agencies do not generally sponsor actions that contradict their own purpose, in applying trade sanctions, the WTO would be doing exactly that.[466] Moreover, as mentioned earlier, the evidence suggests that one of the main reasons for lowering labour standards is the lack of compensation for the higher costs involved in observing stricter labour standards and the subsequent loss of competitive advantage. Since sanctions aim at changing behaviour that is considered illegal or wrong by the international community, they would not reach the core of the problem in cases where the reason for low labour standards lies in the lack of opportunities to offset the costs involved in having higher standards.

In summary, it is preferable to seek a solution that addresses the trade-related issue, for example, by creating incentives in the form of tariff reductions or technology transfer.[467]

The recent example of the so-called "conflict diamonds" illustrates how the WTO is struggling to accommodate the trade sanctions agreed upon by (some) Member States in different international forums. In reaction to documented, egregious and regular violations of human rights by rebel groups involved in the diamond trade in Western Africa, especially Angola, Sierra Leone and Liberia,[468] and following the realisation that such trade prolonged the devastating civil wars, the Kimberly Process was initiated by the South African government. It brought together governments, NGOs and representatives of the diamond industries. The Kimberly Process resulted in a certification scheme for rough diamonds exported to and imported from participating countries. By isolating trade in conflict diamonds from the general legitimate trade in rough diamonds, the scheme is an attempt to end human rights violations that are linked to trade in conflict diamonds.[469] The scheme was adopted on 5 November 2002 by the Interlaken Declaration and entered into force on 1 January 2003.

The scheme calls on participants to "ensure that no shipment of rough diamonds is imported from or exported to a non-Participant." This provision amounts to limiting trade between the participants of the Kimberley scheme to non-conflict diamonds on the one hand, and to a complete prohibition of trade between participants and non-participants on the other. Since most of the participants in the scheme are WTO members, conflict arises between the obligations under the Kimberley Process and obligations under the WTO agreements, especially Articles I, XI and XIII GATT on non-discriminatory market

[466] Charnovitz (2001) 810. See also Cleveland (2002) 148.

[467] GSP regimes, if applied consistently and equally, could also be an appropriate and efficient tool.

[468] For a detailed analysis, see Nadakavukaren Schefer (2005).

[469] The Kimberley Process Certification Scheme (available at http://www.kimberleyprocess.com) defines conflict diamonds in section I as "rough diamonds used by rebel movements or their allies to finance conflict aimed at undermining legitimate governments, as described in relevant United Nations Security Council (UNSC) resolutions insofar as they remain in effect, or in other similar UNSC resolutions which may be adopted in the future, and as understood and recognised in United Nations General Assembly (UNGA) Resolution 55/56, or in other similar UNGA resolution which may be adopted in the future."

access. Instead of applying Article XX(a) GATT, which in this case would most certainly have justified possible violations of the GATT, the WTO members opted for granting a waiver to all participants of the scheme.[470] With this solution the WTO avoided a debate about the extent to which trade sanctions are conceptually compatible with liberalising trade.[471]

3.4. DEMOCRACY AND SOVEREIGNTY

The emergence of networks of experts and MNEs as new players as discussed in the first section of this chapter, together with the potential linkage of trade and human rights across geographical boundaries and different areas of law that has been analysed in this and the previous chapter, raises questions of legitimacy regarding the actors and consistency of norms.

Foreign trade and finance are essentially undemocratic fields, because decisions are prepared by experts and usually taken without consultation with citizens even though the decision can seriously affect them. Alienation is often the result, finding expression in the extremes of political lethargy on the one hand or violent protests, such as the regular anti-globalisation protests that have taken place since the 1999 WTO meeting in Seattle, on the other hand.

In addition, cross-border economic activities and the increasing interdependences of a global society raise the question as to whether national policies that are based on the concept of territorial nation-states can still be effective. While international organisations can—to some extent—compensate for the loss of national competences from an efficiency point of view, the institutional mechanisms that provide for legitimacy within the nation-state are lacking. Without such mechanisms, state policy is replaced by market pressure, and, if taken to the extreme, power and political authority will be replaced by money. The result is a vicious circle: only power can be limited and "governed" by democratic institutions; money cannot.[472]

For lawyers, the key is whether law can provide a solution and define a substantial role for the state.[473] A reformulation of the relationship between domestic and international law may be the answer: the dualistic system in the United Kingdom and the United States is seen by some authors as a tool to compensate for the lack of legitimacy in international law by providing a system of checks and balances against its abuses.[474] The tension between these different international players and systems will be addressed in chapter 4 from a legal point of view.

[470] Waiver Concerning Kimberley Process Certification Scheme for Rough Diamonds: Communication, G/C/W/432/Rev.1, 24 February 2003. For a detailed analysis, see Pauwelyn (2003b).

[471] For a detailed discussion of the conceptual conflicts between sanctions and liberalising trade see Charnovitz (2001).

[472] Habermas (1998) 107–10, 119.

[473] Koskenniemi (2000) 33–34 draws a parallel from the current situation to the work of Carl Schmitt and Hans Morgenthau, concluding that "we have been here before".

[474] Jackson (2003) 793; Kamarck (2000) 229, 250.

4

Reconciling Conflicting Interests: The Roles of Nation States and the International Community

> Without the ability to articulate political visions and critiques, international law becomes pragmatism all the way down, an all-encompassing internalization, symbol, and reaffirmation of power . . . International law's energy and hope lies in its ability to articulate existing transformative commitment in the language of rights and duties and thereby to give voice to those who are otherwise routinely excluded.
>
> Martti Koskenniemi[1]

THE PRECEDING CHAPTERS have identified trade and policy-making conflicts at both international and national levels. International economic organisations pursue objectives that often conflict with the protection of core labour rights. While it is undisputed that global institutions are needed to solve the collective problems arising from globalisation, such powerful institutions and the resultant centralisation raise concerns with respect to individual liberty and—given the absence of a global *demos*—cultural diversity. This conflict between the need for global regulation and the fear of a central decision-making authority that is far removed from the people who are to be governed has been described as the "globalization paradox",[2] or in the words of Robert Keohane, the "government dilemma".[3] It is in this context that recent debates on "governance without government" or "reinventing government" projects must be placed.[4]

In addition to friction at the international level between institutions that are governed by international law, globalised markets and the increasing influence of international economic organisations may also have an impact at the *domestic* level by changing the role of the state and leaving many people feeling powerless and disenfranchised. In fact, the seeds of the problem lie not within the nation state but at the inter-state level. If we were to accept that transnational networks have taken over the role previously played by states and international

1 Koskenniemi (2002a) 516–17.
2 Slaughter (2004) 8–9.
3 Keohane (2001) 1.
4 For an overview, see Walter (2002) 170–75.

organisations such as the UN, then the relationships between citizens and the state or its "replacement" structure, as well as the role of the NGOs need to be renegotiated.[5] In other words, the governance dilemma becomes a *tri-lemma*: global rules should not be set solely by centralised institutions but should involve government actors who can be held accountable by democratic processes. Democracy requires state interaction with citizens as well as other stakeholders such as corporations and NGOs.[6]

Obviously, transnational networks need to be examined more closely as a potential solution in relation to the criteria mentioned above. Yet there may be solutions that can still be based on the concept of the nation state while simultaneously taking account of new needs in a globalised world. In this chapter, I will propose a system of multilevel consistency that, with its checks and balances, could be seen as an intergovernmental social contract.

Chapter 4 will therefore look first at the horizontal level by addressing the conflict between the objectives of international economic organisations and the concept of core labour rights; it will then turn to the vertical dimension, ie the relationship and interaction between international bodies and the nation state.

4.1. THE HORIZONTAL DIMENSION: CORE LABOUR RIGHTS AND INTERNATIONAL ECONOMIC INSTITUTIONS

The previous chapters have identified the lack of consistency between the mandates of international economic institutions and the International Labour Organization (ILO) as one of the major factors that lead to conflicting obligations with respect to core labour rights. This section will proceed by exploring whether and how core labour rights can be considered in international economic institutions.

4.1.1. Conceptual Developments in International Law

As outlined in detail in chapter 2, international consensus on labour rights can be assumed only for the *core* labour rights as they have been defined by the ILO Declaration on Fundamental Principles and Rights at Work. Given their heterogeneous membership, international economic institutions will have to rely on this concept if they attempt to address labour rights at all. This is the approach the World Bank applies when including labour standards in its programmes.

[5] Slaughter (2001a) 2.
[6] Slaughter (2004) 10.

4.1.1.1. *From International Co-operation towards Global Integration*

The international economic organisations that were established at the Bretton Woods Conference in 1944 were based on international co-operation among sovereign states. While this model was an appropriate answer to the failure of the League of Nations and the experiences with the Treaty of Versailles, international relations have now changed again: the trend towards integration is going beyond international co-operation and bringing about a shift from the national legislator to the international expert. This is particularly the case for economic legislation, but can also be observed in the areas of taxation and migration.

At present, international law is ill-suited to accommodate these developments.[7] The lack of appropriate constitutional structures at the global level explains why international organisations are not co-ordinated or embedded in an overarching system. In international law, there is only one source of positive law: treaties. Unlike in national constitutional law, there are no other instruments of written positive law at a lower level. This is one reason for the recent significant increase in non-binding and soft law instruments such as declarations and codes of conduct.

Integration can be observed not as a general phenomenon, but in very specific areas of law. Examples are WTO law and the recent practice of the UN Security Council on sanctions. The latter has seemingly led to a consensus that a resolution by the Security Council is necessary for the legitimacy of sanctions, thus emphasising the integrative approach. These developments in international relations point towards further integration; yet at the same time, international law is undergoing a process of fragmentation that needs to be examined further.

4.1.1.2. *The Fragmentation of International Law*

Chapter 3 has shown how international law has recently become subject to increased fragmentation/diversification.[8] While the reasons for this fragmentation are manifold,[9] two factors play a key role in the context of core labour rights: the development of highly specialised legal regimes within the ILO and international economic institutions on the one hand, and the different structure of these norms on the other.

Core labour rights and specialised international economic institutions do share a common origin: the Atlantic Charter of 1941, a joint declaration by Winston Churchill and F D Roosevelt that contained their vision of a peaceful

[7] For a detailed analysis, see Paulus (2001).

[8] Report of the Study Group of the International Law Commission: Fragmentation of International Law: Difficulties Arising from the Diversification and Expansion of International Law, finalised by Martti Koskenniemi, UN Doc A/CN.4/L.682, 13 April 2006.

[9] Hafner (2002) 326–31.

world order after World War II.[10] Of the three pillars—trade, finance and peace (including human rights)—the first two were further developed at the conference at Bretton Woods in 1944, while human rights and the establishment of a legal and institutional framework for a peaceful post-war order were left to the new United Nations.

As cases in point, WTO law—with the exception of the TRIPS Agreement—is based on the classical concept of international law as reciprocal obligations between states, whereas the ILO's core labour rights approach implies legal rights of individuals and thereby follows a relatively new notion of international law as imposing not only negative but also affirmative obligations on states.[11]

Attempts to increase the efficiency and effectiveness of international law[12] have led to the establishment of sophisticated follow-up mechanisms: the procedures for ensuring compliance with the ILO Declaration of Fundamental Principles and Rights at Work and the WTO dispute settlement mechanism are striking examples of how this trend further fosters specialisation.

It is undisputed that international law is no longer a homogenous body of rules. What is less clear is the impact of fragmentation on the legitimacy of international law.[13] If the different specialised regimes cannot be reconciled, the resulting disintegration of the international legal order could jeopardise the credibility and authority of international law.

In the context of labour rights, fragmentation occurs both with respect to substantive, primary rules and with regard to procedural, secondary provisions. In an attempt to reconcile labour rights with the objectives of international economic institutions, two fundamental questions need to be addressed: are there labour rights that can be considered universal and thus valid throughout specialised legal regimes, and if so, can they be incorporated into the activities of international economic organisations? Thus can their statutes be interpreted in such a way as to include the consideration of core labour rights? Following these fundamental questions we will have to consider the possible effects that such a mainstreaming approach might have on the content of core labour rights.

4.1.2. The Role and Limits of Interpretation

4.1.2.1. The Role of Interpretation in International Economic Organisations

In contrast to other international organisations, international *economic* organisations tend to have statutes that limit their mandate. In order to determine

[10] The Charter is reprinted in Rosenman (1938) 314; see also Introduction above, note 51 and accompanying text.

[11] Tomuschat (2003) 84–85.

[12] Dupuy, P-M (1999) 795.

[13] The complexity of this problem is underlined by the fact that the International Law Commission established a study group with the objective of providing guidelines for "international judges and practitioners in coping with the consequences of the diversification in international law". "Report of the Study Group on Fragmentation of International Law", note 8 above, paras 17–20.

whether the consideration of core labour rights is covered by the mandate, the relevant provisions need to be interpreted according to the rules of general treaty interpretation in international law. These rules are codified in the 1969 Vienna Convention on the Law of Treaties (VCLT) and repeated in the 1986 Vienna Convention on the Law of Treaties between States and International Organisations or between International Organisations. They have gained the status of customary international law.[14]

Articles 31–33, which are identical in both of the Vienna Conventions, combine different methods of interpretation, with an emphasis on the ordinary meaning of a provision within its context and in light of its object and purpose. The articles of agreement of the World Bank and the IMF on the other hand require that all their decisions, including decisions on interpretation "shall be guided by the purpose".[15] At first glance this preference for teleological interpretation might seem incompatible with Article 31 of the Vienna Conventions. However, as Ibrahim F Shihata has pointed out, since the purpose is defined in the respective Articles of Agreement of the World Bank and the IMF, any interpretation of what is covered by the purpose still has to rely on wording.[16]

With respect to the WTO, Article 3.2 DSU states that clarification of existing provisions has to be sought in accordance with customary rules of interpretation of public international law, which results in the application of the Vienna Conventions. Neither Article 3.2 nor the Vienna Conventions prescribe the applicable law but rather methods of interpretation.[17] Thus the next question to arise is: should the WTO Appellate Body look at the state of international law at the time of the conclusions of the WTO agreement or at the time that a provision is being interpreted?

In practice, drawing the line between interpretation and amendment of rules, between *evolutionary* and *revolutionary* interpretation, is a delicate task. Since it is often difficult to amend the charters of international organisations, interpretation is used to accommodate new developments as far as possible. An example is the demise of the gold standard, which was addressed with an amendment of the Articles of Agreement in the IMF but by means of interpretation in the World Bank.[18] In the WTO, a controversy about the admissibility of *amicus curiae* briefs in dispute settlement procedures launched a debate on the limits of interpretation.[19]

[14] *Case concerning Kasikili/Sedudu Island (Botswana/Namibia)*, International Court of Justice, 13 December 1999, ICJ Reports 1999, 1059.

[15] Article I of the Articles of Agreement for the IMF and the World Bank.

[16] Shihata (2000c) at 7.

[17] In the same sense, see Steger (2004) 144–45. Trachtman (2004) 139–42 reaches the same conclusions with different reasoning. For a contrary view, see Pauwelyn (2003a) 478–86, who holds that WTO panels and the Appellate Body can also apply other international law in two cases: if a question is not regulated in the WTO treaty itself and if other international law is invoked in defence of a claim of a violation of WTO law.

[18] Shihata (1995b) at 77–83.

[19] Ehlermann (2002) 615–18.

Generally, international economic organisations tend to refer questions of interpretation to their governing bodies: for the World Bank, the Articles of Agreement state in Article IX(a) and (b) that any question of interpretation of the Agreement arising between any member and the Bank or between members of the Bank shall be submitted to the Executive Directors for their decision. Appeals against their decision can be made to the Board of Governors whose decision shall be final. A similar solution can be found in the IMF.[20] As for the WTO, Article IX.2 of the Marrakesh Agreement gives the authority to adopt binding interpretations of the multilateral trade agreements to the Ministerial Conference and the General Council. This authority to give binding interpretations is conceptually different from the implied powers that are vested in intergovernmental organisations under general international law[21] and include the necessary tools to conduct the business of these organisations.

4.1.2.2. Limits: Material and Temporal Scope

Members of international economic organisations have on several occasions expressed their concern that teleological or evolutionary interpretations could expand the mandate of the organisation and thus impose new obligations on members at the expense of their sovereignty.[22] The rules of the Vienna Conventions reflect these concerns to some extent by emphasising the importance of textual interpretation. In this light, an interpretation against the explicit wording of the text or going in a new direction that is not related to the declared objective of the text, would appear problematic.[23]

Taking such concerns seriously raises three important questions.[24] What type of rules can be referred to when defining treaty obligations? Are all obligations under international law relevant, regardless of their legal status? Or should only general principles of international law or even just *ius cogens* be applicable? The second question is *inter-temporal* in nature: should state obligations be interpreted in light of international law at the time of the conclusions of the treaty,

[20] Article XXIX of the IMF's Articles of Agreement.

[21] See the ICJ, "Reparation for Injuries Suffered in the Service of the United Nations", Advisory Opinion of 11 April 1949, ICJ Reports 1949 [hereinafter *Reparations for Injuries*] 174, at 17; see also chapter 2 above, note 224 and accompanying text.

[22] After the Appellate Body issued rules about the admissibility of *amicus curiae* briefs in the *EC—Asbestos* case (*European Communities—Measures Affecting Asbestos and Asbestos-Containing Products,* AB 2000-11, Report of the Appellate Body, 12 March 2001, WT/DS135/AB/R), Egypt, supported by several developing countries, called for an extraordinary meeting of the WTO General Council. Developing countries expressed their concern about the Appellate Body overstepping its mandate. International Centre for Trade and Sustainable Development (ed), *Bridges between Trade and Sustainable Development*, 4(9) Nov–Dec 2000, at 4. Similar discussions took place in the BWIs in the context of including core labour rights into programmes. See chapter 2 above, notes 266–69 and accompanying text.

[23] Shihata (2000c) at 8–9 goes even further in stating that such an interpretation would amount to an actual amendment and thus go beyond the powers of the interpreters.

[24] Pauwelyn (2003a) 254–68.

or should new developments at the time of its interpretation be taken into account?

Consider as an example a case where the Appellate Body must decide whether restrictions on trade of products manufactured with exploitative child labour are justified by public morals under Article XX(a) GATT. The ILO Declaration on Fundamental Principles and Rights at Work and/or ILO Convention No 182 on Worst Forms of Child Labour could be important in establishing a notion of public morals that includes the prohibition of exploitative child labour. However, both instruments were adopted *after* the conclusions of the WTO Agreements. Following the traditional "principle of contemporaneity",[25] the meaning of the notion "public morals" at the time the GATT was concluded would have to be taken into account by the Appellate Body.

Adopting an *evolutionary* approach on the other hand would lead the Appellate Body to interpret "public morals" in light of contemporary concerns about the welfare of children, thus allowing for consideration of the above-mentioned ILO Declaration and Convention No 182. Such an evolutionary approach has been applied by the ICJ on several occasions.[26] In *US—Shrimp/Turtles* the Appellate Body interpreted the notion of "exhaustible natural resources" in Article XX(g) GATT in an evolutionary manner—without, however, referring to the VCLT.[27]

At first glance, the evolutionary and revolutionary approaches to interpretation hence appear to be mutually exclusive.

4.1.3. Conclusions: The Problem at the Horizontal Level

The difficulties at the horizontal level between different international organisations can be summarised as follows. The development of international organisations with very specific mandates and specialised expertise in a particular area has, *inter alia*, led to the fragmentation of international law. This phenomenon may result in conflicts between the objectives of international economic organisations and core labour rights. The key is whether existing rules on treaty interpretation as they are codified in the Vienna Conventions allow for an

[25] This principle goes back to an early case brought to arbitration before the Permanent Court of International Justice in 1928. In this *Island of Palmas* decision, the sole arbitrator, Justice Max Huber, held that "the act creative of a right" has to be judged by the "law in force at the time the right arises": 2 UN Rep International Arbitral Awards 829, at 845. Nevertheless, he continued to state that the existence of that right at the time of the dispute should have followed the evolution of international law.

[26] "Legal Consequences for States of the Continued Presence of South Africa in Namibia (South West Africa) notwithstanding Security Council Resolution 276 (1970)", Advisory Opinion, ICJ Reports 1971, 31; *Aegean Sea Continental Shelf*, ICJ Reports 1978, 3, at pp 32–34, paras 77–80 and pp 68–69. See Pauwelyn (2003a) 266 note 84.

[27] *United States—Import Prohibition of Certain Shrimp and Shrimp Products*, Report of the Appellate Body, WT/DS58/AB/R, adopted 6 November 1998 [hereinafter *US—Shrimp/Turtles*], paras 128–32.

interpretation that co-ordinates and integrates the different objectives. Such an interpretation may however be limited not only by the applicable method of interpretation as outlined above—ie, textual versus teleological and contextual interpretation, contemporary versus evolutionary interpretation—but also by the concerns of Member States about their sovereignty. The latter aspect will be addressed in the following section.

If the problems of interpretation can be solved, then the next issue is identifying which labour rights can be integrated into the activities of international economic organisations. As pointed out in chapter 2 above, universal consensus on the content of labour rights can only be assumed for the core labour rights enshrined in the ILO Declaration on Fundamental Principles and Rights at Work. It is necessary to decide which organisation should have the power to define authoritatively the concrete content of these rights.

4.2. THE VERTICAL DIMENSION: STATES AND INTERNATIONAL LEGAL OBLIGATIONS

Globalisation affects national law and, in particular, the constitutional order. Developments at the international level, such as the establishment of the WTO, create new sets of rights and obligations, some of which resemble constitutional principles and contain elements of global governance. However, these provisions are applicable only in specific areas. From a national perspective, two crucial questions need to be answered. First, how much room for manoeuvre is generally left for national policies? Answering this question entails analysing the different—and often conflicting—layers of international obligations. Second, the role of international economic organisations with regard to decision-making needs to be examined: is there a change in the notion of sovereignty, moving away from the Westphalian concept towards a more participation-oriented approach?

4.2.1 Do States have Room to Manoeuvre?

4.2.1.1. Layers of International Obligations

As we have seen in chapters 1 and 2, several layers of obligations restrict the state's room for manoeuvre with regard to core labour rights. First, national constitutional law is intended to balance individual liberties (freedom *from*) with distributive polices (right *to*). However, this first choice is already influenced by international institutions, in the form of legal obligations or expert recommendations. Various human rights instruments, as discussed in chapter 1, define the substantial core labour rights and add to national constitutional provisions. This *constitutional* function of international law is accompanied by a *systemic* effect, led by international economic organisations.

While the choice of parameters for the "economic constitution" *(Wirtschaftsverfassung)* used to be one of the classic prerogatives of the Westphalian nation state, under the auspices of the BWIs,[28] the OECD[29] and the WTO,[30] a liberalised, market-oriented framework is no longer optional. Concrete examples are the reviews conducted by the IMF under Article IV of the IMF Statute. These reviews are part of the fund's mandate for surveillance of member countries' economic and financial policies. Experiences with the financial crises in Mexico 1994 and East Asia in the late 1990s led to several efforts to strengthen surveillance mechanisms. On the basis of Article IV, the IMF holds consultations with each of its members, normally every year. These consultations focus on members' exchange rate, fiscal and monetary policies; their balance of payments and external debt developments; the influence of policies on external accounts; the international and regional implications of those policies; and potential vulnerabilities. Consultations are not limited to macroeconomic policies but rather touch on all policies that significantly affect the macroeconomic performance of a country, which, depending upon circumstances, may include labour and environmental policies and the economic aspects of governance.[31] The reports issued by IMF staff regularly contain detailed recommendations on competition policy or labour market strategy.[32]

Similar criteria are applied in the context of conditionality in loan agreements. Although the Washington Consensus no longer serves as a general guiding principle,[33] trade liberalisation and the opening up of markets are still of crucial importance. While the preamble to the Convention on the OECD explicitly states that it aims at consistency with the other international obligations of its Member States, there is no similar provision in the Articles of Agreement for the IMF and the World Bank.

For the state, these developments result in differing obligations of international law: obligations to comply with core labour rights on the one hand and requirements to pursue economic policies that aim at market liberalisation and increased growth on the other hand. The next section will explore further how the advice and recommendations of international economic organisations, in spite of their legally non-binding nature, nonetheless influence domestic regulation.

[28] Articles I and VIII of the IMF's Articles of Agreement; Articles I and II(1) of the Articles of Agreement for the World Bank.

[29] Article 2 of the Convention on the Organisation for Economic Co-operation and Development.

[30] A concrete example is the Protocol on the Accession of the People's Republic of China, 23 November 2001, WT/L/432.

[31] For an overview see IMF, "Fact Sheet on Surveillance", September 2005, available at http://www.imf.org.

[32] This is not only the case for borrowing countries but also for industrialised countries. See for example the country review for Switzerland: "Switzerland—Selected Issues", IMF Country Report No 05/188, June 2005.

[33] See chapter 2 above, note 95 and accompanying text. For a critical account of the Washington Consensus, see Stiglitz (2002) 53–88.

4.2.1.2. The Role of International Economic Institutions: Regulation by Expertise

In some situations, the IMF goes beyond general recommendations or comments and explicitly requires countries to amend legislation—or as in the case of Argentina, to repeal existing laws—in order to improve macroeconomic conditions. Over the years, the IMF and other international economic institutions have come to realise that reforms are sustainable only if they are supported by the authorities and ideally by society as a whole. Nevertheless, Anne Krueger, the former First Deputy Managing Director of the Fund, has made clear that

> . . . ownership is necessary for a programme but it is not sufficient. It has to make sense economically. At the end of the day, a country is responsible for the policies it chooses—and we are responsible for deciding whether to lend in support of them.[34]

In legal terms, countries are not bound to follow the advice of international economic organisations such as the BWIs or the OECD. However, in reality, the situation is more complex. First, IMF recommendations tend to have a considerable impact on financial markets by creating expectations. Therefore, a country that is already facing an economic crisis can rarely afford not to follow the Fund's advice. This can lead to political tensions with regard to domestic policy. For example, Argentina was advised by the IMF to amend its tax law.[35] Because of the substantial role that would be given to provinces in the regulation of taxes, the proposed law was amended by Parliament; but in order to comply with the Fund's conditions for a loan, Parliament had to withdraw the amendments.

International economic organisations are increasingly consulting with domestic experts when reviewing a country's economic policy or assessing conditions for loans. Yet expertise often travels on a one-way street: international experts influence a country's economic and legal situation with their advice; but mechanisms that take domestic political processes or social considerations into account are still rare. Thus, the membrane between international expertise and domestic political systems is only semi-permeable, allowing for travel in only one direction—a phenomenon that biologists know as osmosis. This osmotic effect lies at the heart of the debate on the role of international economic organisations.

Whether in Argentina or elsewhere, international expert networks play a key role in defining the framework for economic policy. Depending on national law involved, parliaments are included in the decision-making process, but—particularly in structural adjustment processes—their role is often reduced to that of a supporting actor.[36] To illustrate the role of the experts and their influence on democratic decision-making procedure, it is worth looking at a less

[34] Anne Krueger in IMF Survey, vol 31, No 15, 5 August 2002, at 242.
[35] Musa (2004) 320–26.
[36] Cottier (1997) 230–31.

dramatic example than Argentina, which took place in Switzerland when the constitutional provision on monetary policy was revised.

The Swiss National Bank had a policy of pursuing price stability but had no specific mandate to do so. Following recommendations from the IMF and OECD as well as leading economic theory, the first draft of the new constitutional provision not only affirmed the independence of the central bank but also explicitly declared price stability to be the goal of monetary policy. Since it was unclear whether the project to revise completely the Constitution would eventually be successful, the idea was to go ahead with the provisions on monetary policy, thus to apply a "fast-track" procedure.[37]

While the independence of the central bank was undisputed, proclaiming the goal of price stability met with fierce political opposition. As a result, the draft had to be amended, and the final version now requires the Swiss National Bank "to follow a monetary policy which serves the *general interest* of the country".[38] The main concern of the opponents was that price stability should not be considered as a goal on its own but rather as a *tool* to achieve prosperity, including full employment. Unemployment was high in Switzerland and all over Europe at the time the deliberations took place. The opponents of the goal of price stability therefore wanted to commit the central bank to a policy that would effectively reduce and prevent unemployment.

The whole debate must be seen in the broader context of the discussion about the European Monetary Union. Although economic theory points to the failure of central banks to influence unemployment *in the long term*, it was politically unthinkable at the time to ignore the high unemployment rates. New economic evidence had also shown that central banks that were independent from governments and followed policies of price stability could contribute to higher growth rates.[39] As a result, a compromise was found in the Maastricht Treaty:

> Article 4(2):
>
> Concurrently with the foregoing, and as provided in this Treaty and in accordance with the timetable and the procedures set out therein, these activities shall include the irrevocable fixing of exchange rates leading to the introduction of a single currency, the ECU, and the definition and conduct of a single monetary policy and exchange rate policy the *primary objective of both of which shall be to maintain price stability* and, *without prejudice to this objective*, to support the *general economic policies* in the Community, in accordance with the principle of an open market economy with free competition.[40]

[37] Das neue Nationalbankgesetz, Bericht und Entwurf der Expertengruppe Reform der Währungsverfassung vom 16. März 2001, pp 8–9.

[38] Article 99(2) of the Constitution (emphasis added). Vallender (2001) § 61 Rz 22.

[39] See study by Cukierman, Kalaitzidakis, Summers and Webb (1993).

[40] Article 4 of the Treaty establishing the European Community (emphasis added).

After lengthy debates, a similar formula was included in the revised Federal Law on the Swiss National Bank.[41] The IMF was disappointed that price stability was not included in the Constitution but was pleased with the constitutional guarantee of the central bank's independence.

As this example shows, economic expertise cannot be translated into legislation in isolation from political circumstances. Recommendations and advice by international economic organisations can have a significant impact on democratic institutions, but the process is more complex than simply limiting legislative options.

In their consultations with member countries, experts from international economic organisations quite often communicate with their peers at the domestic level, thus with specialists in government agencies and central banks. Not surprisingly, such exchanges generally focus on technical issues and leave political considerations aside. This procedure complies with the usually clearly defined mandate such specialised agencies are given by the government.

"Regulation by experts" therefore has two important aspects. First, the high reputation of international economic organisations in financial markets creates an economic necessity for states to comply with their recommendations and advice by adjusting domestic legislation accordingly. This can regrettably reduce parliamentary deliberations and adoption of legislation to formalities.[42] In constitutional terms, because they participate in international organisations and their expert groups, the administrative and executive branches are strengthened at the cost of parliament.

The second important aspect of "regulation by experts" is the fact that networks of international and domestic experts operate mainly behind closed doors and provide limited opportunities for the public to learn about their activities. While this is undoubtedly an appropriate procedure for deliberating market-sensitive issues of economic policy, it prevents the inclusion of other considerations such as core labour rights. It is often argued that parliamentary adoption of legislation that is prepared by such networks compensates for the lack of democratic participation at an earlier stage. However, this argument overlooks two important points: as mentioned above, where economic measures are suggested by international economic organisations, in particular the IMF, factual pressure by markets usually prevents parliaments from opting against such measures. Where trade legislation is harmonised at the international or regional level, different issues are often tied together into a "package" that can only be adopted as a whole. Examples include the first set of bilateral treaties between Switzerland and the European Communities or the results of the Uruguay Round in the WTO. This so called "package deal

[41] Article 5(1) of the Law on the Swiss National Bank, SR 951.11; Bericht der Expertengruppe, note 37 above, pp 97–101.

[42] Cottier and Germann (2002) Rz 22

approach"[43] seriously limits the influence of parliament and in Switzerland leads to a *de facto* restriction of the right to referendum.

In summary, we are observing a silent change in the constitutional order with a strengthening of the executive and administrative branch at the international level and a loss of power for parliaments due to the *de facto* legislative influence of international economic institutions and the "package deal approach" to harmonising international trade regulation.

We therefore need to ask whether there are mechanisms to bridge the gap between the observed *de facto* legislation by international economic organisations and constitutional democratic procedures. Two options will be suggested in the following section: strengthening the participation of parliament in the formulation of foreign policy (section 4.2.1.3. below) and increasing transparency and accountability (section 4.2.1.4. below).

4.2.1.3. *Strengthening Mechanisms for Participation of Parliament*

The increasing influence of international organisations has led to a call for strengthening instruments of direct democracy.[44] In the European Union, the introduction of the principle of subsidiarity in the treaty of Maastricht as well as the increasing number of referenda in Member States is seen as a counterweight to centralisation of power within the Community. This development is comparable to the democratic movement of the Swiss cantons between 1848 and 1874 when they sought to strengthen their position relative to an increasingly powerful federal government by enhancing democratic institutions.[45] Nevertheless, these attempts had the opposite effect: democratisation left the cantons incapable of reacting quickly to new developments. As a result, the position of the federal government was further consolidated.[46]

Similarly, proponents of direct democracy today overlook that it does not enhance the capability of the state to act efficiently at the international level. In fact, instruments of direct democracy can slow down internal decision-making processes to an extent that seriously limits a state's options for active participation in international organisations.[47] In addition, if it is to be effective, direct democracy requires a well-defined community, which at the international level does not

[43] *Ibid* Rz 4.

[44] For example, the discussion in the context of the European Convention: See Report of the Initiative and Referendum Institute Europe, Voices of Europe, IRI Report on the growing importance of Initiatives and Referendums in the European integration process, edited by Heidi Hautala, Bruno Kaufmann and Diana Wallis, Brussels 7 November 2002. Available at http://www.iri-europe.org/?reports/?referendumchallenge.pdf. Also Article I-46 of the draft Treaty establishing a Constitution for Europe, provisional consolidated version, Conference of the Representatives of the Governments of the Member States, CIG 86/04, 25 June 2004.

[45] Fleiner (1941b) 202.

[46] Schindler (1996) 285.

[47] More than 30 years ago Kurt Eichenberger called direct democracy a "*Staatsform der Langsamkeit*", ie a "state form of slowness", Tschannen (1995) para 680 with further references.

exist.[48] There is no global *demos* that can represent the will of the people across state borders.[49] For this reason, international organisations can only address states. The participation of the citizen or parliament is—with the exception of first attempts in the EU[50]—a matter of national law. The role of the parliament would be further weakened if instruments of direct democracy went beyond the decisions on fundamental principles. Rather the participation of the parliament in defining the key elements of foreign policy should be strengthened.[51]

In this light, the recently adopted extension of the right to hold a referendum against international agreements that contain important legal provisions or require implementation in the form of a federal law in Switzerland[52] does not deal with the issue in all its complexity. It merely underscores the need for referendum on international treaties to occur at earlier stages of the ratification process rather than at the implementation stage, thereby helping to prevent the government from taking on international obligations that cannot be complied with domestically.[53]

In the United States, with the 2002 Trade Promotion Authority Act (TPA 2002),[54] Congress passed legislation that attempts to balance on the one hand the need for comprehensive presidential authority to negotiate trade agreements ("fast track"), especially in the ongoing round at the WTO, with on the other hand, ensuring the participation of Congress. This goal is achieved by several means. First, the Act defines the objectives of US trade policy,[55] thereby binding the administration to fundamental principles, including, among many others, the promotion of core labour standards.[6] Secondly, the TPA specifies which trade agreements can be negotiated by the President without first seeking the approval of Congress, thus providing for a clear regulation of competences.[57]

[48] Schindler (1996) 285.

[49] In its decision on the Treaty of Maastricht, the German Constitutional Court held that at this stage there was no European people but that the European Union's democratic legitimacy was mainly derived from the people of the Member States through the national parliaments. BVerfG 89, 155 (1994), paras 96, 100–1 and 108: "Der Unions-Vertrag begründet [. . .] einen Staatenverbund zur Verwirklichung einer immer engeren Union der—staatlich organisierten—Völker Europas [. . .], keinen sich auf ein europäisches Staatsvolk stützenden Staat."

[50] Direct election of the European Parliament still reflects the will of the people in the Member States and not that of a common European people. The European Convention, which was established by the Laeken European Council in December 2001, aimed at including citizens and civil society in the creation of a European Constitution. Laeken Declaration on the Future of the European Union, Presidency Conclusions of the European Council meeting in Laeken, 14/15 December 2001, SN 300/1/01/REV 1, Annex I, chapter III.

[51] Cottier (1997) 230–31; Ehrenzeller (1999) 89.

[52] Article 141(1) lit. d (3) of the Swiss Constitution, in force since 1 August 2003.

[53] Parlamentarische Initiative (Kommission 96.091 SR) Beseitigung von Mängeln der Volksrechte, Bericht der Staatspolitischen Kommission des Ständerates vom 2. April 2001, BBl 2001 4803, at 4825.

[54] Bipartisan Trade Promotion Authority adopted on 1 August 2002, Trade Act of 2002, Pub L No 107-210, 116 Stat 993, codified in 19 USC § 3802 [hereinafter TPA 2002].

[55] TPA 2002, sec 2102(a) and (b).

[56] TPA 2002, sec 2102(b.11), (c.1) and (c.2).

[57] TPA 2002, sec 2103.

Several provisions that require consultations with congressional committees ensure that even where the President is granted authority to negotiate and enter trade agreements, Congress does not completely give up its power.[58] In addition, in domestically sensitive areas such as labour market policies, the President is required to provide Congress with specific reports on the implications of trade agreements on the domestic market.[59]

In Switzerland, Article 166 of the Constitution serves as a framework for enhancing the co-operation between the Federal Council and Parliament.[60] The Federal Council is required by law to inform parliamentary commissions in a timely manner on developments in foreign policy. In addition, it has to consult with parliamentary foreign policy commissions when new domestic law is created by negotiations with international organisations.[61] What is lacking, however, is the institutionalised, substantial participation of Parliament in the processes of defining trade and foreign policy goals. Overall, the chosen approach reflects the traditional law-making procedures in international law, ie treaty-making. Yet, it does not address the new, less formal ways of creating international legal obligations that were discussed earlier.

Strengthening the role of Parliament is also on the agenda of the European Union. Like national legislation, all international agreements require the consultation of the European Parliament, and many also require its consent.[62] In addition, extensive consultation with the Council takes place within the framework of the Common Foreign and Security Policy. Although the European Parliament has few "hard" competences in foreign policy, it takes a firm stand in international trade policy by, *inter alia*, calling for the establishment of a consultative parliamentary assembly in the WTO[63] and the compliance of the WTO with ILO core labour standards.[64]

4.2.1.4. *Transparency and Accountability*

A) The National Level The weakening of the role of parliaments leads to a loss of transparency and accountability, two key elements of democracy. Transparency is diminished because country's representatives to expert groups

[58] TPA 2002, sec 2102(d) and sec 2104.

[59] TPA 2002, sec 2102(c.5) on the implications on the domestic labour market and sec 2102(c.8), which asks for a "meaningful" labour rights report of the countries with which the President is negotiating.

[60] Biaggini (1999) 725–26.

[61] Article 152 ParlG, Federal law on the parliament, SR 171.10; Saladin (1995) 33.

[62] Article 300 EC Treaty. Consent of the European Parliament is required for agreements establishing a specific institutional framework by organising co-operation procedures, agreements having important budgetary implications, and agreements entailing amendment of an act adopted under the co-decision procedure referred to in Article 251.

[63] European Parliament resolution on the Fourth WTO Ministerial Conference, 25 October 2001, paras 10–11.

[64] European Parliament resolution on openness and democracy in international trade (2001/2093 (INI)), 25 October 2001, para 42.

of international economic organisations are generally not elected, and the proceedings of such groups are often not open to the public.[65]

Accountability is the constitutional counterweight to institutional independence.[66] It includes accountability to the government and—in the case of independent economic agencies such as central banks—the parliament and the public.

The new Swiss National bank law[67] illustrates how accountability of independent economic agencies can be achieved. Article 7 on "Accountability and Information" requires the Bank to discuss regularly the state of the economy, monetary policy and current issues of federal economic policy with the Federal Council. In addition, Article 7 obliges the Bank and the Federal Council to inform each other *before* taking decisions of economic or monetary significance. Mutual information does not imply that decisions have to be co-ordinated, and the independence of the central bank, which must not be instructed by the government, can therefore be safely maintained.[68]

The idea of delegating monetary policy to an independent central bank stems from the fact that such banks are assumed to base their decisions on expertise and economic considerations, to act impartially and not under the influence of current political developments. Given the implications of monetary policy for the welfare of a country, the responsibility of a central bank is considerable.[69] Experiences in Switzerland in the late 1980s, when decisions on monetary policy further escalated an already deepening recession, led to a call from Parliament to hold the central bank accountable. The new law requires the central bank to explain the state of the economy as well as its intentions on monetary policy to commissions of Parliament.[70]

Compared to the EU,[71] the United States[72] and other countries that require testimonies before parliamentary committees not only on a regular basis but

[65] In some cases the documents are made public after a delay. For example, the documents relating to the 1995–98 negotiations on a multilateral investment agreement in the OECD were published by the OECD on 19 February 2002 in response "to the interest of stakeholders and civil society . . . [The publication] is designed to help interested parties gain a full understanding of the history and substance of these negotiations." OECD Press Release of 19 February 2002, available at http://www.oecd.org.

[66] Lastra (1996) 49.

[67] Bundesgesetz über die Schweizerische Nationalbank, SR 951.11.

[68] Botschaft über die Revision des Nationalbankgesetzes vom 26. Juni 2002, BBl 2002, at 6097–303, at 6190.

[69] If a central bank applies an over-restrictive monetary policy during a recession it can further limit economic growth and slow down recovery. In retrospect, this was the case in Switzerland during 1991–96.

[70] Article 7(2), note 67 above.

[71] The European Parliament may hold a general debate on the Annual Report of the ECB .The President of the ECB and the other members of the Executive Board may, at the request of the European Parliament or on their own initiative, present their views to the competent committees of the European Parliament. Such hearings generally take place each quarter. In addition, a member of the European Commission has the right to take part in the meetings of the Governing Council and the General Council, but not to vote. As a rule, the Commission is represented by the commissioner responsible for economic and financial matters. Article 15 Protocol on the Statute of the European Central Bank.

[72] Under the Humphrey-Hawkins Act of 1978 (Full Employment and Balanced Growth Act, 15

also at the request of the committees, the new Swiss solution seems rather timid. However, it does not prevent members of the Swiss Parliament from asking questions and thus expanding the subject of the discussion. In addition, the new law addresses the third stakeholder in monetary policy, the public. Article 7(3) requires the Bank to inform the public regularly on the conduct of monetary policy. Also, an annual report is published in addition to quarterly publications on economic and monetary developments.

Finally, it is often argued that one of the most efficient non-electoral tools for holding governments accountable is markets. Rating agencies help to consolidate and publicise a number of market judgments about firms. As a result, governments with low ratings, for instance because of corruption, find it more difficult to attract investment. In the aftermath of the Asian crisis it was market pressure, not intergovernmental agreements, that led to far-reaching reforms.[73] However, the problem with relying on markets for accountability is twofold. First, markets do not operate democratically: the different interests and stakeholders are not all represented, and the "votes" are not distributed equally. Second, efficient market mechanisms may under certain circumstances collide with values agreed upon in a democratic constitution, such as social policies. Therefore, the benchmarks against which markets hold governments accountable are not necessarily those of civil society.

In conclusion, the democratic deficits induced by the shift of power from parliaments to the executive and administrative branch can be partially compensated for by introducing mechanisms for transparency and accountability such as parliamentary hearings and the publication of reports and information. In addition, informal processes such as the activities of NGOs can initiate the release of information to the public.

B) International Economic Institutions Recent efforts by international economic institutions to increase transparency beyond the national context have focused on the general public. The BWIs as well as the OECD publish ample information about their activities on their web sites. The WTO, long known for its restrictive release of information to the public, launched an initiative to become more transparent in May 2002 and now publishes all official documents without restriction unless a member requests otherwise.[74] In addition, all international economic organisations arrange forums for discussions with NGOs.

USCA § 3101, 3132), the Board of Governors must submit a report on the economy and the conduct of monetary policy to Congress by 20 February and 20 July of each year. The Chairman of the Board of Governors is called to testify on the report before the Senate Committee on Banking, Housing and Urban Affairs and the House Committee on Banking, Finance and Urban Affairs.

[73] Head (1998) at note 51 and accompanying text.

[74] "Procedures for the Circulation and De-restriction of WTO Documents", WT/L/452, 16 May 2002. Restricted documents are automatically de-restricted after 60 days unless otherwise requested by a member.

Nonetheless, with respect to national parliaments, none of the above-mentioned international economic organisations provides for institutional participation or accountability procedures. The OECD offers discussions with members of the Parliamentary Assembly of the Council of Europe (including OECD members that are not members of the Council of Europe) but does not give them a formal right to participate in negotiations. In the context of the WTO, suggestions have been made, namely by Ernst-Ulrich Petersmann[75] and the European Parliament itself,[76] that a parliamentary assembly should be created following the model of the European Union. In addition, several countries have submitted detailed proposals for enhancing transparency particularly in dispute settlement.[77]

4.2.1.5. *Systemic Issues*

The next step is to examine how different sets of rules in international economic law interrelate with core labour rights. Are they self-contained regimes that operate independently, or are there possibilities for reconciling the increasingly fragmented areas of international law?

The different obligations in international law are consistent if looked at individually or seen as *self-contained regimes*. Bruno Simma has applied this term to international legal theory in the context of state responsibility. According to Simma, self-contained regimes provide for their own remedies and exclude more or less totally the application of the general legal consequences of wrongful acts.[78] As such, they would exclude the application of general international law outside of their own systems. However, from a state's perspective they set different goals, which inevitably lead to conflicts at both the national and international levels. From a trade law point of view, such conflicting goals can result in protectionist outcomes when free trade is restricted in order to protect core labour rights. Human rights advocates on the other hand will argue that the pressure to reduce labour costs in the wake of globalisation potentially undermines core labour standards.[79] Therefore, the question remains: how can one decide between the different values?

[75] Petersmann (2002a) 646–47.

[76] European Parliament resolution on the Fourth WTO Ministerial Conference, 25 October 2001, paras 10–11. Note 63 above and accompanying text.

[77] European Parliament resolution on openness and democracy in international trade (2001/2093 (INI)), 25 October 2001; "Contribution of the European Communities and its Member States to the Improvement of the WTO Dispute Settlement Understanding", 13 March 2002, TN/DS/W/1; "Contribution of the United States to the Improvement of the Dispute Settlement Understanding of the WTO Related to Transparency", 22 August 2002, TN/DSW/13. The US Congress included the objective of transparency in the 2002 Trade Promotion Authority Act, Bipartisan Trade Promotion Authority adopted on 1 August 2002, Trade Act of 2002, Pub L No 107-210, 116 Stat 993, Sec 2102, para 5, codified in 19 USC § 3802.

[78] The broader term of "subsystems" on the other hand, includes a full set of secondary rules: see Simma (1985) 117.

[79] For an analysis of the areas of conflict between human rights and WTO law, see Dommen (2002) 13–15.

We have seen that the market is unable to manage adequately the social problems arising from liberalisation and globalisation. Law is often considered a tool to provide an infrastructure for the market, especially in organisations such as the BWIs. Hence, globalised markets require the legal framework to be competitive. With regulatory competition between different legal orders, the freedom to choose core values—a key element of democracy—becomes limited. This leaves the state in an awkward and defensive position: regulatory choices are to some extent no longer based on constitutional values but on market strategies. In other words, factual pressure can replace normative concepts.[80]

Modern systems theory teaches us that there is no system that can provide valid statements about its own functioning without referring to elements (such as values) outside the system.[81] In other words, in order for a system to be legitimate, it must refer to accepted values, ethics or theoretical instruments such as the hypothetical basic norm *(hypothetische Grundnorm)* developed by Hans Kelsen.[82]

In domestic law, the Constitution usually provides a framework that links these different values and co-ordinates conflicting interests.[83] Since there is no global constitution, other means must be found to integrate the different areas of international and domestic law and the conflicting interests that ensue. General principles of law such as the principle of good faith can serve as instruments for linking the different and often conflicting layers of law and integrate them into a coherent system.[84] Another avenue is to revisit the traditional notion of government and analyse the recent changes in the concept of sovereignty. This is where the different concepts of governance come into play. The next section will look at the relationship between the increasing influence of international organisations and the notion of national sovereignty.

4.2.2. Balancing International Law and National Sovereignty

Any discussion of national sovereignty in the context of international law inevitably raises the question of compliance. States observe a loss of sovereignty when they feel obliged to comply with international law.[85] In attempting to find a model for integrating the different areas of international legal obligations into

[80] Habermas (1992).
[81] The famous example is the *Epimenides Paradox*. First scientifically established by the German mathematician Kurt Gödel, the concept was later applied to social sciences including law by Niklas Luhmann. Gunther Teubner further developed Luhmann's approach with his autopoietic theory of law. Teubner (1989) 42; Hofstadter (1985) 19, 530–33.
[82] Kelsen (1960) 203–4. For an excellent analysis of Kelsen's concept, see Koskenniemi (2002a) 238–49.
[83] Saladin (1995) 38–50.
[84] *Ibid*, 189–215, describing the increasing difficulties of the state in fulfilling this mandate. See also Cottier (1997) 235–36.
[85] Marti (2003) 165–75.

a consistent system, we first need to understand why nations comply with international law and how such compliance can best be achieved.

The issue of state compliance underlies all discussions of how international legal norms ought to be formulated so as to provide incentives for states to comply with them. Is it the fear of sanctions or the threatened loss of reputation that lies behind compliance? Influenced by transnational legal process theory and Kantian philosophy, legitimacy has become one of the crucial elements in recent studies of state compliance with international law.[86]

In order better to situate the discussion, a brief overview of various theoretical approaches to compliance with international law is necessary.[87] Since the fall of the iron curtain and the end of the cold war, four major, but partially overlapping, "schools" have evolved. The first is the rationalist/instrumentalis approach as represented by Robert Keohane and Kenneth Abbott. In this view, international law is a regime that serves national interests and solves prisoner's dilemma situations on a national scale. Compliance with international law is therefore a winning strategy that nations will follow by rational choice as long as they see the benefits.

On the other side of the spectrum is Kantian philosophy. Two main threads exist here: one is based on Thomas Franck's concept of *rule-legitimacy*; the other, represented *inter alia* by Anne-Marie Slaughter, emphasises the importance of national identity. *Liberalism* is the key concept in the latter, which maintains that compliance is strongly dependent on whether or not the state can be characterised as liberal in identity, ie whether it has a form of representative government, guarantees of civil and political rights and a judicial system dedicated to the rule of law.[88] According to this theory, liberal democracies are more likely to have relationships based on law, while relations between liberal and illiberal states will more likely take place in political zones.[89]

Reviving Kantian philosophy, Franck's fairness approach builds on the ideas of Ronald Dworkin, John Rawls and Jürgen Habermas. His concept of fairness encompasses rationalist (benefit of nations), constructivist (power of norms for identity), legal process (fair process and state perception as elements of legitimacy) and Kantian philosophy (application of Rawls' ideas to international law with principles of right process and distributive justice).[90] His core notion of the legitimacy of legal rules depends on four conditions: rule clarity or determinacy, symbolic validation of the rule by rituals and formalities, conceptual coherence and the adherence to "right process", ie compliance with the international rule system.[91] Legitimacy is characterised as follows:

86 An excellent analysis of compliance in international monetary affairs can be found in Simmons (2000a) 819–32.

87 For an overview, see Koh (1997) 2614–35.

88 Slaughter's uncritical concept of a liberal state has been widely criticised: Marks (2000) 90–92; Alvarez (2001) 192–93; Koskenniemi (2000) 29–34.

89 Slaughter (1995) 522–26.

90 Koh (1997) 2642.

91 Franck (1995) 26, 30–41.

> People expect more than food. They also expect peace, good order, and security, and to be free of the stress of perpetual revolution, even if that revolution has benevolent redistributive intent. They expect that decisions about distributive and other entitlements will be made by those duly authorized, in accordance with procedures which protect against corrupt, arbitrary, or idiosyncratic decision-making or decision-executing. The fairness of international law, as of any other legal system, will be judged, first by the degree to which the rules satisfy the participant's expectations of justifiable distribution of costs and benefits, and secondly, by the extent to which the rules are made and applied in accordance with what the participants perceive as right process.[92]

Located somewhere between the staunchly rationalist/instrumentalist theory of state compliance and the Kantian approaches of Slaughter and Franck, there lies the *constructivist* school of thought. Based on Grotian heritage, the role of law here is seen as a determining factor in forming identity and building an international society.

During the cold war, "transnational" issues emerged where interstate co-operation persisted despite political controversies and tensions. The theoretical reply to these developments was *Transnationalism*. A textbook entitled *Transnational Legal Problems*, published by Henry Steiner and Detlev Vagts in 1968, focused on transnational legal process and abandoned the traditional dichotomy between public and private, domestic and international law.[93] Instead of politics, the key was now law and law's normativity.

Since this seminal publication, transnationalism has taken many forms. Most notable for our purposes here is the work of Abram Chayes and Antonia Handler Chayes, who start from a functionalist, process-oriented perspective. In their monograph *New Sovereignty*, Chayes and Chayes suggest a managerial approach to compliance.[94] Instead of relying on traditional enforcement mechanisms to secure compliance with international law, they propose a co-operative model that relies on processes of justification, discourse and persuasion. What is needed is a regime—a manager—such as a treaty and a discourse, thus a process. Their model builds on the assumption that nations comply with international law not because they fear sanctions but because they no longer define themselves by territorial control but as members of the international community. As such, it is the possible loss of reputation that induces compliance with international law.[95] Referring to international legal processes, the mechanisms suggested by Chayes and Chayes include transparency, reporting and data collection, verification and monitoring, dispute settlement and capacity-building.

[92] *Ibid*, 7.

[93] The current edition is Steiner, Henry J, Vagts, Detlef F and Koh, Harold Hongju, 4th edn (New York, Foundation Press, 1994).

[94] Chayes and Chayes (1995) 229–49.

[95] This argument has recently been taken up by Oona Hathaway in a very controversial study on compliance with human rights: see Hathaway (2003a); and Hathaway (2003b) with a reply to some of the critics of her first study.

The study does not cover the internalisation of international norms into domestic law.

In an attempt to reconcile the different ways of explaining why states comply with international norms, the enforcement and alternative compliance strategies in particular, Harald Koh has suggested what he calls the "transnational legal process". His focus is on norm internalisation, the missing link in the concepts of Franck and the Chayeses. Koh applies a three-step approach. First, a party should promote an interpretation of a norm. By so-doing, the moving party implicitly exercises pressure on other parties to internalise the new interpretation into national law. The goal is to bind the other parties to follow the new interpretation as part of their internal value sets. In Koh's view, transnational actors create patterns of behaviour in their interactions that ripen into institutions, regimes and transnational networks.[96] As a result, it is important first to empower more actors to participate. Second, if the goal of interaction is to produce interpretation of human rights norms, suitable forums need to be established, or existing ones such as international courts can be adapted. Third, he raises the question of how international human rights norms can best be internalised into national law. Koh acknowledges that the relationships among social, political and legal internalisation can be challenging.[97]

With these general theoretical developments about state compliance in mind, we can now consider the recent debate on governance. The effects of globalisation and the increasing influence of experts and markets on regulation have been analysed by scholars from different angles. On the one hand is a theory of "governance" that focuses on the shift in the meaning of government. This new process of governing leads to a rebuilding of politics as an alternative to law, thus blurring the lines between law and politics and between national and international law.[98] In this view, the international regime is understood more as a process or multilevel game than as government by legal norms. On the other hand, opponents of this recent mainstream approach are more concerned with the distribution of wealth and power in a global society. In contrast to those who focus on governance, they concentrate more on norms and sanctions than on communication and persuasion.

4.2.2.1. The Theory of Governance

Governance has become somewhat of a buzzword that encompasses various meanings. Traditionally, governance was used as a synonym for government. However, more recently the meaning has shifted to the process of creating conditions for ordered rule and collective action. It does not offer a new normative theory but an organising framework for understanding changing processes of

[96] Koh (1997) 2654.
[97] *Ibid*, 2656–57.
[98] Kennedy (2000) 389, 411; Koskenniemi (2000) 25–34.

governing.[99] For the purposes of this study, the term governance will be used as encompassing what David Kennedy has referred to as the "new" school of anti-formalist international law.[100] Its basic claim is that the international regime is better understood as a process or multilevel game than as a government by legal norms.

There seems to be wide agreement that governance refers to the development of governing styles whereby boundaries between and within the public and private sectors are now blurred. The new understanding of governance challenges conventional assumptions, which focus on government as if it were a "stand-alone" institution divorced from wider societal forces. For some, governance is just about a "reinvented" form of government that is better managed, ie what in Europe we refer to as New Public Management.[101] However, for our purposes here, governance will be understood in the broader meaning described above and as it has been defined by the Commission on Global Governance:

> Governance is the sum of the many ways individuals and institutions, public and private, manage their common affairs. It is a continuing process through which conflicting or diverse interests may be accommodated and co-operative action may be taken. It includes formal institutions and regimes empowered to enforce compliance, as well as informal arrangements that people and institutions either have agreed to or perceive to be in their interest.[102]

Because of its relevance for the labour rights discussion, the following sections will concentrate on the concept of "transgovernmental networks" and touch only briefly on other approaches.

A) Transgovernmental Networks and Democracy With the concept of transgovernmental networks, Anne-Marie Slaughter seeks to reconcile the declining importance of national governments and the increasing significance of international institutions.[103] She describes the phenomenon as a "disaggregated world order" that requires a new conception of democracy:[104]

> It is a horizontal conception of government, resting on the empirical fact of mushrooming private governance regimes in which individuals, groups and corporate entities in domestic and transnational society generate the rules, norms, and principles they are prepared to live by. It is a conception in which uncertainty and unintended consequences are facts of life, facts that individuals can face without relying on a higher authority. They have the necessary resources within themselves and with each other. They only need to be empowered to draw on them.[105]

99 Stoker (1998) 17–18.
100 Kennedy (2000) 389.
101 Stoker (1998) 18.
102 Commission on Global Governance (1995) at 2.
103 Slaughter (1997) 183–97; Slaughter (2004) 131–65.
104 In doing so, Slaughter further elaborates on her concept of disaggregated democracy in Slaughter (2001a) 32.
105 Slaughter (2004) 194–95.

The core concept in Slaughter's "new world order" is transgovernmentalism as a complement to intergovernmentalism.[106] On the basis of the different contexts in which they arise and operate, she identifies three types of transnational regulatory networks,[107] which need to be integrated in order to serve as a foundation for world order. Such integration takes place horizontally by establishing "networks of networks" and vertically by making individual government institutions responsible for the implementation of rules created by a supranational institution.[108] Before we explore the relationship between the different networks and the state, a look at existing networks is necessary.

a) Government Networks within International Organisations: The Club Model

When considering the real world, there are first networks that develop within the context of established international organisations such as the BWIs, the WTO or the OECD and that can be described as the "club model" of international institutions.[109] The club model became particularly important after the Second World War when international institutions facilitated co-operation by reducing the costs of making agreements, through established rules and practices, and by providing information. Ministers working on similar issues collaborated to make rules: "Trade ministers dominated GATT; finance ministers ran the IMF".[110]

Since only a relatively small number of like-minded ministers were involved after the War, this mode of operation was very convenient for participating governments. Officials working in other fields, whether at the national or international levels, were excluded from the negotiations. Because such exclusion worked in a reciprocal way, by which they were able to exclude outsiders from their own negotiations, it was acceptable. For example, environmental, labour rights and finance experts did not regularly participate in WTO negotiations. Another striking example is the OECD, which brings government officials together for the purpose of addressing a specific common problem and making recommendations or promulgating a model code for its solution.[111] In the club model, negotiations take place behind closed doors, making accountability difficult. However, from the perspective of multilateral co-operation, the club model can be judged a success.[112]

How then can voters make sure that their government officials are advancing their interests and not those of other citizens or interest groups? Following traditional theory, international organisations that are established by treaties and

[106] Slaughter (2004) 162.
[107] *Ibid*, 45–51; Slaughter (2001b) 355–60.
[108] Slaughter (2004) 131–65.
[109] Keohane and Nye (2001) 265–67.
[110] *Ibid*, 266.
[111] An example is the Financial Action Task Force (FATF) against money laundering, the world's leading institution in the fight against money laundering
[112] Keohane and Nye (2001) 267. For the WTO see the detailed analysis by Robert Hudec: Hudec (1999) 11–14.

comply with national ratification procedures exercise only powers delegated from the Member States and therefore do not raise any accountability concerns. Obviously, as the protests in Seattle showed, this view is not supported by public opinion. What we see, for example with the BWIs, are not international organisations with a clearly defined mandate that can easily be understood by citizens, but a rather rudimentary legal framework, which is constantly being interpreted and further developed by international groups of experts. When Switzerland applied to become a member of the BWIs, the information sent to voters described the organisations' mandate in very general terms. There was no mention of the possible infringements on democracy that might result from decisions taken by the Board of Governors or the effects of Article IV consultations.

Reliance on these examples is not intended to suggest that it is not legitimate for governments to delegate the authority to negotiate to ministers of finance or to central banks. However, such delegations require the public to be informed about what is being delegated and what actions the delegated agents have taken. Only then can the governments be held accountable in elections. This also implies that accountability at the domestic level needs to be strengthened.[113] Finally, increased legislative control over policy at the supranational level can enhance accountability. However, such increased control usually creates difficulties when negotiating international agreements because the national governments need room for manoeuvre. In fact, the bill for the renewal of the US President's authority to negotiate trade agreements (the "fast-track procedure") illustrates this dilemma: in order to compensate for the lack of democratic control and congressional influence, the bill includes a negotiating objective on labour and the environment.[114] While this approach seems to satisfy unions, it might create difficulties under WTO law.

b) **Government Networks within the Framework of an Executive Agreement**

In addition to networks within established institutions, transgovernmental activities also take place in less visible frameworks. Executive agreements, ie those negotiated by heads of state and not by legislative branches of government, may serve as an umbrella for the co-operation of national regulators. The most prominent example in this context is the New Transatlantic Agenda of 1995 and the Transatlantic Economic Partnership agreement of 1998 between the United States and the European Union.[115]

Equally important with regard to economic policy and labour rights are the networks that have emerged as an answer to the calls for a new financial architecture for the twenty-first century in the wake of the Russian and East Asian financial crises of 1997 and 1998.[116] In order to include officials from developing

[113] See section 4.2.1.4.A. above.

[114] Bipartisan Trade Promotion Authority adopted on 1 August 2002, Trade Act of 2002, Pub L No 107-210, 116 Stat 933, Sec 2102, codified in 19 USC § 3802, ss 5 and 6.

[115] Pollack and Shaffer (2001b) 14–17.

[116] Weber (2001) 250–65.

countries in the discussions, and to create a counterweight to the G-7, the Basel Committee and the IMF's Interim Committee, the United States pushed for the creation of the G-22. The group was originally comprised of the G-7 and 15 emerging market countries. It is now known as the G-20 and serves as a forum for co-operation and consultation on matters pertaining to the international financial system.[117]

c) **Spontaneous Government Networks** Probably the most "suspicious" transgovernmental activities are those that take place outside formal agreements and thus cannot be linked to a particular treaty or an executive agreement. The most cited example is the Basel Committee on Banking Regulations and Supervisory Practices,[118] where banking supervisors and senior central bank officials of the G-10 countries come together.[119] The group was created by the Bank for International Settlements (BIS) in 1974, following the collapse of the Herstatt Bank. The Basel Capital Accord adopted by the Basel Committee sets the legal standard for banking activities worldwide. Because of its risk assessments, it has considerable influence on financial markets.[120]

The International Organization of Securities Commissions (IOSCO) pursues similar objectives in harmonising security rules. The IOSCO has no charter and was not established by a treaty but by a private bill of the Quebec National Assembly.[121]

The third and youngest organisation in the context of financial regulation is the International Association of Insurance Supervisors (IAIS). Founded in 1994, partly on request by the Basel Committee, the IAIS is a non-profit organisation incorporated in Illinois. It does not explicitly pursue the goal of harmonising rules but serves as a forum for exchange of information and experience among insurance supervisors across the world. However, the IAIS may very well become an international financial regulator in the future.[122]

Another example is the Financial Stability Forum, which was established in 1999 to improve the functioning of financial markets and to reduce systemic risks through enhanced information exchange and international co-operation among the authorities responsible for maintaining financial stability.[123]

[117] President Clinton and leaders of the Asia-Pacific Economic Forum (APEC) announced the creation of the Group of 22, on a temporary basis, at their meeting in Vancouver in November 1997. For current activities of the G-20 see http://www.g20.org.

[118] For a detailed analysis, see Zaring (1998) 287–91.

[119] For Switzerland, the director of the Federal Banking Commission, the supervisory body for financial institutions, and a representative of the central bank are members of the Basel Committee.

[120] For an overview of the developments within the Basel Committee, see Picciotto (1996) 1039–45.

[121] Zaring (1998) 292 with further references.

[122] *Ibid*, 297–301.

[123] The Financial Stability Forum has 40 members: 25 senior representatives of national authorities responsible for financial stability in 11 significant international financial centres (Australia, Canada, France, Germany, Hong Kong, Italy, Japan, The Netherlands, Singapore, the United Kingdom and the United States), six senior representatives of four international financial institutions (BIS, IMF, OECD and the World Bank), six senior representatives of three international

The typical tools applied by such spontaneous networks are Memoranda of Understanding, which are not strictly legally binding but can be implemented by the regulators themselves.

Interestingly, despite of the crucial influence of the Basel Committee on domestic and international legislation, there are—at least in the case of Switzerland—no institutionalised consultations with the legislative branch on pending issues. Such developments have been seen as a removal of issues from the domestic political sphere through deliberate technocratic de-politicisation and thus carry the risk of a possible "runaway technocracy". Yet it must be said that scientific and objective language can also be a tool to facilitate acceptance; it need not be a tactic to avoid domestic bureaucratic battles in a way that excludes domestic voters from the discussion.[124]

B) Governance without Government? An extension of the network concept, the idea of "governance without government" has emerged. It refers to the fact that territoriality is no longer the determining criterion for defining state sovereignty and that national borders do not confine markets. Consequently, nation states are no longer capable of playing a significant role in regulating global relationships; instead, markets, alliances and networks are taking over. Government is seen as seriously weakened, incapable of "steering" as it has in the past.[125] Together with this comes a shift in responsibilities onto the private sectors and citizens.

Because of the pre-eminent role of the government in the welfare state in Europe, the debate started there, mainly in the context of New Public Management concepts, which aim to redefine the relationship between government and the private sector. As with Slaughter's theory, the notion of governance without government gives precedence to networks. Governance without government goes further though, because networks not only influence government policy but go so far as taking over the business of government.[126]

Self-governing networks face the problem of accountability in much the same way as transgovernmentalism. Here, the accountability deficit emerges at two levels: members of a network might disagree with the objectives agreed upon by the leaders, or they might be dissatisfied by the leaders' performance. Even if all members of a network are satisfied, there remains the problem of outsiders who are excluded from the network. Networks are by definition driven by the self-interest of their members rather than a wider concern with public interest.[127]

regulatory and supervisory bodies (Basel Committee on Banking Supervision, IOSCO and IAIS); a representative from each of two committees of central bank experts (Committee on the Global Financial System and Committee on Payment and Settlement Systems) and the Chairperson.

124 Picciotto (1996) 1037 gives the example of the Bretton Woods Conference where foreign policy goals were translated into calculations in order to facilitate their acceptance.

125 Peters and Pierre (1998) 224.

126 In a New Public Management approach, the only traditional role remaining for elected officials is that of setting goals and priorities. *Ibid*, 227.

127 Stoker (1998) 24.

The presumption that technocratic cosmopolitan governance has no stake in local disputes beyond stability and acts without political entanglement seems simply naïve. New accountability mechanisms are therefore necessary.

C) Conclusions and Critique For Slaughter, transgovernmentalism, combined with efficient accountability mechanisms, offers a response to the challenges that countries face as a result of their loss of regulatory power and the democratic deficit that follows economic globalisation.[128] Partly in reaction to strong criticism,[129] Slaughter now increasingly focuses on accountability[130] and what she calls "disaggregated sovereignty", which theoretically empowers institutions below the state level to fulfil their mandate at the international level.[131]

Are transgovernmental networks really the solution? Can they bridge the gap between obligations to comply with substantive rights such as labour rights on the one hand and requirements to maintain open markets on the other hand? There are several challenges to Slaughter's approach, and in her most recent work, she addresses these in a chapter entitled "A Just World Order".[132]

An early critic of Slaughter's model, Alston has pointed out two major problems.[133] First, it is necessary to identify the global agenda: what are the key global problems? Do they include terrorism in the wake of 11 September 2001? Or poverty? Are they both equally important? Second, who sets and implements that agenda? In addition, problems arise with respect to accountability and transparency.

Most recently, technocracy and lack of transparency have become the focal point of discussions. In Slaughter's concept, interest groups determine what the real problems are. Because of her focus on highly specialised networks nurtured mainly by government and central bank officials, issues that are not represented by such groups are not on the agenda. This is especially true for human rights. Poor people have no voice in these networks, and as a result, poverty is not on the agenda. However, this stems not only from *global technocracy* but also from the underlying power problem: empowering government networks shifts the domestic political balance of power and reinforces existing power asymmetries between nations. In other words, technocratic government networks privilege those nations that have technocrats.

One attempt to address this issue is the capacity-building programmes that are currently being supported by the WTO and individual member countries. A striking example is the Trade Law Centre for Southern Africa (Tralac), which was established with support from the Swiss government. Within a short period of time Tralac has become one of the leading think tanks in international trade law and a unique resource for training and research in Africa.

[128] Slaughter (2004) 261–71.
[129] Alvarez (2001); Alston (1997) 438–47.
[130] Slaughter (2001b) note 3.
[131] Slaughter (2004) 266–71.
[132] *Ibid*, 216–60.
[133] Alston (1997) 439.

Reliance on self-governing networks leads to an economisation of labour rights. The leading criteria are no longer rights and duties but economic efficiency and market mechanisms. Scholars such as Slaughter and Keohane are trying to overcome this problem by accompanying their concept with normative elements of democracy and liberalism.[134] By so doing, they are introducing a theory of rational choice that implies that every state should follow a liberal concept because this is—from a theoretical point of view—the best tool to address the challenges created by the increasing informalisation of international relations. This assumption has been strongly criticised as the "liberal hybris".[135] It reduces international relations to scientific laws and thereby creates a new form of rational or cynical imperialism.[136]

Real life is not about economising rights by giving them an objective, measurable content that is beyond dispute; instead, it is about the political contestation of distribution and justice:

> Governing an international order means making choices among groups—between finance and production, capital and labor, these and those distributors, these and those consumers, and male and female workers. Some of these choices will be national, of course—between Thai and Malaysian producers—but most will not. Development policy means preferring these investors to those and these public officials to those, not the technocratic extension of a neutral "best practice". To make these choices we need a world that is open to a politics of identity and to struggles over affiliation and distribution among the conflicting and intersecting patterns of group identity in the newly opened international regime.[137]

The theory of transgovernmental networks does not provide adequate solutions to these problems. If markets and experts are the driving forces, we need to judge them, as with the global political order, by their distributive effect among the different global stakeholders.[138] In her most recent work on a new world order, Slaughter acknowledges this deficiency in her original formulation and suggests a set of "informal global norms regulating government networks".[139] By emphasising the informal character of her proposed norms, Slaughter clearly distinguishes her approach from the constitutionalist concepts as developed *inter alia* by Ernst-Ulrich Petersmann.

Participation and representation, which form part of the most significant challenges to the idea of transgovernmental networks, are addressed by Slaughter with the principle of global deliberative equality, a concept developed by Michael Ignatieff.[140] While this principle states that all affected people should be represented when essential decisions about their lives are being taken,

134 Slaughter (1993) 205–39; Slaughter (1995) 504.
135 Alvarez (2001).
136 Koskenniemi (2002a) 491–92.
137 Kennedy (2000) 418.
138 *Ibid*, 419.
139 Slaughter (2004) 244–57.
140 Ignatieff (2001) 94–95.

due to the informality of Slaughter's concept, it does not solve the problem of accountability and distributive justice. According to Slaughter, the participants in networks develop and define the "norms" governing their relationship. Given that there is no central world government in the transgovernmental network concept, this seems logical. However, it does not solve the problem of who should decide which decisions are important, nor how the group of affected people should be defined. The principle can work in practice only if the different stakeholders are already represented in the networks, which is precisely what the principle requires. Therefore, additional elements such as a theory of distributive justice as developed by John Rawls,[141] need to be developed or integrated. Thus, even with the new global "norms" added to Salughter's model, the basic questions raised by Philip Alston in 1997 still go unanswered.

In summary, it seems that global informal norms are not sufficient to overcome the deficiencies of transgovernmental network theory and the governance without government model. Law is necessary because neither natural society nor the markets can resolve the conflicts described above.[142] Law creates an artificial order that requires compromises to accommodate different interests.[143]

4.3. SYNTHESIS: MULTILEVEL CONSISTENCY AS AN ALTERNATIVE APPROACH

The previous chapters have shown that globalisation and the fragmentation of international law lead to frictions and contradictions between the objectives of international economic organisations and the protection of core labour rights. These conflicts need to be resolved if international law is to provide a reliable and credible system of norms.[144] Moreover, globalisation has an impact on the role of the nation state,[145] and in responding to globalisation, the traditional nation state faces several challenges. First, in the international context, national (constitutional) law has partially lost its role as a steering tool. With increasing interdependence, international institutions and organisations and even markets compete in setting objectives for domestic policies. As a result, the traditional notion of national sovereignty as a formal legal concept needs to be reviewed. Might a concept of substantial sovereignty that is based on participation rather than formal independence be more appropriate?

Second, internationalisation of the law-making process is changing the constitutional distribution of power between parliaments on the one hand and

141 Rawls (1999).

142 With respect to markets, law is seen as a tool that provides the necessary infrastructure. See section 4.2.1.5. above.

143 "Everyone knows that politics are not 'really' about translating natural rights into positive law; that at issue are struggle and compromise, power and ideology, and not derivations from transparent and automatically knowable normative demands." Koskenniemi (1999) 115.

144 Similarly, see Hafner (2002) 331–33.

145 For a comprehensive overview, see Pernthaler (1998) 76–79.

executive and administrative branches on the other. Since a substantial part of legislation and harmonisation of regulations is being negotiated internationally, administrative and executive branches of government are becoming more important. This development together with the increasing use of the package deal approach limits the possibility of parliaments actively and creatively influencing the law-making process.

However, to some extent, globalisation has also widened the scope of national jurisdiction because territorial borders no longer define the limits of national sovereignty. An example is the protection of (fundamental) human rights.

This chapter will argue that the challenges raised by globalisation are not organisational but normative in nature. The key lies therefore in reconciling the different layers of legal obligations and at the same time finding mechanisms for legitimising expert advice and regulations, thereby transforming them into accountable legal standards.

In developing a concept of multilevel consistency, an analysis of how treaty interpretation can assist in resolving conflicts between different obligations of international law will first be considered. This will be followed by a look at the compatibility of international obligations with domestic law. Finally, an attempt will be made to bring the different requirements of consistency together in a comprehensive model, the suggested multilevel-consistency approach.

4.3.1. The Scope of Treaty Obligations

4.3.1.1. Treaty Interpretation

The general rule for the interpretation of treaty obligations is Article 31 of the Vienna Convention on the Law of Treaties (VCLT). Article 31 states:

1 A treaty shall be interpreted in good faith in accordance with the ordinary meaning to be given to the terms of the treaty in their context and in the light of its object and purpose.
2 The context for the purpose of the interpretation of a treaty shall comprise, in addition to the text, including its preamble and annexes: [. . .]
3 There shall be taken into account together with the context:

   a) any subsequent agreement between the parties regarding the interpretation of the treaty or the application of its provisions
   b) any subsequent practice in the application of the treaty which establishes the agreement of the parties regarding its interpretation;
   c) any relevant rules of international law applicable in the relations between the parties [. . .]

As we have seen, core labour rights are defined in treaties such as the fundamental ILO Conventions that derive from more general human rights instruments. Nevertheless, trade-related regimes[146] such as the WTO and GATT Agreement can also have a significant impact on the enforcement of core labour rights. With regard to the relationship between these two spheres, Article 31 allows for two conclusions. Article 31(2) requires us to consider the preamble when interpreting trade agreements such as the WTO and GATT. That Article 31 VCLT applies to WTO dispute settlement derives from Article 3(2) of the Rules on the Settlement of Disputes:

> The dispute settlement system of the WTO is a central element in providing security and predictability to the multilateral trading system. The Members recognize that it serves to preserve the rights and obligations of Members under the covered agreements, and to clarify the existing provisions of those agreements *in accordance with customary rules of interpretation of public international law*. Recommendations and rulings of the DSB cannot add to or diminish the rights and obligations provided in the covered agreements.[147]

By becoming a WTO member a country agrees to adhere to the WTO dispute settlement mechanism and, with the above-cited Article 3, accepts the customary rules of interpretation of public international law regardless of whether or not it has ratified the VCLT.[148] In other words, the WTO dispute settlement rules declare the provisions of the VCLT on interpretation applicable to all its members. In the context of the WTO, discussion of whether and which of the VCLT provisions on treaty interpretation form part of customary international law therefore becomes obsolete.[149]

Referring to this provision, the Appellate Body has confirmed on several occasions that Article 31 VCLT is of crucial importance in the WTO dispute settlement process.[150] The Marrakesh Agreement establishing the WTO is the umbrella agreement for the entire WTO system and thus has a special status. Its preamble is the most comprehensive statement of the objectives of the WTO system,[151] and the Appellate Body was therefore able to rely on it heavily in *US—Shrimp/Turtles* for the definition of the term "exhaustible resources".[152] However, the preamble does not mention human rights. Instead, both the

146 Finance-related instruments such as the IMF or World Bank statute are set aside for the moment because these instruments do not create direct legal obligations but serve as basis for "expert activities" that lead to concrete obligations for states.

147 Understanding on Rules and Procedures Governing the Settlement of Disputes, Annex 2 to the Marrakesh Agreement Establishing the World Trade Organization, SR 0.632.20 (emphasis added).

148 Eg France has not ratified the VCLT.

149 Sinclair (1984) 10–21.

150 *Japan—Taxes on Alcoholic Beverages*, Report of the Appellate Body, 4 October 1996, WT/DS8/AB/R, WT/DS10/AB/R, WT/DS11/AB/R [hereinafter *Japan—Alcoholic Beverages*], at 10–12; *United States—Standards for Reformulated and Conventional Gasoline*, Report of the Appellate Body, 29 April 1996 WT/DS2/AB/R, [hereinafter *US—Gasoline*], at 17; *Korea—Measures Affecting Imports of Fresh, Chilled and Frozen Beef*, Report of the Appellate Body, 11 December 2000, WT/DS161/AB/R, WT/DS169/AB/R [hereinafter *Korea—Beef*], at paras 96, 159.

151 Howse and Mutua (2000) 12–13.

152 *US—Shrimp/Turtles*, note 27 above, at paras 129–31.

GATT and the Marrakesh Agreement state raising standards of living and full employment as goals. Where core labour rights enhance development, they are therefore covered by the preamble. As we have seen in chapter 2,[153] sustainable development and human rights go hand in hand. However, concluding that the preamble of the Marrakesh Agreement therefore encompasses human rights, core labour rights in particular, seems to go a little too far.[154]

In light of this somewhat inconclusive result regarding the (lack of a) direct connection between core labour rights and sustainable development, let us move on to Article 31(3)c. This provision states that in interpreting a treaty provision, all other international legal obligations to which the parties have adhered must be considered. The issue here is consistency. Treaty provisions should not be interpreted in a way that is contradictory to other international legal obligations between the parties. Also, the International Court of Justice allows for treaty interpretation in the light of international law as it has evolved and developed since the treaty was concluded:

> An international instrument has to be interpreted and applied within the framework of the entire legal system prevailing at the time of the interpretation.[155]

In practice, many conflicts arise from different obligations in different legal instruments. In fact, Article 31(3)c is more than just a rule for co-ordination. It requires states to act in good faith and to comply with the obligations they have accepted. For example, Article 31(3)c instructs us to consider the Fundamental ILO Conventions when interpreting the meaning of public morals in Article XX GATT if the parties to the conflict are also ILO Member States. In so doing, Article 31(3)c prevents states from "cherry-picking", ie from choosing the treaty that best fits their needs in specific situations.[156] We currently encounter such problems in the context of the General Agreement on Trade in Services (GATS),

[153] Section 2.2.6. above.

[154] Howse and Mutua (2000) 13, quoting Amartya Sen but leaving open the question of whether the preamble should be interpreted as including human rights.

[155] "Legal Consequences for States of the Continued Presence of South Africa in Namibia (South West Africa) Notwithstanding Security Council Resolution 276 (1970)", ICJ Reports 1971, 31, para 53.

[156] Mauritius recently set an example for this problem in the WTO: Mauritius has invoked the right to food with reference to, *inter alia*, Article 11 of the ICESCR and Article 25 of the Universal Declaration of Human Rights in the context of the issues of food security and non-trade concerns for developing countries. Mauritius has argued that Article 20 and the Preamble of the Agreement on Agriculture require that non-trade concerns should be taken into account in the continuation of the reform process and that such non-trade concerns include the developing countries' right to food. In the view of Mauritius, the government has a clear legal obligation to promote the right to food; yet the international conventions leave the choice of an appropriate policy instruments to the state. Therefore, the instruments provided by WTO law should be used to achieve this goal. G/AG/NG/W/36/Rev.1. In its reasoning, Mauritius applied an approach that has been suggested by the High Commissioner of Human Rights in her report "Globalization and its Impact on the Full Enjoyment of Human Rights", 15 January 2002, E/CN.4/2002/54, para 44, which addresses the WTO Agreement on Agriculture and the Report on the liberalization of trade in services and human rights of 25 June 2002, E/CN.4/Sub.2/2002/9, para 11.

with some developing countries declining to offer preferences, stating that such concessions would conflict with the conditions imposed on them by IMF structural adjustment programmes.[157]

Similar problems arise in the context of bilateral investment agreements. Such agreements include provisions for investor–state dispute settlement as mixed arbitration. Under these agreements, foreign investors can challenge human rights-inspired measures imposed on them by host states. Several cases concerning environmental provisions arose under NAFTA,[158] raising considerable concern that domestic regulations related to human health, environmental protection or public safety may be successfully challenged in this way. While no case concerning human rights has yet been brought before an arbitration panel, the South African government has been threatened with challenges to its racial empowerment legislation under bilateral investment agreements.[159]

With regard to the WTO, it is important to note that interpreting its provisions in their contemporary context, ie in an evolutionary manner, does not imply that these rules are of a constitutional nature. The WTO today is only "constitutional" in the sense that it has developed into an international organisation that is working on an international legal order for international trade and that needs increasing legitimacy and transparency. It is not constitutional in the sense exported from national law, ie as an organisation that pursues objectives that go beyond the interests of the Member States or that creates legal norms that are not amendable by the states.[160]

Since the relationship between labour rights conventions and trade agreements cannot be clarified sufficiently by treaty interpretation according to Article 31(3)c VCLT, we will now look at Article 30 VCLT and Article 103 of the UN Charter.

4.3.1.2. Conflicting Treaty Obligations: The Question of Coherence

Article 30 VCLT deals with successive treaties relating to the same subject matter:

[157] An argument similar to Mauritius's claim was put forward by Argentina. It stated that the provisions of the Memorandum of Understanding with the IMF and the provisions of Article VIII GATT were irreconcilable. However, the Appellate Body held that since the GATT does not contain any IMF-related exceptions under Article VIII GATT, independent IMF rules such as the Memorandum cannot justify Argentina's violation of Article VIII GATT. *Argentina—Measures Affecting Imports of Footwear, Textiles, Apparel and Other Items, Report of the Appellate Body, 27 March 1998*, WT/DS56/AB/R, [hereinafter *Argentina—Footwear*], at para 69. See Ahn (2000) 8–11 and 23–29; Siegel (2002) 561–99.

[158] *Metalclad Corporation v United Mexican States*, Final Award, 30 August 2000, ICSID Case No ARB (AF)/97/1, published in: (2001) 40 ILM 36; *SD Myers Inc v Government of Canada*, NAFTA Arbitration under the UNCITRAL Arbitration Rules, Partial Award, 13 November 2000.

[159] Peterson (2003) 25.

[160] Pauwelyn (2003a) 264–67.

1 Subject to Article 103 of the Charter of the United Nations, the rights and obligations of States parties to successive treaties relating to the same subject-matter shall be determined in accordance with the following paragraphs.
2 When a treaty specifies that it is subject to, or that it is not to be considered as incompatible with, an earlier or later treaty, the provisions of that other treaty prevail.
3 When all the parties to the earlier treaty are parties also to the later treaty but the earlier treaty is not terminated or suspended in operation under article 59, the earlier treaty applies only to the extent that its provisions are compatible with those of the latter treaty.
4 When the parties to the later treaty do not include all the parties to the earlier one:

a) as between States parties to both treaties the same rule applies as in paragraph 3;
b) as between a State party to both treaties and a State party to only one of the treaties, the treaty to which both States are parties governs their mutual rights and obligations.

5 Paragraph 4 is without prejudice to article 41, or to any question of the termination or suspension of the operation of a treaty under article 60 or to any question of responsibility which may arise for a State from the conclusions or application of a treaty the provisions of which are incompatible with its obligations towards another State under another treaty.

Article 30 is largely a reflection of existing rules of customary international law.[161] However, by reference to Article 103 UN Charter,[162] these principles are inapplicable in the case of conflicts between the UN Charter and other agreements concluded by Member States.[163]

The Charter contains an obligation to ensure human rights in Articles 1(3) and 55(c). These obligations prevail over any contradictory treaty provision between Member States. However, Article 103 does not tell us what the legal consequences for conflicting provisions are. Are they suspended or void? As a consequence of the constitutional character of Article 103,[164] conflicting treaty

[161] Bernhardt in Simma (2002) note 3 on Article 103.

[162] Article 103 UN Charter states:

> In the event of a conflict between the obligations of the Members of the United Nations under the present Charter and their obligations under any other international agreement, their obligations under the present Charter shall prevail.

[163] Article 30(1) VCLT. The 1986 Vienna Convention on the Law of Treaties with and between International Organisations contains a similar provision in Article 30(6): "The preceding paragraphs are without prejudice to the fact that, in the event of a conflict between obligations under the Charter of the United Nations and obligations under a treaty, the obligations under the Charter shall prevail". This provision takes into account that international organisations cannot be parties to the UN Charter. Bernhardt in Simma (2002) note 5 on Article 103.

[164] Whether the UN Charter as a whole can serve as a constitutional framework for the international community is controversial. Yet most authors agree that it contains at least some provisions with constitutional character, allowing the Charter to be considered as a starting point for the development of a constitution for the international community. For a detailed discussion, see Fassbender (1998) 568–85; Macdonald (1999) 213 argues that Article 103—among other provisions in the Charter—assigns to the Charter a quasi-constitutional relevance. See also Simma and Paulus (1998) 274; Petersmann (1999) 765–70. For critical views, see Arangio-Ruiz (1997) 1–28; Crawford (1997) 12.

provisions between Member States become inapplicable. This reflects the practice of most federal states when dealing with conflicting laws at state level.[165]

In practice, cases of prima facie conflicting provisions in treaties between UN Member States are rare.[166] As discussed above, friction between core labour rights on the one hand and trade and finance regulation on the other, arises with respect to their application. Here, Article 103 asks for an interpretation in accordance with the obligations of the Charter. Again, constitutional elements in the UN Charter determine the criteria for treaty interpretation. As mentioned earlier, a dynamic, evolutionary interpretive approach is required to take into account the dynamic character and inherent incompleteness of any Constitution.[167] As a result, we find a hierarchy of norms at the international level, with the provisions of the UN Charter serving as guiding principles. The precedence of the Charter has been confirmed by the ICJ.[168]

> World peace itself may depend on respect for the higher rank and binding force of the Charter as emphasized by Article 103. Developments in the world since 1988 can be considered to have strengthened the role of the UN and its Charter, which may become a real and effective constitution for the international community.[169]

As discussed in detail in chapter 1 above, core labour rights can be traced back to the UN Charter. They are the basic human rights for the labour market and thus must be considered obligations under the UN Charter.

4.3.2. Consistency with Domestic Law

Another source of conflict is domestic social policies that are difficult to reconcile with international trade regimes. As discussed earlier, many states have provisions in their constitutions or domestic laws that require certain minimum standards with regard to core labour rights. Such situations are addressed by Article 46 VCLT, which aims at resolving conflicts with international law:

> 1 A State may not invoke the fact that its consent to be bound by a treaty has been expressed in violation of a provision of its internal law regarding competence to conclude treaties as invalidating its consent unless that violation was manifest and concerned a rule of its internal law of fundamental importance.
>
> 2 A violation is manifest if it would be objectively evident to any State conducting itself in the matter in accordance with normal practice and in good faith.

165 For an excellent comparative analysis, see Halberstam (2001a).

166 The differentiation between member and non-member states became obsolete after the Swiss vote on membership of the UN on 3 March 2002; only the Vatican now remains outside the UN.

167 "Legal Consequences for States of the Continued Presence of South Africa in Namibia (South West Africa) Notwithstanding Security Council Resolution 276 (1970)", ICJ Reports 1971, 16, 31, para 53.

168 ICJ, Case concerning questions of interpretation and application of the 1971 Montreal Conventions arising from the aerial incident at Lockerbie (*Libyan Arab Jamahiriya v United Kingdom*) ICJ Reports 1992, 3 [hereinafter *ICJ, Lockerbie*], at 15, para 39.

169 Bernhardt in Simma (2002) note 25 on Article 103.

Article 46 states an exception to the general rule in Article 27, which prohibits states from invoking provisions of internal law as justification for the failure to comply with a treaty. Based on the principle of good faith, a treaty is valid unless the violation of internal law is manifest, ie obvious to the other states, *and* the internal provisions are of fundamental importance. Yet Article 46 refers only to internal provisions that concern the conclusions of treaties. Such norms are of two types: rules of a *procedural* nature that concern the internal decision-making process and the way in which decisions are represented to other countries; and *substantial* norms limiting the treaty-making power. While the coverage of the first category by Article 46 is not disputed, the second is controversial.

With regard to procedural provisions, Article 46 thus significantly limits the presumption contained in Article 7 that heads of state, heads of governments and foreign ministers are competent to conclude treaties.[170] It applies when, for example, a head of state adheres to a treaty even though the Constitution requires the agreement of Parliament and this requirement is well known to the other party of the contract.

Many states have rules that exclude certain fundamental issues such as human rights or the rule of law completely from the treaty-making power of the state in an attempt to protect these basic values against abuses. The idea derives from the rationale of Ulysses who, when approaching the island of the Sirens and knowing of their dangerousness, ordered his companions to bind him to the mast and not release him under any circumstance.[171] As Petersmann has pointed out, the underlying "pre-commitments" are based on the experience that human rationality is imperfect and exposed to short-term temptations (such as temporary trade benefits or competitive advantages) that might be inconsistent with long-term interests (such as the protection of core labour rights).[172] The state thus binds itself in order to prevent abuse of freedom.

Several constitutions, namely those of European states, declare some of their provisions to be unamendable.[173] One of the most prominent examples is Article 79(3) of the German Basic Law of 1949, which was a result of the experiences in the Weimar Republic. Switzerland abides by the concept of so-called substantial limitations to constitutional amendments *(materielle Schranken der Verfassungsrevision)*.[174] Over time, the scope of such provisions has gradually

170 Müller, JP (1971) 196–97.

171 Elster (2000) 94–96.

172 Petersmann (1998) 1.

173 For an overview, see Häberle (1992) 597; Fassbender (1998) 602.

174 VEB 29, 1959–60, Nr. 3, 22: "Sicher können auf dem Wege des Staatsvertrages nicht fundamentale Normen der Bundesverfassung abgeändert oder aufgehoben werden. Es ist nicht angängig, auf diese Weise die grundlegende Struktur des schweizerischen Staatsrechts umzustürzen." Articles 139(3) and 193(4) of the Constitution state international *ius cogens* as limitation to constitutional amendments. The provision has been interpreted as possibly also including obligations *erga omnes* or international crimes, although they do not form part of international *ius cogens*: Thürer (2001b) §11 Rz 14–15; Cottier and Hertig (2000) 18–22.

expanded. Following a study undertaken by Peter Häberle, democracy, human dignity and human rights are today considered the foundation of constitutionalism and may not be altered or interfered with.[175]

A state that is bound in this way therefore cannot adhere to international treaties that violate fundamental constitutional provisions. Article 46 addresses the cases in which states nevertheless enter into such international obligations. In its commentary on the draft provision that later became Article 46, the International Law Commission explicitly stated that *any* constitutional limitations of treaty-making power fall within the scope of Article 46: its applicability is thus not limited to procedural provisions.[176] There are no indications that the Vienna Conference followed a different approach. Many national constitutional courts have confirmed this principle.[177]

Another argument in favour of the view that Article 46 applies to constitutional provisions regardless of their procedural or material nature relates to the ratification of the VCLT itself. A state that limits the exercise of treaty-making power in its domestic law cannot ratify an international convention that nullifies precisely this limitation. In doing so the state would be exercising the power the constitution explicitly takes away from its authority and would thereby be overturning the constitutional order.[178]

It is this line of argument that the ECJ pursued in its opinions on the compatibility of the Treaty on the European Economic Area with the EC Treaty.[179] Moreover, in its landmark decision *Matthews v United Kingdom*,[180] the European Court of Human Rights held that members of the European Convention on Human Rights (ECHR) are bound by the Convention when transferring powers to an international organisation. In the view of the court, Member States remain responsible under the Convention even after the transfer of power to a supranational institution.[181] In the above-mentioned case, the UK had excluded the population living in Gibraltar, one of its dependent territories, from having the right to elect members to the European Parliament. This exclusion of Gibraltar was in essence based on a decision by the European Council[182]

175 Häberle (1992) 600–9.

176 ILC Yearbook 1966 II, 240, para 1 on Article 43 of the draft.

177 For Germany see the decision on the compatibility of the Maastricht Treaty with the German Grundgesetz: BVerfGE 89, 155; for the European Union see the *Bananas* decision, [1994] ECR I-4973; for Switzerland see Achermann (2001) 43–74; for the US see *Reid v Covert* 354 USR 1 (1957).

178 See VEB 29, 1959–60, Nr. 3, 22, quoted in note 174 above.

179 Case 1/91, Opinion Delivered Pursuant to the Second Subparagraph of Article 228(1) of the EEC Treaty [1991] ECR I-6079; Case 1/92, Opinion Delivered Pursuant to the Second Subparagraph of Article 228(1) of the EEC Treaty [1992] ECR I-282. The court stated that Article 238 of EC Treaty does not authorise the amendment of fundamental institutions of Community law. See also the comments by Breining-Kaufmann (1992) 639–41.

180 *Matthews v United Kingdom* (Application No 24833/94), European Court of Human Rights, 18 February 1999, 28 ECtHR 361 (1999).

181 *Ibid*, para 32.

182 Council Decision 76/787/ECSC, EEC, Euratom, OJ L 278/1, 8 October 1976.

and the related specific provisions.[183] The court did not accept as valid the UK's reasoning that the restriction of the right to vote was based on European law rather than domestic law. Instead, it held that the UK entered the respective treaty commitments under Community law after its ratification of the ECHR and therefore could not argue that it had no control over the state of affairs.[184]

In summary, if a treaty violates fundamental provisions of domestic law that limit treaty-making power, and the violation is obvious to the other contracting parties (*violation manifeste*),[185] a state can invoke the treaty's invalidity.[186] What does invalid mean in such cases? Article 69 VCLT generally states that an invalid treaty is void *ab initio*, thus has no legal force for the party concerned. However, if the parties have already acted in good faith in reliance on such a treaty, the acts will not be invalid. It is difficult to imagine such acts given that Article 46 already requires that the violation of fundamental domestic law be manifest, thus obvious to the other parties. In other words, Article 46 itself is based on the principle of good faith, which is reiterated in Article 69. Similarly, this concept is of crucial importance—both, legally and economically—in the context of GATT. Article XXIII:1(b) GATT protects legitimate expectations even if the GATT itself is not violated.[187]

For treaties between states and international organisations, the Vienna Convention on the Law of Treaties between States and International Organizations or between International Organizations (1986) is applicable. Its Article 46(1) is identical to Article 46(1) VCLT. Because of the strict requirements, cases in which Article 46 is applicable are rare. However, Article 46 comes into play if, for example, a loan agreement between a state and the IMF were to require the state seriously to restrict the right to collective bargaining in order to liberalise labour markets. If core labour rights, including the right to bargain collectively, were constitutionally non-amendable, and the IMF were aware of the legal situation in the country, the agreement would be void.

4.3.3. Multilevel Consistency

The solutions suggested by Article 46 VCLT and Article 103 UN Charter follow the traditional conflict of laws resolution model: the collision rule is used to decide which of the conflicting norms prevails. However, from the perspective of the state, in many cases such a result is not satisfying. Instead, an *integrative*

[183] Act Concerning the Election of Representatives of the European Parliament by Direct Universal Suffrage of 20 September 1976, Annex II. The Act is attached to Council Decision 76/787, *ibid.*

[184] *Matthews v United Kingdom*, note 180 above, para 34. Bröhmer (1999) 201.

[185] Müller, JP (1971) 201.

[186] Verdross and Simma (1984) § 691 with further references.

[187] *Japan—Measures Affecting Consumer Photographic Film and Paper*, Report of the Panel, 31 March 1998, WT/DS44/R [hereinafter *Japan—Film*], para 10.218. In the first case in which the Appellate Body had the occasion to interpret Article XXIII:1(b), it did not examine the concept of legitimate expectations: *EC—Asbestos*, note 22 above, at para 190.

approach would allow for the inclusion and reconciliation of the different legitimate interests involved. How could such an approach work? The pluralistic solution suggested here involves two key features: interpretation in accordance with international law, human rights law specifically, and the consideration of consistency as an additional criterion for treaty interpretation.[188]

4.3.3.1. Human Rights-compatible Interpretation ("menschenrechtskonforme Auslegung")

As discussed earlier, Article 31 VCLT requires treaty provisions to be read in their context and in light of existing international law. In practice, this principle has been confirmed for international environmental law by the Appellate Body.[189] With regard to the significance of textual interpretation and the question of whether the historical or the contemporary context at the time the dispute settlement takes place should be considered, the Appellate Body opted for an evolutionary dynamic approach of interpretation. In *US—Shrimp/Turtles* it held that the term "exhaustible resources" must be read "in the light of contemporary concerns of the community of nations about the protection and conservation of the environment."[190]

The Appellate Body cited the ICJ's statement in the *Namibia Advisory Opinion* that some terms are not static but rather "by definition evolutionary".[191] It then moved on to include the relevant provisions in the United Nations Convention on the Law of the Sea (UNCLOS), which were considered as reflecting customary international law by the United States even though the US had not ratified this convention. Similar to the WTO agreements, which are considered the international legal order for international trade, UNCLOS is often referred to as a constitutional framework for the law of the seas.

Following the Namibia case, the ICJ further developed its concept of evolutionary interpretation. In *Oil Platforms*, the court had to interpret the scope of the notion of measures "necessary" to protect a party's essential security interests in the Treaty of Amity between the US and the Islamic Republic of Iran.[192] It confirmed that according to Article 31(3) VCLT an interpretation of the respective provision in the Treaty of Amity had to take into account any relevant rules of international law applicable in the relations between the parties. It then referred to the UN Charter and customary international law to determine whether the disputed measures could be justified as self-defence or whether they

[188] For a pluralistic approach in the European context, see Scharpf (2001) 1–5.

[189] *US—Shrimp/Turtles*, note 27 above, at paras 129–31.

[190] *Ibid*, at para 129 (emphasis added); White (1999) 324–25.

[191] "Legal Consequences for States of the Continued Presence of South Africa in Namibia (South West Africa) Notwithstanding Security Council Resolution 276 (1970)", ICJ Reports 1971, 31, para 53. See also note 155 above and accompanying text.

[192] *Case Concerning Oil Platforms, Islamic Republic of Iran v United States of America*, ICJ 2003, 6 November 2003, General List No 90, reprinted in (2003) 42 ILM 1334 [hereinafter *Oil Platforms*].

resulted in an unlawful use of force.[193] As a consequence, despite the broad notion of security interests, the parties could not agree on measures that would go beyond what is allowed under the UN Charter as self-defence. The reasoning of the IJC becomes even clearer in Judge Simma's separate opinion:

> To interpret [the respective provision of the Treaty of Amity] more liberally would be both absurd and destructive: absurd, because our provision could then be read to mean that parties to treaties of, among other things "amity" could be allowed to contract one of the most fundamental of all obligations under present international law, namely the prohibition on the threat or use of force—an obligation which States owe any other State even if they cannot muster any degree of "amity" for each other. Furthermore, such a reading [of the respective provision of the Treaty of Amity] would be destructive because it would allow a mutual "emancipation" from some of the most cogent of all rules of international law.[94]

So far, there have been no decisions by the Appellate Body relating to human rights. In light of the Appellate Body's jurisprudence, the general rule of Article 31 is applicable as well. Yet in situations where core labour rights might be an issue,[195] Member States have argued that their consideration by WTO dispute settlement organs would be contrary to the Singapore Declaration and its recent restatement at the Doha Conference.[196]

This argument is flawed in several respects: the Singapore Declaration was a reply to requests by some members, in particular the EU and the US, to include a social clause in the WTO agreements. It therefore addresses the *institutional* question of whether labour rights should be included into the WTO law. In other words, the declaration is about the *substance* of WTO law, not about its application. By considering core labour rights when applying WTO law, the WTO dispute settlement organs would neither create new obligations for nor expand the existing WTO obligations of the Member States, since ILO Member States are already bound by the core labour rights.[197] Instead, the Appellate Body would comply with what Article 3(2) DSU requires, namely "to clarify the existing provisions of those agreements". Such an approach would be in line with the ICJ decision in *Oil Platforms*.

Admittedly, further detailed studies are necessary to clarify the concrete content of core labour rights in the trade context.[198] Currently only the general

[193] *Ibid*, paras 40–41.

[194] *Ibid*, separate opinion of Judge Simma, para 10.

[195] The most recent example is the discussion of the Belgian labelling program in the TBT Committee: Committee on Technical Barriers to Trade, Minutes of the discussions in G/TBT/?M/?23, 8 May 2001 and G/TBT/M/24, 14 August 2001; see also chapter 3 above, note 391 and accompanying text.

[196] WTO, Singapore Ministerial Declaration, adopted on 13 December 1996, WT/MIN (96)/DEC, and WTO, Doha Ministerial Declaration, adopted on 14 November 2001, WT/MIN(01)/DEC/W/1.

[197] The argument that the decision in *Oil Platforms* (note 192 above) could expand WTO obligations was made by Joost Pauwelyn in his presentation at the ASIL annual meeting 2004. Pauwelyn (2004) 137.

[198] Alston (2004) 483–90.

principles are available. Here again, the Singapore Declaration steps in: the ILO as the leading institution for labour issues will have to develop benchmarks for determining when core labour rights are being violated in order to provide the dispute settlement organs with reliable indicators. Allocating the power for authoritative interpretation of the content of core labour rights to the ILO considerably reduces the danger of economising them, which we identified earlier in the context of mainstreaming programmes.[199] Substantial work has already been done in this field by the United Nations Development Program (UNDP) and the World Bank.[200] In fact, although the challenge being faced by the WTO dispute settlement organs may seem new to international trade lawyers, it is already familiar to constitutional courts and the human rights community. The UN Committee on Economic, Social and Cultural Rights[201] has been working on establishing a set of benchmarks for quite some time.[202] In the fight against poverty, the OECD, the World Bank and the UN have joined forces to agree on indicators for monitoring progress towards the targets.[203] At the national level, constitutional courts in both developing[204] and developed[205] countries have established benchmarks to determine the extent of violations of social and economic rights.

In summary, provisions in international economic law must be interpreted in light of the existing human rights obligations of the parties involved, thus providing for coherence between two different set of rules at the international level.[206] The Singapore Declaration does not prevent the WTO dispute settlement organs from doing this. Where clarifications on the content of core labour rights are necessary, the ILO is the competent authority to fill in such gaps.

4.3.3.2. Consistency as an Evolving Principle of International Law

A) From Co-existence to Co-operation to Integration Globalisation and sovereignty are often seen as contrasting and even conflicting concepts. Developments in international law from laws of co-existence to laws of co-operation after 1945 and the current shift in international relations towards integration have changed the nature of sovereignty. For those who complain about the end of the nation

199 McCrudden (2005) 9–28.

200 Of particular importance is the Human Development Index, developed by the UNDP and published in its annual Human Development Report.

201 Committee on Economic Social and Cultural Rights, General Comment No 1 (1989), UN Doc HRI/GEN/1/Rev.3 (1997), p 56, para 3 names the "establishment of priorities which reflect the provisions of the Covenant" as one of the functions of reporting procedures.

202 Alston (1999a) at 15–18.

203 UNDP (1998) at 15.

204 *Government of the Republic of South Africa v Grootboom* (2000) 11 BCLR 1169 (CC); (2001) 1 SA 46 (CC), 4 October 2000.

205 BGE 105 V 63; Müller, JP (1999) 173–78.

206 This notion of coherence differs from that used by Franck (1995) 38–40, who uses the example of GSP, which in his view is inconsistent with MFN but in keeping with the underlying purpose of GATT.

state, the new world order should contain a universally accepted set of rules, a "world constitution". This concept is very different from the traditional liberal version of the rule of law: because an abstract, verifiable definition of "the good" proved to be impossible, liberals relied on process as the basis for legality. To some extent, shifting the focus from substance to process and institutions has also become a way of avoiding discussions on different values. The Singapore Declaration must be seen in this context. By dividing competences between the WTO and the ILO, none of the organisations have really had to take a stand on the delicate question of the link between trade and labour rights.[207]

Current international law is inadequate for addressing the new developments in international relations. The classic principles of international law that are universally accepted, including sovereignty, self-determination, territorial integrity, non-intervention and consent, are still state-based concepts.[208] They all reaffirm statehood as the law's creative centre.[209] A core function of the Westphalian state is the translation of domestic conflicts into reasoned compromise by its legal order. The problem is that conflicts often result in the delicate task of restricting one sovereign state's freedom in favour of that of another. Here, the concept of statehood does not provide a solution. Globalisation has amplified this challenge by adding new actors such as multinational corporations, markets and international networks, who previously did not figure in the traditional notion of the nation-state. As a result, the policy *capacity* of national governments has been reduced as well as the policy *legitimacy*. Under the Westphalian system, an act of sovereignty by a recognised government would never have prompted any "second-guessing" with regard to legitimacy.[210]

B) Sovereignty as Participation? Today, equality of sovereign states is just one of the key principles of international law. As we have seen, globalisation has altered the meaning of sovereignty by changing the state's sphere of influence and also by re-interpreting the notion of legitimacy. Sovereignty is limited by the prohibition of the use of force and by international human rights. The *Pinochet* case[211] and the trial against former Serbian president Milosevic are examples.[212]

Like the developments regarding the use of force and the interpretation of Article 2.4 of the UN Charter,[213] international economic integration has also limited national sovereignty to the extent that it has shifted legal issues, particularly

[207] Koskenniemi (1991) 403 gives the example of the UN Convention on the Law of the Sea, which defers decisions on the permissible uses of the oceans to established mechanisms.

[208] Under the Westphalian System, a body of treaty law emerged that reaffirmed the primacy of sovereignty, because no sovereign country could be forced to accept what it had not consented to. Valaskakis (2001) 51.

[209] Koskenniemi (1991) 406.

[210] The term "second-guessing" is from Valaskakis (2001) 57.

[211] Decision by the House of Lords, 24 March 1999, *Regina v Bow Street Stipendiary Magistrate, ex parte Pinochet Ugarte (No 3)* [1999] 2 WLR 827.

[212] Müller, JP (2002) 143–45.

[213] For a detailed discussion in the context of the Kosovo intervention Koskenniemi (2002b) 160.

in international trade law, from the national to the international level. Growing economic interdependence limits a state's options for autonomous legislation and policy decisions—key elements of the traditional notion of sovereignty. In addition, internationalisation induces restrictions on democratic participation of the people. This latter issue needs to be explored further.

The lack of democratic legitimacy in traditional international law was inherent to its concept as a legal order of co-existence between sovereign states. As such it related to the executive, which was perceived as representative of the state.[214] With democratisation and after the French Revolution, treaty-making power moved from sovereign princes to parliaments.[215] Because of the increasing legal harmonisation brought about by international treaties, in Switzerland the right to referendum had to be expanded in 1977 to include not only treaties that were concluded for a duration of more than 15 years, but also treaties that aimed at the country's participation in international organisations.[216] In other words, the criterion shifted from the duration of the treaty to a qualitative notion of integration. While the former reflects the concept of international law as a law of co-existence based on territorial nation states, the latter must be seen in the context of the move from international co-operation to international integration.

Since we do not have a constitutional structure at the international level, democratic legitimacy needs to be enhanced *within* states. What makes this problematic is that instruments of direct democracy can seriously hamper international regulation and thereby further weaken the position of the state in international negotiations. Switzerland is a "good" example in the sense that it shows how institutions of direct democracy can prevent a country's integration in the international community. In other words, the expansion of direct democratic participation in international law-making was affordable only because of the country's relative international isolation.[217]

Where do these developments leave us with regard to the sovereignty of the nation state? Obviously, sovereignty is no longer absolute in terms of Jean Bodin's concept of an indivisible authority.[218] Because of the complexity of current problems—for example, the need to protect the environment and to combat international terrorism—the power of the national state to determine independently its own course of action must be replaced by an obligation to co-operate at the international level.[219] Put differently, such a new notion of sovereignty would emphasise participation rather than the negative concept of preserving territorial authority.

[214] Thürer (2001b) Rz 44.
[215] Schindler (1998b) 615–16.
[216] Thürer (2001) Rz 45–46. For a detailed analysis including the several attempts to reform the referendum, see Zellweger (2001) 281–93.
[217] Schindler (1996) 286–87.
[218] Bodin (1977) vol I, chapitre VIII de la souveraineté. See also Beaulac (2003) 237–42.
[219] For a similar idea, see Saladin (1995) 121–24.

C) Consistency as an Element of Democratic Governance Are we on the way to a "new world order" as described by Anne-Marie Slaughter? Undoubtedly, the responses of the Westphalian System and the concept of *Rechtsstaat* to the economic disparities that result from increasing globalisation are now inadequate. As discussed earlier, such conflicts cannot be solved by simply letting one side win over the other. If we consider the international labour rights and trade regulation systems as being "multileveled", we need a multileveled approach that reconciles the different layers of international obligations instead of unilaterally determining which one should prevail. The reason is legitimacy: state actions are considered legitimate not only because they are taken in compliance with procedural rules but because they actually contribute to solving pressing problems.[220] Thus democratic governance does not stop at providing access to justice but requires a procedure for creating authenticity and identity. This is where legitimacy comes in. Understood as a tool to facilitate the implementation and efficiency of the legal order, legitimacy forces states to address their citizens' needs. Because it is very difficult to define a universal set of values, most scholars now focus on process when discussing legitimacy.

As a result, the function of the state is no longer limited to translating conflicts into civilised procedures but includes bridging the gap between its citizens on the one hand and actors at the transnational level on the other hand. In other words, the state is the institutional means by which citizens can participate in globalisation. This is a fundamental principle that flows directly from the concept of democratic governance.

With regard to core labour rights and competing legal regimes such as trade and finance, the acknowledgment of the right to democratic governance requires an inclusive interpretation of these regimes. Multilevel consistency therefore involves all actors: in the relationship between state and citizens, the state is bound by core labour rights whether acting at the national or international level. Acting in a different forum such as the IMF or in an informal context does not suspend these obligations. Depending on the point of view, the principle of consistency both limits and protects sovereignty. If we look at the example of import restrictions for products produced by child labour, consistency requires the WTO to respect—under certain conditions as described earlier—this state policy, thus protecting state sovereignty. However, if a state bans *all* products from a country where child labour occurs, consistency requires the WTO to intervene because such a general regime would be over-inclusive and thus in violation of the GATT.

In fact, the obligations for international organisations and dispute settlement organs are similar to those for the state. Although they are not formally bound by core labour rights, they must respect them as universally accepted standards and because of the principle of a consistent legal order. This principle can therefore be said to have an "external effect" in imposing certain obligations on

[220] For international monetary affairs, see Simmons (200b) 591–601.

international bodies. These obligations as we have seen consist of an interpretation of conflicting international obligations compatible with the protection of human rights.

Finally, from a citizen's perspective, the state is the connecting link between the national legal order and developments at the international level, whether they take place in a formal setting such as the WTO or in informal networks. Trade regulation and core labour rights will only be legitimate from the citizen's point of view if a holistic approach can be pursued in implementing them. What is needed is not a reinterpretation of Rousseau's theory of the general will but a model of governance that ensures the participation of all concerned in the globalisation process.[221] Such a model could work as a new system of checks and balances in the transgovernmental process.

Before this model is described in detail, a look at the legal nature of the principle of multilevel consistency is necessary.

D) Legal Qualification of the Principle of Multilevel Consistency So far, we have referred to multilevel consistency as an "evolving principle" but have not yet clarified its possible status among the sources of international law. Is it a general principle of international law according to Article 38.1(c) of the ICJ statute? Article 38.1(c) includes several categories of general principles. There are principles that stem from domestic law[222] and are transferable to international relations such as the principle of acquiescence[223] and estoppel. In addition, Article 38.1(c) refers to principles that have been developed by the international community. Examples include Resolutions adopted by the General Assembly of the UN that together with the *opinio iuris* of the Member States can become binding principles of international law. Finally, there are principles that find their origin in the structure and logic of international law. Such principles are the equality of the states, the concept of equity[224] and *pacta sunt servanda*. The rules on treaty interpretation could also be included in this category if they are considered tools or "logical devices" to be weighed against each other rather than absolute legal rules.[225]

Seen as a tool for treaty interpretation, the principle of consistency would fit into the latter category of general principles of international law. Such a qualification is based on the assumption that although international law is not a complete system it is nevertheless required to provide a framework for reconciling

221 As Slaughter (2001a) convincingly points out, no philosophical theory—however compelling—will change the views of those who perceive themselves as disenfranchised through globalisation.

222 For an analysis of the joint-and-several liability doctrine see the separate opinion of Judge Simma in *Oil Platforms*, note 192 above, paras 66–74.

223 *Case concerning the Temple of Préah Vihear (Cambodia v Thailand)*, ICJ Reports 1962, 6, at pp 32–33.

224 *Case concerning the Continental Shelf (Tunisia v Libyan Arab Jamahiriya)*, ICJ Reports 1982, 18 at p 60, para 71.

225 Pauwelyn (2003a) 126 with further references.

different sub-regimes in order to maintain its credibility. This is true regardless of the underlying concept of international law and thus regardless of whether one sees international law as a set of substantial rules or merely as providing a decision-process that allows controlled treatment of a situation.[226]

E) A Model for a Principle of Multilevel Consistency The principle of multilevel consistency applies with regard to the state as well as to international organisations. Figure 4.1. illustrates the different mechanisms.

The process begins with citizens, who in a democratic process decide on basic values, usually by formulating constitutional principles. These principles are then binding on the state in all its actions.

International co-operation can take place in formal ways, ie by means of membership in international organisations or by adherence to treaties. When engaging in such international obligations, the state is bound by the constitutional principles established by its citizens and by its international commitments. Depending on national legislation, parliament must give consent before new obligations are taken on. Thus, as a member of international organisations, a state is bound by its domestic constitutional provisions as well as by its obligations as, for example, a member of the WTO or ILO.

Where obligations are sufficiently well-defined, specific compliance mechanisms are established. Such mechanisms can be either of a formal nature, for example, a binding dispute settlement procedure as found in the WTO, or may consist of more informal reporting mechanisms such as those used in the ILO. According to the suggested principle of multilevel consistency, in both cases, dispute settlement organs or compliance bodies would interpret the obligations in "their" agreements in the context of other existing obligations of international law. For trade rules, this implies an interpretation that is compatible with the existing core labour rights obligations of the parties involved.

As we have seen, in some cases, treaties and organisational statutes do not go beyond basic substantial legal principles, focusing on technical requirements such as the compliance with economic standards. This is the case not only for the IMF and the World Bank, but also for informal networks such as the Basel Committee. From a democratic perspective, this is a more delicate constellation. The formulation of technical standards is usually left to expert groups with specific knowledge in the relevant area. These specialists are neither elected nor otherwise held accountable to Member States. Their advice can lead to national legislation or to the implementation of special policies, for example in the context of structural adjustments. Since in such cases rule-making is *de facto* taken out of parliament's realm, special accountability mechanisms are necessary to ensure the democratic legitimacy of the rules adopted or the measures taken.

The principle of multilevel consistency requires that parliament is involved in all legislation according to national provisions in order to ensure democratic

[226] For an overview on the different concepts of international law, see Koskenniemi (2002b) 163–71.

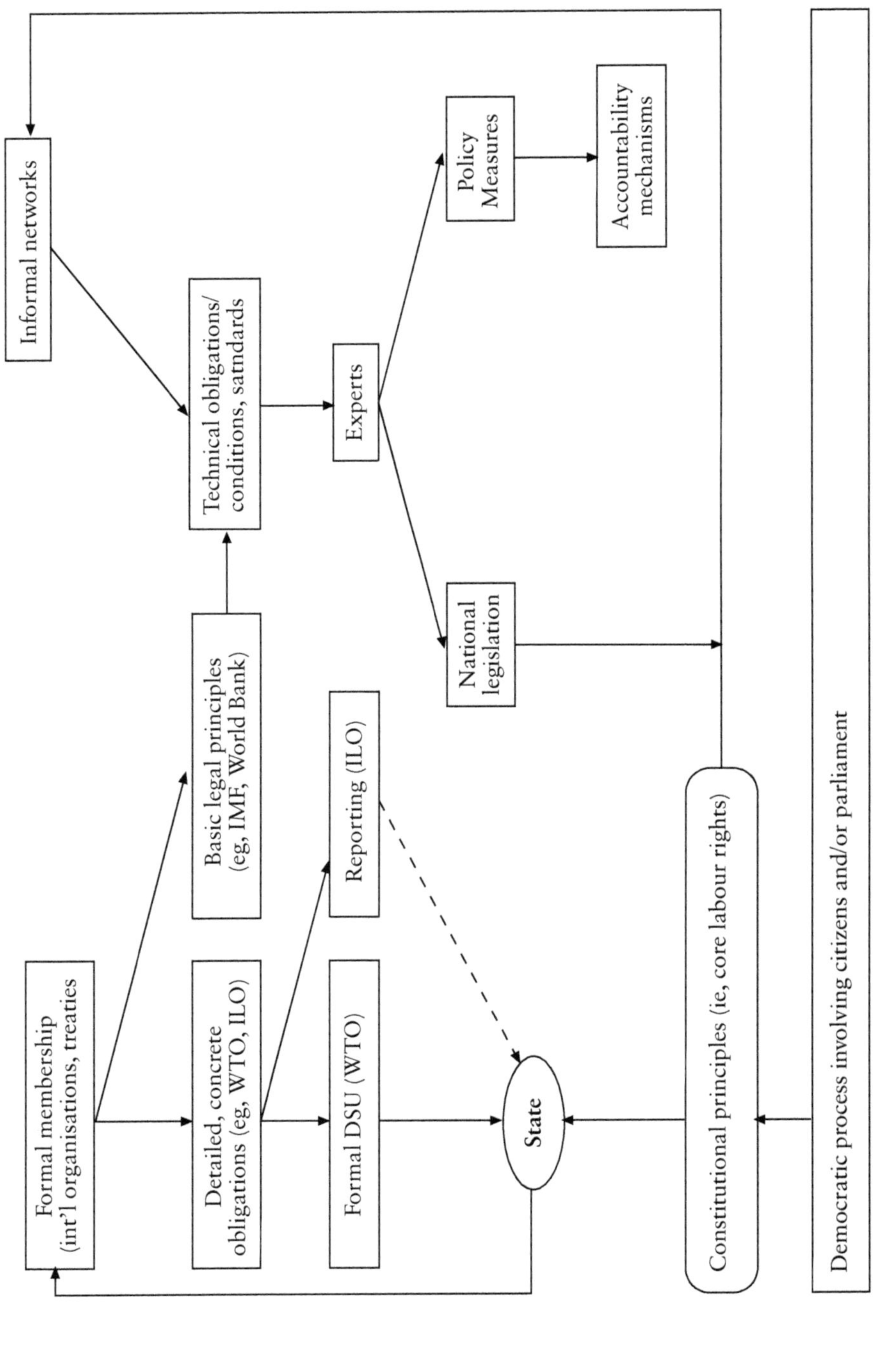

Figure 4.1. *Checks and Balances in a System of Multilevel Consistency*

participation. It is here that the impact of globalisation on national sovereignty plays an important role: if a state wishes to be considered a reliable partner in international organisations and forums, it needs a certain margin of discretion in making decisions during negotiations. Delegation of power from parliament to the executive, alongside accountability mechanisms, is therefore crucial. To be most efficient, parliamentary involvement should focus on strategic decisions, not on the details; these should be left to the government so as not to weaken its position in negotiations.

Accountability, ie an *ex post* review, is of particular importance with regard to measures adopted in informal networks. Experience shows that expert groups tend to neglect the broader implications of their decisions; therefore institutionalised procedures for ad hoc consultation during negotiations, eg parliamentary commissions, appear desirable.

4.4. IMPLEMENTING MULTILEVEL CONSISTENCY: PRACTICAL IMPLICATIONS

Now that we have described the principle of multilevel consistency as a conceptual tool for reconciling different international legal regimes such as core labour rights and the law of international trade and finance, the question remains as to how the protection of core labour rights in international economic institutions can be enhanced *in practice*. The following section summarises the practical implications of the concept.

4.4.1. Enhancing Core Labour Rights in International Economic Institutions

Since the WTO and the BWIs are quite different with regard to their legal frameworks, this section will look at them individually.

4.4.1.1. The WTO

In the WTO, core labour rights can become an issue in various contexts, such as the application of Article XX GATT exceptions, the introduction of labelling schemes under the TBT and the compatibility of GSP systems with the principle of non-discrimination. The multilevel consistency model requires the consideration of core labour rights when interpreting WTO law, but in practice one of the problems lies in the fact that these rights are not very concrete. When, for example, should child labour be considered exploitative? Article 3.2 DSU limits the jurisdiction of WTO panels to claims under the covered WTO agreements and prohibits the dispute settlement organs from adding new obligations to those in the covered agreements. Therefore, WTO dispute settlement organs have no jurisdiction to rule on claims of violation of core labour rights and cannot actively enforce them.[227]

The Singapore Declaration made it clear that the ILO is the competent authority for dealing with labour issues; claims about violations of core labour rights must therefore be brought before this body. However, the Singapore Declaration by no means prevents the application of core labour rights by the WTO dispute settlement organs. This argument is further strengthened by the fact that unlike the Convention on the Law of the Sea and the Statute of the ICJ,[228] the DSU does not include an explicit provision on applicable law. In practice, problems will arise when it comes to interpreting core labour rights in light of the WTO agreements.

The methods of interpretation described earlier and the principle of multilevel consistency will, in most cases, be able to solve "conflicts" between WTO law and core labour rights. However, they cannot fill the fairly abstract concept of core labour rights with concrete details and clearer obligations for the parties. This task has to be fulfilled by the ILO.[229] When the ILO comes to a conclusion, for example under an Article 33 procedure such as in the case of Burma/Myanmar, there is no room for a legal review by the WTO.[230] In other words, since the ILO already provides mechanisms for further developing core labour standards as well as compliance procedures, the "mandate" of the WTO dispute settlement organs with regard to core labour rights is limited to their application in concrete cases in which violations of WTO law are argued by a Member State.

What is required to enhance the protection of core labour rights within the WTO is not the creation of new legal rules but firstly the improvement of institutional co-operation with the ILO. The first informal steps were taken recently when a delegation from the WTO Secretariat taught a seminar on WTO law for ILO staff at the ILO Headquarters in Geneva. Similarly, the visit of the WTO Director-General to the ILO in Geneva in March 2002 has been perceived as a major (preliminary) step in enhancing institutional relations.

4.4.1.2. The BWIs

The Bretton Woods Institutions face a situation quite different from that of the WTO: while there is currently no legal framework for including the ILO concept of core labour rights into the work of the BWIs, considerable progress has been made at the operational level. However, in order to improve substantially the protection of *all* core labour rights, the pragmatic approach chosen so far is inadequate. Instead, emphasis must be put on strengthening the *legal* frame-

[227] Pauwelyn (2001) 554.
[228] United Nations Convention on the Law of the Sea (LOS Convention), 10 December 1982, 1833 UNTS 397, Article 291; ICJ Statute Article 38.
[229] Alston (2004) 471–76.
[230] Brupbacher (2002) 179.

work, by formally including the concept of core labour rights into the programmes of the BWIs.

This study has shown that the Articles of Agreement of the IMF and the World Bank do not preclude such legal engagement. It is often argued that the World Bank is not a body for the enforcement of human rights but a development agency. This argument mistakenly leads to the conclusion that the Bank can—because of its mandate—address only core labour rights that have a proven record of being economically beneficial for the country.[231] Like the WTO, the BWIs, in considering the legal obligations of its Member States within the ILO framework, does not turn into human rights agencies. This study does not ask for the BWIs to impose sanctions on countries that are violating core labour rights but to include these rights into their programmes.

World Bank programmes are one of the very few instruments available where the improvement of core labour rights can be situated within the broader context of social policy measures and is not limited to the discussion of the imposition of sanctions. As this study shows, this is a crucial element in putting core labour rights into practice. On the basis of a clear legal framework, core labour rights audits could be performed before programmes are implemented.

4.4.2. Conclusions

The principle of multilevel consistency provides a framework for addressing conflicts between core labour rights and the objectives of international economic organisations. In addition, steps that will vary between the different institutions are necessary to make it work in practice.

In the WTO, the issue of core labour rights will arise in a legal context and can be addressed with methods of legal interpretation. What is still lacking is a translation of the legal concept into standards that are applicable in the trade context. This is where the ILO must provide guidance. The former General Counsel to the World Bank, the late Ibrahim Shihata, articulated the Bank's role in transforming

> . . . many *ideals of the UN declarations and covenants* regarding economic, social and cultural rights [. . ., through] its policy dialogue with its borrowing members, and through its research, publications and co-operation with governments and other agencies *into realities*.[232]

This role could also apply to the ILO with regard to co-operation with the WTO.

[231] "The Bank's contribution to the achievement of economic, social and cultural human rights is a *by-product*, not an immediate or direct goal". Schlemmer-Schulte (1999a) 241 (emphasis added). See also Schlemmer-Schulte (2001b) 693–94.

[232] Shihata (1995a) 568 (emphasis added).

On the other hand, within the BWIs and in particular the World Bank, we observe a need for a clear legal framework and legal commitment while operational guidelines and co-operation with the ILO seem to work quite well in practice.

4.5. THE CHANGING ROLE OF THE STATE

We have seen that the principle of multilevel consistency can serve as a conceptual tool to reconcile national and international obligations as well as to resolve frictions between different international regimes. However, it has also been demonstrated that the role of the state is seriously affected in several respects.

At the institutional level, the role of parliament is affected by a shift in legislation from the national to the international level. To accommodate this shift, new mechanisms in decision-making and policy definition between the executive and parliament need to be established. To compensate for the loss of influence in the process of law-making, parliaments need to be more involved in the formulation of foreign economic policy objectives. In addition, feedback mechanisms need to be developed to keep parliaments up-to-date with current negotiations.

For a country with strong direct democratic institutions such as Switzerland, additional changes at the institutional level seem unavoidable: such a high level of direct democratic participation is too burdensome a procedure to keep up with developments at the global level. If integration is a declared state objective, direct democratic institutions need to focus on key strategic decisions rather than on detailed regulations. On the other hand, countries with weak institutions or no institutions of direct democracy will feel a need to increase democratic legitimacy, for example by introducing referenda on key decisions such as the adherence to the European Monetary Union, the Treaty of Nice[233] and the new European Constitution.[234]

Since many decisions that, in the traditional Westphalian model of the sovereign state, were made within the realm of domestic policy are now taken at the international level, structural changes in the relationship between the state and the international community are inevitably taking place. This study has shown that the traditional notion of sovereignty as formal independence is increasingly being replaced by a concept that is based on participation. This requires several

233 Section 20 of the Danish Constitution requires a referendum for ceding sovereignty to international organisations unless Parliament (*folketing*) accepts it by a 5/6 majority. This is why two referenda took place on Denmark's accession to the Treaty of Maastricht. In Ireland, a majority vote by the people is required for transferring sovereignty to the EU: Irish Supreme Court, *Crotty v An Taoiseach* [1987] IR 713, 24 December 1986. Ireland was the only EU Member State that submitted the Treaty of Nice to a referendum. In the first referendum on 21 June 2001, the treaty was rejected, but it was then adopted on 19 October 2002.

234 Treaty Establishing a Constitution for Europe, CIG 87/1/04 Rev 1, 13 October 2004, signed on 29 October 2004. The treaty has not yet been ratified.

adjustments at the state level: because of increasing specialisation and delegation of regulation to expert groups, governments need to become more involved in the work of these groups by establishing mechanisms for holding experts accountable and—in co-operation with parliaments, as outlined above—by formulating strategic guidelines for national representatives in such groups.

Put differently, globalisation affects the state at all levels and requires a redistribution of tasks among parliament, the executive and ultimately citizens.

5

Conclusions

1. The definition of core labour rights is the result of an attempt to reconcile different conflicting interests in a world of work that is faced with the challenge of globalisation. An analysis of existing international labour rights instruments shows that universal consensus can be found only with respect to process-oriented rights. States therefore remain responsible for establishing substantive labour rights provisions such as minimum wages and maximum working hours. To allow for flexibility in the labour market, developed nations such as Switzerland often frame such substantive labour standards as social goals or objectives.
2. The core labour rights as defined by the International Labour Organization (ILO) Declaration on Fundamental Principles and Rights at Work (1998) can be traced back to the Universal Declaration of Human Rights (1948). In other words, the ILO Declaration further develops a concept of labour rights that is already contained in the Universal Declaration. The ILO Declaration, although not legally binding, was adopted by an overwhelming majority of 273 votes against 19 abstentions; most of the abstaining countries have since co-operated in the implementation of the Declaration. This study therefore argues that the ILO formulation of core labour rights reflects a universal consensus, bringing these rights close to *obligations erga omnes*.
3. International organisations outside the ILO follow different approaches in dealing with core labour rights.

   a) The Bretton Woods Institutions (BWIs) generally follow a "do no harm policy"; in other words, they respect core labour rights in their own activities but do not routinely include them into their programmes for member countries. Exceptions are made for child labour and gender equality, which are now routinely incorporated into World Bank programmes. This mainstreaming approach is based on the economically-driven conviction that gender equality and the abolition of child labour contribute to economic welfare. In this study, this phenomenon is referred to as *the economisation of core labour rights*. It bears the danger of further restricting an already narrow concept of core labour rights.
   b) Similarly, the Organisation for Economic Co-operation and Development (OECD) does not follow a legal concept when addressing core labour rights but relies on *soft law* such as the guidelines for multinational enterprises and expert advice. OECD reports have a considerable impact

on the policies and reputations of states and can also influence international rating agencies. This book has critically assessed the lack of a clear legal framework for labour rights.

c) In contrast, the World Trade Organization (WTO) is governed by detailed legal rules and still relies on the concept of sovereign nation-states. An analysis of the basic principles of the General Agreement on Tariffs and Trade (GATT), and especially the exception clause in Article XX, shows that from a theoretical point of view there is—under specific circumstances—room for the consideration of core labour rights as long as they are not invoked for protectionist purposes. In particular, it is argued that the WTO dispute settlement organs have to interpret WTO law according to the Vienna Convention on the Law of Treaties. Therefore they have to apply general principles and customary international law.

4. Globalisation affects states at several levels. This study has looked at the two main examples, namely, the role of multinational enterprises and the relationship between labour rights and trade regulation.

   a) The ILO and OECD address the responsibility of multinational enterprises for complying with core labour rights at home and abroad with specific, non-legally-binding guidelines. While the ILO Tripartite Declaration on Principles concerning Multinational Enterprises and Social Policy has relatively low standing within the hierarchy of ILO norms, the OECD Guidelines for Multinational Enterprises were adopted by the Council of Ministers after a participatory process that included social partners as well as civil society. Given the high reputation of OECD standards, the Guidelines seem to have a considerable impact in practice. However, both instruments are soft law.

   b) In order to overcome the stalemate reached after unsuccessful attempts to link trade and labour by including a social clause in the WTO agreements, the United Nations Secretary-General Kofi Annan launched the Global Compact in 1999. The idea is to encourage business leaders to incorporate core labour rights into their economic activities. Because there are no formal enforcement or accountability mechanisms, the Compact is at risk of being abused for public relations purposes.

   c) The study concludes that an international legally binding instrument to hold multinational enterprises accountable would be unlikely to achieve the necessary international consensus. However, the OECD and ILO guidelines as well as the new proposed UN Norms on corporate responsibility show that there are some emerging general principles. By incorporating these guidelines into domestic law, states can play an important role in the building of an international law of business responsibility.

5. Many states have taken measures to link core labour rights and trade. This book discusses the examples of the United States, the European Union and

Switzerland. It then explores how core labour rights could become an issue within the WTO and examines the implications of the Agreement on Technical Barriers to Trade (TBT) and Government Procurement Agreement (GPA).

a) Social labelling programmes are covered by the TBT Agreement. Using the example of the Belgian law on socially responsible production, the study shows what is needed by such measures in order for them to be compatible with WTO law. It shows that the Singapore Declaration (1996) does not prevent the application of core labour rights by WTO dispute settlement organs.
b) With respect to the GPA, this book examines how core labour rights are part of a universal concept of "public order" and thus covered by the respective exception in Article XXIII. Therefore, measures to protect core labour rights that would otherwise violate the GPA can be justified by the protection of "public order".

6. Linking trade and labour rights inevitably raises the question of regulatory competition and the possible "race to the bottom". The problem consists of two elements that need to be addressed differently: global commons and market access.

   a) The public goods problem can be best addressed by the ILO, which has the competence to establish, interpret and enforce core labour rights. While the Singapore Declaration confirms that the WTO has no mandate to address the issue of core labour rights as global public goods, it does not prevent the WTO dispute settlement organs from applying standards that are set by the ILO.
   b) From a market access point of view, the feared race to the bottom can be avoided if the comparative advantage of the countries concerned is maintained. This study shows how this can be achieved by using existing non-violation complaints under WTO law.

7. Once the feasibility of links between trade and core labour rights has been established, the question of whether trade sanctions are the appropriate means of enforcing compliance with core labour rights arises. For two reasons trade sanctions are not considered an appropriate means of enforcement. First, from a humanitarian point of view they are unlikely to affect the responsible authorities who could effectively improve the situation with regard to core labour rights. Second, in most cases, countries choose not to tighten labour standards for economic, trade-related reasons, such as the lack of opportunities to offset the higher costs involved in complying with higher standards. Trade sanctions would not effectively address this problem and would moreover be counter to the purpose of the WTO regime.
8. International trade and finance are partially undemocratic regimes because decisions are based on the opinions of experts and are often taken without consultation with citizens. Similar deficiencies exist at the state level, where

expert bodies take over functions that have traditionally been performed by the nation state. Particularly affected are the executive and administrative branches, which, at the expense of parliament, play an increasingly important role at the international level. New instruments to secure parliamentary participation in foreign policy—and thus democratic legitimacy—have therefore been discussed. This study concludes that instruments of direct democratic participation must focus on strategic decisions in order not to hinder international integration.

9. In considering the loss of sovereignty in the Westphalian sense, it is argued that the traditional concept of independence is increasingly being replaced by a more positive notion of *sovereignty as participation*.
10. In summary, this study concludes that these difficulties can be overcome not by a new social contract but by a model of multilevel consistency that encompasses the principle of a consistent legal order. The principle of a consistent legal order has different implications at different levels:

    a) First, it obliges a state to adhere to only those international treaties that are in compliance with its fundamental domestic (constitutional) provisions.
    b) Second, once such obligations are accepted, the state must comply with them under all circumstances, ie not only at the bilateral level but also as a member of international organisations and informal networks. The principle of a consistent legal order applies to the relationship between the state and its citizens; it cannot be suspended simply because the state acts in a different context.
    c) Third, a consistent legal order is a fundamental principle of democratic governance and as such forms part of the public order.
    d) Fourth, because the notion of statehood becomes meaningless without a consistent legal order, this principle is inalienable. It can be embedded in a broader notion of state sovereignty. International dispute settlement organs must therefore interpret conflicting provisions, taking into account not only international human rights such as core labour rights but also the principle that fundamental international obligations are complementary, forming a coherent set of universal rules and not a series of isolated regimes.
    e) Fifth, international organisations must take core labour rights into account when establishing programmes in other fields such as trade and finance. The reason is simple: since the Member States are bound by these principles, the international organisations—although not technically bound by these rights themselves—must act in a way so as at least not to impede Member State compliance with these rights. In practice, this means, for example, that labour rights audits should occur before International Monetary Fund or World Bank programmes are established.

Appendix

Selected Labour Rights Provisions

A.1. Universal Declaration of Human Rights (1948)

Article 22

Everyone, as a member of society, has the right to social security and is entitled to realization, through national effort and international cooperation and in accordance with the organization and resources of each State, of the economic, social and cultural rights indispensable for his dignity and the free development of his personality.

Article 23

1. Everyone has the right to work, to free choice of employment, to just and favourable conditions of work and to protection against unemployment.
2. Everyone, without any discrimination, has the right to equal pay for equal work.

3. Everyone who works has the right to just and favourable remuneration ensuring for himself and his family an existence worthy of human dignity, and supplemented, if necessary, by other means of social protection.
4. Everyone has the right to form and to join trade unions for the protection of his interests.

Article 24

Everyone has the right to rest and leisure, including reasonable limitations of working hours and periodic holidays with pay.

Article 25

1. Everyone has the right to a standard of living adequate for the health and wee-being of himself and of his family, including food, clothing, housing and medical care and necessary social services, and the right to security in the event of unemployment, sickness, disability, widowhood, old age or other lack of livelihood in circumstances beyond his control.
2. Motherhood and childhood are entitled to special care and assistance. All children, whether born in or out of wedlock, shall enjoy the same social protection.

A.2. International Covenant on Economic, Social and Cultural Rights (ICESCR) (1966)

Article 6

1. The States Parties to the present Covenant recognize the right to work, which includes the right of everyone to the opportunity to gain his living by work which he freely chooses or accepts, and will take appropriate steps to safeguard this right.
2. The steps to be taken by a State Party to the present Covenant to achieve the full realization of this right shall include technical and vocational guidance and training programmes, policies and techniques to achieve steady economic, social and cultural development and full and productive employment under conditions safeguarding fundamental political and economic freedoms to the individual.

Article 7

The States Parties to the present Covenant recognize the right of everyone to the enjoyment of just and favourable conditions of work which ensure, in particular:

(a) Remuneration which provides all workers, as a minimum, with:

   (i) Fair wages and equal remuneration for work of equal value without distinction of any kind, in particular women being guaranteed conditions of work not inferior to those enjoyed by men, with equal pay for equal work;

   (ii) A decent living for themselves and their families in accordance with the provisions of the present Covenant;

(b) Safe and healthy working conditions;
(c) Equal opportunity for everyone to be promoted in his employment to an appropriate higher level, subject to no considerations other than those of seniority and competence;
(d) Rest, leisure and reasonable limitation of working hours and periodic holidays with pay, as well as remuneration for public holidays.

Article 8

1. The States Parties to the present Covenant undertake to ensure:
    (a) The right of everyone to form trade unions and join the trade union of his choice, subject only to the rules of the organization concerned, for the promotion and protection of his economic and social interests. No restrictions may be placed on the exercise of this right other than those prescribed by law and which are necessary in a democratic society in the interests of national security or public order or for the protection of the rights and freedoms of others;
    (b) The right of trade unions to establish national federations or confederations and the right of the latter to form or join international trade-union organizations;
    (c) The right of trade unions to function freely subject to no limitations other than those prescribed by law and which are necessary in a democratic society in the interests of national security or public order or for the protection of the rights and freedoms of others;
    (d) The right to strike, provided that it is exercised in conformity with the laws of the particular country.
2. This article shall not prevent the imposition of lawful restrictions on the exercise of these rights by members of the armed forces or of the police or of the administration of the State.
3. Nothing in this article shall authorize States Parties to the International Labour Organisation Convention of 1948 concerning Freedom of Association and Protection of the Right to Organize to take legislative measures which would prejudice, or apply the law in such a manner as would prejudice, the guarantees provided for in that Convention.

Article 9

The States Parties to the present Covenant recognize the right of everyone to social security, including social insurance.

Article 10

The States Parties to the present Covenant recognize that:

1. The widest possible protection and assistance should be accorded to the family, which is the natural and fundamental group unit of society, particularly for its establishment and while it is responsible for the care and education of dependent children. Marriage must be entered into with the free consent of the intending spouses.

2. Special protection should be accorded to mothers during a reasonable period before and after childbirth. During such period working mothers should be accorded paid leave or leave with adequate social security benefits.
3. Special measures of protection and assistance should be taken on behalf of all children and young persons without any discrimination for reasons of parentage or other conditions. Children and young persons should be protected from economic and social exploitation. Their employment in work harmful to their morals or health or dangerous to life or likely to hamper their normal development should be punishable by law. States should also set age limits below which the paid employment of child labour should be prohibited and punishable by law.

A.3. International Covenant on Civil and Political Rights (ICCPR) (1966)

Article 8

1. No one shall be held in slavery; slavery and the slave-trade in all their forms shall be prohibited.
2. No one shall be held in servitude.
3. (a) No one shall be required to perform forced or compulsory labour;
   (b) Paragraph 3(a) shall not be held to preclude, in countries where imprisonment with hard labour may be imposed as a punishment for a crime, the performance of hard labour in pursuance of a sentence to such punishment by a competent court;
   (c) For the purpose of this paragraph the term "forced or compulsory labour" shall not include:
      (i) Any work or service, not referred to in subparagraph (b), normally required of a person who is under detention in consequence of a lawful order of a court, or of a person during conditional release from such detention;
      (ii) Any service of a military character and, in countries where conscientious objection is recognized, any national service required by law of conscientious objectors;
      (iii) Any service exacted in cases of emergency or calamity threatening the life or well-being of the community;
      (iv) Any work or service which forms part of normal civil obligations.

Article 22

1. Everyone shall have the right to freedom of association with others, including the right to form and join trade unions for the protection of his interests.
2. No restrictions may be placed on the exercise of this right other than those which are prescribed by law and which are necessary in a democratic society in the interests of national security or public safety, public order (*ordre public*), the protection of public health or morals or the protection of the rights and freedoms of others. This article shall not prevent the imposition of lawful restrictions on members of the armed forces and of the police in their exercise of this right.
3. Nothing in this article shall authorize States Parties to the International Labour Organisation Convention of 1948 concerning Freedom of Association and Protection

of the Right to Organize to take legislative measures which would prejudice, or to apply the law in such a manner as to prejudice, the guarantees provided for in that Convention.

A.4. Convention on the Elimination of All Forms of Discrimination against Women (1979)

Article 11

1. States Parties shall take all appropriate measures to eliminate discrimination against women in the field of employment in order to ensure, on a basis of equality of men and women, the same rights, in particular:

   (a) The right to work as an inalienable right of all human beings;
   (b) The right to the same employment opportunities, including the application of the same criteria for selection in matters of employment;
   (c) The right to free choice of profession and employment, the right to promotion, job security and all benefits and conditions of service and the right to receive vocational training and retraining, including apprenticeships, advanced vocational training and recurrent training;
   (d) The right to equal remuneration, including benefits, and to equal treatment in respect of work of equal value, as well as equality of treatment in the evaluation of the quality of work;
   (e) The right to social security, particularly in cases of retirement, unemployment, sickness, invalidity and old age and other incapacity to work, as well as the right to paid leave;
   (f) The right to protection of health and to safety in working conditions, including the safeguarding of the function of reproduction.

2. In order to prevent discrimination against women on the grounds of marriage or maternity and to ensure their effective right to work, States Parties shall take appropriate measures:

   (a) To prohibit, subject to the imposition of sanctions, dismissal on the grounds of pregnancy or of maternity leave and discrimination in dismissals on the basis of marital status;
   (b) To introduce maternity leave with pay or with comparable social benefits without loss of former employment, seniority or social allowances;
   (c) To encourage the provision of the necessary supporting social services to enable parents to combine family obligations with work responsibilities and participation in public life, in particular through promoting the establishment and development of a network of child-care facilities;
   (d) To provide special protection to women during pregnancy in types of work proved to be harmful to them.

3. Protective legislation relating to matters covered in this article shall be reviewed periodically in the light of scientific and technological knowledge and shall be revised, repealed or extended as necessary.

A.5. Convention on the Rights of the Child (1989)

Article 32

1. States Parties recognize the right of the child to be protected from economic exploitation and from performing any work that is likely to be hazardous or to interfere with the child's education, or to be harmful to the child's health or physical, mental, spiritual, moral or social development.
2. States Parties shall take legislative, administrative, social and educational measures to ensure the implementation of the present article. To this end, and having regard to the relevant provisions of other international instruments, States Parties shall in particular:

   (a) Provide for a minimum age or minimum ages for admission to employment;
   (b) Provide for appropriate regulation of the hours and conditions of employment;
   (c) Provide for appropriate penalties or other sanctions to ensure the effective enforcement of the present article.

Article 35

States Parties shall take all appropriate national, bilateral and multilateral measures to prevent the abduction of, the sale of or traffic in children for any purpose or in any form.

A.6. Optional Protocol to the Convention on the Rights of the Child on the Sale of Children, Child Prostitution and Child Pornography (2000)

Article 2

For the purposes of the present Protocol:

(a) Sale of children means any act or transaction whereby a child is transferred by any person or group of persons to another for remuneration or any other consideration;
(b) Child prostitution means the use of a child in sexual activities for remuneration or any other form of consideration;
(c) Child pornography means any representation, by whatever means, of a child engaged in real or simulated explicit sexual activities or any representation of the sexual parts of a child for primarily sexual purposes.

Article 3

1. Each State Party shall ensure that, as a minimum, the following acts and activities are fully covered under its criminal or penal law, whether such offences are committed domestically or transnationally or on an individual or organized basis:

   (a) In the context of sale of children as defined in article 2:

      (i) Offering, delivering or accepting, by whatever means, a child for the purpose of:

a. Sexual exploitation of the child;
b. Transfer of organs of the child for profit;
c. Engagement of the child in forced labour;

(ii) Improperly inducing consent, as an intermediary, for the adoption of a child in violation of applicable international legal instruments on adoption;

(b) Offering, obtaining, procuring or providing a child for child prostitution, as defined in article 2;
(c) Producing, distributing, disseminating, importing, exporting, offering, selling or possessing for the above purposes child pornography as defined in article 2.

A.7. ILO Convention (No 29) Concerning Forced Labour (1930)

Article 2

1. For the purposes of this Convention the term "forced or compulsory labour" shall mean all work or service which is exacted from any person under the menace of any penalty and for which the said person has not offered himself voluntarily. 2. Nevertheless, for the purposes of this Convention the term "forced or compulsory labour" shall not include:

(a) Any work or service exacted in virtue of compulsory military service laws for work of a purely military character;
(b) Any work or service which forms part of the normal civic obligations of the citizens of a fully self-governing country;
(c) Any work or service exacted from any person as a consequence of a conviction in a court of law, provided that the said work or service is carried out under the supervision and control of a public authority and that the said person is not hired to or placed at the disposal of private individuals, companies or associations;
(d) Any work or service exacted in cases of emergency, that is to say, in the event of war or of a calamity or threatened calamity, such as fire, flood, famine, earthquake, violent epidemic or epizootic diseases, invasion by animal, insect or vegetable pests, and in general any circumstance that would endanger the existence or the well-being of the whole or part of the population;
(e) Minor communal services of a kind which, being performed by the members of the community in the direct interest of the said community, can therefore be considered as normal civic obligations incumbent upon the members of the community, provided that the members of the community or their direct representatives shall have the right to be consulted in regard to the need for such services.

A.8. ILO Convention (No 105) Concerning the Abolition of Forced Labour (1957)

Article 1

Each Member of the International Labour Organisation which ratifies this Convention undertakes to suppress and not to make use of any form of forced or compulsory labour:

(a) As a means of political coercion or education or as a punishment for holding or expressing political views or views ideologically opposed to the established political, social or economic system;
(b) As a method of mobilising and using labour for purposes of economic development;
(c) As a means of labour discipline;
(d) As a punishment for having participated in strikes;
(e) As a means of racial, social, national or religious discrimination.

Article 2

Each Member of the International Labour Organisation which ratifies this Convention undertakes to take effective measures to secure the immediate and complete abolition of forced or compulsory labour as specified in article 1 of this Convention.

A.9. ILO Convention (No 87) on Freedom of Association and Protection of the Right to Organise (1948)

Article 1

Each Member of the International Labour Organisation for which this Convention is in force undertakes to give effect to the following provisions.

Article 2

Workers and employers, without distinction whatsoever, shall have the right to establish and, subject only to the rules of the organisation concerned, to join organisations of their own choosing without previous authorisation.

Article 3

1. Workers' and employers' organisations shall have the right to draw up their constitutions and rules, to elect their representatives in full freedom, to organise their administration and activities and to formulate their programmes.
2. The public authorities shall refrain from any interference which would restrict this right or impede the lawful exercise thereof.

Article 8

1. In exercising the rights provided for in this Convention workers and employers and their respective organisations, like other persons or organised collectivities, shall respect the law of the land.
2. The law of the land shall not be such as to impair, nor shall it be so applied as to impair, the guarantees provided for in this Convention.

Article 10

In this Convention the term *organisation* means any organisation of workers or of employers for furthering and defending the interests of workers or of employers.

Article 11

Each Member of the International Labour Organisation for which this Convention is in force undertakes to take all necessary and appropriate measures to ensure that workers and employers may exercise freely the right to organise.

A.10. ILO Convention (No 98) on the Right to Organise and Collective Bargaining (1949)

Article 1

1. Workers shall enjoy adequate protection against acts of anti-union discrimination in respect of their employment.
2. Such protection shall apply more particularly in respect of acts calculated to—
   (a) make the employment of a worker subject to the condition that he shall not join a union or shall relinquish trade union membership;
   (b) cause the dismissal of or otherwise prejudice a worker by reason of union membership or because of participation in union activities outside working hours or, with the consent of the employer, within working hours.

Article 2

1. Workers' and employers' organisations shall enjoy adequate protection against any acts of interference by each other or each other's agents or members in their establishment, functioning or administration.
2. In particular, acts which are designed to promote the establishment of workers' organisations under the domination of employers or employers' organisations, or to support workers' organisations by financial or other means, with the object of placing such organisations under the control of employers or employers' organisations, shall be deemed to constitute acts of interference within the meaning of this Article.

Article 3

Machinery appropriate to national conditions shall be established, where necessary, for the purpose of ensuring respect for the right to organise as defined in the preceding Articles.

Article 4

Measures appropriate to national conditions shall be taken, where necessary, to encourage and promote the full development and utilisation of machinery for voluntary negotiation between employers or employers' organisations and workers' organisations, with a view to the regulation of terms and conditions of employment by means of collective agreements.

Article 5

1. The extent to which the guarantees provided for in this Convention shall apply to the armed forces and the police shall be determined by national laws or regulations.
2. In accordance with the principle set forth in paragraph 8 of article 19 of the Constitution of the International Labour Organisation the ratification of this Convention by any Member shall not be deemed to affect any existing law, award, custom or agreement in virtue of which members of the armed forces or the police enjoy any right guaranteed by this Convention.

Article 6

This Convention does not deal with the position of public servants engaged in the administration of the State, nor shall it be construed as prejudicing their rights or status in any way.

A.11. ILO Convention (No 100) on Equal Remuneration (1951)

Article 2

1. Each Member shall, by means appropriate to the methods in operation for determining rates of remuneration, promote and, in so far as is consistent with such methods, ensure the application to all workers of the principle of equal remuneration for men and women workers for work of equal value.
2. This principle may be applied by means of—

   (a) national laws or regulations;
   (b) legally established or recognised machinery for wage determination;
   (c) collective agreements between employers and workers; or
   (d) a combination of these various means.

Article 3

1. Where such action will assist in giving effect to the provisions of this Convention measures shall be taken to promote objective appraisal of jobs on the basis of the work to be performed.
2. The methods to be followed in this appraisal may be decided upon by the authorities responsible for the determination of rates of remuneration, or, where such rates are determined by collective agreements, by the parties thereto.
3. Differential rates between workers which correspond, without regard to sex, to differences, as determined by such objective appraisal, in the work to be performed shall not be considered as being contrary to the principle of equal remuneration for men and women workers for work of equal value.

Article 4

Each Member shall co-operate as appropriate with the employers' and workers' organisations concerned for the purpose of giving effect to the provisions of this Convention.

A.12. ILO Convention (No 111) on Discrimination (Employment and Occupation) (1958)

Article 1

1. For the purpose of this Convention the term *discrimination* includes—
   (a) any distinction, exclusion or preference made on the basis of race, colour sex, religion, political opinion, national extraction or social origin, which has the effect of nullifying or impairing equality of opportunity or treatment in employment or occupation;
   (b) such other distinction, exclusion or preference which has the effect of nullifying or impairing equality of opportunity or treatment in employment or occupation as may be determined by the Member concerned after consultation with representative employers' and workers' organisations, where such exist, and with other appropriate bodies.
2. Any distinction, exclusion or preference in respect of a particular job based on the inherent requirements thereof shall not be deemed to be discrimination.
3. For the purpose of this Convention the terms employment and occupation include access to vocational training, access to employment and to particular occupations, and terms and conditions of employment.

A.13. ILO Convention (No 138) on Minimum Age (1973)

Article 1

Each Member for which this Convention is in force undertakes to pursue a national policy designed to ensure the effective abolition of child labour and to raise progressively the minimum age for admission to employment or work to a level consistent with the fullest physical and mental development of young persons.

Article 2

1. Each Member which ratifies this Convention shall specify, in a declaration appended to its ratification, a minimum age for admission to employment or work within its territory and on means of transport registered in its territory; subject to Articles 4 to 8 of this Convention, no one under that age shall be admitted to employment or work in any occupation.
2. Each Member which has ratified this Convention may subsequently notify the Director-General of the International Labour Office, by further declarations, that it specifies a minimum age higher than that previously specified.

3. The minimum age specified in pursuance of paragraph 1 of this Article shall not be less than the age of completion of compulsory schooling and, in any case, shall not be less than 15 years.
4. Notwithstanding the provisions of paragraph 3 of this Article, a Member whose economy and educational facilities are insufficiently developed may, after consultation with the organisations of employers and workers concerned, where such exist, initially specify a minimum age of 14 years.
5. Each Member which has specified a minimum age of 14 years in pursuance of the provisions of the preceding paragraph shall include in its reports on the application of this Convention submitted under article 22 of the constitution of the International Labour Organisation a statement—

   (a) that its reason for doing so subsists; or
   (b) that it renounces its right to avail itself of the provisions in question as from a stated date.

Article 3

1. The minimum age for admission to any type of employment or work which by its nature or the circumstances in which it is carried out is likely to jeopardise the health, safety or morals of young persons shall not be less than 18 years.
2. The types of employment or work to which paragraph 1 of this Article applies shall be determined by national laws or regulations or by the competent authority, after consultation with the organisations of employers and workers concerned, where such exist.
3. Notwithstanding the provisions of paragraph 1 of this Article, national laws or regulations or the competent authority may, after consultation with the organisations of employers and workers concerned, where such exist, authorise employment or work as from the age of 16 years on condition that the health, safety and morals of the young persons concerned are fully protected and that the young persons have received adequate specific instruction or vocational training in the relevant branch of activity.

Article 4

1. In so far as necessary, the competent authority, after consultation with the organisations of employers and workers concerned, where such exist, may exclude from the application of this Convention limited categories of employment or work in respect of which special and substantial problems of application arise.
2. Each Member which ratifies this Convention shall list in its first report on the application of the Convention submitted under article 22 of the Constitution of the International Labour Organisation any categories which may have been excluded in pursuance of paragraph 1 of this Article, giving the reasons for such exclusion, and shall state in subsequent reports the position of its law and practice in respect of the categories excluded and the extent to which effect has been given or is proposed to be given to the Convention in respect of such categories.
3. Employment or work covered by Article 3 of this Convention shall not be excluded from the application of the Convention in pursuance of this Article.

A.14. ILO Convention (No 182) on Worst Forms of Child Labour (1999)

Article 1

Each Member which ratifies this Convention shall take immediate and effective measures to secure the prohibition and elimination of the worst forms of child labour as a matter of urgency.

Article 2

For the purposes of this Convention, the term *child* shall apply to all persons under the age of 18.

Article 3

For the purposes of this Convention, the term *the worst forms of child labour* comprises:

(a) all forms of slavery or practices similar to slavery, such as the sale and trafficking of children, debt bondage and serfdom and forced or compulsory labour, including forced or compulsory recruitment of children for use in armed conflict;
(b) the use, procuring or offering of a child for prostitution, for the production of pornography or for pornographic performances;
(c) the use, procuring or offering of a child for illicit activities, in particular for the production and trafficking of drugs as defined in the relevant international treaties;
(d) work which, by its nature or the circumstances in which it is carried out, is likely to harm the health, safety or morals of children.

Article 4

1. The types of work referred to under Article 3(d) shall be determined by national laws or regulations or by the competent authority, after consultation with the organizations of employers and workers concerned, taking into consideration relevant international standards, in particular Paragraphs 3 and 4 of the Worst Forms of Child Labour Recommendation (1999).
2. The competent authority, after consultation with the organizations of employers and workers concerned, shall identify where the types of work so determined exist.

The list of the types of work determined under paragraph 1 of this Article shall be periodically examined and revised as necessary, in consultation with the organizations of employers and workers concerned.

Article 7

1. Each Member shall take all necessary measures to ensure the effective implementation and enforcement of the provisions giving effect to this Convention including the provision and application of penal sanctions or, as appropriate, other sanctions.
2. Each Member shall, taking into account the importance of education in eliminating child labour, take effective and time-bound measures to:

(a) prevent the engagement of children in the worst forms of child labour;
(b) provide the necessary and appropriate direct assistance for the removal of children from the worst forms of child labour and for their rehabilitation and social integration;
(c) ensure access to free basic education, and, wherever possible and appropriate, vocational training, for all children removed from the worst forms of child labour;
(d) identify and reach out to children at special risk; and
(e) take account of the special situation of girls.

3. Each Member shall designate the competent authority responsible for the implementation of the provisions giving effect to this Convention.

A.15. ILO Declaration on Fundamental Principles and Rights at Work (1998)

Whereas the ILO was founded in the conviction that social justice is essential to universal and lasting peace;

Whereas economic growth is essential but not sufficient to ensure equity, social progress and the eradication of poverty, confirming the need for the ILO to promote strong social policies, justice and democratic institutions;

Whereas the ILO should, now more than ever, draw upon all its standard-setting, technical cooperation and research resources in all its areas of competence, in particular employment, vocational training and working conditions, to ensure that, in the context of a global strategy for economic and social development, economic and social policies are mutually reinforcing components in order to create broad-based sustainable development;

Whereas the ILO should give special attention to the problems of persons with special social needs, particularly the unemployed and migrant workers, and mobilize and encourage international, regional and national efforts aimed at resolving their problems, and promote effective policies aimed at job creation;

Whereas, in seeking to maintain the link between social progress and economic growth, the guarantee of fundamental principles and rights at work is of particular significance in that it enables the persons concerned to claim freely and on the basis of equality of opportunity their fair share of the wealth which they have helped to generate, and to achieve fully their human potential;

Whereas the ILO is the constitutionally mandated international organization and the competent body to set and deal with international labour standards, and enjoys universal support and acknowledgement in promoting fundamental rights at work as the expression of its constitutional principles;

Whereas it is urgent, in a situation of growing economic interdependence, to reaffirm the immutable nature of the fundamental principles and rights embodied in the Constitution of the Organization and to promote their universal application;

The International Labour Conference,

1. Recalls:

   (a) that in freely joining the ILO, all Members have endorsed the principles and rights set out in its Constitution and in the Declaration of Philadelphia, and have undertaken to work towards attaining the overall objectives of the Organization to the best of their resources and fully in line with their specific circumstances;
   (b) that these principles and rights have been expressed and developed in the form of specific rights and obligations in Conventions recognized as fundamental both inside and outside the Organization.

2. Declares that all Members, even if they have not ratified the Conventions in question, have an obligation arising from the very fact of membership in the Organization, to respect, to promote and to realize, in good faith and in accordance with the Constitution, the principles concerning the fundamental rights which are the subject of those Conventions, namely:

   (a) freedom of association and the effective recognition of the right to collective bargaining;
   (b) the elimination of all forms of forced or compulsory labour;
   (c) the effective abolition of child labour; and
   (d) the elimination of discrimination in respect of employment and occupation.

3. Recognizes the obligation on the Organization to assist its Members, in response to their established and expressed needs, in order to attain these objectives by making full use of its constitutional, operational and budgetary resources, including by the mobilization of external resources and support, as well as by encouraging other international organizations with which the ILO has established relations, pursuant to article 12 of its Constitution, to support these efforts:

   (a) by offering technical cooperation and advisory services to promote the ratification and implementation of the fundamental Conventions;
   (b) by assisting those Members not yet in a position to ratify some or all of these Conventions in their efforts to respect, to promote and to realize the principles concerning fundamental rights which are the subject of those Conventions; and
   (c) by helping the Members in their efforts to create a climate for economic and social development.

4. Decides that, to give full effect to this Declaration, a promotional follow-up, which is meaningful and effective, shall be implemented in accordance with the measures specified in the annex hereto, which shall be considered as an integral part of this Declaration.
5. Stresses that labour standards should not be used for protectionist trade purposes, and that nothing in this Declaration and its follow-up shall be invoked or otherwise used for such purposes; in addition, the comparative advantage of any country should in no way be called into question by this Declaration and its follow-up.

Bibliography

AARONSON, SUSAN ARIEL (2001) "Oh Behave! Voluntary Codes Can Make Corporations Model Citizens" 15 *The International Economy* 40–47.

AARONSON, SUSAN and REEVES, JAMES (2002) "The European Response to Public Demands for Corporate Responsibility" *National Policy Association Report*, February.

ACADEMY OF INTERNATIONAL LAW (ed) (1994) *Recueil des Cours, Vol 250/1994–VI* (The Hague, Brill).

ACHERMANN, ALBERTO (2001) "Der Vorrang des Völkerrechts im schweizerischen Recht" in Thomas Cottier, Alberto Achermann, Daniel Wüger and Valentin Zellweger (eds), *Der Staatsvertrag im schweizerischen Verfassungsrecht* (Bern, Stämpfli Verlag).

Agora: The United States Constitution and International Law (2004) 98 *American Journal of International Law* 42–108 (with contributions by Harold Hongju Koh, Roger Alford, Michael Ramsey, Gerald Neuman and Alexander Aleinikoff).

AHN, DUKGEUN (2000) "Linkages between International Financial and Trade Institutions: IMF, World Bank and WTO" 34 *Journal of World Trade* 1–35.

ALFREDSSON, GUDMUNDUR and EIDE, ASBJØRN (eds) (1999) *The Universal Declaration of Human Rights: A Common Standard of Achievement* (The Hague, Martinus Nijhoff Publishers).

ALLOTT, PHILIP (2002) *The Health of Nations: Society and Law beyond the State* (Cambridge, Cambridge University Press).

ALSTON, PHILIP (1980) "Linking Trade and Human Rights" 23 *German Yearbook of International Law* 126–58.

—— (1982) "International Trade as an Instrument of Positive Human Rights Policy" 4 *Human Rights Quarterly* 155–83.

—— (1993) "Labor Rights Provisions in US Trade Law: 'Aggressive Unilateralism'?" 15 *Human Rights Quarterly* 1–35.

—— (1997) "The Myopia of the Handmaidens: International Lawyers and Globalization" 8 *European Journal of International Law* 435–48.

—— (1999a) "International Governance in the Normative Areas", *UNDP Background Papers: Human Development Report 1999*, 15–18.

—— (ed) (1999b) *The EU and Human Rights* (Oxford, Oxford University Press).

—— (2002) "Resisting the Merger and Acquisition of Human Rights by Trade Law: A Reply to Petersmann" 13 *European Journal of International Law* 815–44.

—— (2004) "'Core Labour Standards' and the Transformation of the International Labour Rights Regime" 15 *European Journal of International Law* 457–521.

—— (2005a) "Facing Up to the Complexities of the ILO's Core Labour Standards Agenda" 16 *European Journal of International Law* 467–80.

—— (ed) (2005b) *Labour Rights as Human Rights* (Oxford, Oxford University Press).

—— (2005c) "Labour Rights as Human Rights: The Not So Happy State of the Art" in Philip Alston (eds), *Labour Rights as Human Rights* (Oxford, Oxford University Press).

ALSTON, PHILIP and QUINN, GERARD (1987) "The Nature and Scope of States Parties' Obligations under the International Covenant on Economic, Social and Cultural Rights" 9 *Human Rights Quarterly* 157–229.

ALVAREZ, JOSE E (2001) "Do Liberal States Behave Better? A Critique of Slaughter's Liberal Theory" 12 *European Journal of International Law* 183–246.

AMANN, DIANE MARIE (2004) "'Raise the Flag and Let It Talk': On the Use of External Norms in Constitutional Decision Making" 2 *International Journal of Constitutional Law* 597–610.

AMBROSE, KATHLEEN A (2000) "Science and the WTO" 31 *Law and Policy in International Business* 861–68.

ANDERES, SABRINA (2001) *Fremde im eigenen Land: Die Haftbarkeit transnationaler Unternehmen für Menschenrechtsverletzungen an indigenen Völkern* (Zürich, Schulthess).

ANDREASSEN, BARD-ANDERS (1992) "Article 22" in Asbjørn Eide, Gudmundur Alfredsson, Göran Melander, Lars Adam Rehof and Allan Rosas (eds), *The Universal Declaration of Human Rights: A Commentary* (Oslo, Scandinavian University Press).

ANGHIE, ANTONY (2000) "Time Present and Time Past: Globalization, International Financial Institutions, and the Third World" 32 *New York University Journal of International Law and Politics* 243–90.

ANNAN, KOFI A (2000) *We the Peoples—The Role of the United Nations in the 21st Century* (New York, United Nations).

APPLEBAUM, HERBERT (1995) "The Concept of Work in Western Thought" *Meanings of Work—Considerations for the 21st Century* 46–78.

APPLETON, ARTHUR (2000) "Environmental Labelling Schemes: WTO Law and Developing Country Implications" in Gary P Sampson and Bradnee W Chambers (eds), *Trade, Environment, and the Millennium* (Tokyo, United Nations University Press).

ARANGIO-RUIZ, GAETANO (1997) "The Federal Analogy and UN Charter Interpretation" 8 *European Journal of International Law* 1–28.

ARENDT, HANNAH (1958) *The Human Condition* (Chicago, University of Chicago Press).

ARROWSMITH, SUE and DAVIES, ARWEL (eds) (1998) *Public Procurement, Global Revolution* (London, Kluwer Law International).

AUBERT, JEAN-FRANÇOIS (1987a) "Kommentar zu Artikel 2 BV" in Jean-François Aubert, Kurt Eichenberger, Jörg-Paul Müller, René Rhinow and Dietrich Schindler (eds), *Kommentar zur Bundesverfassung der Schweizerischen Eidgenossenschaft vom 29. Mai 1874* (Zürich, Schulthess).

—— (1987b) "Kommentar zu Artikel 34ter BV" in Jean-François Aubert, Kurt Eichenberger, Jörg-Paul Müller, René Rhinow and Dietrich Schindler (eds), *Kommentar zur Bundesverfassung der Schweizerischen Eidgenossenschaft vom 29. Mai 1874* (Zürich, Schulthess).

—— (1991) "La Constitution, son contenu, son usage" 110 II *Zeitschrift für Schweizerisches Recht NF* 9–141.

AUBERT, JEAN-FRANÇOIS, EICHENBERGER, KURT, MÜLLER, JÖRG-PAUL, RHINOW, RENÉ and SCHINDLER, DIETER (eds) (1987) *Kommentar zur Bundesverfassung der Schweizerischen Eidgenossenschaft vom 29. Mai 1874* (Zürich, Schulthess).

BAEHR, PETER, FLINTERMAN, CEES and SENDERS, MIGNON (eds) (1999) *Innovation and Inspiration: Fifty Years of the Universal Declaration of Human Rights* (Amsterdam, Royal Netherlands Academy of Arts and Sciences).

BAGWELL, KYLE and STAIGER, ROBERT W (2000) "GATT-Think", *NBER Working Paper No 8005*.
—— (2001a) "National Sovereignty in the World Trading System: Labor, Environment, and the WTO" 22 *Harvard International Review* 54–59.
—— (2001b) "The WTO as a Mechanism for Securing Market Access Property Rights: Implications for Global Labor and Environmental Issues, May 2001" 15 *Journal of Economic Perspectives* 69–88.
—— (2002) *The Economics of the World Trading System* (Cambridge, MA, MIT Press).
BARENBERG, MARK (2000) "Labor Federalism in the United States: Lessons for International Labor Rights" 3 *Journal of International Economic Law* 303–29.
BARTELS, LORAND (2002) "Article XX of GATT and the Problem of Extraterritorial Jurisdiction: The Case of Trade Measures for the Protection of Human Rights" 36 *Journal of World Trade* 358–65.
—— (2003) "The WTO Enabling Clause and Positive Conditionality in the European Community's GSP Program" 6 *Journal of International Economic Law* 507–32.
BARTENHAGEN, ERIK P (1997) "The Intersection of Trade and the Environment: An Examination of the Impact of the TBT Agreement on Ecolabeling Programs" 17 *Virgina Environmental Law Journal* 51–81.
BARTOLOMEI DE LA CRUZ, HÉCTOR, SWEPSTON, LEE and VON POTOBSKY, GERALDO W (1996) *The International Labor Organization, the International Standards System and Basic Human Rights* (Boulder, Westview Press).
BASU, KAUSHIK (1999) "Child Labor: Cause, Consequence, and Cure, with Remarks on International Labor Standards" vol XXXVII *The Journal of Economic Literature* 1083–119.
—— (2001) "On the Goals of Development" in Gerald M Meier and Joseph E Stiglitz (eds), *Frontiers of Development Economics—The Future in Perspective* (Washington DC, World Bank/Oxford University Press).
BASU, KAUSHIK, HORN, HENRIK, ROMAN, LISA and SHAPIRO, JUDITH (eds) (2003) *International Labor Standards: History, Theory, and Policy Options* (Malden, MA, Blackwell Publishing).
BAUM, GREGORY (ed) (1982) *The Priority of Labor* (New York, Paulist Press).
BEAULAC, STÉPHANE (2003) "Emer de Vattel and the Externalization of Sovereignty" 5 *Journal of the History of International Law* 237–92.
BECK, ULRICH (1997) *Was ist Globalisierung* (Frankfurt aM, Suhrkamp).
BELLACE, JANICE R (2001) "The ILO Declaration on Fundamental Principles and Rights at Work" 17 *International Journal of Comparative Labour Law and Industrial Relations* 269–87.
BERCUSSON, BRIAN (2001) "Regulatory Competition in the EU System: Labour" in Daniel C Esty and Damien Geradin (eds), *Regulatory Competition and Economic Integration—Comparative Perspectives* (Oxford, Oxford University Press).
BERNHARDT, RUDOLF (ed) (1995) *Encyclopedia of Public International Law* (Amsterdam, North-Holland Publishing Company).
BETCHERMAN, GORDAN and ISLAM, RIZWANUL (eds) (2001) *East Asian Labor Markets and Economic Crisis: Impacts, Responses, and Lessons* (Washington DC, World Bank, International Labour Office).
BHAGWATI, JAGDISH and HIRSCH, MATHIAS (eds) (1998) *The Uruguay Round and Beyond: Essays in Honour of Arthur Dunkel* (Ann Arbor, Springer Verlag).

BHAGWATI, JAGDISH and PATRICK, HUGH T (eds) (1990) *Aggressive Unilateralism* (Ann Arbor, University of Michigan Press)

BIAGGINI, GIOVANNI (1996) 'schweizerische und europäische Wirtschaftsverfassung im Vergleich—Über Strukturprobleme zweier wettbewerbsorientierter Wirtschaftsverfassungen" 97 *Schweizerisches Zentralblatt für Staats- und Verwaltungsrecht* 49–82.

—— (1999) "Das Verhältnis der Schweiz zur Internationalen Gemeinschaft" 8 *Aktuelle Juristische Praxis*, 722–29.

—— (2000) "Die Idee der Verfassung—Neuausrichtung im Zeitalter der Globalisierung?" 119 *Zeitschrift für Schweizerisches Recht NF* 445–76.

BIAGGINI, GIOVANNI, MÜLLER, GEORG, RICHLI, PAUL, ZIMMERLI, ULRICH (2005) *Wirtschaftsverwaltungsrecht des Bundes*, 4th edn (Basel, Genf, München, Helbling & Lichtenhahn)

BLACK, CHARLES (1999) *A New Birth of Freedom* (New Haven, Yale University Press).

BLACK, JULIA (2002) "Critical Reflections on Regulation" 27 *Australian Journal of Legal Philosophy* 1–35.

BLACKETT, ADELLE (1999) "Wither Social Clause? Human Rights, Trade Theory and Treaty Interpretation" 31 *Columbia Human Rights Law Review* 1–80.

BLANK, ANNET and GABRIELLE, MARCEAU (1997) "A History of Multilateral Negotiations on Procurement: From ITO to WTO" in Bernard M Hoekman and Petros C Mavroidis (eds), *Law and Policy in Public Purchasing—The WTO Agreement on Government Procurement* (Ann Arbor, University of Michigan Press).

BLANPAIN, ROGER (1999) "European Social Policies: One Bridge too Short" 20 *Comparative Labor Law and Policy Journal* 497–504.

BODIN, JEAN (1977) *Les six livres de la République (1577)* (Aalen, Scientia).

BORDO, MICHAEL D (1993) "The Gold Standard, Bretton Woods and Other Monetary Regimes: A Historical Appraisal" 75 *Review, Federal Reserve Bank, St Louis* 123–99.

—— (2002) "Globalization in Historical Perspective" 37 *Business Economics* 20–29.

BOUGHTON, JAMES M (2000) "The IMF and the Silent Revolution—Global Finance and Development in the 1980s" (Washington DC, International Monetary Fund).

—— (2001) *Silent Revolution: The International Monetary Fund, 1979–1989* (Washington DC, International Monetary Fund).

BRADLOW, DANIEL D (1996) 'Symposium: Social Justice and Development: Critical Issues Facing the Bretton Woods System: The World Bank, the IMF and Human Rights" 6 *Transnational Law & Contemporary Problems* 47–90.

—— (2001) "Stuffing New Wine into Old Bottles: The Troubling Case of the IMF" 3 *Journal of International Banking Regulation* 9–36.

BRANDTNER, BARBARA and ALLAN, ROSAS (1999) "Trade Preferences and Human Rights" in Philip Alston (ed), *The EU and Human Rights* (Oxford, Oxford University Press).

BRATTON, WILLIAM W, MCCAHERY, JOSEPH, PICCIOTTO, SOL and SCOTT, CRAIG (eds) (1996) *International Regulatory Competition and Co-Ordination* (Oxford, Clarendon Press).

BREINING-KAUFMANN, CHRISTINE (1991) *Hunger als Rechtsproblem: Völkerrechtliche Aspekte eines Rechtes auf Nahrung* (Zürich, Schulthess).

—— (1992) "Zur Vereinbarkeit von EWR–Vertrag und EG–Recht" 2 *Aktuelle Juristische Praxis* 639–41.

—— (1994) "Deregulierung und Europaverträglichkeit als Maximen der Gesetzgebung im Wirtschaftsrecht" in Hans-Ulrich Walder, Tobias Jaag and Dieter Zobl (eds), *Aspekte des Wirtschaftsrechts, Festgabe zum Schweizerischen Juristentag 1994* (Zürich, Schulthess).

—— (2001) "Ein Sieg für die Umwelt? Der Entscheid der WTO im Asbest–Streit zwischen Kanada und der Europäischen Union" 10 *Aktuelle Juristische Praxis* 669–80.

—— (2005) "The Legal Matrix of Trade and Human Rights Law: State Obligations versus Private Rights and Obligations" in Thomas Cottier, Joost Pauwelyn and Elisabeth Bürgi (eds), *Human Rights and International Trade* (Oxford, Oxford University Press).

BREINING-KAUFMANN, CHRISTINE, WEBER, ROLF H. (2007) Reconciling Liberalized Trade in Financial Services and Domestic Regulation, in Mads Andenas and Kern Alexander (eds), *The World Trade Organization and Trade in Services* (Den Haag, Brill and Martinus Nijhof Publishers).

BRÖHMER, JÜRGEN (1999) "Das Europäische Parlament: Echtes Legislativorgan oder blosses Hilfsorgan im legislativen Prozess? Zur Matthews–Entscheidung des Europäischen Gerichtshofs für Menschenrechte" 2 *Zeitschrift für europarechtliche Studien* 197–217.

BRUPBACHER, STEFAN (2002) *Fundamentale Arbeitsnormen der Internationalen Arbeitsorganisation: Eine Grundlage der sozialen Dimension der Globalisierung* (Bern, Stämpfli Verlag).

BUCHER, EUGEN, CANARIS, CLAUS-WILHELM, HONSELL, HEINRICH and KOLLER, THOMAS (eds) (2005) *Norm und Wirkung: Beiträge zum Privat– und Wirtschaftsrecht aus heutiger und historischer Perspektive. Festschrift für Wolfgang Wiegand zum 65. Geburtstag* (Bern, Stämpfli Verlag).

BUCHANAN, JAMES M (1975) *The Limits of Liberty: Between Anarchy and Leviathan* (Chicago, University of Chicago Press).

—— (1987) "Constitutional Economics" in Peter Newman, John Eatwell and Murray Milgate (eds), *The New Palgrave: A Dictionary of Economics*, vol 1, 585–588 (London, Palgrave Macmillan).

BUERGENTHAL, THOMAS (1999) "The World Bank and Human Rights" in Edith Brown Weiss, Andres Rigo Sureda and Laurence Boisson de Chazournes (eds), *The World Bank, International Financial Institutions, and the Development of International Law: A Symposium Held in Honor of Dr Ibrahim F I Shihata* (Washington DC, American Society of International Law).

BYERS, MICHAEL (ed) (2000) *The Role of Law in International Politics: Essays in International Relations and International Law* (Oxford, Oxford University Press).

BYRNES, ANDREW (1997) "Slow and Steady Wins the Race? The Development of an Optional Protocol to the Women's Convention" 91 *American Society of International Law, Proceedings* 383.

CASS, DEBORAH Z (2001) "The 'Constitutionalization' of International Trade Law: Judicial Norm-generation as the Engine of Constitutional Development in International Trade" 12 *European Journal of International Law* 39–75.

—— (2005) *The Constitutionalization of the World Trade Organization: Legitimacy, Democracy, and Community in the International Trading System* (Oxford, Oxford University Press).

CHARLESWORTH, HILARY (1998) "The Mid-life Crisis of the Universal Declaration of Human Rights" 55 *Washington & Lee Law Review* 781–96.

CHARLESWORTH, HILARY and CHINKIN, CHRISTINE (2000) *The Boundaries of International Law: A Feminist Analysis* (Manchester, Juris Publishing).

CHARNOVITZ, STEVE (1987) "The Influence of International Labor Standards on the World Trading System: A Historical Overview" 126 *International Labour Review* 565–84.

—— (1997) "Trade, Employment and Labour Standards: The OECD Study and Recent Developments in the Trade and Labour Standards Debate" 11 *Temple International and Comparative Law Journal* 131–63.

—— (1998) "The Moral Exception in Trade Policy" 38 *Virginia Journal of International Law* 689–745.

—— (2001) "Rethinking WTO Trade Sanctions" 95 *American Journal of International Law* 792–832.

CHARNOVITZ, STEVE ((2002a) "WTO Cosmopolitics" 34 *New York University Journal of International Law and Politics* 299–354.

—— (2002b) "The Law of Environmental 'PPMs' in the WTO: Debunking the Myth of Illegality" 27 *Yale Journal of International Law* 59–110.

CHARNOVITZ, STEVE, BARTELS, LORAND, HOWSE, ROBERT, BRADLEY, JANE, PAUWELYN, JOOST and REGAN, DONALD (2004) "The Appellate Body's GSP Decision (Internet Roundtable)" 3 *World Trade Review* 239–65.

CHARNY, DAVID (2000) "Regulatory Competition and the Global Coordination of Labor Standards" 3 *Journal of International Economic Law* 281–302.

CHAYES, ABRAM and CHAYES, ANTONIA HANDLER (1995) *The New Sovereignty* (Cambridge, Cambridge University Press).

CHEMERINSKY, ERWIN (1997) *Constitutional Law—Principles and Policies* (New York, Aspen Publishers).

CHINKIN, CHRISTINE (1999) "A Critique of the Public/Private Dimension" 10 *European Journal of International Law* 387–95.

—— (2001) "The United Nations Decade for the Elimination of Poverty: What Role for International Law?" in Michael D A Freeman (ed), *Current Legal Problems* (Oxford, Oxford University Press).

CIOCARI, JOHN D (2000) "The Lawful Scope of Human Rights Criteria in World Bank Credit Decisions: An Interpretive Analysis of the IBRD and IDA Articles of Agreement" 33 *Cornell International Law Journal* 331–71.

CLAPHAM, ANDREW (2006), *Human Rights Obligations of Non-State Actors* (Oxford: Oxford University Press)

CLAPHAM, ANDREW and JERBI, SCOTT (2001) "Categories of Corporate Complicity in Human Rights Abuses" 24 *Hastings International and Comparative Law Review* 339–49.

CLAUSSEN, DETLEF, NEGT, OSKAR and WERZ, MICHAEL (eds) (2001) *Hannoversche Schriften 4: Philosophie und Empirie* (Frankfurt aM, Verlag Neue Kritik).

CLEVELAND, SARAH H (1998) "Global Labor Rights and the Alien Tort Claims Act" 76 *Texas Law Review* 1533–79.

—— (2001) "Norm Internalization and US Economic Sanctions" 26 *Yale Journal of International Law* 1–92.

—— (2002) "Human Rights Sanctions and International Trade: A Theory of Compatibility" 5 *Journal of International Economic Law* 133–89.

—— (2003) "Why International Labor Standards?" in Robert J Flanagan and William B Gould (eds), *International Labor Standards: Globalization, Trade, and Public Policy* (Stanford, Stanford University Press).

Commission on Global Governance (1995) *Our Global Neighborhood: The Report of the Commission on Global Governance* (Oxford, Oxford University Press).

Committee on Economic, Social and Cultural Rights (1998) "Statement on Globalization and Economic, Social and Cultural Rights", May 1998.

COMPA, LANCE A (1995) "Going Multilateral: The Evolution of US Hemispheric Labor Rights

Policy under GSP and NAFTA" 10 *Connecticut Journal of International Law* 337–64.

COMPA, LANCE A and DIAMOND, STEPHEN F (eds) (1996) *Human Rights, Labor Rights and International Trade* (Philadelphia, University of Pennsylvania Press).

CONAGHAN, JOANNE, FISCHL, RICHARD MICHAEL and KLARE, KARL E (eds) (2002) *Labour Law in an Era of Globalization: Transformative Practices and Possibilities* (Oxford, Oxford University Press).

CONNOR, TIM (2001) "Still Waiting for Nike to Do It—Nike's Labor Practices in the Three Years since CEO Phil Knight's Speech to the National Press Club" (San Francisco, Global Exchange)

COOTER, ROBERT and ULEN, THOMAS (2004) *Law and Economics*, 4th edn (Boston, Pearson Addison Wesley).

CORNIA, GIOVANNI ANDREA, JOLLY, RICHARD and STEWART, FRANCES (1987) *Adjustment with a Human Face: Protecting the Vulnerable and Promoting Growth. A Study by UNICEF* (Oxford, Oxford University Press).

COTESTA, VITTORIO (1999) *Sociologia di conflitti etnici—Razzismo, immigrazione e società multiculturale* (Bari, Laterza).

COTTIER, THOMAS (1996) "The Challenge of Regionalization and Preferential Relations in World Trade Law and Policy" 2 *European Foreign Affairs Review* 149–67.

—— (1997) "Die Globalisierung des Rechts—Herausforderungen für Praxis, Ausbildung und Forschung" 133 *Zeitschrift des Bernischen Juristenvereins* 217–41.

—— (2000) "Limits to International Trade: The Constitutional Challenge" 94 *American Society of International Law Proceedings* 220–22.

—— (2002) "Trade and Human Rights: A Relationship to Discover" 5 *Journal of International Economic Law* 111–32.

COTTIER, THOMAS, ACHERMANN, ALBERTO, WÜGER, DANIEL and ZELLWEGER, VALENTIN (eds) (2001) *Der Staatsvertrag im schweizerischen Verfassungsrecht: Beiträge zu Verhältnis und methodischer Angleichung von Völkerrecht und Bundesrecht* (Bern, Stämpfli Verlag).

COTTIER, THOMAS and GERMANN, CHRISTOPHE (2002) "Die Partizipation bei der Aushandlung neuer völkerrechtlicher Bindungen: verfassungsrechtliche Grundlagen und Perspektiven" in Daniel Thürer, Jean–François Aubert and Jörg Paul Müller (eds), *Verfassungsrecht der Schweiz* (Zürich, Schulthess).

COTTIER, THOMAS and HERTIG, MAYA (2000) "Das Völkerrecht in der neuen Bundesverfassung: Stellung und Auswirkungen" in Ulrich Zimmerli (ed), *Die neue Bundesverfassung, Konsequenzen für Praxis und Wissenschaft, Berner Tage für die juristische Praxis 1999* (Bern, Stämpfli Verlag).

—— (2003) "The Prospects of 21st-Century Constitutionalism" 7 *Max Planck Yearbook of United Nations Law* 261–328.

COTTIER, THOMAS and OESCH, MATTHIAS (eds) (2002) *Die sektoriellen Abkommen Schweiz—EG, Berner Tage für die juristische Praxis* (Bern, Stämpfli Verlag).

COTTIER, THOMAS, PAUWELYN, JOOST and BÜRGI, ELISABETH (eds) (2005) *Human Rights and International Trade* (Oxford, Oxford University Press).

Council of Europe, European Committee for Equality (1998) *Gender Mainstreaming: Conceptual Framework, Methodology and Presentation of Good Practice* (Strasbourg, Council of Europe).

COXSON, CHRISTOPHER R (1999) "The 1998 ILO Declaration on Fundamental Principles and Rights at Work: Promoting Labor Law Reforms Through the ILO as an

Alternative to Imposing Coercive Trade Sanctions" 17 *Dickinson Journal of International Law* 469–504.

CRAVEN, MATTHEW (1998) *The International Covenant on Economic, Social and Cultural Rights—A Perspective on its Development* (Oxford, Clarendon Press).

—— (2002) "Humanitarianism and the Quest for Smarter Sanctions" 13 *European Journal of International Law* 43–61.

CRAWFORD, JAMES (1997) "The Charter of the United Nations as a Constitution" in Hazel Fox (ed), *The Changing Constitution of the United Nations* (London, British Institute of International and Comparative Law).

CUKIERMAN, ALEX, KALAITZIDAKIS, PANTELIS, SUMMERS, LAWRENCE H and WEBB, STEVEN B (1993) "Central Bank Independence, Growth Investment and Real Rates" 39 *Carnegie-Rochester Conference Series on Public Policy* 95–140.

CUTS, Centre for International Trade, Economics & Environment (1999) "Eradicating Child-Labour while Saving the Child—Who Will Pay the Costs?" 5 *Briefing Papers.*

D'ANTONA, MASSIMO (2002) "Labour Law at the Century's End: An Identity Crisis?" in Joanne Conaghan, Richard Michael Fischl and Karl E Klare (eds), *Labour Law in an Era of Globalization: Transformative Practices and Possibilities* (Oxford, Oxford University Press).

DANKWA VICTOR, FLINTERMAN, CEES and LECKIE, SCOTT (1998) "Commentary to the Maastricht Guidelines on Violations of Economic, Social and Cultural Rights" 20 *Human Rights Quarterly* 705–29.

DARROW, MAC (2003) *Between Light and Shadow: The World Bank, the International Monetary Fund and International Human Rights Law* (Oxford, Hart Publishing).

DAVIES, ANNE C L (2005) "Should the EU Have the Power to Set Minimum Standards for Collective Labour Rights in the Member States?" in Philip Alston (ed), *Labour Rights as Human Rights* (Oxford, Oxford University Press).

DE BÚRCA, GRÁINNE and Scott, Joanne (eds) (2001) *The EU and the WTO—Legal and Constitutional Issues* (Oxford, Hart Publishing).

DELBRÜCK, JOST (2001) "Structural Changes in the International System and its Legal Order: International Law in the Era of Globalization" 11 *Schweizerische Zeitschrift für Internationales und Europäisches Recht* 1–36.

DETRICK, SHARON (1999) *A Commentary on the United Nations Convention on the Rights of the Child* (The Hague, Martinus Nijhoff Publishers).

DEUTSCHE GESELLSCHAFT FÜR VÖLKERRECHT (ed) (1998) *Die Wirkungskraft der Grundrechte bei Fällen mit Auslandsbezug* (Heidelberg, Verlag CF Müller).

DILLER, JANELLE M (1999) "A Social Conscience in the Global Marketplace? Labour Dimensions of Codes of Conduct, Social Labelling and Investor Initiatives" 138 *International Labour Review* 99–129.

DILLER, JANELLE M and LEVY, DAVID A (1997) "Child Labor, Trade and Investment: Toward the Harmonization of International Law" 91 *American Journal of International Law* 663–96.

DOMMEN, CAROLINE (2002) "Raising Human Rights Concerns in the World Trade Organization: Actors, Processes and Possible Strategies" 24 *Human Rights Quarterly* 1–50.

DOXEY, MARGARET (1999) "United Nations Sanctions: Lessons of Experience" in Swiss Federal Office for Foreign Economic Affairs (seco) (ed), *2nd Interlaken Seminar on Targeting United Nations Financial Sanctions, 29–31 March 1999* (Bern, Department of Economy).

DRAHOS, PETER (2004) "The Regulation of Public Goods" 7 *Journal of International Economic Law* 321–39.

DRIESEN, DAVID M (2001) "What is Free Trade? The Real Issue Lurking behind the Trade and Environment Debate" 41 *Virginia Journal of International Law* 279–368.

DUNNING, HAROLD (1998) "The Origins of Convention No 87 on Freedom of Association and the Right to Organize" 137 *International Labour Review* 149–67.

DUNOFF, JEFFREY L and TRACHTMAN, JOEL P (1999) "Economic Analysis of International Law" 24 *Yale Journal of International Law* 1–59.

DUPUY, PIERRE-MARIE (1999) "The Danger of Fragmentation or Unification of the International Legal System and the International Court of Justice" 31 *New York University Journal of International Law and Politics* 791–807.

DUPUY, RENÉ-JEAN (ed) (1999) *Mélanges en l"honneur de Nicolas Valticos—Droit et justice* (Paris, Pedone).

DUVIGNEAU, JOHANN LUDWIG (2001) "Die Konstitutionalisierung des WTO-Rechts" 56 *Aussenwirtschaft* 295–325.

EUROPEAN COMMUNITIES COMMISSION (2001) Promoting Core Labour Standards and Improving Social Governance in the Context of Globalisation—Communication from the Commission to the Council, the European Parliament and the Economic and Social Committee, COM(2001) 416 final, 2001.

EHLERMANN, CLAUS-DIETER (2002) "Six Years on the Bench of the 'World Trade Court': Some Personal Experiences as a Member of the Appellate Body of the World Trade Organization" 36 *Journal of World Trade* 605–39.

EHRENZELLER, BERNHARD (1999) "Möglichkeiten und Grenzen der direkten Demokratie" *Basler Juristische Mitteilungen (BJM)* 65–91.

EICHENBERGER, KURT (1991) "Sinn und Bedeutung einer Verfassung" 110 II *Zeitschrift für Schweizerisches Recht NF* 143–273.

EIDE, ASBJØRN (1992) "Article 25" in Eide, Asbjørn, Alfredsson, Gudmundur, Melander, Göran, Rehof, Lars Adam and Rosas, Allan (eds), *The Universal Declaration of Human Rights: A Commentary* (Oslo, Scandinavian University Press).

—— (1998) "Freedom from Want: Taking Economic and Social Rights Seriously" in Barend Van der Heijden and Bahia Tahzib-Lie (eds), *Reflections on the Universal Declaration of Human Rights* (The Hague, Martinus Nijhoff Publishers).

EIDE, ASBJØRN, ALFREDSSON, GUDMUNDUR, MELANDER, GÖRAN, REHOF, LARS ADAM and ROSAS, ALLAN (eds) (1992) *The Universal Declaration of Human Rights: A Commentary* (Oslo, Scandinavian University Press).

ELLIOTT, KIMBERLY ANN (1999) "Analysing the Effects of Targeted Financial Sanctions" in Swiss Federal Office for Foreign Economic Affairs (seco) (eds), *2nd Interlaken Seminar on Targeting United Nations Financial Sanctions, 29–31 March, 1999* (Bern, Department of Economy).

ELSTER, JON (2000) *Ulysses Unbound* (Cambridge, Cambridge University Press).

ENGERMAN, STANLEY L (2003) "The History and Political Economy of International Labor Standards" in Kaushik Basu, Henrik Horn, Lisa Román and Judith Shapiro (eds), *International Labor Standards: History, Theory and Policy Options* (Malden, MA, Blackwell).

ENGLE, KAREN (2000) "Culture and Human Rights: The Asian Value Debate in Context" 32 *New York University Journal of International Law and Politics* 291–333.

ESTY, DANIEL C and GERADIN, DAMIEN (eds) (2001) *Regulatory Competition and Economic Integration—Comparative Perspectives* (Oxford, Oxford University Press).

FALLON, PETER and TZANNATOS, ZAFIRIS (1998) *Child Labor: Issues and Directions for the World Bank* (Washington DC, World Bank).

FASSBENDER, BARDO (1998) "The United Nations Charter as Constitution of the International Community" 36 *Columbia Journal of Transnational Law* 529–619.

FAWCETT, JAMES E S (1960) "The Place of Law in an International Organization" 36 *British Yearbook of International Law* 321–42.

FAZIOLI, FABRIZIO (ed) (1996) *Il lavoro di domani—Le incognite e le speranze di una profonda trasformazione* (Bellinzona, Edizioni Casagrande).

FEDDERSEN, CHRISTOPH T (1998) "Focusing on Substantive Law in International Economic Relations: The Public Morals of GATT's Article XX(a) and 'Conventional' Rules of Interpretation" 7 *Minnesota Journal of Global Trade* 75–122.

FEDDERSEN, CHRISTOPH T (2002) *Der ordre public in der WTO: Auslegung und Bedeutung des Art. XX lit. a) GATT im Rahmen der WTO-Streitbeilegung* (Berlin, Duncker & Humblot).

FINE, SIDNEY (1969) *Sit-down: The General Motors strike of 1936–1937* (Ann Arbor, University of Michigan Press).

FISCHER, STANLEY (ed) (2004a) *IMF Essays from a Time of Crisis: The International Financial System, Stabilitzation, and Development* (Cambridge, MA, MIT Press).

—— (2004b) "ABCDE: Past Ten Years, Next Ten Years. Annual World Bank Conference on Development Economics 1998" in Stanley Fischer (ed), *IMF Essays from a Time of Crisis: The International Financial System, Stabilization and Development* (Cambridge, MA, MIT Press).

FLANAGAN, ROBERT J and GOULD, WILLIAM B (eds) (2003) *International Labor Standards: Globalization, Trade, and Public Policy* (Stanford, Stanford Law and Politics).

FLEINER, FRITZ (ed) (1941a) *Ausgewählte Schriften und Reden* (Zürich, Schulthess).

—— (1941b) "Zentralismus und Föderalismus in der Schweiz" in Fritz Fleiner (ed), *Ausgewählte Schriften und Reden* (Zürich, Schulthess).

FOX, HAZL (ed) (1997) *The Changing Constitution of the United Nations* (London, British Institute of International and Comparative Law).

FRANCK, THOMAS M (1992) "The Emerging Right to Democratic Governance" 86 *American Journal of International Law* 46–91.

—— (1995) *Fairness in International Law and Institutions* (Oxford, Clarendon Press).

FREDMAN, SANDRA, MCCRUDDEN, CHRISTOPHER and FREEDLAND, MARK (2000) "An EU Charter of Fundamental Rights" *Public Law* 178–86.

FREEMAN, MICHAEL (1999) "Fifty Years of Development of the Concept and Contents of Human Rights" in Peter Baehr, Cees Flinterman and Mignon Senders (eds), *Innovation and Inspiration: Fifty Years of the Universal Declaration of Human Rights* (Amsterdam, Royal Netherlands Academy of Arts and Sciences).

FREY, BRUNO S (1984) "The Public Choice View of International Political Economy" 38 *International Organizations* 199–223.

FRIEDMAN, THOMAS L (2000) *The Lexus and the Olive Tree* (New York, Anchor).

FRIEDMANN, WOLFGANG GASTON (1964) *The Changing Structure of International Law* (New York, Columbia University Press).

FROWEIN, JOCHEN A and PEUKERT, WOLFGANG (1996) *Europäische Menschenrechtskonvention: EMRK-Kommentar* (Kehl am Rhein, Strassbourg).

FUKUYAMA, FRANCIS (1992) *The End of History and the Last Man* (New York, Free Press).

FULLER, LON L (1969) *The Morality of Law*, revised edn (New Haven, Yale University Press).

GERNIGON, BERNARD, ODERO, ALBERTO and GUIDO, HORACIO (2000) "ILO Principles Concerning Collective Bargaining" 139 *International Labour Review* 33–55.

GERSTENBERG, OLIVER (2002) "Expanding the constitution Beyond the Court: The Case of Euro-Constitutionalism" 8 *European Law Journal* 172–92.

GHAI, YASH (1995) "Human Rights and Governance: The Asia Debate" 15 *Australian Yearbook of International Law* 1–34.

GHAZI SHARIAT PANAHI, BAHRAM (2005) The IMF, the World Bank Group, and the Question of Human Rghts (Ardsley, NY Transnational Publishers).

GIANVITI, FRANÇOIS (2002), Economic, Social and Cultral Rights and the International Monetary Fund, paper presented at the IMF Seminar on Current Developments in Monetary and Financial Law, Washington D.C., May 7–17, 2002. Available at www.imf.org, Washington D.C.

GIDDENS, ANTHONY (1990) *The Consequences of Modernity* (Stanford, Stanford University Press).

GOLD, JOSEPH (1996) *Interpretation: The IMF and International Law* (Boston, Kluwer Law International).

GOLDSMITH, JACK L and POSNER, ERIC A (1999) "A Theory of Customary International Law" 66 *University of Chicago Law Review* 1113–77.

GOLUB, STEPHEN S (1997) "International Labor Standards and International Trade", *IMF Working Paper WP/97/37.*

GORZ, ANDRÉ (1989) *Critique of Economic Reason* (London, Verso).

—— (1999a) "A New Task for the Unions: The Liberation of Time from Work" in Roland Munck and Peter Waterman (eds), *Labour Worldwide in the Era of Globalization* (New York, Macmillan).

—— (1999b) *Reclaiming Work—Beyond the Wage-Based Society* (Cambridge, Polity Press).

GYGI, FRITZ and RICHLI, PAUL (1997) *Wirtschaftsverfassungsrecht* (Bern, Stämpfli Verlag).

GYSIN, CHARLOTTE (1999) *Der Schutz des Existenzminimums in der Schweiz* (Basel, Helbing & Lichtenhahn).

HABERMAS, JÜRGEN (1992) *Faktizität und Geltung—Beiträge zur Diskurstheorie des Rechts und des demokratischen Rechtsstaates* (Frankfurt aM, Suhrkamp).

—— (1998) *Die postnationale Konstellation* (Frankfurt aM, Suhrkamp).

HAFNER, GERHARD (2002) "Risks Ensuing from Fragmentation of International Law", *Official Records of the United Nations General Assembly*, 55th Session Supplement No 10 (A/55/10), Annex, 321–29.

HAFNER, GERHARD, BÖCKSTIEGEL, KARL-HEINZ, FOLZ, HANS-ERNST and MÖSSNER, JÖRG MANFRED (1998) *Liber amicorum Professor Ignaz Seidl-Hohenveldern in Honour of His 80th Birthday* (The Hague, Kluwer Law International).

HAGGARD, STEPHAN (2000) *The Political Economy of the Asian Financial Crisis* (Washington DC, Institute for International Economics).

HALBERSTAM, DANIEL (2001a) "Comparative Federalism and the Issue of Commandeering" in Kalypso Nicolaidis and Robert Howse (eds), *The Federal Vision: Legitimacy and Levels of Governance in the US and the EU* (Oxford, Oxford University Press).

—— (2001b) "The Foreign Affairs of Federal Systems: A National Perspective on the Benefits of State Participation" 46 *Villanova Law Review* 1015–68.

HALL, STUART, HELD, DAVID and MCGREW, TONY (eds) (1992) *Modernity and its Futures* (Cambridge, Polity Press).

HALLER, WALTER and KÖLZ, ALFRED (2004) *Allgemeines Staatsrecht*, 3rd edn (Basel, Helbing & Lichtenhahn).

HANDL, GUNTHER (1998) "The Legal Mandate of Multilateral Development Banks as Agents for Change toward Sustainable Development" 92 *American Journal of International Law* 642–65.

HANSKI, RAIJA and SUKSI, MARKKU (eds) (1999) *An Introduction to the International Protection of Human Rights* (Turku, Abo Akademi University).

HARVEY, COLIN J (ed) (2005) *Human Rights in the Community: Rights as Agents for Change* (Oxford, Hart Publishing).

HATHAWAY, OONA A (2003a) "Do Human Rights Treaties Make a Difference?" 111 *Yale Law Journal* 1935–2042.

—— (2003b) "Testing Conventional Wisdom" 14 *European Journal of International Law* 185–200.

HÄBERLE, PETER (1984) "Vielfalt der Property Rights und der verfassungsrechtliche Eigentumsbegriff" in Manfred Neumann (ed), *Ansprüche, Eigentums- und Verfügungsrechte, Arbeitstagung des Vereins für Socialpolitik in Basel 1983* (Basel, Duncker & Humblot).

HÄBERLE, PETER (1992) *Verfassungsrechtliche Ewigkeitsklauseln als verfassungsstaatliche Identitätsgarantien. Rechtsvergleichung im Kraftfeld des Verfassungsstaates* (Berlin, Duncker & Humblot).

HÄFELIN, ULRICH and HALLER, WALTER (2005) *Schweizerisches Bundesstaatsrecht* 6th edn (Zürich, Schulthess).

HEAD, JOHN W (1998) "Lessons from the Asian Financial Crisis: The Role of the IMF and the United States" 7 *Kansas Journal of Law and Public Policy* 70–99.

—— (2005) *The Future of the Global Economic Organizations: An Evaluation of Criticisms Leveled at the IMF, the Multilateral Development Banks, and the WTO* (Ardsley, NY, Transnational Publishers).

HEISKANEN, VEIJO (2004) "The Regulatory Philosophy of International Trade Law" 38 *Journal of World Trade* 1–36.

HELD, DAVID, MCGREW, ANTHONY, GOLDBLATT, DAVID and PERRATON, JONATHAN (1999) *Global Transformations—Politics, Economics and Culture* (Cambridge, Polity Press).

HENCKAERTS, JEAN-MARIE and DOSWALD-BECK, LOUISE (2005) *Customary International Humanitarian Law* (Cambridge, Cambridge University Press).

HENKIN, LOUIS (1978) *The Rights of Man Today* (Boulder, Westview Press).

HEPPLE, BOB (ed) (2002) *Social and Labour Rights in a Global Context: International and Comparative Perspectives* (Cambridge, Cambridge University Press).

—— (2005) *Labour Laws and Global Trade* (Oxford, Hart Publishing).

HESSE, HELMUT (1994) "Moral der Stabilitätspolitik" in Helmut Hesse and Otmar Issing (eds), *Geld und Moral* (München, Vahlen).

HESSE, HELMUT and OTMAR, ISSING (eds) (1994) *Geld und Moral* (München, Vahlen).

HILF, MEINHARD (2001) "Power, Rules and Principles—Which Orientation for the WTO/GATT Law?" 4 *Journal of International Economic Law* 111–30.

HINSCH, WILFRIED (2002) *Gerechtfertigte Ungleichheiten: Grundsätze sozialer Gerechtigkeit* (Berlin, de Gruyter).

HIRST, PAUL and THOMPSON, GRAHAME (1999) "Globalization—Frequently Asked Questions and Some Surprising Answers" in Peter Leisink (ed), *Globalization and Labour Relations* (Cheltenham, Edward Elgar Publishing).

HOBE, STEPHAN (2002) "The Era of Globalisation as a Challenge to International Law" 40 *Duquesne Law Review* 655–65.

HOEKMAN, BERNARD M and MAVROIDIS, PETROS C (eds) (1997a) *Law and Policy in Public Purchasing—The WTO Agreement on Government Procurement* (Ann Arbor, University of Michigan Press).

—— (1997b) "Basic Elements of the Agreement on Government Procurement" in Bernard M Hoekman and Petros C Mavroidis (eds), *Law and Policy in Public Purchasing—The WTO Agreement on Government Procurement* (Ann Arbor, University of Michigan Press).

HOFSTADTER, DOUGLAS R (1985) *Gödel, Escher, Bach* (Stuttgart, Klett-Cotta).

HOLTON, ROBERT (1998) *Globalization and the Nation-state* (New York, Macmillan Press).

HOLZMANN, ROBERT and JORGENSEN, STEEN (1999) "Social Protection as Social Risk Management: Conceptual Underpinnings for the Social Protection Sector Strategy Paper" 11 *Journal of International Development* 1005–27.

—— (2001) "Social Risk Management: A New Conceptual Framework for Social Protection, and Beyond" 8 *International Tax and Public Finance* 529–56.

HORTON, SUSAN and MAZUMDAR, DIPAK (2001) "Vulnerable Groups and the Labor Market: The Aftermath of the Asian Financial Crisis" in Gordan Betcherman and Rizwanul Islam (eds), *East Asian Labor Markets and Economic Crisis: Impacts, Responses, and Lessons* (Washington DC, World Bank, International Labour Office).

HOWSE, ROBERT (1999) "The World Trade Organization and the Protection of Workers' Rights" 3 *The Journal of Small & Emerging Business Law* 131–72.

—— (2002a) "The Road to Baghdad is Paved with Good Intentions" 13 *European Journal of International Law* 89–92.

—— (2002b) "Human Rights in the WTO: Whose Rights, What Humanity? Comment on Petersmann" 13 *European Journal of International Law* 651–59.

—— (2003a) "India's WTO Challenge to Drug Enforcement Conditions in the European Community Generalized System of Preferences" 4 *Chicago Journal of International Law* 385–405.

—— (2003b) "Back to Court after *Shrimp/Turtle*? Almost But Not Quite Yet: India's Short-lived Challenge to Labor and Environmental Exceptions in the European Union's Generalized System of Preferences" 18 *American University International Law Review* 1333–81.

HOWSE, ROBERT and LANGILLE, BRIAN (2000) "The World Trade Organization and Labour Rights", paper presented at the Conference on Trade and Labor Rights, University of Wisconsin, November 2000.

HOWSE, ROBERT and MUTUA, MAKAU (2000) *Protecting Human Rights in a Global Economy: Challenges for the World Trade Organization* (Montreal, Rights & Democracy International Centre for Human Rights and Democratic Development).

HOWSE, ROBERT and NICOLAIDIS, KALYPSO (2001) "Legitimacy and Global Governance: Why Constitutionalizing the WTO is a Step Too Far" in Roger B Porter, Pierre Sauvé, Arvind Subramanian and Beviglia Americo Zampetti (eds), *Efficiency, Equity and Legitimacy: The Multilateral Trading System at the Millennium* (Washington DC, Brookings Institution Press).

HOWSE, ROBERT and REGAN, DONALD (2000) "The Product/Process Distinction—An Illusory Basis for Disciplining Unilateralism in Trade Policy" 11 *European Journal of International Law* 249–89.

HOWSE, ROBERT and TREBILCOCK, MICHAEL (1996) "The Fair Trade–Free Trade Debate: Trade, Labor, and the Environment" 16 *International Review of Law and Economics* 61–79.

HOWSE, ROBERT and TUERK, ELISABETH (2001) "The WTO Impact on Internal Regulations—A Case Study of the *Canada—EC Asbestos* Dispute" in Gráinne De Búrca and Joanne Scott (eds), *The EU and the WTO—Legal and Constitutional Issues* (Oxford, Hart Publishing).

HUBER, EVELYNE, RUESCHEMEYER, DIETRICH and STEPHENS, JOHN D (1993) "The Impact of Economic Development on Democracy" 7 *Journal of Economic Perspectives* 71–85.

HUDEC, ROBERT E (1998a) "GATT/WTO Constraints on National Regulation: Requiem for an 'Aim and Effects' Test" 32 *International Lawyer* 619–48.

—— (1998b) "The Role of the GATT Secretariat in the Evolution of the WTO Dispute Settlement Procedure" in Jagdish Bhagwati and Mathias Hirsch (eds), *The Uruguay Round and Beyond: Essays in Honour of Arthur Dunkel* (Ann Arbor, Springer Verlag).

—— (1999) "The New WTO Dispute Settlement Procedure: An Overview of the First Three Years" 8 *Minnesota Journal of Global Trade* 1–53.

HUGHES, CHRISTOPHER W (2000) "Globalisation and Security in the Asia-Pacific: An Initial Investigation", CSGR Working Paper No 61/00.

Human Rights Watch (2001) "Trading Away Rights—The Unfulfilled Promise of NAFTA's Labor Side Agreement" *Human Rights Watch Publication* 13 No 2 (B), April 2001.

HUNT, JOHN GABRIEL (eds) (1995) *The Essential Franklin Delano Roosevelt* (New York, Gramercy).

ICHRP (International Council on Human Rights Policy) (2002) *Beyond Voluntarism—Human Rights and the Developing International Legal Obligations of Companies* (Versoix, International Council on Human Rights Policy).

IGNATIEFF, MICHAEL (2001) *Human Rights as Politics and Idolatry* (Princeton, Princeton University Press).

International Labour Organization (ILO) (1986) *General Survey of the Reports on the Equal Remuneration Convention (No 100) and Recommendation (No 90), 1951: Report* (Geneva, International Labour Office).

—— (1994) *General Survey of the Reports on the Freedom of Association and the Right to Organize Convention (No 87), 1948 and the Right to Organize and Collective Bargaining Convention (No 98), 1949: Report of the Committee of Experts* (Geneva, International Labour Office).

—— (1996) *Freedom of Association, Digest of Decisions of the Freedom of Association Committee of the Governing Body of the ILO* (Geneva, International Labour Office).

—— (1997) *The ILO, Standard Setting, and Globalization, Report of the Director-General: International Labour Conference, 85th Session* (Geneva, International Labour Office).

—— (1999a) *Human Resource Implications of Globalization and Restructuring in Commerce—Report for Discussion at the Tripartite Meeting on the Human Resource Implications of Globalization and Restructuring in Commerce* (Geneva, International Labour Office).

—— (1999b) *Decent Work: Report of the Director-General, Juan Somavia, International Labour Conference, 87th Session* (Geneva, International Labour Office).

—— (2000a) *Your Voice at Work: Global Report under the Follow-up to the ILO Declaration on Fundamental Principles and Rights at Work* (Geneva, International Labour Office).

—— (2000b) *Private Initiatives and Labour Standards: A Global Look* (Geneva, International Labour Office).

—— (2001a) *Stopping Forced Labour: Global Report under the Follow-up to the ILO Declaration on Fundamental Principles and Rights at Work* (Geneva, International Labour Office).

—— (2001b) *Reducing the Decent Work Deficit—A Global Challenge, Report of the Director-General, Juan Somavia, International Labour Conference, 89th Session* (Geneva, International Labour Office).

—— (2002) *A Future without Child Labour: Global Report under the Follow-up to the ILO Declaration on Fundamental Principles and Rights at Work* (Geneva, International Labour Office).

—— (2003) *Time for Equality at Work: Global Report under the Follow-up to the ILO Declaration on Fundamental Principles and Rights at Work* (Geneva, International Labour Office).

—— (2004a) *Organizing for Social Justice: Global Report under the follow-up to the ILO-Declaration on Fundamental Principles and Rights at Work.* (Geneva, International Labour Office).

—— (2004b) *A Fair Globalization: The Role of the ILO, Report of the Director-General on the World Commission on the Social Dimension of Globalization, International Labour Conference, 92nd Session* (Geneva, International Labour Office).

—— (2005) *A Global Alliance against Forced Labour: Global Report under the Follow-up to the ILO Declaration on Fundamental Principles and Rights at Work* (Geneva, International Labour Office).

—— (2006) *The end of child labour: Within reach: Global Report under the follow-up to the Declaration on Fundamental Principles and Rights at Work* (Geneva, International Labour Office).

Jaag, Tobias (2002) "Institutionen und Verfahren" in Daniel Thürer, Rolf H Weber and Roger Zäch (eds), *Bilaterale Verträge Schweiz—EG: Ein Handbuch* (Zürich, Schulthess).

Jackson, John H (1997) *The World Trading System* (Cambridge, MA, MIT Press).

—— (1998) *The World Trade Organization: Constitution and Jurisprudence* (London, Royal Institute of International Affairs).

—— (2000) "Comments on *Shrimp/Turtle* and the Product/Process Distinction" 11 *European Journal of International Law* 303–7.

—— (2003) "Sovereignty-Modern: A New Approach to an Outdated Concept" 97 *American Journal of International Law* 782–802.

Jenks, Wilfried C (1963) *Law, Freedom and Welfare* (London, Stevens and Sons).

Kamarck, Elaine Ciulla (2000) "Globalization and Public Administration Reform" in Joseph S Nye and John D Donahue (eds), *Governance in a Globalizing World* (Cambridge, MA, Brookings Institution Press).

Kälin, Walter (1994a) *Das Verfahren der staatsrechtlichen Beschwerde* (Bern, Stämpfli Verlag).

—— (1994b) "Menschenrechtsverträge als Gewährleistungen einer objektiven Ordnung" 33 *Berichte der Deutschen Gesellschaft für Völkerrecht, Aktuelle Probleme des Menschenrechtsschutzes* 9.

—— (2002) "Die Bedeutung des Freizügigkeitsabkommens für das Ausländerrecht" in Thomas Cottier and Matthias Oesch (eds), *Die sektoriellen Abkommen Schweiz—EG, Berner Tage für die juristische Praxis* (Bern, Stämpfli Verlag).

KÄLIN, WALTER, MALINVERNI, GIORGIO and NOWAK, MANFRED (eds) (1997) *Die Schweiz und die UNO-Menschenrechtspakte* (Basel, Helbing & Lichtenhahn).

KÄLLSTRÖM, KENT (1992) "Article 23" in Asbjørn Eide, Gudmundur Alfredsson, Göran Melander, Lars Adam Rehof and Allan Rosas (eds), *The Universal Declaration of Human Rights: A Commentary* (Oslo, Scandinavian University Press).

KANT, IMMANUEL (1982) *Die Metaphysik der Sitten, Werkausgabe*, Wilhelm Weischedel (ed), vol VIII, 5th edn (Frankfurt aM, Suhrkamp).

KELSEN, HANS (1960) *Reine Rechtslehre. Mit einem Anhang: Das Problem der Gerechtigkeit* (Wien, Verlag Franz Deuticke).

KEMPE, MARTIN (2001) "A Comeback for 'Taylorism'? Report from Germany" 38 *World of Work* 18–20.

KENNEDY, DAVID (1999) "The Disciplines of International Law and Policy" 12 *Leiden Journal of International Law* 9–133.

—— (2000) "When Renewal Repeats: Thinking Against the Box" 32 *New York University Journal of International Law and Politics* 335–500.

KEOHANE, ROBERT (2001) "Governance in a Partially Globalized World: Presidential Address, American Political Science Association" 95 *American Political Science Review* 1–13.

KEOHANE, ROBERT and NYE, JOSEPH S (2001) "The Club Model of Multilateral Cooperation and Problems of Democratic Legitimacy" in Roger B Porter, Pierre Sauvé, Arvind Subramanian and Beviglia Americo Zampetti (eds), *Efficiency, Equity and Legitimacy: The Multilateral Trading System at the Millennium* (Washington DC, Brookings Institution Press).

KEYNES, JOHN MAYNARD (1919) *The Economic Consequences of the Peace* (London, Macmillan).

KIRCHGÄSSNER, GEBHARD (1998) "Zur Ethik des Arbeitsmarkts: Einige Bemerkungen aus nicht-kognitivistischer Perspektive" *Universität St. Gallen, Volkswirtschaftliche Abteilung, Diskussionspaper Nr 9809.*

KIRCHGÄSSNER, GEBHARD, FIELD, LARS P and SAVIOZ, MARCEL R (1999) *Die direkte Demokratie—Modern, erfolgreich, entwicklungs- und exportfähig* (Basel, Helbing & Lichtenhahn).

KLEY-STRULLER, ANDREAS (1995) "Der Anspruch auf unentgeltliche Rechtspflege" 5 *Aktuelle Juristische Praxis* 179–91.

—— (1996) "Anerkennung eines selbständigen Rechts auf Existenzsicherung als neues ungeschriebenes Recht der Bundesverfassung" 6 *Aktuelle Juristische Praxis* 756–59.

KOH, HAROLD HONGJU (1997) "Why Do Nations Obey International Law?" 106 *Yale Law Journal* 2599–659.

KOHLER, GEORG and MARTI, URS (eds) (2003) *Konturen der neuen Welt(un)ordnung: Beiträge zu einer Theorie der normativen Prinzipien internationaler Politik* (Berlin, de Gruyter).

KOKOTT, JULIANE (1998) "Grund- und Menschenrechte als Inhalt eines internationalen ordre public" in Berichte der Deutschen Gesellschaft für Völkerrecht (ed), *Die Wirkungskraft der Grundrechte bei Fällen mit Auslandsbezug* (Heidelberg, Verlag CF Müller).

KÖLZ, ALFRED (1992a) *Quellenbuch zur neueren schweizerischen Verfassungsgeschichte: Vom Ende der Alten Eidgenossenschaft bis 1848* (Zürich, Stämpfli Verlag).

—— (1992b) *Neuere Schweizerische Verfassungsgeschichte* (Bern, Stämpfli Verlag).

KOSKENNIEMI, MARTTI (1991) "The Future of Statehood" 32 *Harvard International Law Journal* 397–410.

—— (1999) "The Effect of Rights on Political Culture" in Philip Alston (ed), *The EU and Human Rights* (Oxford, Oxford University Press).

—— (2000) "Carl Schmitt, Hans Morgenthau, and the Image of Law in International Relations" in Michael Byers (ed), *The Role of Law in International Politics, Essays in International Relations and International Law* (Oxford, Oxford University Press).

—— (2002a) *The Gentle Civilizer of Nations—The Rise and Fall of International Law 1870–1960* (Cambridge, Cambridge University Press).

—— (2002b) "'The Lady Doth Protest Too Much': Kosovo and the Turn to Ethics in International Law" 65 *The Modern Law Review* 159–75.

KRAJEWSKI, MARKUS (2001) *Verfassungsperspektiven und Legitimation des Rechts der Welthandelsorganisation (WTO)* (Berlin, Duncker & Humblot).

KRISTOF, NICHOLAS D and WUDUNN, SHERYL (1994) *China Wakes: The Struggle for the Soul of a Rising Power* (New York, Vintage).

—— (2000) *Thunder from the East: Portrait of a Rising Asia* (New York, Vintage).

KRUEGER, ANNE O (1998) "Whither the World Bank and the IMF?" 26 *Journal of Economic Literature* 1983–2020.

KÜNZLI, JÖRG and KÄLIN, WALTER (1997) "Die Bedeutung des UNO-Paktes über wirtschaftliche, soziale und kulturelle Rechte für das schweizerische Recht" in Walter Kälin, Giorgio Malinverni and Manfred Nowak (eds), *Die Schweiz und die UNO-Menschenrechtspakte* (Basel, Helbing & Lichtenhahn).

LANGILLE, BRIAN A (1999) "The ILO and the New Economy: Recent Developments" 15 *International Journal of Comparative Labour Law and Industrial Relations* 229–58.

—— (2005) "Core Labour Rights—The True Story (Reply to Alston)" 16 *European Journal of International Law* 409–37.

LANSKY, MARK (1997) "Perspectives on Child Labour: How the Challenge is Being Met" 136 *International Labour Review* 233–57.

LASTRA, ROSA MARIA (1992) "The Independence of the European System of Central Banks" 33 *Harvard International Law Journal* 475–519.

—— (1996) Central Banking and Banking Regulation (London, Financial Markets Group, London School of Economics and Political Science).

—— (2000) "The International Monetary Fund in Historical Perspective" 3 *Journal of International Economic Law* 507–23.

LAUTERPACHT, HERSCH (1950) *International Law and Human Rights* (London, Stevens and Sons).

LEARY, VIRGINIA A (1996) "The Paradox of Workers' Rights as Human Rights" in Lance A Compa and Stephen F Diamond (eds), *Human Rights, Labor Rights and International Trade* (Philadelphia, University of Pennsylvania Press).

—— (2003) "'Form Follows Function': Formulations of International Labor Standards—Treaties, Codes, Soft Law, Trade Agreements" in Robert J Flanagan and William B Gould (eds), *International Labor Standards: Globalization, Trade, and Public Policy* (Stanford, University of Stanford).

LEISINK, PETER (1999) *Globalization and Labour Relations* (Cheltenham, Edward Elgar Publishing).

LEVINE, MARVIN J (1997) *Worker Rights and Labor Standards in Asia's Four New Tigers—A Comparative Perspective* (New York, Plenum Press).

LEVINSON, JEROME (1992) "Multilateral Financing Institutions: What Form of Accountability?" 8 *American Journal of International Law and Policy* 39–63.

LIEBHOLD, PETER and RUBENSTEIN, HARRY R (1998) "Between a Rock and a Hard Place" 9 *Labor's Heritage (George Meany Memorial Archives)* 4–25.

LOPEZ-HURTADO, CARLOS (2002) "Social Labelling and WTO Law" 5 *Journal of International Economic Law* 719–46.

LUCKE, KARIN (2005) "States' and Private Actors' Obligations under International Human Rights Law and the Draft UN Norms" in Thomas Cottier, Joost Pauwelyn and Elisabeth Bürgi (eds), *Human Rights and International Trade* (Oxford, Oxford University Press).

MACDONALD, RONALD (1999) "The Charter of the United Nations in Constitutional Perspective" 20 *Australian Yearbook of International Law* 205–31.

MACKLEM, PATRICK (2005) "The Right to Bargain Collectively in International Law: Workers' Right, Human Right, International Right?" in Philip Alston (eds), *Labour Rights as Human Rights* (Oxford, Oxford University Press).

MADER, LUZIUS (1999) "Die Sozial- und Umweltverfassung" 8 *Aktuelle Juristische Praxis* 698–705.

MALAMUD, DEBORAH C (1998) "Engineering the Middle Classes: Class Line-drawing in the New Deal Hours Legislation" 96 *Michigan Law Review* 2212–321.

MALINVERNI, GIORGIO (1987) "Kommentar zu Artikel 56 BV" in Jean-François Aubert, Kurt Eichenberger, Jörg-Paul Müller, René Rhinow and Dietrich Schindler (eds), *Kommentar zur Bundesverfassung der Schweizerischen Eidgenossenschaft vom 29. Mai 1874* (Zürich, Schulthess).

—— (1998) "L'indépendance de la Suisse dans un monde interdépendant" 117 II *Zeitschrift für Schweizerisches Recht NF* 1–137.

MARCEAU, GABRIELLE (1995) "Transition from GATT to WTO—A Most Pragmatic Operation" 29 *Journal of World Trade* 147–63.

—— (2002) "The WTO Dispute Settlement and Human Rights" 13 *European Journal of International Law* 753–814.

MARKS, SUSAN (2000) *The Riddle of All Constitutions* (Oxford, Oxford University Press).

MARTI, URS (2003) "Souveränität und Globalisierung" in Georg Kohler and Urs Marti (eds), *Konturen der neuen Welt(un)ordnung: Beiträge zu einer Theorie der normativen Prinzipien internationaler Politik* (Berlin, de Gruyter).

MARTIN, JOHN P (1998) "What Works among Active Labour Market Policies: Evidence from OECD Countries' Experiences", Labour Market and Social Policy Occasional Papers No 35.

MASKUS, KEITH E (1997) "Should Core Labour Standards Be Imposed through International Trade Policy?", World Bank Working Paper (Washington DC, World Bank).

MAUPAIN, FRANCIS (2000) "International Labor Organization Recommendations and Similar Instruments" in Dinah Shelton (ed), *Commitment and Compliance—The Role of Non-binding Norms in the International Legal System* (Oxford, Oxford University Press).

—— (2005a) "Revitalization Not Retreat: The Real Potential of the 1998 ILO Declaration for the Universal Protection of Workers" Rights" 16 *European Journal of International Law* 439–65.

—— (2005b) "Is the ILO Effective in Upholding Workers' Rights? Reflections on the Myanmar Experience" in Philip Alston (ed), *Labour Rights as Human Rights* (Oxford, Oxford University Press).

McCrudden, Christopher (1998) "Social Policy Issues in Public Procurement: A Legal Overview" in Sue Arrowsmith and Arwel Davies (eds), *Public Procurement: Global Revolution* (London, Kluwer Law International).

—— (1999a) "Mainstreaming Equality in the Governance of Northern Ireland" 22 *Fordham International Law Journal* 1696–775.

—— (1999b) "International Economic Law and the Pursuit of Human Rights: A Framework for Discussion of the Legality of 'Selective Purchasing' Laws under the WTO Government Procurement Agreement" 2 *Journal of International Economic Law* 3–48.

—— (2005) "Mainstreaming Human Rights" in Colin J Harvey (ed), *Human Rights in the Community: Rights as Agents for Change* (Oxford, Hart Publishing).

McCrudden, Christopher and Davies, Anne (2000) "A Perspective on Trade and Labor Rights" 3 *Journal of International Economic Law* 43–62.

McGrew, Anthony (1992) "A Global Society?" in Stuart Hall, David Held and Tony McGrew (eds), *Modernity and its Futures* (Cambridge, Polity Press).

McRae, Donald M (2000) "The WTO in International Law: Tradition Continued or New Frontier?" 3 *Journal of International Economic Law* 27–41.

Mehmet, Ozay, Mendes, Errol and Sinding, Robert (eds) (1998a) *Towards a Fair Global Labour Market: Avoiding a New Slave Trade* (London, Routledge).

—— (1998b) "Cultural Relativism and Human Rights: The Debate Over Labour Standards and 'Asian Values'" in Ozay Mehmet, Errol Mendes and Robert Sinding (eds), *Towards a Fair Global Labour Market: Avoiding a New Slave Trade* (London, Routledge).

Meier, Gerald M and Stiglitz, Joseph E (eds) (2000) *Frontiers of Development Economics—The Future in Perspective* (Washington DC, World Bank and Oxford University Press).

Melander, Göran (1992) "Article 24" in Asbjørn Eide, Gudmundur Alfredsson, Göran Melander, Lars Adam Rehof and Allan Rosas (eds), *The Universal Declaration of Human Rights: A Commentary* (Oslo, Scandinavian University Press).

Meltzer, Allan H (2004) "The Report of the International Financial Institution Advisory Commission: Comments on the Critics" in David Vines and Christopher L Gilbert (eds), *The IMF and its Critics: Reform of Global Financial Architecture* (Cambridge, Cambridge University Press).

Meyer-Blaser, Ulrich and Gächter, Thomas (2001) "Der Sozialstaatsgedanke" in Daniel Thürer, Jean-François Aubert and Jörg Paul Müller (eds), *Verfassungsrecht der Schweiz* (Zürich, Schulthess).

Milner, Helen (1990) "The Political Economy of US Trade Policy: A Study of the Super 301 Provision" in Jagdish Bhagwati and Hugh T Patrick (eds), *Aggressive Unilateralism* (Ann Arbor, University of Michigan Press).

Mishra, Ramesh (1999) *Globalization and the Welfare State* (Cheltenham, Elgar Publishing).

Moggridge, Donald Edward (1971) *The Collected Writings of John Maynard Keynes* (London, Macmillan Press).

Moor, Pierre (2001) "Principes de l'activité étatique et responsabilité de l"Etat" in Daniel Thürer, Jean-François Aubert and Jörg Paul Müller (eds), *Verfassungsrecht der Schweiz* (Zürich, Schulthess).

MORGENTHAU, HANS (1935) "Théorie des sanctions internationales" 3/XVI *Revue de droit international et de législation comparée* 473–503, 809–36.

MORICI, PETER and EVAN, SCHULZ (2001) *Labor Standards in the Global Trading System* (Washington DC, Economic Strategy Institute).

MORIS, HALIM (1997) "The World Bank and Human Rights: Indispensable Partnership or Mismatched Alliance?" 4 *ILSA Journal of International & Comparative Law* 173–200.

MOSER, CAROLINE O N, TORNQUVIST, ANNIKA and VAN BRONKHORST, Bernice (1998) *Mainstreaming Gender and Development in the World Bank—Progress and Recommendations* (Washington DC, The International Bank for Reconstruction and Development/The World Bank).

MUCHLINSKI, PETER T (2001) "Human Rights and Multinationals: Is There a Problem?" 77 *International Affairs* 31–47.

MÜLLER, GEORG (2001) "Rechtssetzung und Staatsverträge" in Daniel Thürer, Jean-François Aubert and Jörg Paul Müller (eds), *Verfassungsrecht der Schweiz* (Zürich, Schulthess).

MÜLLER, JÖRG PAUL (1971) *Vertrauensschutz im Völkerrecht* (Köln, Carl Heymann Verlag).

—— (1981) *Soziale Grundrechte in der Verfassung?* (Basel, Helbing & Lichtenhahn).

—— (1997) "Wandel des Souveränitätsbegriffs im Lichte der Grundrechte—dargestellt am Beispiel von Einwirkungen des internationalen Menschenrechtsschutzes auf die schweizerische Rechtsordnung" in René Rhinow, Stephan Breitenmoser and Bernhard Ehrenzeller (eds), *Fragen des internationalen und nationalen Menschenrechtsschutzes, Symposium zum 60. Geburtstag von Luzius Wildhaber* (Basel, Helbing & Lichtenhahn).

—— (1999) *Grundrechte in der Schweiz* (Bern, Stämpfli Verlag).

—— (2002) Die Demokratische Verfassung—Zwischen Verständigung und Revolte (Zürich, Verlag Neue Zürcher Zeitung).

—— (2005) "Grundrechte juristischer Personen" in Eugen Bucher, Claus-Wilhelm Canaris, Heinrich Honsell and Thomas Koller (eds), *Norm und Wirkung: Beiträge zum Privat- und Wirtschaftsrecht aus heutiger und historischer Perspektive. Festschrift für Wolfgang Wiegand zum 65. Geburtstag* (Bern, Stämpfli Verlag).

MUNCK, RONALDO and WATERMAN, PETER (eds) (1999) *Labour Worldwide in the Era of Globalization: Alternative Models in The New World Order* (London, Macmillan Press).

MURPHY, JOSETTE (1997) Mainstreaming Gender in World Bank Lending—An Update (Washington DC, World Bank).

MUSA, MICHAEL (2004) "Argentina and the Fund: Anatomy of a Policy Failure" in David Vines and Christopher L Gilbert (eds), *The IMF and its Critics: Reform of the Global Financial Architecture* (Cambridge, Cambridge University Press).

MUTUA, MAKAU WA (1996) "The Ideology of Human Rights" 36 *Virginia Journal of International Law* 589–657.

NADAKAVUKAREN SCHEFER, KRISTA (2005) "Stopping Trade in Conflict Diamonds: Exploring the Trade and Human Rights Interface with the WTO Waiver for the Kimberley Process" in Thomas Cottier, Joost Pauwelyn and Elisabeth Bürgi (eds), *Human Rights and International Trade* (Oxford, Oxford University Press).

NEUMANN MANFRED (ed) (1984) *Ansprüche, Eigentums- und Verfügungsrechte, Arbeitstagung des Vereins für Socialpolitik in Basel 1983* (Basel, Duncker & Humblot).

Newman, Peter, Eatwell, John and Milgate, Murray (eds) (1987) *The New Palgrave—A Dictionary of Economics* (London, Palgrave Macmillan).

Nogueras, Diego J Liñan and Hinosojosa, Martínez Luis M (2001) "Human Rights Conditionality in the External trade of the European Union: Legal and Legitimacy Problems" 7 *Columbia Journal of European Law* 307–36.

Nowak, Manfred (2005) *UN Covenant on Civil and Political Rights: CCPR Commentary*, 2nd edn (Kehl am Rhein, Engel).

Nye, Joseph S and Donahue, John D (eds) (2000) *Governance in a Globalizing World: Visions of Governance for the 21st Century* (Cambridge, MA, Brookings Institution Press).

O'Higgins, Paul (1997) "Labour is Not a Commodity: An Irish Contribution to International Labour Law" 26 *Industrial Law Journal* 225–34.

—— (2002) "The Interaction of the ILO, the Council of Europe and European Union Labour Standards" in Bob Hepple (ed), *Social and Labour Rights in a Global Context: International and Comparative Perspectives* (Cambridge, Cambridge University Press).

Oates, Wallace E (1997) "On Environmental Federalism: Discussion of Environmental Federalism in a Global Economy" 83 *Virginia Law Review* 1321–29.

OECD (1996a) *Trade, Employment and Labour Standards: A Study of Core Workers' Rights and International Trade* (Paris, OECD Publishing).

—— (1996b) "Process and Production Methods (PPMs): Conceptual Framework and Considerations on Use of PPM-Based Trade Measures" OCDE/GD(97)137.

—— (2000) *International Trade and Core Labour Standards* (Paris, OECD Publishing).

—— (2001a) *The Development Dimensions of Trade* (Paris, OECD Publishing).

—— (2001b) *Employment Outlook* (Paris, OECD Publishing).

OECD Directorate for Education, Employment, Labour and Social Affairs (1998) "Key Employment Policy Challenges Faced by OECD Countries", Labour Market and Social Policy Occasional Papers No 31.

Oppermann, Thomas (1999) *Europarecht* (München, Beck).

Otto, Dianne (1997) "Rethinking the 'Universality' of Human Rights Law" 29 *Columbia Human Rights Law Review* 1–46.

Paulus, Andreas L (2001) *Die internationale Gemeinschaft im Völkerrecht eine Untersuchung zur Entwicklung des Völkerrechts im Zeitalter der Globalisierung* (München, Beck).

Pauwelyn, Joost (2001) "The Role of Public International Law in the WTO: How Far Can We Go?" 95 *American Journal of International Law* 535–78.

—— (2003a) *Conflict of Norms in Public International Law: How WTO Law Relates to Other Rules of International Law* (Cambridge, Cambridge University Press).

—— (2003b) "WTO Compassion or Superiority Complex? What to Make of the WTO Waiver for 'Conflict Diamonds'" 24 *Michigan Journal of International Law* 1177–207.

—— (2004) "The Jurisdiction of the World Trade Organization" 98 *American Society of International Law Proceedings* 135–38.

Pérez Sainz, J P (1998) "The New Faces of Informality in Central America" 30 *Journal of Latin American Studies* 157–79.

Pernthaler, Peter (1998) "Die Globalisierung als Herausforderung an eine moderne Staatslehre" in Heinz Schäffer, Walter Berka, Harald Stolzlechner and Josef Werndl (eds), *Staat—Verfassung—Verwaltung, Festschrift anlässlich des 65. Geburtstages von Friedrich Koja* (Wien, Springer).

PETERS, B GUY and PIERRE, JOHN (1998) "Governance without Government? Rethinking Public Administration" 8 *Journal of Public Administration Research and Theory* 223–43.

PETERSMANN, ERNST-ULRICH (1991) Constitutional Functions and Constitutional Problems of International Economic Law: International and Domestic Foreign Trade Law and Foreign Trade Policy in the United States, the European Community and Switzerland (Fribourg, University Press).

—— (1996) "Constitutionalism and International Organizations" 17 *Northwestern Journal of International Law and Business* 398–469.

—— (1997) *International Trade Law and the WTO Dispute Settlement System* (London, Kluwer Law International).

—— (1998) "How to Constitutionalize International Law and Foreign Policy for the Benefit of Civil Society?" 20 *Michigan Journal of International Law* 1–30.

—— (1999) "Constitutionalism and International Adjudication: How to Constitutionalize the UN Dispute Settlement System?" 31 *New York University Journal of International Law and Politics* 753–89.

—— (2001) "Human Rights and International Economic Law in the 21st Century—The Need to Clarify Their Interrelationships" 4 *Journal of International Economic Law* 3–39.

—— (2002a) "Time for a United Nations 'Global Compact' for Integrating Human Rights into the Law of Worldwide Organizations: Lessons from European Integration" 13 *European Journal of International Law* 621–50.

—— (2002b) "Taking Human Dignity, Poverty and Empowerment of Individuals More Seriously: Rejoinder to Alston" 13 *European Journal of International Law* 845–51.

—— (2003) "Constitutional Economics, Human Rights and the Future of the WTO" 58 *Aussenwirtschaft* 49–91.

PETERSON, LUKE ERIC (2003) "International Human Rights in Bilateral Investment Treaties and in Investment Treaty Arbitration", Research Paper prepared by the International Institute for Sustainable Development (IISD) for the Swiss Department of Foreign Affairs (Canada, International Institute for Sustainable Development).

PICCIOTTO, SOL (1996) "Networks in International Economic Integration: Fragmented States and the Dilemmas of Neo-liberalism" 17 *Northwestern Journal of International Law and Business* 1014–56.

POLLACK, MARK A and SHAFFER, GREGORY C (eds) (2001a) *Transatlantic Government in the Global Economy* (Lanham, Rowman & Littlefield).

—— (2001b) "Introduction: Transatlantic Governance in Historical and Theoretical Perspective" in Mark A Pollack and Gregory C Shaffer (eds), *Transatlantic Government in the Global Economy* (Lanham, Rowman & Littlefield).

POPE JOHN PAUL II (1982) "Laborem Exercens, Encyclical Letter" in Gregory Baum (ed), *The Priority of Labor* (New York, Paulist Press).

PORTER, ROGER B, SAUVÉ, PIERRE, SUBRAMANIAN, ARVIND and ZAMPETTI, Americo Beviglia (eds) (2001) *Efficiency, Equity and Legitimacy: The Multilateral Trading System at the Millennium* (Washington DC, Brookings Institution Press).

PORTMANN, WOLFGANG (2002) "Flankierende Massnahmen zum Abkommen über die Freizügigkeit" in Daniel Thürer, Rolf H Weber and Zäch Roger (eds), *Bilaterale Verträge Schweiz—EG, Ein Handbuch* (Zürich, Schulthess).

RAGAZZI, MAURIZIO (1997) *The Concept of International Obligations Erga Omnes* (Oxford, Clarendon Press).

RAWLS, JOHN (1999) *A Theory of Justice* (Cambridge, MA, Belknap Press of Harvard University Press).

RAWLS, JOHN (2001) *Law of Peoples* (Cambridge, MA, Harvard University Press).

REES, TERESA (1998) *Mainstreaming Equality in the European Union* (London, Routledge).

REGAN, DONALD H (1986) "The Supreme Court and State Protectionism: Making Sense of the Dormant Commerce Clause" 84 *Michigan Law Review* 1091–287.

—— (1995) "How to Think about the Federal Commerce Power and Incidentally Rewrite *United States v Lopez*" 94 *Michigan Law Review* 554–614.

—— (2001) "Judicial Review of Member-State Regulation of Trade within a Federal or Quasi-federal System: Protectionism and Balancing, Da Capo" 99 *Michigan Law Review* 1853–902.

—— (2002) "Regulatory Purpose and 'Like Products' in Article III:4 of the GATT (with Additional Remarks on Article III:2)" 36 *Journal of World Trade* 443–78.

RHINOW, RENÉ (1987) "Kommentar zu Artikel 31bis BV" in Jean-François Aubert, Kurt Eichenberger, Jörg Paul Müller, René Rhinow and Dieter Schindler (eds), *Kommentar zur Bundesverfassung der Schweizerischen Eidgenossenschaft vom 29. Mai 1874* (Zürich, Schulthess).

—— (ed) (1995) *Die schweizerische Sicherheitspolitik im internationalen Umfeld* (Basel, Helbing & Lichtenhahn).

—— (2000) "Wirtschafts-, Sozial- und Arbeitsverfassung" *Die neue Bundesverfassung, Konsequenzen für Praxis und Wissenschaft, Berner Tage für die juristische Praxis 1999* 157–82.

RHINOW, RENÉ, BREITENMOSER, STEPHAN and EHRENZELLER, BERNHARD (eds) (1997) *Fragen des internationalen und nationalen Menschenrechtsschutzes, Symposium zum 60. Geburtstag von Luzius Wildhaber* (Basel, Helbing & Lichtenhahn).

RHINOW, RENÉ, SCHMID, GERHARD and BIAGGINI, GIOVANNI (1998) *Oeffentliches Wirtschaftsrecht* (Basel, Helbing & Lichtenhahn).

RICHLI, PAUL (2000) *Interdisziplinäre Daumenregeln für eine faire Rechtssetzung: Ein Beitrag zur Rechtssetzungslehre im liberalen sozial und ökologisch orientierten Rechtsstaat* (Basel, Helbing & Lichtenhahn).

RODRIK, DANI (1997) "Sense and Nonsense in the Globalization Debate" *Foreign Policy, Summer* 19–36.

ROESSLER, FRIEDER (1998) "Domestic Policy Objectives and the Multilateral Trade Order: Lessons from the Past" 19 *University of Pennsylvania Journal of International Economic Law* 513–32.

ROOSEVELT, FRANKLIN DELANO (1940) *The Public Papers and Addresses of Franklin D Roosevelt* (New York, Random House).

ROSENAU, JAMES NATHAN and CZEMPIEL, ERNST-OTTO (eds) (2000) *Governance without Government: Order and Change in World Politics* (Cambridge, Cambridge University Press).

ROSENMAN, SAMUEL IRVING (ed) (1938) *The Public Papers and Addresses of Franklin D Roosevelt* (New York, Random House).

SACHAROFF, ARIADNE K (1998) "Multinationals in Host Countries: Can They be Held Liable under the Alien Tort Claims Act for Human Rights Violations?" 23 *Brooklyn Journal of International Law* 927–64.

SALADIN, PETER (1995) *Wozu noch Staaten? Zu den Funktionen eines modernen demokratischen Rechtsstaats in einer zunehmend überstaatlich orientierten Welt* (Bern, Stämpfli Verlag).

SALCEDO, JUAN CARRILLO (1995) "Human Rights, Universal Declaration (1948)" in Rudolf Bernhardt (ed), *Encyclopedia of Public International Law* (Amsterdam, North Holland Publishing Company).

SALZMAN, JAMES (2000) "Labor Rights, Globalization and Institutions: The Role and Influence of the Organization for Economic Cooperation and Development" 21 *Michigan Journal of International Law* 769–848.

SAMPSON, GARY P and CHAMBERS, W BRADNEE (eds) (2000) *Trade, Environment, and the Millennium* (Tokyo, UN University Press).

SAMSON, KLAUS and SCHINDLER, KENNETH (1999) "The Standard-setting and Supervisory System of the International Labour Organisation" in Raija Hanski and Markku Suksi (eds), *An Introduction to the International Protection of Human Rights* (Turku, Abo Akademi University).

SCHARPF, FRITZ W (2001) "Notes toward a Theory of Multilevel Governing in Europe" 24 *Scandinavian Political Studies* 1–26.

SCHÄFFER, HEINZ, BERKA, WALTER, STOLZLECHNER, HARALD and WERNDL, JOSEF (eds) (1998) *Staat — Verfassung — Verwaltung, Festschrift anlässlich des 65. Geburtstages von Friedrich Koja* (Wien, Springer).

SCHERMERS, HENRICUS GERHARD and BLOKKER, NIELS M (1995) *International Institutional Law: Unity within Diversity* (The Hague, Martinus Nijhoff Publishers).

SCHIESSER-GACHNANG, DORIS (1999) *Konditionalität als Element der Kreditvergabe des Internationalen Währungsfonds* (Zürich, Swiss National Bank).

SCHINDLER, DIETRICH (1991) "Probleme des humanitären Völkerrechts und der Neutralität im Golfkonflikt 1990/91" 1 *Schweizerische Zeitschrift für Internationales und Europäisches Recht* 3–23.

—— (1992) "Changing Conceptions of Neutrality in Switzerland" *Austrian Journal of Public and International Law* 105–16.

—— (1996) "Zwischenstaatliche Interdependenz und Demokratie" in Piermarco Zen-Ruffinen and Andreas Auer (eds), *De la constitution—Études en l'honneur de Jean-François Aubert* (Basel, Helbing & Lichtenhahn).

—— (1999a) "Neutrality and Morality: Developments in Switzerland and in the International Community" 14 *American University International Law Review* 155–70.

—— (1998b) "Völkerrecht und Demokratie" in Gerhard Hafner, Karl-Heinz Böckstiegel, Hans-Ernst Folz and Jörg Manfred Mössner (eds), *Liber amicorum Professor Ignaz Seidl-Hohenveldern in Honour of his 80th Birthday* (The Hague, Kluwer Law International).

SCHINDLER, DIETRICH, HERTIG, GÉRARD, KELLENBERGER, JAKOB, THÜRER, DANIEL and ZÄCH, ROGER (eds) (1990) *Die Europaverträglichkeit des schweizerischen Rechts* (Zürich, Schulthess).

SCHLEMMER-SCHULTE, SABINE (1998) "The World Bank's Experience with its Inspection Panel" 58 *Zeitschrift für ausländisches öffentliches Recht und Völkerrecht* 353–88.

—— (1999a) "The World Bank and Human Rights" 4 *Austrian Review of International & European Law* 230–68.

—— (1999b) "The World Bank's Role in Fighting Child Labor" in Eugeen Verhellen (ed), *Understanding Children's Rights—Proceedings of the Fourth International Disciplinary Course on Children's Rights held at the University of Ghent, December 1999* (Gent, Centrum voor de Rechten van het Kind).

—— (2000) "Introductory Note to the Conclusions of the Second Review of the World Bank Inspection Panel" 39 *International Legal Materials* 243–46.

—— (2001a) "The World Bank's Role in the Promotion of the Rule of Law in Developing Countries" in Sabine Schlemmer-Schulte and Ko-Yung Tung (eds), *Liber Amicorum Ibrahim F Shihata* (The Hague, Kluwer Law International).

—— (2001b) "The Impact of Civil Society on the World Bank, the International Monetary Fund and the World Trade Organization: The Case of the World Bank" 7 *ILSA Journal of International & Comparative Law* 399–428.

SCHLEMMER-SCHULTE, SABINE and TUNG, KO-YUNG (eds) (2001a) *Liber Amicorum Ibrahim F Shihata* (The Hague, Kluwer Law International).

SCHOENBERGER, KARL (2000) *Levis's Children* (New York, Atlantic Monthly Press).

SCHUMANN, MICHAEL (2001) "Kritische Industriesoziologie -Theoretische Anknüpfungspunkte, exemplarische Befunde, neue Aufgaben" in Detlef Claussen, Oskar Negt and Michael Werz (eds), *Hannoversche Schriften 4: Philosophie und Empirie* (Frankfurt aM, Verlag Neue Kritik).

SEN, AMARTYA KUMAR (1997a) "Human Rights and Asian Values: What Kee Kuan Yew and Le Peng Don't Understand about Asia" 217 *The New Republic* 33–41.

—— (1997b) *Resources, Values and Development* (Cambridge, MA, Harvard University Press).

—— (1999) *Development as Freedom* (London, Oxford University Press).

—— (2000) "Work and Rights" 139 *International Labour Review* 119–28.

—— (2001) "What Is Development About?" in Gerald M Meier and Joseph E Stiglitz (eds), *Frontiers of Development Economics—The Future in Perspective* (Washington DC, World Bank and Oxford University Press).

SENGENBERGER, WERNER and CAMPBELL, DUNCAN (eds) (1994) *Creating Economic Opportunities: The Role of Labour Standards in Industrial Restructuring* (Geneva, International Labour Office).

SENNETT, RICHARD (1998) *Der flexible Mensch* (Berlin, Berlin Verlag).

SENTI, RICHARD (2000) *WTO—System und Funktionsweise der Welthandelsordnung* (Zürich, Schulthess).

SETHURAMAN, S V (1982) *The Urban Informal Sector in Developing Countries: Employment, Poverty and Environment* (Geneva, International Labour Office).

SETSER, BRAD, GELPERN, ANNA (2006) 'Pathways through Financial Crisis: Argentina, 12 Global Governance (forthcoming issue 4).

SHELTON, DINAH (ed) (2000) *Commitment and Compliance—The Role of Non-binding Norms in the International Legal System* (Oxford, Oxford University Press).

SHIHATA, IBRAHIM F I (1995a) "The World Bank and Human Rights" in Ibrahim F I Shihata (ed), *The World Bank in Changing World, Volume II* (The Hague, Martinus Nijhoff Publishers).

—— (ed) (1995b) *The World Bank in a Changing World, Volume II* (The Hague, Martinus Nijhoff Publishers).

—— (2000a) *The World Bank Inspection Panel in Practice* (Washington DC, World Bank).

—— (2000b) "The World Bank's Protection and Promotion of Children's Rights" in Ibrahim F I Shihata (ed), *The World Bank in a Changing World, Volume III* (The Hague, Martinus Nijhoff Publishers).

—— (ed) (2000c) *The World Bank in a Changing World, Volume III* (The Hague, Martinus Nijhoff Publishers).

SHUMAN, MICHAEL H (1994) "GATTzilla versus Communities" 27 *Cornell International Law Journal* 527–52.

SIEGEL, DEBORAH E (2002) "Legal Aspects of the IMF/WTO Relationship: The Fund's Articles of Agreement and the WTO Agreements" 96 *American Journal of International Law* 561–99.

SIMMA, BRUNO (1985) "Self-contained Regimes" XVI *Netherlands Yearbook of International Law* 111–36.

—— (1994) "From Bilateralism to Community Interest in International Law" in Academy of International Law (ed), *Recueil des Cours, Vol 250/1994–VI* (Den Haag, Brill).

—— (ed) (2002) *The Charter of the United Nations: A Commentary* (New York, Oxford University Press).

SIMMA, BRUNO and ALSTON, PHILIP (1992) "The Sources of Human Rights Law: Custom, *jus cogens* and General Principles" 12 *Australian Yearbook of International Law* 82–107.

SIMMA, BRUNO and PAULUS, ANDREAS L (1998) "The 'International Community': Facing the Challenge of Globalization" 9 *European Journal of International Law* 266–77.

SIMMONS, BETH (2000a) "International Law and State Behavior: Commitment and Compliance in International Monetary Affairs" 94 *American Political Science Review* 819–35.

—— (2000b) "The Legalization of International Monetary Affairs" 54 *International Organization* 573–602.

SINCLAIR, IAN (1984) *The Vienna Convention on the Law of Treaties* (Manchester, Manchester University Press).

SINGH, NIRVIKAR (2003) "The Impact of International Labor Standards: A Survey of Economic Theory" in Kaushik Basu, Henrik Horn, Lisa Román and Judith Shapiro (eds), *International Labor Standards: History, Theory, and Policy Options* (Malden, MA, Blackwell).

SKOGLY, SIGRUN I (2001) *The Human Rights Obligations of the World Bank and the International Monetary Fund* (London, Cavendish).

SLAUGHTER, ANNE-MARIE (1992) "Toward an Age of Liberal Nations" 33 *Harvard International Law Journal* 393–405.

—— (1993) "International Law and International Relations Theory: A Dual Agenda" 87 *American Journal of International Law* 205–39.

—— (1995) "International Law in a World of Liberal States" 6 *European Journal of International Law* 503–38.

—— (1997) "The Real New World Order" 76 *Foreign Affairs* 183–97.

—— (2001a) "Global Governance Networks, Global Information Agencies, and Disaggregated Democracy", Harvard Law School Public Law Working Paper No 18.

—— (2001b) "The Accountability of Government Networks" 8 *Indiana Journal of Global Legal Studies* 347–67.

—— (2004) *A New World Order* (Princeton, Princeton University Press).

SMITH, ADAM (1976) *An Inquiry into the Nature and Causes of the Wealth of Nations, 1776, Glasgow Edition* (Oxford, Clarendon Press).

SOHN, LOUIS B (1999) "The Contribution of the International Labor Organization to the Development of the Concept of Economic, Social and Cultural Rights" in René-Jean Dupuy (ed), *Mélanges en l'honneur de Nicolas Valticos—Droit et justice* (Paris, Pedone).

SOMAVIA, JUAN (1999) "Decent Work for All in a Global Economy: An ILO Perspective", submission by Mr Juan Somavia, Director-General, International Labour Office, to the Third WTO Ministerial Conference in Seattle, 30 Nov–3 Dec 1999 (Geneva, International Labour Office).

—— (2000) "Decent Work for All in a Global Economy", World Bank UN Lecture Series, 2 March 2000 (Geneva, International Labour Office).

SPANN, GIRARDEAU A (2000) *The Law of Affirmative Action* (New York, New York University Press).

STEGER, DEBRA P (2004) "The Jurisdiction of the World Trade Organization: Remarks" 98 *American Society of International Law Proceedings* 142–46.

STEIN, ERIC (2001) "International Integration and Democracy: No Love at First Sight" 95 *American Journal of International Law* 489–534.

STEINER, HENRY J (1998) "Social Rights and Economic Development: Converging Discourses?" 4 *Buffalo Human Rights Law Review* 25–42.

STEINER, HENRY J and ALSTON, PHILIP (2000) *International Human Rights in Context—Law, Politics, Morals* (Oxford, Oxford University Press).

STIGLITZ, JOSEPH (2000) "Democratic Development as the Fruits of Labor", keynote address, Industrial Relations Research Association, Boston, January 2000.

—— (2002) *Globalization and Its Discontents* (New York, WW Norton).

STILWELL, MATTHEW and VAN DYKE, BRENNAN (1999) *An Activist's Handbook on Genetically Modified Organisms and the WTO*, 2nd edn (Geneva, Center for International Environmental Law).

STOKER, GERRY (1998) "Governance as Theory: Five Propositions" 50 *International Social Science Journal* 17–28.

STOLZ, PETER (1968) *Politische Entscheidungen in der Versammlungsdemokratie Untersuchungen zum kollektiven Entscheid in der athenischen Demokratie, im schweizerischen Landsgemeindekanton Glarus und im Kibbuz* (Bern, Haupt).

STONER, JAMES REIST (2003) *Common-Law Liberty: Rethinking American Constitutionalism* (Lawrence, University Press of Kansas).

STRANGE, SUSAN (1998) *The Retreat of the State* (Cambridge, Cambridge University Press).

STREULI, ELISA and BAUER, TOBIAS (2001) "Working Poor in der Schweiz" 5 *info/social* 43–47.

SUMMERS, CLYDE (1999) "NAFTA's Labor Side Agreement and International Labor Standards" 3 *Journal of Small and Emerging Business Law* 173–87.

SWEPSTON, LEE (1998) "Human Rights Law and Freedom of Association: Development through ILO Supervision" 137 *International Labour Review* 169–94.

SYKES, ALAN O (1992) "Constructive Unilateral Threats in International Commercial Relations: The Limited Case for Section 301" 23 *Law and Policy in International Business* 263–317.

—— (1999) "Regulatory Protectionism and the Law of International Trade" 66 *University of Chicago Law Review* 1–46.

TAPIOLA, KARI (2000) "The ILO Declaration on Fundamental Principles and Rights at Works and its Follow-up" 37 *Bulletin of Comparative Labour Relations* 9–16.

TEMIN, PETER (1999) "Globalization" 15 *Oxford Review of Economic Policy* 76–89.

TEUBNER, GUNTHER (1989) *Recht als autopoietisches System* (Frankfurt aM, Suhrkamp).

THOMAS, KEITH (ed) (1999) *The Oxford Book of Work* (Oxford, Oxford University Press).

THÜRER, DANIEL (1992) "UN Enforcement Measures and Neutrality: The Case of Switzerland (Comment)" 30 *Archiv des Völkerrechts* 63–85.

—— (1993) "Von der sog. 'Europaverträglichkeit': Rechtsgestaltungsprinzip aus Verlegenheit oder Vehikel zur 'Stillen Revolutionierung' der schweizerischen Rechtsordnung?" 112 I *Zeitschrift für Schweizerisches Recht NF* 91–94.

—— (2000) "Globalisierung der Wirtschaft: Herausforderung zur 'Konstitutionalisierung' von Macht und Globalisierung von Verantwortlichkeit—Oder: Unterwegs zur 'Citizen Corporation'" 119 I *Zeitschrift für Schweizerisches Recht NF* 107–22.

Thürer, Daniel, Aubert, Jean-François and Müller, Jörg Paul (eds) (2001a) *Verfassungsrecht der Schweiz* (Zürich, Schulthess).

—— (2001b) "Verfassungsrecht und Völkerrecht" in Daniel Thürer, Jean-François Aubert and Jörg Paul Müller (eds), *Verfassungsrecht der Schweiz* (Zürich, Schulthess).

Thürer, Daniel and Hillemanns, Carolin (2002) "Allgemeine Prinzipien" in Daniel Thürer, Rolf H Weber and Roger Zäch (eds), *Bilaterale Verträge Schweiz—EG: Ein Handbuch* (Zürich, Schulthess).

Thürer, Daniel and Kaufmann, Christine (1990) "Ausländerrecht" in Dietrich Schindler, Gérard Hertig, Jakob Kellenberger, Daniel Thürer and Roger Zäch (eds), *Die Europaverträglichkeit des schweizerischen Rechts* (Zürich, Schulthess).

Thürer, Daniel, Weber, Rolf H and Zäch, Roger (eds) (2002) *Bilaterale Verträge Schweiz—EG: Ein Handbuch* (Zürich, Schulthess).

Tietje, Christian (1995) "Voluntary Eco-labelling Programmes and Questions of State Responsibility in the WTO/GATT Legal System" 29 *Journal of World Trade* 123–58.

Tomei, Manuela (1999) *Freedom of Association, Collective Bargaining and Informalization of Employment: Some Issues* (Geneva, International Labour Office).

Tomuschat, Christian (1981) "Is Universality of Human Rights Standards an Outdated and Utopian Concept?" in Roland Bieber (ed), *Gedächtnisschrift für Christoph Sasse, Band II* (Kehl, Engel).

—— (2003) *Human Rights: Between Idealism and Realism* (Oxford, Oxford University Press).

Trachtman, Joel P (2004) "The Jurisdiction of the World Trade Organization: Remarks" 98 *American Society of International Law Proceedings* 139–42.

Trebilcock, Michael J and Howse, Robert (1998) "Trade Liberalization and Regulatory Diversity: Reconciling Competitive Markets with Competitive Politics" 6 *European Journal of Law and Economics* 5–37.

—— (2005) *The Regulation of International Trade* 3rd edn (London, Routledge).

Tschannen, Pierre (1995) *Stimmrecht und politische Verständigung* (Basel, Helbing & Lichtenhahn).

Tschudi, Hans Peter (1989) "Die Ordnung der Arbeit durch die Bundesverfassung" in Walter Haller, Alfred Kölz, Georg Müller and Daniel Thürer (eds), *Im Dienst an der Gemeinschaft, Festschrift für Dietrich Schindler zum 65. Geburtstag* (Basel, Helbing & Lichtenhahn).

Ulrich, Dave (1997) *Human Resource Champions* (Boston, Harvard Business School Press).

United Nations Committee on Economic Social and Cultural Rights (2001) "Effects of Strucutral Adjustment Policies and Foreign Debt on the Full Enjoyment of all Human Rights, Particularly Economic, Social and Cultural Rights", Commission on Human rights resolution 2001/27, UN Doc E/CN.4/RES/2001/27, 20 April 2001.

United Nations Development Programme (UNDP) (1998) *Overcoming Human Poverty: Poverty Report 1998* (New York, UNDP).

—— (1999) *Globalization with a Human Face: Human Rights Development Report 1999* (New York, UNDP).

URMINSKY, MICHAEL (2002) "Self-regulation in the Workplace: Codes of Conduct, Social Labeling and Socially Responsible Investment", MCC Working Paper No 1.

VALASKAKIS, KIMON (2001) "Long-term Trends in Global Governance: From 'Westphalia' to 'Seattle'" in OECD (ed), *Governance in the 21st Century* (Paris, OECD Publishing).

VALLENDER, KLAUS A (1999) "Grundzüge der 'neuen' Wirtschaftsverfassung" 8 *Aktuelle Juristische Praxis* 677–86.

—— (2001) "Wirtschaft" in Daniel Thürer, Jean-François Aubert and Jörg Paul Müller (eds), *Verfassungsrecht der Schweiz* (Zürich, Schulthess).

VALTICOS, NICOLAS and VON POTOBSKY, GERALDO (1995) *International Labour Law* (Boston, Kluwer Law and Taxation).

VAN BOVEN, THEO (1999) "Fifty Years Universal Declaration of Human Rights—Balance and Challenges of the International Protection of Human Rights" in Peter Baehr, Cees Flinterman and Mignon Senders (eds), *Innovation and Inspiration: Fifty Years of the Universal Declaration of Human Rights* (Amsterdam, Royal Netherlands Academy of Arts and Sciences).

VAN BUEREN, GERALDINE (1995) *The International Law on the Rights of the Child* (Dordrecht, Martinus Nijhoff Publishers).

VAN DER HEIJDEN, BAREND AND TAHZIB-LIE, BAHIA (1998) *Reflections on the Universal Declaration of Human Rights* (The Hague, Martinus Nijhoff Publishers).

VAN WEZEL STONE, KATHERINE (1996) "Labour in the Global Economy: Four Approaches to Transnational Labour Regulation" in William W Bratton, Joseph McCahery, Sol Picciotto and Craig Scott (eds), *International Regulatory Competition and Co-ordination* (Oxford, Clarendon Press).

—— (1999) "To the Yukon and Beyond: Local Laborers in a Global Market" 3 *Journal of Small & Emerging Business Law* 93–130.

VAZQUEZ, CARLOS MANUEL (2003) "Trade Sanctions and Human Rights—Past, Present, and Future" 6 *Journal of International Economic Law* 797–839.

—— (2005) "Claims against Corporations under the Alien Tort Statute" in Thomas Cottier, Joost Pauwelyn and Elisabeth Bürgi (eds), *Human Rights and International Trade* (Oxford, Oxford University Press).

VASQUEZ, IAN (1996) "The Brady Plan and Market-based Solutions to Debt Crises" 16 *CATO Journal* 233–44.

VERDROSS, ALFRED and SIMMA, BRUNO (1984) *Universelles Völkerrecht* (Berlin, Duncker & Humblot).

VERHELLEN, EUGEEN (ed) (1999) *Understanding Children's Rights—Proceedings of the Fourth International Disciplinary Course on Children's Rights held at the University of Ghent, December 1999* (Gent, Centrum voor de Rechten van het Kind).

VILLIGER, KASPAR (1995) "Aktuelle Herausforderungen der schweizerischen Sicherheitspolitik" in René Rhinow (ed), *Die schweizerische Sicherheitspolitik im internationalen Umfeld* (Basel, Helbing & Lichtenhahn).

VINES, DAVID and GILBERT, CHRISTOPHER L (eds) (2004a) *The IMF and its Critics: Reform of Global Financial Architecture* (Cambridge, Cambridge University Press).

—— (2004b) "The IMF and International Financial Architecture: Solvency and Liquidity" in David Vines and Christopher L Gilbert (eds), *The IMF and its Critics* (Cambridge, Cambridge University Press).

WALKER, NEIL (2001) "The EU and the WTO: Constitutionalism in a New Key" in Gráinne De Búrca and Scott Joanne (eds), *The EU and the WTO—Legal and Constitutional Issues* (Oxford, Hart Publishing).

WALTER, CHRISTIAN (2002) "Constitutionalizing (Inter)national Governance—Possibilities for and Limits to the Development of an International Constitutional Law" 44 *German Yearbook of International Law* 170–201.

WATRIN, CHRISTIAN (1985) "Staatsaufgaben—Die ökonomische Sicht" 34 *Zeitschrift für Wirtschaftspolitik* 131–59.

—— (1986) *"Marktversagen" versus "Staatsversagen"* (Zürich, Vorort des Schweizerischen Handels- und Industrie-Vereins).

WEBER, ROLF H (2001) "Challenges for the New Financial Architecture" 31 *Hong Kong Law Journal* 241–65.

—— (2003), Ethik im Aussenwirtschaftsrecht—Überlegungen am Beispiel der Politik von IWF und Weltbank' 12 *Aktuelle Juristische Praxis* 1338–52.

WEBER-DÜRLER, BEATRICE (2000) "Grundrechtseingriffe" in Ulrich Zimmerli (ed), *Die neue Bundesverfassung, Konsequenzen für Praxis und Wissenschaft, Berner Tage für die juristische Praxis 1999* (Bern, Stämpfli Verlag).

WEILER, JOSEPH H H (1991) "The Transformation of Europe" 100 *Yale Law Journal* 2403–83.

—— (1999) *The Constitution of Europe: "Do the New Clothes have an Emperor?" and Other Essays on European Integration* (Cambridge, Cambridge University Press).

WEISS, EDITH BROWN, RIGO SUREDA, Andres and Boisson de Chazournes, Laurence (eds) (1999) *The World Bank, International Financial Institutions, and the Development of International Law: A Symposium Held in Honor of Dr Ibrahim F I Shihata* (Washington DC, American Society of International Law).

WEISSBRODT, DAVID and KRUGER, MURIA (2003) "Current Developments: Norms on the Responsibilities of Transnational Corporations and Other Business Enterprises with Regard to Human Rights" 97 *American Journal of International Law* 901–22.

WHITE, GILLIAN (1999) "Treaty Interpretation: The Vienna Convention 'Code' as Applied by the World Trade Organization Judiciary" 20 *Australian Yearbook of International Law* 319–40.

WHITFIELD, KEITH and STRAUSS, G (eds) (1998) *Researching the World of Work—Strategies and Methods in Studying Industrial Relations* (Ithaca, ILR Press).

WILLIAMSON, JOHN (ed) (1990) *Latin American Adjustment: How Much Has Happened?* (Washington DC, Institute for International Economics).

World Bank (1991) *World Development Report 1991: The Challenge of Development* (Washington DC, World Bank).

—— (1998) *Development and Human Rights: The Role of the World Bank* (Washington DC, World Bank).

—— (1999) *Principles and Good Practice in Social Policy* (Washington DC, World Bank).

—— (2000a) *Global Economic Prospects and the Developing Countries* (Washington DC, World Bank).

—— (2000b) *Engendering Development Through Gender Equality in Rights, Resources and Voice—Summary* (Washington DC, World Bank).

—— (2001a) *Advancing Gender Equality—World Bank Action since Beijing* (Washington DC, World Bank).

—— (2001b) *Social Protection Sector Strategy: From Safety Net to Springboard* (Washington DC, World Bank).

—— (2001c) *World Development Indicators 2001* (Washington DC, World Bank).

WOUTERS, JAN and DE MEESTER, BART (2003) "The Role of International Law in Protecting Public Goods. Regional and Global Challenges", LIRGIAD, Leuven Interdisciplinary Research Group on International Agreements and Development.

WTO Secretariat (1995) "Negotiating History of the Coverage of the Agreement on Technical Barriers to Trade with Regard to Labelling Requirements, Voluntary Standards, and Processes and Production Methods Unrelated to Product Characteristics—Note by the Secretariat" G/TBT/W/11, 29 August 1995.

WÜGER, DANIEL (2001) "Die direkte Anwendbarkeit staatsvertraglicher Normen" in Thomas Cottier, Alberto Achermann, Daniel Wüger and Valentin Zellweger (eds), *Der Staatsvertrag im schweizerischen Verfassungsrecht* (Bern, Stämpfli Verlag).

WYSS, MARTIN PHILIPP (2001) *Oeffentliche Interessen—Interessen der Oeffentlichkeit?* (Bern, Stämpfli Verlag).

ZARING, DAVID (1998) "International Law by Other Means: The Twilight Existence of International Financial Regulatory Organizations" 33 *Texas International Law Journal* 281–330.

ZELLWEGER, VALENTIN (2001) "Die demokratische Legitimation staatsvertraglichen Rechts" in Thomas Cottier, Alberto Achermann, Daniel Wüger and Valentin Zellweger (eds), *Der Staatsvertrag im schweizerischen Verfassungsrecht* (Bern, Stämpfli Verlag).

ZEN-RUFFINEN, PIERMARCO and AUER, ANDREAS (eds) (1996) *De la constitution—études en l'honneur de Jean-François Aubert* (Basel, Helbing & Lichtenhahn).

ZIMMERLI, ULRICH (ed) (2000) *Die neue Bundesverfassung, Konsequenzen für Praxis und Wissenschaft, Berner Tage für die Juristische Praxis, BTJP 1999* (Bern, Stämpfli Verlag).

Index

www.ingramcontent.com/pod-product-compliance
Ingram Content Group UK Ltd.
Pitfield, Milton Keynes, MK11 3LW, UK
UKHW020831290926
15470UKWH00009B/1845/J

9 781841 135991